Elevate Your Audio Production with REAPER

An extensive guide to recording, editing, and mixing with a powerful DAW

Marco Galvan

Christopher Bolte

<packt>

Elevate Your Audio Production with REAPER

Th e authors acknowledge the use of cutting-edge AI (such as ChatGPT and Grammarly), with the sole aim of enhancing the language and clarity within the book, thereby ensuring a smooth reading experience for readers. It's important to note that the content itself has been craft ed by the authors and edited by a professional publishing team.

Portfolio Director: Pavan Ramchandani
Relationship Lead: Neha Pande, Larissa Pinto
Program Manager: Divij Kotian
Project Manager: Arul Viveaun S
Content Engineer: Shreya Sarkar
Technical Editor: K Bimala Singha, Vidhisha Patidar
Proofreader: Shreya Sarkar
Copy Editor: Safi s Editing
Indexer: Hemangini Bari
Production Designer: Prashant Ghare
Marketing Owner: Nivedita Pandey, Priya Bhanushali

First published: March 2025

Production reference: 2281125

Published by Packt Publishing Ltd.
Grosvenor House
11 St Paul's Square
Birmingham
B3 1RB, UK.

ISBN 978-1-83588-542-0

www.packtpub.com

Thank God for giving me the gift of being able to learn so many things I love and for allowing me to share them with others through teaching.

I dedicate this book to my family. To my wife, Liliana, who has always shown me her love by supporting me in all my projects and inspiring me with her love for books. To my children, Hannah and Jonathan, whom I hope this book will inspire and help them achieve all their dreams. To my parents, who always did everything in their power to help me succeed.

– Marco Galvan

I would like to dedicate this book to my amazing and incredibly supportive wife, Sarah, and to my family who have always had my back throughout the many twists and turns of life and work. Furthermore, I want to dedicate it to anyone trying to make their mark in the world of audio in increasingly uncertain times in the hopes that it will add another invaluable tool to your palette, helping you to stay nimble and versatile as the scope of work of audio professionals remains ever-changing.

– Christopher Bolte

Contributors

About the authors

Marco Galvan, with over 20 years in the music and audio industry, holds an engineering degree with a specialization in acoustics from the **Instituto Politecnico Nacional (IPN)**. A professional musician and composer, he studied at Berklee College of Music and is certified in musical theory and keyboards by the ABRSM and Trinity College London. His audio credentials include courses at Alchemea College in London, and certifications such as Pro Tools Operator and Meyer Sound System Design, among others. Currently, he works as a Dolby Atmos mixing and mastering engineer and serves as an associate professor at Universidad Anáhuac, where he teaches audio and music production using REAPER and other digital audio workstations (DAWs).

Christopher Bolte (BØLT) is a sound designer for video games, a passionate field recordist, and a mixing engineer. He holds a degree in jazz performance and education from Hochschule Osnabrück and Berklee College of Music and has been recording audio for most of his life – or 20 years to be precise. As a sound designer, he is currently working on indie and "AA" games while still finding time to pursue a degree in sound design, create sound effects libraries and sample packs, and contribute to global SFX crowdsourcing projects. He always strives to be a helpful voice in the global game audio community through blog posts, mentorship, resource sharing, outreach, and by contributing to this very book. Chris helps run the Game Audio Boston networking group and is part of the **Game Audio Network Guild** (G.A.N.G.).

I want to thank Jusstin Frankel, John Schwartz, and everyone else who has contributed to the creation of REAPER and made it so incredibly versatile, powerful, and shapeable; The REAPER community for always having their user's backs and being so proactive in creating unique and clever workflow helpers; LKC, nvk.tools, Bird's Things, Tadej Supukovic, Oded Davidof, Aaron Cendan, Kusa, and all the other REAPER extension developers who make my daily work so much easier; Greg Lester, Liam Cameron, Giorgio Vezzini, and Matt Besler for many great lessons and chats that helped me tremendously in getting my bearings in game audio; and Kenny Gioia for providing some of the best REAPER insights and tutorials around!

About the reviewers

Tornike Katsarava is a musician, sound designer, and sound engineer who has worked as a sound engineer for more than 7 years on live events, as well as recording/mixing music, audio post-production, and audiobook production. An experienced audio engineer in the broadcasting industry, including television and radio companies, Tornike has previously worked with Proxy Live Solutions; Elia Production; Radio CRT; and the Palitra News TV company. Currently, Tornike works as an audio visual technician at the U.S. Department of State and owns an audio/video production company – Elia Production. Tornike has also translated some chapters from Clarence Barlow's *On Musiquantics*.

Iniyan DG is a passionate audio engineer and sound designer with over three years of professional experience. Specializing in audio recording, editing, and mixing, Iniyan is proficient in leading DAWs and has extensive experience in designing and mixing surround sound, including Dolby Atmos, for film, music, and media. Iniyan holds a master's degree in audio production from the University of Salford, UK, and a bachelor's degree in electronics and instrumentation engineering from Anna University, India. With a strong foundation in both freelance and industry environments, Iniyan excels in delivering high-quality audio for diverse projects.

Table of Contents

5

Mastering and Exporting Projects 119

Part 2: Advanced Production Techniques

6

Exploring Custom Actions and Macros 141

7

Advanced Mixing and Processing 157

8

Working with Video 179

Part 3: Specialized Applications

9

Music Production Techniques 213

Preface

Hello! This book aims to be a guide that will take you step by step along the path of audio production using REAPER software. REAPER is a software within the category called **Digital Audio Workstation** (**DAW**). DAWs are powerful and comprehensive programs that allow you to work on virtually any type of audio project, from recording, editing, mixing, and mastering music, to podcasts, game audio, video audio, immersive sound, and much more.

REAPER has established itself as a very accessible and compatible DAW, with a large number of features that not every DAW offers. For this reason, REAPER is a great tool for anyone who wants to work on any digital audio project on a computer.

Given the vast number of features REAPER has, it can sometimes be a bit confusing to learn how to use it without a good guide. This is where the purpose of this book comes in. Its purpose is to teach you how to use REAPER, starting from the general fundamentals of audio production and guiding you, step by step, through each of the production stages across various types of applications.

You will learn while working on music projects, mixing, mastering, podcasts, video, immersive sound, and more. By the end of this book, you will have enough knowledge to complete audio projects from start to finish using proper procedures, and you will have a solid foundation to continue exploring the many features REAPER has as a tool for audio work.

I hope you have fun and learn a lot along the way!

Who this book is for

This book is aimed at musicians or aspiring music producers who want to learn how to use REAPER from scratch in a clear and simple way. It can also be very useful for content creators, podcasters, video producers, and other audio enthusiasts who want to learn how to record, edit, and mix their audio projects.

The book is designed to start from scratch. However, it can also be very helpful for those who are already familiar with another DAW and want to start using REAPER or incorporating it as a work tool.

What this book covers

Chapter 1, *Getting Started with REAPER*, will teach you the main features of REAPER and the basics to start using it, including its installation and initial setup. You will also learn about the principles of digital audio, which is the main element we manipulate in REAPER. You'll create your first project in REAPER and make the necessary adjustments to customize the software according to your needs.

Chapter 2, Recording Audio and MIDI in REAPER, covers the entire process of audio and MIDI recording, from the key points for achieving a good audio recording to the ways you can program music using MIDI. You will also learn how to import files into your projects to start shaping your audio productions.

Chapter 3, Editing and Arranging, focuses on editing functions, both for audio and MIDI. In this chapter, you'll learn how to use commands to refine and clean up audio recordings, repeat sections, adjust the sizes of takes, and modify note duration and timing, among many other useful functions in the editing process.

Chapter 4, Mixing Procedures in REAPER, explains the general procedures used in mixing, from adjusting levels and panning to various types of audio processing commonly used at this stage. It also covers automation, which is a fundamental feature in modern mixing.

Chapter 5, Mastering and Exporting Projects, describes how to work with a project that has already been mixed, and how to make the final adjustments and processes to prepare it for its distribution. This chapter explains the loudness standards used by current streaming platforms, as well as how to export a project based on your requirements.

Chapter 6, Exploring Custom Actions and Macros, covers various ways to make your work more efficient in REAPER, using custom actions and shortcuts. It also discusses several settings and preferences that can be customized according to each user's tastes or needs.

Chapter 7, Advanced Mixing and Processing, covers the use of more advanced mixing techniques and REAPER functions that will allow you to manage sessions with more tracks more effectively. You will also learn the principles of working on multichannel projects, such as surround sound and audio processing.

Chapter 8, Working with Video, explores how to import video files into REAPER to work on their sound post-production, whether creating a soundtrack or editing and mixing dialogue and sound effects.

Chapter 9, Music Production Techniques, focuses on the most important tools used in music production projects. Topics include pre-production, creating melodies and harmonies, basic MIDI programming, and common editing and mixing techniques used in music production.

Chapter 10, Podcast Production Workflows, explains the podcast creation process from its start to its final distribution. You will learn techniques and procedures to add effects and edit voices for greater clarity and impact in a podcast episode.

Chapter 11, Sound Design for Film and Games, covers the basics of sound production for a movie or video game using common professional techniques. This chapter will teach you the criteria and considerations needed when editing and mixing these types of projects.

Chapter 12, Exploring Immersive Audio, focuses on immersive sound in REAPER, from the types of technologies currently used in this field to a step-by-step explanation of how to create an immersive audio project that can be experienced with headphones.

Chapter 13, Optimizing the Workflow and Troubleshooting in REAPER, discusses various techniques and procedures to solve common problems when working with REAPER. Additionally, it explains extra functions that will help simplify your production work.

To get the most out of this book

To work with this book, you'll need to install REAPER version 7.15 or higher. For this, you will need a computer with Windows XP/Vista/7/8/10/11 (32 or 64-bit, Intel/AMD only). If you're a Mac user, you'll need macOS 10.5 - 14.x (Intel or Apple Silicon).

Software/hardware covered in the book	Operating system requirements
REAPER DAW version 7.15 or higher	Windows, macOS
IEM plugin suite	

To work on *Chapter 12*, which covers immersive sound, you will need to install the free IEM plugin suite, which you can download from `https://plugins.iem.at`.

This book contains several long screenshots. These have been captured to provide an overview of various features. As a result, the text in these images may appear small at 100% zoom. However, you can take a look at the clear images at this link: `https://packt.link/NhBDD`.

Download the example files and assets

You can download the example files and assets for this book from GitHub at `https://github.com/PacktPublishing/Elevate-your-audio-production-with-Reaper`.

We also have other such bundles from our rich catalog of books and videos available at `https://github.com/PacktPublishing/`. Check them out!

Conventions used

There are a number of text conventions used throughout this book.

`Code in text`: Indicates code words in text, database table names, folder names, filenames, file extensions, pathnames, dummy URLs, and user input. Here is an example: "Set the **Highpass** filter to `100 Hz`."

Bold: Indicates a new term, an important word, or words that you see onscreen. For instance, words in menus or dialog boxes appear in **bold**. Here is an example: "If we double-click on an audio item, the **Media Item Properties** window will open."

> **Tips or important notes**
> Appear like this.

Get in touch

Feedback from our readers is always welcome.

General feedback: If you have questions about any aspect of this book, email us at `customercare@packtpub.com` and mention the book title in the subject of your message.

Errata: Although we have taken every care to ensure the accuracy of our content, mistakes do happen. If you have found a mistake in this book, we would be grateful if you would report this to us. Please visit `www.packtpub.com/support/errata` and fill in the form.

Piracy: If you come across any illegal copies of our works in any form on the internet, we would be grateful if you would provide us with the location address or website name. Please contact us at `copyright@packtpub.com` with a link to the material.

If you are interested in becoming an author: If there is a topic that you have expertise in and you are interested in either writing or contributing to a book, please visit `authors.packtpub.com`.

Share Your Thoughts

Once you've read *Elevate Your Audio Production with REAPER*, we'd love to hear your thoughts! Scan the QR code below to go straight to the Amazon review page for this book and share your feedback.

`https://packt.link/r/1835885438`

Your review is important to us and the tech community and will help us make sure we're delivering excellent quality content.

Free Benefits with Your Book

This book comes with free benefits to support your learning. Activate them now for instant access (see the "*How to Unlock*" section for instructions).

Here's a quick overview of what you can instantly unlock with your purchase:

PDF and ePub Copies

- Access a DRM-free PDF copy of this book to read anywhere, on any device.
- Use a DRM-free ePub version with your favorite e-reader.

Next-Gen Web-Based Reader

- **Multi-device progress sync**: Pick up where you left off, on any device.
- **Highlighting and notetaking**: Capture ideas and turn reading into lasting knowledge.
- **Bookmarking**: Save and revisit key sections whenever you need them.
- **Dark mode**: Reduce eye strain by switching to dark or sepia themes

How to Unlock

Scan the QR code (or go to `packtpub.com/unlock`). Search for this book by name, confirm the edition, and then follow the steps on the page.

UNLOCK NOW

Note: Keep your invoice handy. Purchases made directly from Packt don't require one

Part 1: Basic Audio Production

In this first part, you will learn the fundamental concepts of REAPER and audio production in general. You will go step by step through the process of setting up REAPER and creating projects, covering recording, editing, mixing, and mastering audio, so that you can complete a project from start to finish.

This part has the following chapters:

- *Chapter 1, Getting Started with REAPER*
- *Chapter 2, Recording Audio and MIDI in REAPER*
- *Chapter 3, Editing and Arranging*
- *Chapter 4, Mixing Procedures in REAPER*
- *Chapter 5, Mastering and Exporting Projects*

1

Getting Started with REAPER

Audio and music production is a very rewarding and fun creative activity. Nowadays, it's possible to do this on a computer using tools such as **Digital Audio Workstations (DAWs)**. One of the most popular DAWs today is REAPER, as it is an accessible, powerful, and easy-to-use software. REAPER is user-friendly software, compatible with various operating systems, and it has many functions that are hard to find in other DAWs.

Throughout this book, you will learn how to effectively use REAPER to carry out various projects such as music production, podcast production, and audio editing for video. Additionally, you will learn about audio formats, such as immersive sound, that are expected to become more common in the near future.

In this chapter, you will learn about the main features of REAPER and the typical installation process on various systems. You will also learn the basic concepts of digital audio that will allow you to understand the fundamentals of the audio files you will manipulate in REAPER. You will learn how to create new projects and configure REAPER to start working on them.

In this chapter, we will cover the following topics:

- **What is REAPER?**: You will learn some of the main features of this excellent software.
- **Installation and basic configuration**: You will learn the steps to follow to install REAPER on your computer.
- **Principles of digital audio**: You will learn the basic concepts of digital audio.
- **Creating your first project**: You will learn how to create a basic project in REAPER.
- **Customization options**: You will learn about some options and settings that you can adjust to improve your user experience in REAPER.

By the end of this chapter, you will have learned about the most important features of REAPER, as well as the main points that must be taken care of when setting up this software for a new project.

Technical requirements

In this book, we will be working with version 7.20 of REAPER. You can download it from `https://www.REAPER.fm/download.php`.

If you haven't installed REAPER yet and you are a Windows user, your computer should be running Windows XP/Vista/7/8/10/11 (32- or 64-bit, Intel/AMD only). If you are a Mac user, you need macOS 10.5 – 14.x (Intel or Apple Silicon).

What is REAPER?

REAPER is a DAW created by the American company Cockos Incorporated, whose intention from the outset was to create a powerful and accessible DAW and develop lightweight and easily installable software. The result has been more than satisfactory, as the size of the installation file is less than 30 MB and still has a lot of functions included.

REAPER has gradually positioned itself as one of the main contenders in the world of DAWs. In the subsequent sections, let's look at the most important features that have made REAPER the preferred DAW for millions of users around the world.

Compatibility

REAPER is one of the few DAWs that can be used on Mac, Windows, and even Linux computers. This allows it to have project compatibility across different types of systems and for all kinds of users, from young people starting out in the world of music production making music in their bedrooms to experienced audio engineers who require a reliable and powerful tool for demanding tasks.

This DAW is also capable of handling virtually any audio file format, such as ACID, AIFF, AVI, BWF, CAF, CDDA, FLAC, KAR, MIDI, MOV, MUSICXML, MP3, MP4, MPEG, OGG VORBIS, RAW/PCM, REX2, SD2, WAV, and WMV.

This means that you can import any audio file and process or edit it within REAPER.

In addition, REAPER supports virtually any type of audio hardware. For example, on Windows, it can use ASIO drivers, which allow very good performance on these systems. On Mac, it supports hardware with Core Audio drivers, which are part of the macOS operating system.

Efficiency

REAPER is extremely efficient. Its installation file is much smaller than that of any other DAW, so its installation and updates are very quick and simple. Additionally, it is very robust and reliable, which is vital for important recording sessions or live performances.

Internal processing

This DAW handles cutting-edge audio processing technology, such as several pitch-shifting and time-stretching modes, high-quality resampling, and more. This ensures that its audio manipulation is of the highest quality. One might think that, due to its accessible price, REAPER would have some deficiencies in this regard. However, the audio quality and processing capabilities you can achieve with REAPER are comparable to those of any other professional DAW.

Plugin support

Most DAWs support the use of external plugins. A **plugin** is additional software to the DAW that provides specific functionality, for example, adding echo, reverb, or equalization.

REAPER supports most plugin formats (VST, VST3, LV2, AU, CLAP, DX, and JS), making it quite easy to add additional effects or virtual instruments to your productions.

A notable aspect of REAPER is that you can use it to create your own plugins! This is an advanced topic that requires knowledge of programming and digital signal processing; however, it is interesting to know that those who like to create their own software tools can use REAPER to create and use their own plugins.

Advanced recording and editing

REAPER has all the recording and audio editing features expected of a professional DAW. You can make recordings with no track limits; use as many inputs and outputs as required; make composite takes, layers, and much more; configure monitoring setups for multiple musicians; send and receive audio to and from external devices and processors (with a suitable audio interface); and make multichannel, surround, and MIDI recordings.

Regarding editing, it is also a very comprehensive DAW. It has functions for copying, repeating, duplicating, and adjusting the volume of audio files quickly and creating projects that use audio, MIDI, and video. It has extensive automation, mixing, and mastering functions as well.

In *Chapter 3* and *Chapter 9*, you will learn advanced recording and editing techniques.

Customization

Another standout feature of REAPER is its customization. Not only can it change its appearance or window layout, but it also has many keyboard shortcuts that can be programmed to perform virtually any function.

Additionally, REAPER integrates macros and scripts that can be used to automate functions or tasks. For example, with these tools, you can assign effects or processing to different tracks with just one command, or you can even create a complete song in seconds using scripts programmed by you! The limit is truly in your imagination and creativity.

So far, we have seen the main features that make REAPER a great DAW, such as its compatibility, efficiency, and capability to work with simple or complex projects.

Now we will see the steps to install REAPER, both on Windows and on Mac systems.

Installation and basic configuration

If you don't have REAPER installed on your computer yet, this section will demonstrate the steps you should follow.

Head over to the official website of REAPER (`https://www.REAPER.fm`) to download the installer relevant to your operating system. REAPER offers both 64-bit and 32-bit versions. If you're unsure which one to choose, the 64-bit version is generally recommended for most modern computers.

REAPER is constantly updated, so it is very likely that by the time you read this, there will be a newer version. Generally, updates are for bug fixes or minor features, so you should be able to follow the procedures outlined in this book without a problem.

Windows installation

To install REAPER on a Windows machine, follow the next steps:

1. Double-click the downloaded `.exe` file to launch the installer.
2. Agree to the license agreement and follow the on-screen prompts.
3. Choose an installation location (default is usually fine) and click **Next**.
4. You can opt to install additional components (VST support, etc.), but the default selections are sufficient for most users. Click **Install**.
5. Once the installation is complete, you can launch REAPER directly from the installer or find it in your **Start** menu.

Mac installation

To install REAPER on a Mac computer, follow these steps:

1. Open the downloaded `.dmg` file.
2. Drag the *REAPER application* icon to your `Applications` folder.
3. Eject the disk image and launch REAPER from your `Applications` folder.

One of the best features of REAPER is that its installation file is surprisingly small. This is because REAPER does not include sound libraries or virtual instruments, which increase the size of installers of other DAWs. The way Cockos Incorporated have handled the development of REAPER to keep it stable, comprehensive, and easy-to-install is truly a point in their favor.

Another important feature of REAPER is that it only has one version. Most DAWs have different versions at different prices, each with certain limitations or more advanced features depending on the needs of each user. In the case of REAPER, you will find only one version, which includes all the features and which you can use without restrictions during a 60-day trial period. After that period, a very affordable license is available for purchase to continue using the software.

Because the price of REAPER's permanent license is very affordable ($60 USD at the time of writing), REAPER does not offer additional discounts or promotions, such as academic, student, or bulk license purchase discounts. Nevertheless, its price makes it one of the most accessible DAWs on the market, especially considering all its capabilities.

Now that you know how to install REAPER on your computer, let's explore some important concepts of digital audio, which form the foundation for working with a DAW.

Principles of digital audio

To understand the use of a DAW more completely, it's a good idea to grasp some concepts of digital audio. We'll go over some of the most important points in this section.

Digital audio is the representation of sound in the form of binary code. This representation is made using binary digits or **bits** (1, 0). This means that we can represent sound through a stream of ones and zeros. When audio takes this digital or binary form, it can be manipulated and processed in various ways using a computer.

This is precisely what a DAW does: it allows us to record, edit, and process digital audio. The use of DAWs has been part of the revolution in music and audio production. This is because, previously, this could only be done in a professional recording studio. Now, anyone with a moderately powerful computer and a DAW such as REAPER can create highly polished projects.

Now, let's see some fundamental concepts of digital audio that will allow us to better understand the equipment we need.

Audio interfaces

A key point in computer audio production is the audio interface. An **audio interface** is a device that allows audio input and output to a computer.

Several years ago, audio interfaces were simply known as sound cards. These cards had to be installed on the computer's motherboard, or they came integrated into the system. If your computer has a headphone output, then it already has a very basic audio interface. Some of these sound cards also have microphone inputs; in these cases, the interface is more complete.

In this regard, Apple have built a reputation over the years for using good-quality sound cards in their computers. Some PCs may also have decent sound cards; however, it's harder to determine this due to the wide variety of PCs on the market.

Regardless of your computer, the first step to achieving high-quality audio on your computer is to use a good audio interface. But don't worry, if you don't have an audio interface yet, you can still start using REAPER using your computer's sound card.

Currently, most interfaces are connected to computers via USB. There are a wide variety of brands and models of audio interfaces. They generally differ in the number of inputs and outputs they have, as well as the quality of their internal circuits. In this sense, we can find good-quality interfaces ranging from around $100 USD for one- or two-channel interfaces to several thousand dollars for units with many channels and specific features.

Advantages of using an audio interface

The main advantages of using an audio interface are as follows:

- **Superior audio quality**: The audio quality is usually better if we use an audio interface than a computer's sound card due to the quality of the analog-to-digital and digital-to-analog converters of the interface. Most sound cards use basic chips for audio processing, while interfaces feature more specialized chips for this task.
- **Number of inputs**: We can have multiple audio inputs for microphones or instruments. The number of inputs of an interface gives us an idea of how many channels we can record simultaneously. For example, with an 8-channel input interface, we can record 8 microphones at the same time. A typical scenario would be recording a drum kit, where you typically need from 4 to over 10 microphones recording simultaneously. Another example would be recording all the members of a band playing at the same time.
- **Number of outputs**: These can be used to connect multiple speakers, as is the case with immersive sound systems (e.g., Dolby Atmos). We can also use the outputs to connect monitors or headphones for several musicians when recording.
- **Lower latency**: As we will detail later, **latency** is a delay that affects digital audio playback. With good-quality audio interfaces, we can reduce latency when working with a DAW and improve the user experience.
- **Extra processing**: Some audio interfaces have internal processing chips (digital signal processing). This allows them to offload the CPU of the computer when adding effects in the DAW.
- **Advanced monitoring options**: Many interfaces have hardware or software options to control audio monitoring, such as routing audio internally from the web browser to the DAW for recording or streaming.

USB microphones

A tool that has become very popular in recent years, and that can be very useful for those starting in audio production, is a **USB microphone**. These are large-diaphragm microphones that allow very good sound capture quality, but also have an included audio interface.

As the name suggests, these microphones do not have a conventional audio output, but rather a USB connection. They connect directly to the computer and can be used in a DAW such as REAPER without the need for additional hardware. Additionally, they usually have audio output for headphones, similar to what a simple audio interface would offer.

Analog-to-digital conversion

Let's see in a very simple way how a signal from an analog source, such as a microphone or electric guitar, is digitized in an interface, meaning how it goes from being an analog electrical signal to becoming a stream of bits (digital audio).

When the signal comes out of the microphone, this signal has infinite voltage values, as we see in *Figure 1.1*:

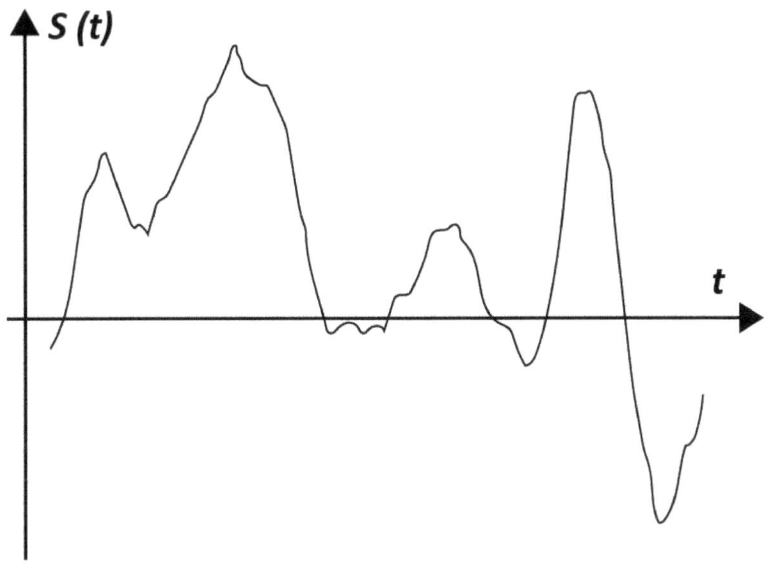

Figure 1.1 – Analog signal

[src: https://commons.wikimedia.org/wiki/File:Analog_digital_series.svg]

In *Figure 1.1*, the clear line that looks similar to a chain of mountains of varying heights represents the voltages delivered by a microphone or an electric instrument. We see that there is an infinite possibility of voltage values as time progresses. Some of them are very high, some very low, some are positive, some are negative, and there are even moments where the signal is at **0** volts (where the clear line crosses the horizontal axis).

An analog signal such as this, with so many possible voltage values, cannot be analyzed or processed by a digital system. A digital system requires precise data to process as time progresses, so it's necessary to take only certain values or samples, as we will see next.

Sampling rate

To digitize the analog signal shown in *Figure 1.1*, the first step is to take samples of it. These samples are represented by the vertical lines shown in *Figure 1.2*:

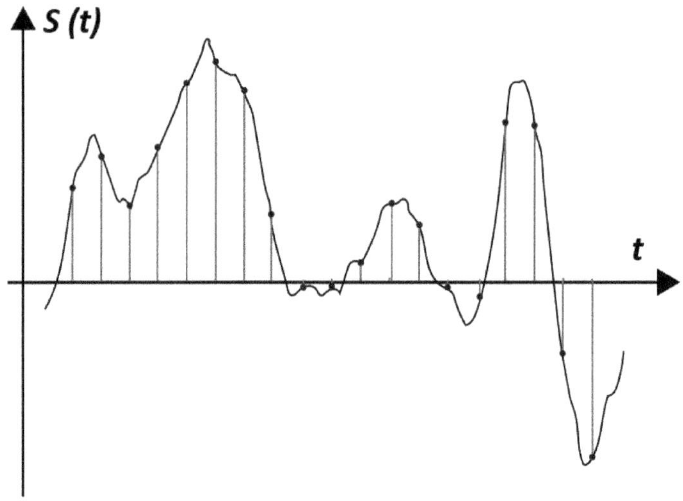

Figure 1.2 – Analog signal being sampled
[src: https://commons.wikimedia.org/wiki/File:Analog_digital_series.svg]

As we can see, at the end of each vertical line, there is a point touching the line of the analog signal—this is the **sampling process**.

During the sampling stage, a specialized circuit inside the audio interface takes values, or samples, of each moment of the analog signal. The speed at which the system takes these samples is known as the **sampling rate**. The sampling rate is expressed in **kilohertz** (**kHz**) and tells us how many audio samples are taken per second. For example, a sampling rate of 10 kHz would take 10,000 samples for every second of audio!

In the audio industry, there are standard sampling rate values. The following list shows the most common sampling rate values nowadays:

44.1 kHz group:

- 44,100 Hz (44.1 kHz)
- 88,200 Hz (88.2 kHz)
- 176,400 Hz (176.4 kHz)

48 kHz group:

- 48,000 Hz (48 kHz)
- 96,000 Hz (96 kHz)
- 192,000 Hz (192 kHz)

As we can see in the preceding list, the values are related to each other, as the value below each one is twice the one above. This is important to consider when creating a new project in REAPER or when exporting a finished file, as we'll see in the subsequent section.

The higher the sampling rate, the more samples are taken per second of audio. This means the digital audio file will be larger too. The advantage of using higher sampling rates is that we can capture higher frequencies. High frequencies are an important component of the clarity of certain sounds, such as those of strings or cymbals.

This effect is outlined in the **Nyquist–Shannon sampling theorem**. In simple terms, it tells us that, to avoid distortion in the digitization process, the sampling rate must be at least twice the frequency we want to digitize. For example, if we want to digitize a sound of 15 kHz, the sampling rate must be at least 30 kHz. In theory, a healthy and young human ear can hear frequencies up to 20 kHz (in some cases even higher). This means that the minimum sampling rate should be around 40 kHz.

Based on this characteristic of our ears, the sampling rates we see in *Figure 1.2* were established. In the early 1980s, the creators of the audio CD agreed that the value of 44.1 kHz be used in that new system. On the other hand, most professional digital audio equipment established a base sampling rate of 48 kHz. Both sampling rates offer very similar audio quality, as they can capture frequencies up to 22.5 kHz and 24 kHz, respectively, which is more than enough for most people. Therefore, these are the most common sampling rates used to date for audio distribution. They offer a very good balance between file size and sound quality.

Choosing a sampling rate

Increasing the sampling rate means that even higher frequencies can be captured, which can provide better audio quality, especially for recordings of instruments with a lot of harmonic richness, such as string instruments, or when recording orchestras.

In fact, this is something we should consider when creating a new project in REAPER, especially because increasing the sampling rate will also increase the size of audio files, as well as the stress on our CPU to process everything. For example, if a computer can handle 40 audio tracks at 48 kHz without any problems, it may not be able to handle the load of those same 40 tracks at 96 kHz because it must do twice as many calculations per second, as it will handle twice the amount of data (samples).

In practice, it is usually sufficient to use sampling rates of 44.1 kHz or 48 kHz for most projects, or 88.2 kHz or 96 kHz for projects that merit that *high definition*, considering that our computer has enough CPU and RAM to handle those sessions.

In the *Creating your first project* section, we will see in more detail when each sampling rate option is convenient.

Bit depth

As samples are taken at the sampling rate speed, it's necessary to measure them to know the voltage value of each one, that is, to know how many volts each point in *Figure 1.2* measures, or what its value is on the vertical axis. This is known as the **quantization process**, where a value is assigned to each sample.

Now, the possible values are determined by the number of bits used in the process. For example, if only 2 bits are used, we'll have *4 possible values* or *combinations (22 = 4)*, as seen in *Figure 1.3*:

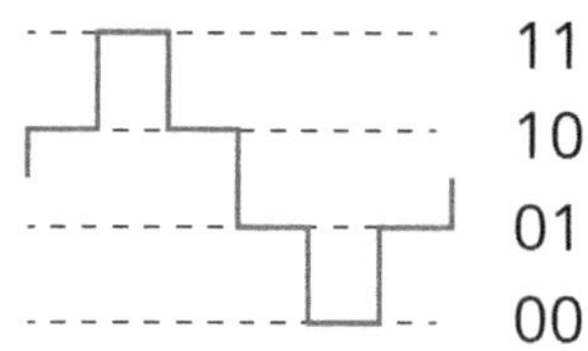

Figure 1.3 – A 2-bit quantization

[src: https://commons.wikimedia.org/wiki/File:2-bit_resolution.png]

The preceding diagram shows a very limited number of combinations, so the conversion process will be of very low quality. If we increase the number of bits to 4, then we'll have 2^4 combinations, meaning 16 possible values, as seen in *Figure 1.4*:

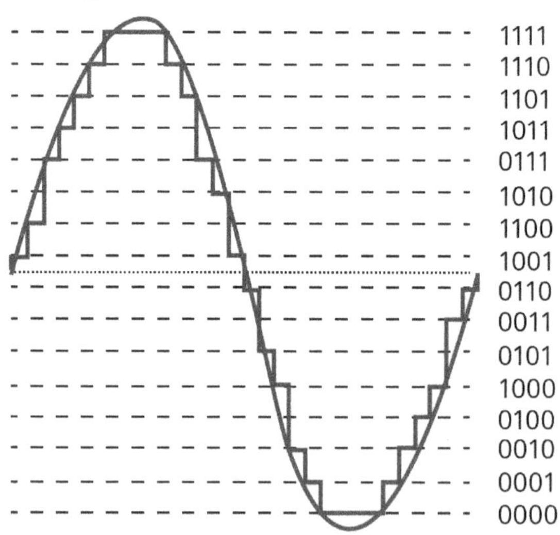

Figure 1.4 – A 4-bit quantization

[src: https://commons.wikimedia.org/wiki/File:4-bit_resolution_analog_comparison.png]

This **bit resolution** or **bit depth** gives us a better result, as the quantized values get closer to the original values of the analog signal.

Similarly, every time we increase the number of bits (n), the possible quantization values will increase based on 2^n. For example, the format of an audio CD uses 16 bits, which translates to 65,536 possible values. A 16-bit digital audio allows quite good quality and is still one of the most common distribution formats today.

The recommended bit depth for audio and music production, in general, is 24 bits. This number of bits is more than sufficient to obtain excellent quality in digital audio and is the value we'll use in the projects in this book.

Now, how does bit depth interact with the sampling rate? For example, if we use digital audio at 16 bits and 44.1 kHz (standard for audio CDs), the system must take 44,100 samples per second. In other words, one sample is taken every 22.7 microseconds (1/44,100), and each of these samples is a 16-bit word (e.g., 1001011001011001).

This gives us an idea of the volume of data that a DAW must process for each second of audio on a single channel using this resolution.

Latency

Latency is a common term in digital audio systems and DAWs. Latency is a delay generated in the conversion process, either analog-to-digital or digital-to-analog, as well as during **digital signal processing** (**DSP**). This latency is perceived when playing an instrument or using a microphone through a DAW. When speaking into the microphone, there will be a delay before hearing the sound through headphones or monitors.

Every digital audio system has latency; the key is knowing how to control or adjust it. For example, when processing digital audio, such as modifying its volume, what's happening behind the scenes is that the CPU is performing thousands of mathematical operations per second with the bits that make up the digital audio. The CPU performs these operations in blocks of bits, performing the necessary calculations one block at a time.

These blocks are stored in temporary memory called a **buffer**. Once the data from the buffer is processed, it exits, and the buffer is refilled with new data to process. This is how the bits of digital audio are generated.

If this *buffer is large*, then the CPU has more time to process the audio and generate the output bits. This results in *higher latency*. On the other hand, if the *buffer is small*, the CPU must process the data faster, resulting in *lower latency*.

The amount of latency is crucial for the proper performance of a musician. Ideally, the latency should be as low as possible so that the musician feels no delay in the sound and can perform well. This involves using a small buffer; however, this will make the CPU work much harder, causing the computer to heat up more.

On the other hand, if the buffer is large, then the CPU can work more *comfortably*, but there will be more latency in the system. The buffer size is one of the first settings we should adjust in a DAW, as we will see later. Typically, a balance is sought by adjusting the buffer to have the lowest latency possible that the CPU can handle.

The type and model of CPU, the type of interface, and its drivers are determining factors in the latency that a system may have. That's why each system can work up to a certain latency value.

Now that you are familiar with basic concepts of digital audio, such as sampling rate, bit depth, and latency, we can start working on creating our first project in REAPER.

Creating your first project

Let's see how to start a new project in REAPER, as well as the settings we need to consider. If we have an audio interface, we must ensure that it is turned on and correctly installed before launching REAPER, as otherwise, we may encounter errors in its configuration.

Many of the current interfaces that connect via USB are usually plug-and-play; however, we should check their documentation to ensure they do not require additional drivers or software to be recognized by the operating system.

When we open REAPER, we will see the main REAPER window, as shown in *Figure 1.5*:

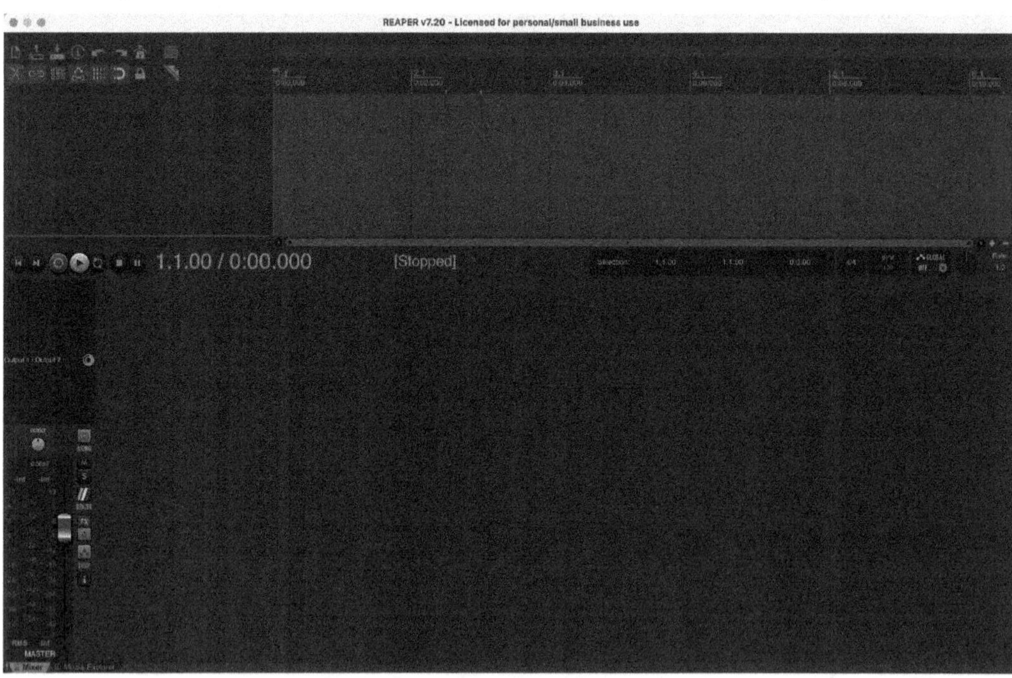

Figure 1.5 – An overview of REAPER's main window

Now let's see how to adjust the device settings to ensure we are using the appropriate audio device.

Audio device settings

The first thing we need to do when using REAPER is to ensure that our audio interface or sound card is recognized by REAPER. To do this, we will go to the **Options** | **Settings** menu at the top. This will take us to the **REAPER Preferences** window.

The **REAPER Preferences** window has several tabs on the left side. Here, we will navigate to the **Audio** | **Device** section, as shown in *Figure 1.6*:

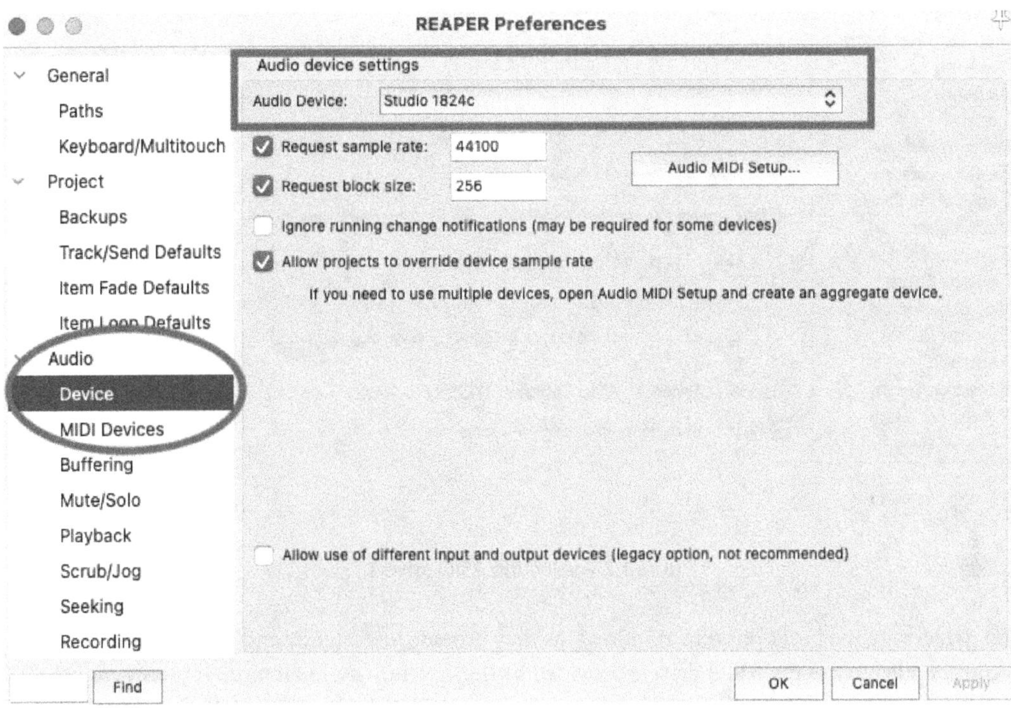

Figure 1.6 – Audio device settings

The contents of this window will vary depending on the type of operating system and interface you are using. In the case of macOS, your interface should appear in the top option labeled **Audio device settings**. In *Figure 1.6*, an example of an interface identified as **Studio 1824c** is shown, but in this menu, several options may appear, such as your computer speakers or headphones.

In the case of Windows, the options are a bit different. Here, what we need to look for are the ASIO drivers for your interface, as shown in *Figure 1.7*:

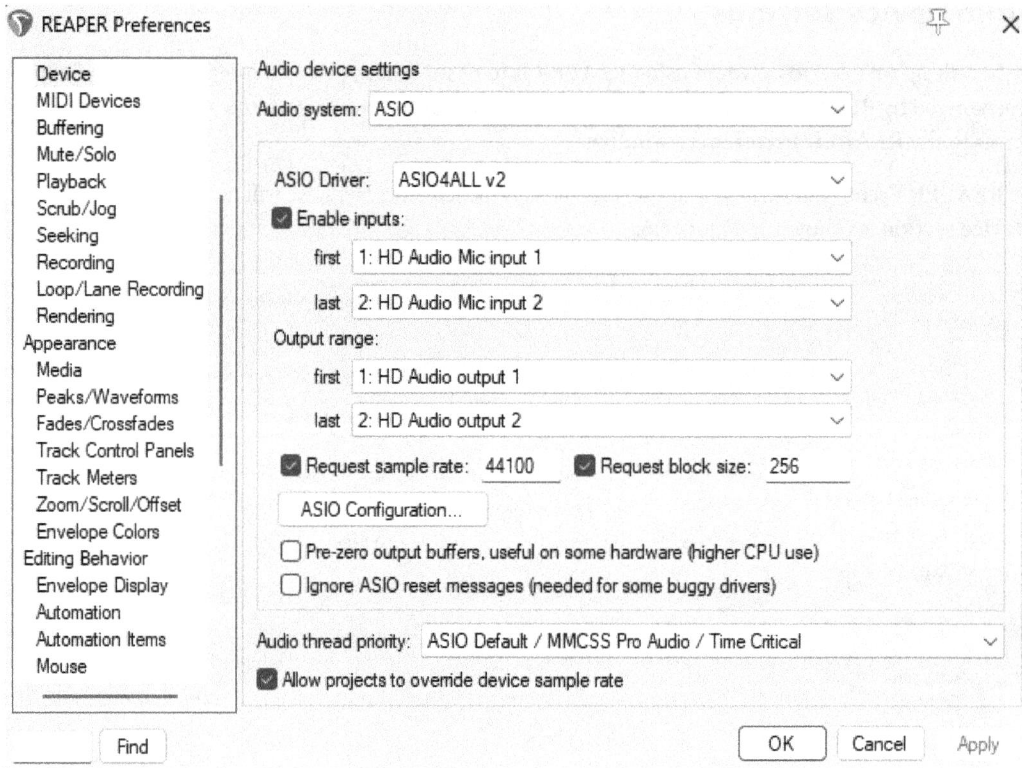

Figure 1.7 – Selecting ASIO drivers

ASIO drivers are the best option in Windows, as they provide low latency and great performance. It is recommended to use the ASIO drivers provided by the interface manufacturer. If there is no ASIO driver available, as shown in *Figure 1.7*, you can use an option such as the one from `asio4all.org`. ASIO4ALL v2 is a free and functional driver that must be downloaded and installed before running REAPER.

Selecting the sampling rate

In the **REAPER Preferences** window, we will also select the sampling rate for our project. We will do this by activating the **Request sample rate** option and entering the desired value, which is `44100`, as shown in *Figure 1.8*:

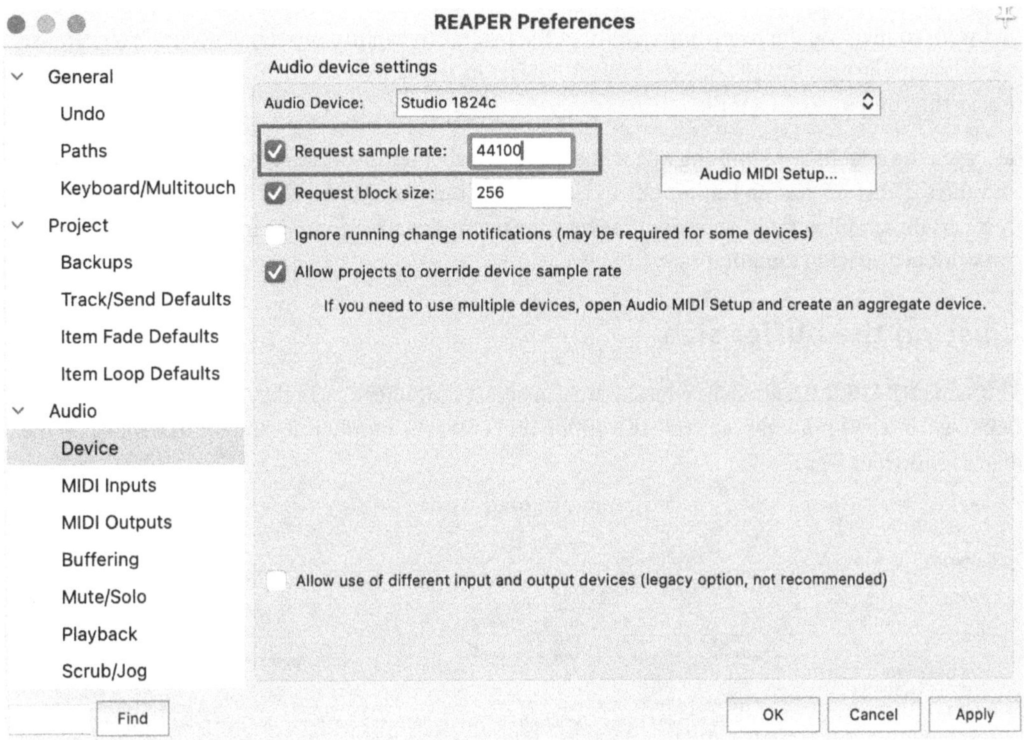

Figure 1.8 – Selecting the sampling rate

As we saw earlier, we have two groups of possible sampling rates: those that are multiples of 44,100 Hz and those that are multiples of 48,000 Hz. For many years, there was a debate about which one was better in quality; however, they are currently considered practically equal.

The choice between them will depend on the type of project we are going to undertake. When it comes to music projects or audio content (e.g., podcasts) intended for distribution on streaming services or for use on a CD, it is advisable to work on the project at 44,100 Hz, as this is the CD standard and has been adopted by most streaming services to date.

For any other type of audio project, such as audio for video, film, video games, immersive sound, or multimedia projects, it is recommended to use 48,000 Hz, as this is the standard for professional audio in general.

> **Tip**
>
> If it is uncertain what the application or distribution of the project will be, it is most advisable to use 48 kHz.

If you want to increase the recording quality of the project to capture more harmonics, you can use twice the sampling rate, that is, 88,200 Hz or 96,000 Hz. As explained earlier, this may limit the number of tracks the computer can handle.

In all cases, the established sampling rate will depend on whether the interface or sound card supports such values. REAPER has no limitations in this regard, but audio interfaces are limited to working only at certain sampling rates. You should review the documentation for your interface to see whether it can work at a specific sampling rate.

Adjusting the buffer size

In this same **REAPER Preferences** window, we can adjust the buffer size in the option labeled **Request block size**. Here, we must also activate the option and enter the number of samples that make up the buffer, as shown in *Figure 1.9*:

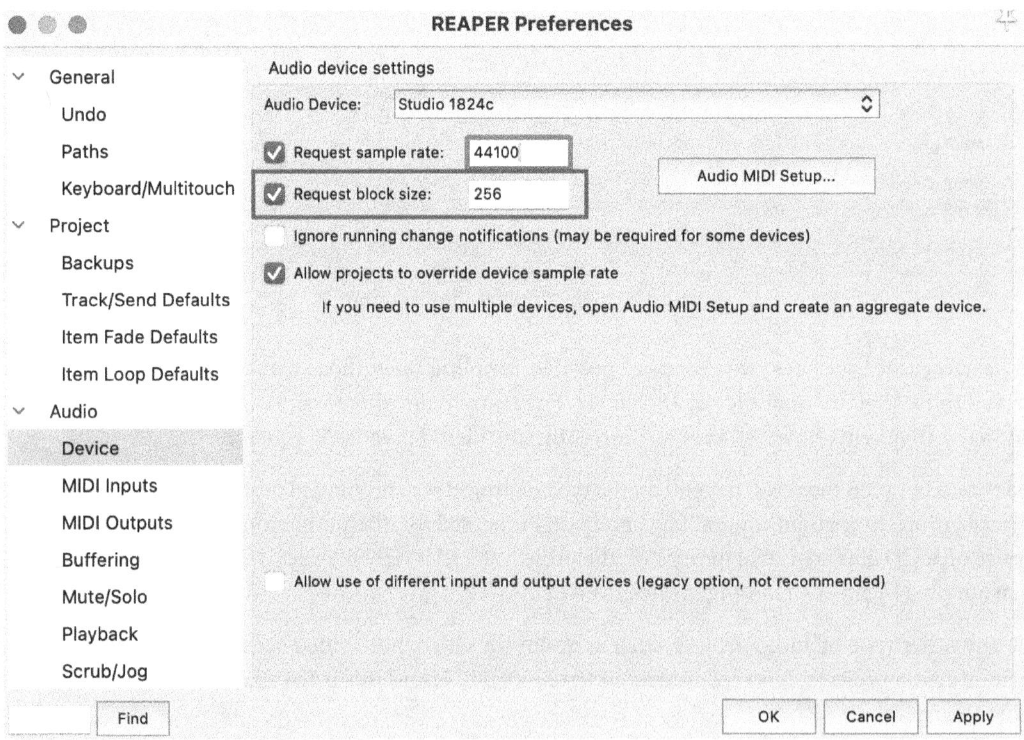

Figure 1.9 – Adjusting the buffer size

As we have seen, the smaller this number is, the less latency we will have when monitoring the audio; however, our CPU will work more intensively.

Ideally, we want to find the smallest buffer size that our system supports. A good starting point is 256 samples.

> **Important note**
>
> It is advisable to adjust this value in numbers related to the binary system, such as 32, 64, 128, 256, 512, or 1,024.

When the buffer is too small for the system, clicks and audio dropouts may be heard while playing. This is an indication that the buffer size needs to be increased. This is a trial-and-error process that should be undertaken for each system and project.

In the REAPER *menu bar*, we can see an indicator that tells us the sampling rate we are working with, as well as the latency in milliseconds, as shown in *Figure 1.10*:

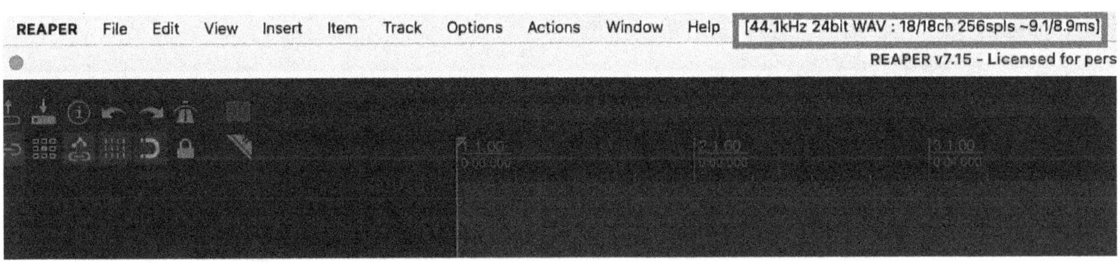

Figure 1.10 – REAPER's project data

In the preceding screenshot, we see that the project is set to **44.1** kHz and **24** bits and that the buffer of **256** samples we have selected gives us around 9 milliseconds of latency. Most musicians can comfortably record with latencies lower than 10 ms; however, with longer delays, it can become uncomfortable and difficult to play music with the correct timing.

Project settings

Another window that we must always adjust at the beginning of each project is **Project Settings**. This window can be accessed from the **File** | **Project Settings** menu. This window has several tabs, as seen in *Figure 1.11*:

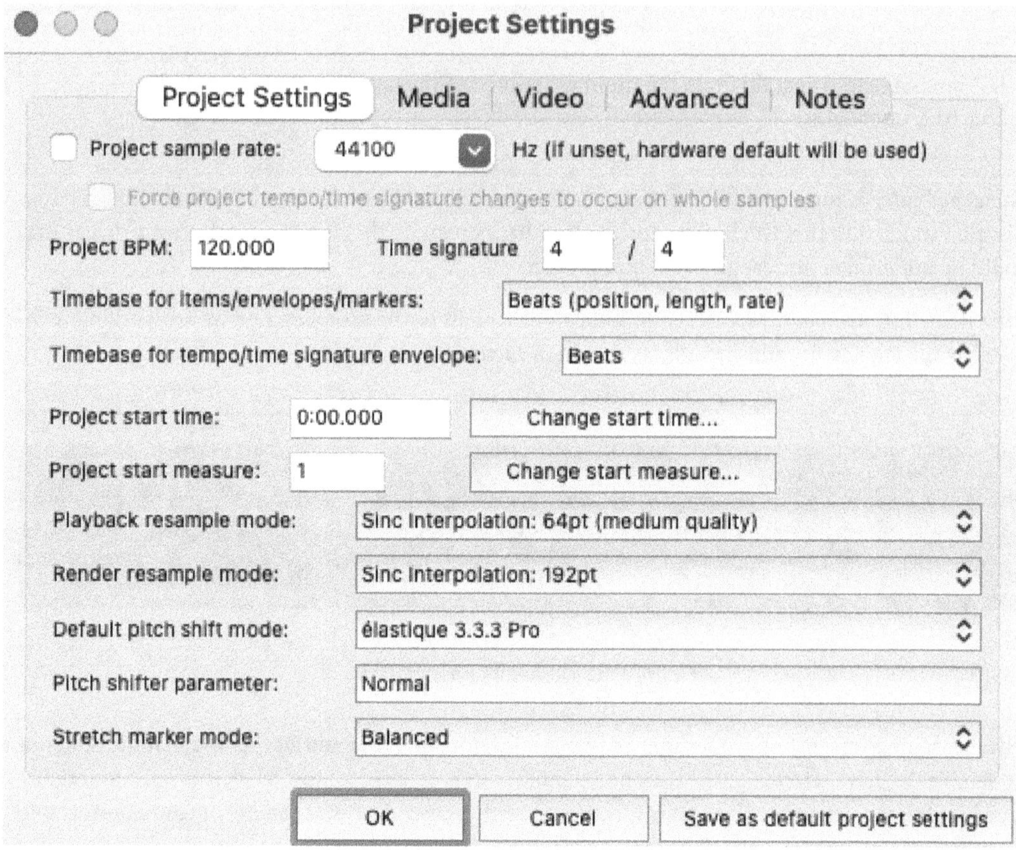

Figure 1.11 – Project Settings window

In the **Project Settings** tab, we can set a different sampling rate than the system's if necessary (which is not recommended). Also, here we will define the **Project BPM** (the project's tempo in beats per minute or BPM), the **Time signature** used, and other advanced settings.

An important adjustment is found in the **Media** tab. In these options, we can define the path where the audio and video files used in the project will be saved. By default, the `Media` folder will be created within the project folder.

Finally, in the **Recording** section under the **Media** tab, we can choose the type of audio file that will be generated when recording in REAPER. The recommendation here is to use WAV files, as they are of the highest quality and compatibility, as shown in *Figure 1.12*:

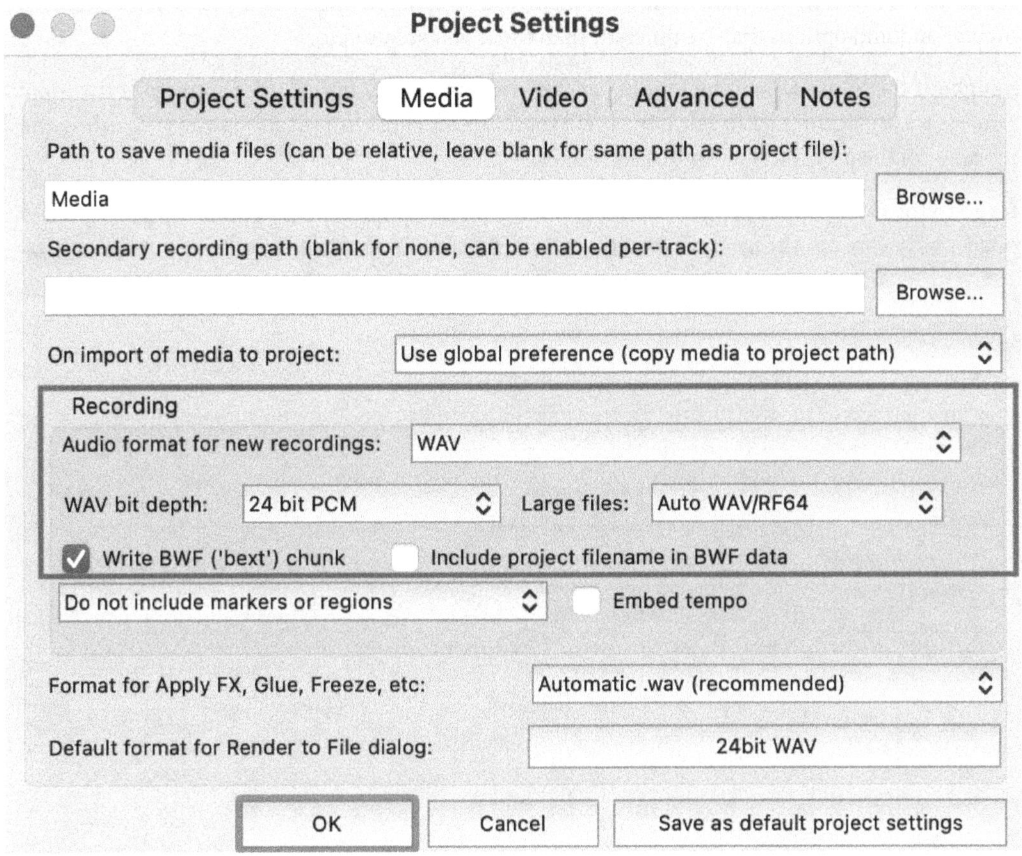

Figure 1.12 – Media tab

Here, we can also select the bit depth of the recordings. Although 16 bits is often a good option overall, it is recommended to use 24 bits to achieve the best audio quality when recording. Values higher than this are usually not necessary in most projects.

The most important settings when creating a new project are choosing the audio device and its driver, the sampling rate and bit depth of the project, as well as the type of audio file we will record.

Now let's look at some preferences related to the appearance of REAPER while working with it.

Customization options

One of REAPER's most notable features is its customizability. In fact, REAPER can be customized so much that in some cases it can be counterproductive, as you might open REAPER on someone else's computer and find options that are different than those you are used to.

Throughout the book, we will be looking at the most important options depending on the topic or project we are dealing with. For now, I will mention the most important options regarding the appearance of the user interface in this section.

If we go to the **Options** | **Settings** menu, the first tab on the left is called **General**, as we can see in *Figure 1.13*. Here we can change the **Language** of REAPER, the **Undo settings**, and the **Startup settings**.

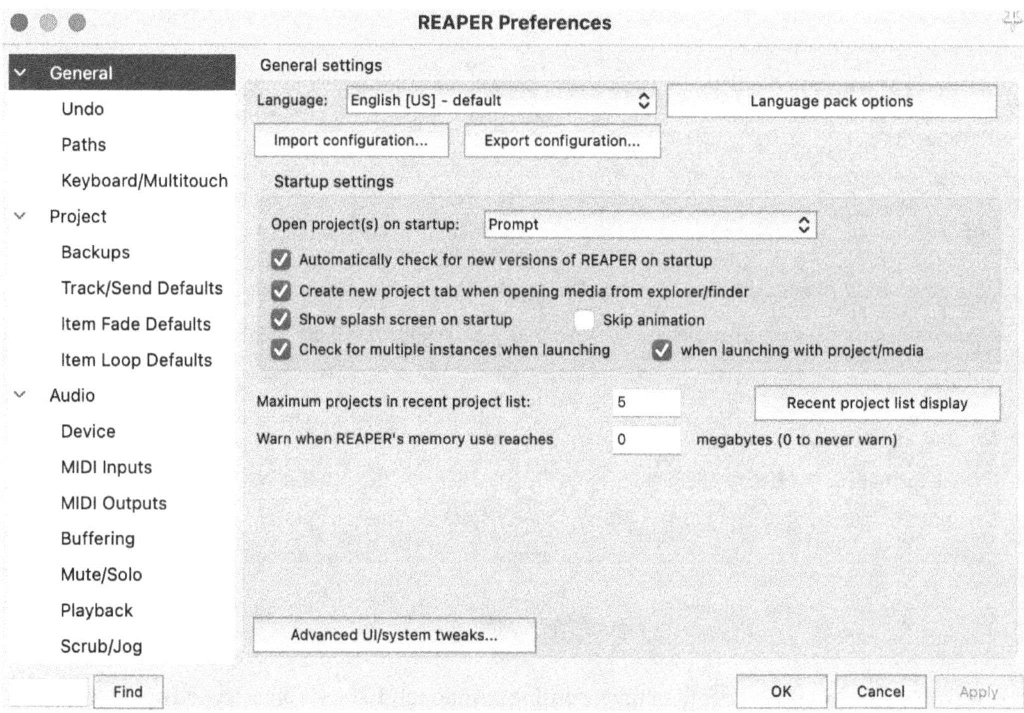

Figure 1.13 – General preferences

In the **General** section, there are also options to adjust the keyboard and multitouch pad if you have one.

Next, in the **Appearance** section, we find many options that we can change according to our preferences or needs. Among the most prominent of these is **Tooltips**, which makes it easier to understand the REAPER interface, as we see in *Figure 1.14*:

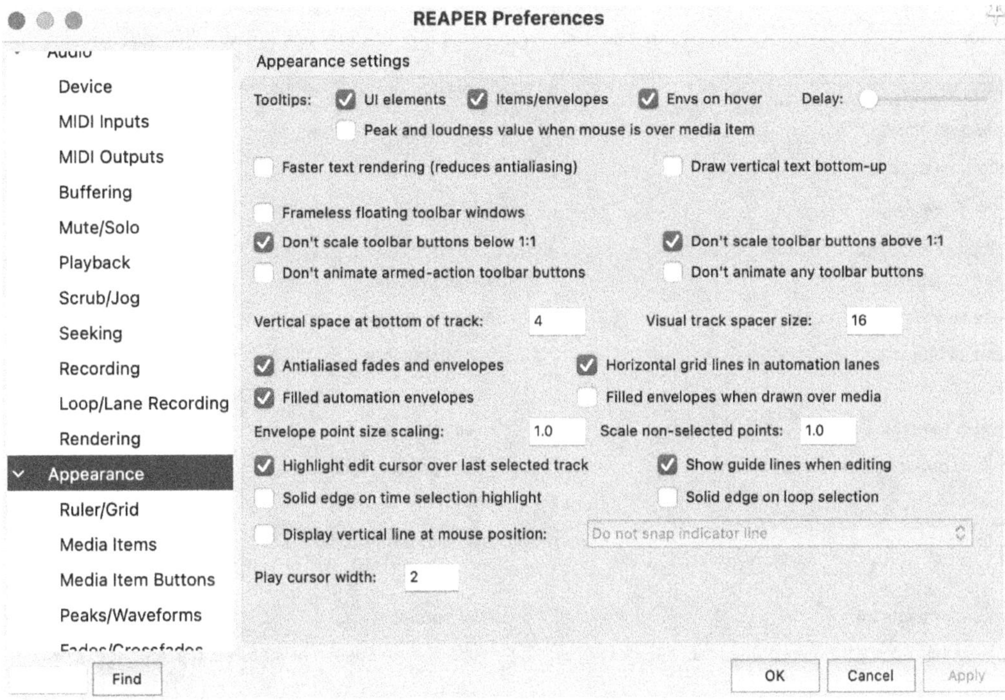

Figure 1.14 – Appearance section

In this window, we can also adjust the cursor width and the space between tracks. As we can see, there are many options; however, REAPER provides a general explanation of each at the bottom of the window when we hover the mouse over them.

> **Note**
>
> It is important to mention that in Windows, the content of the **Appearance** section may vary slightly.

If we go to the **Options** | **Customize menus/toolbars** menu, a window will appear where we can adjust the content of each menu in REAPER, as shown in *Figure 1.15*:

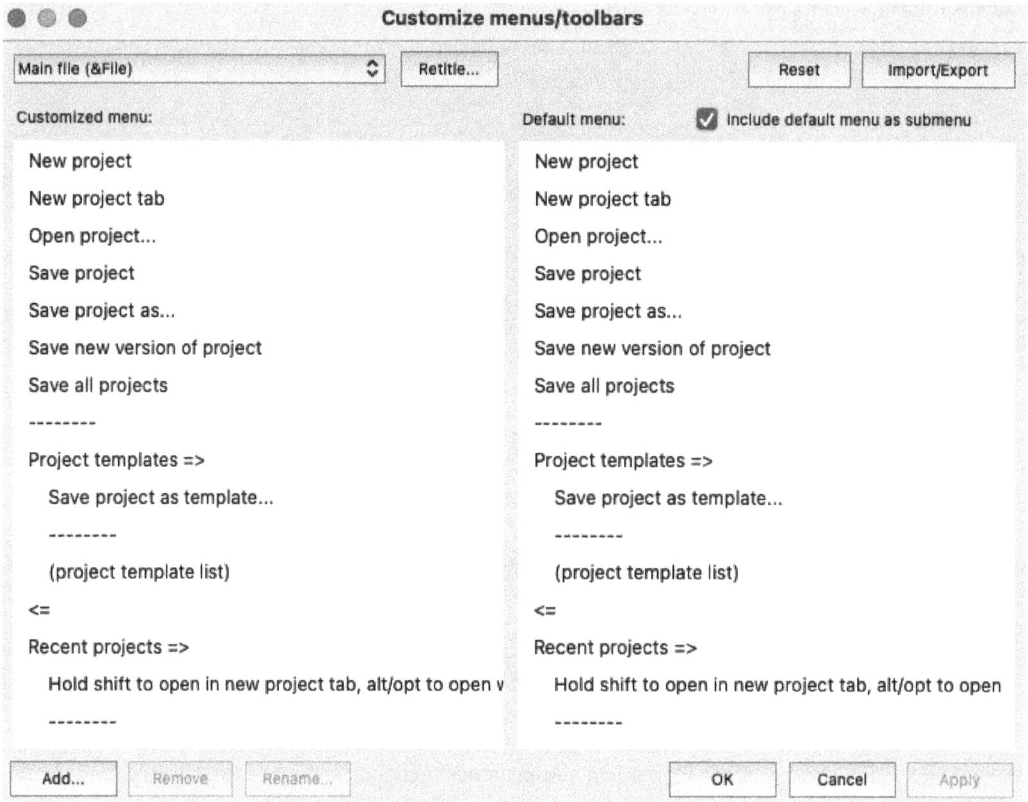

Figure 1.15 – Custom menus tool

This is a window where the available functions can be radically changed, so caution must be exercised not to remove options that may be useful.

Finally, in the **Options** | **Themes** menu, we will find the themes that come by default in REAPER, as well as a **Theme Adjuster** to change the colors of each part of the program. It is worth mentioning that REAPER has a highly active online community (`https://forum.cockos.com/`), where we can find many options shared by other users, such as themes and icon sets.

Throughout the book, we will focus on the functions that come by default in REAPER, but it is important to know that as you become familiar with REAPER, you have the option to customize it in a detailed way.

Summary

In this chapter, we have seen the major features that make REAPER a different and, in many cases, unique DAW. We have also covered important concepts of digital audio, such as latency, sampling rate, and bit depth, so you can set up your projects using the correct resolution. Now you know how to configure REAPER to use your audio interface, as well as access the menus to customize some aspects of it.

In the next chapter, we will start working by importing and recording audio and MIDI, which is the first step in a music or audio project.

2

Recording Audio and MIDI in REAPER

Recording is the first stage in the production process. During recording, the takes that will form the material we will work with are captured. In recording, it is important to take care of the technical aspect to avoid noise or distortion that may affect the quality of the take; however, it is also very important to seek the appropriate performance, one that has the required intention or feeling. Although this last point is beyond the scope of this book, it is important to mention it.

In this chapter, we will begin to generate content for our project in REAPER. To do this, you will learn how to perform three basic activities: importing audio files, recording audio files, and recording MIDI sequences. Each of these actions offers us different characteristics and advantages, depending on what we need in our production.

In this chapter, we will cover the following main topics:

- **Importing audio files**: This will allow us to use previously recorded content, such as audio from libraries or other projects.
- **Recording audio files**: This will allow us to capture sounds from musical instruments or voices. It is often the most common way to work on an audio production.
- **Recording MIDI sequences:** This will allow us to make recordings using synthesizers or virtual instruments, which will greatly expand the sound palette available to a modern music producer.
- **Troubleshooting**: This section will give us useful information about common problems found while recording (such as noise, distortion, etc.), and how to solve them.

By the end of this chapter, you will know how to perform different types of recordings properly. This will give you a lot of versatility and options to work with all kinds of sound material in your productions. The rest of the content of this book is based on having recorded material of good quality, so it is very important to carry out the correct procedures, such as those you will learn about in this chapter.

Technical requirements

To be able to carry out the activities in this chapter, it is necessary to have installed an audio interface with microphone or instrument input. You can use a USB interface similar to the **Focusrite Scarlett**, **Behringer U-Phoria**, **PreSonus Studio**, and **Arturia MiniFuse**, among others. The computer's sound card can also be used if it has a microphone or line input.

You can use audio from a microphone connected to the interface, or from an instrument, such as an electric guitar or keyboard.

You may find it useful to use the project created in the previous chapter to apply the concepts of this chapter.

Importing audio files

In REAPER, we have different ways of getting audio content into our project (importing audio, recording audio, and recording MIDI). The first way we will see this is by importing audio files, as this is the easier one.

Importing files means adding previous recordings made either by ourselves or by someone else. There are many possible sources of audio files, including the following:

- Audio files from other REAPER projects or another DAW. This is a good option if you want to reuse material from past projects.
- Files downloaded from an audio portal on the internet (e.g., `freesound.org`, `pixabay.com`, etc.). This will give you a lot of options that you can search, depending on your needs.
- Audio files from commercial libraries or packs (e.g., `splice.com`, `loopmasters.com`, etc.). These are usually organized by genre, mood, or musical instrument.
- Files recorded on other systems, such as mobile devices (cell phones or tablets) or portable recorders. Sometimes, you may record something in the field and wish to use that recording in a project.

As we can see, importing files allows us to obtain a large source of resources that we can use in a production, without the need to record them ourselves.

Saving projects

Once we have created a new project, it is advisable to save it to ensure that all the files we use are in order. For this, we can go to the **File** | **Save project** menu. You can use *Cmd* + *S* on Mac or *Ctrl* + *S* on Windows. Most shortcuts are written next to each menu command, as seen in *Figure 2.1*. So, you can learn them as you use them on your operating system.

> **Tip**
> It is highly recommended to always use keyboard shortcuts to work faster in REAPER.

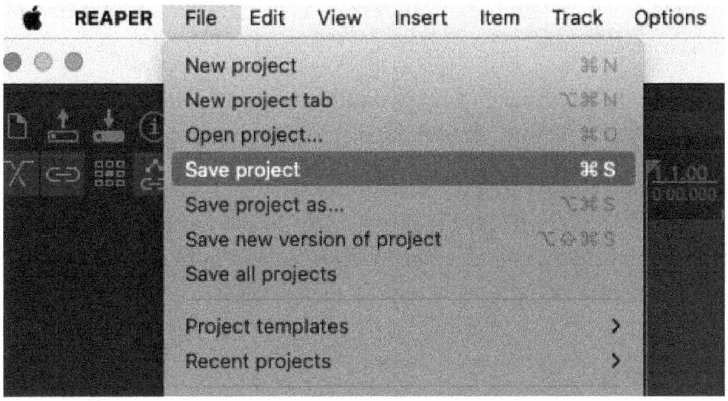

Figure 2.1 – Keyboard shortcuts

Then, after clicking on **Save project**, a window will appear on which we must name the project and indicate where it will be saved (see *Figure 2.2*). The extension for REAPER projects is `.RPP`.

There are a couple of options worth selecting in this dialog: **Create subdirectory for project** and **Copy all media into project directory, using**. These will help us keep our projects organized.

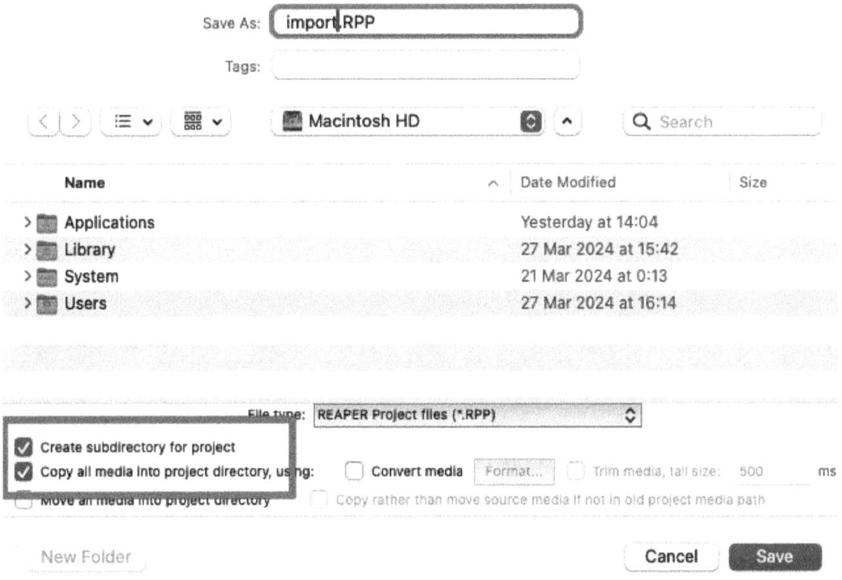

Figure 2.2 – Saving a project

REAPER will create a folder with the project name and the `.RPP` file in it; this file contains all the project information. It is important to clarify that `.RPP` files do not include any audio files; they only include session information, edits, mixing and automation information, and so on. The audio files will be in the `Media` subfolder, which is automatically created when the **Create subdirectory for project** option is activated, as seen in *Figure 2.2*.

This means that if we want to move our project to another computer, we must copy the entire project folder, not just the `.RPP` file! This way, we will also take the corresponding audio files with us.

Once the project is saved, we must ensure that all imported files are automatically copied to the `Media` subfolder. To do this, go to **REAPER Preferences** in the **Options | Settings** menu, then to the **Media | Import** section, and activate the **Copy imported media to project media directory (can be overridden in project settings)** option, as seen in *Figure 2.3*:

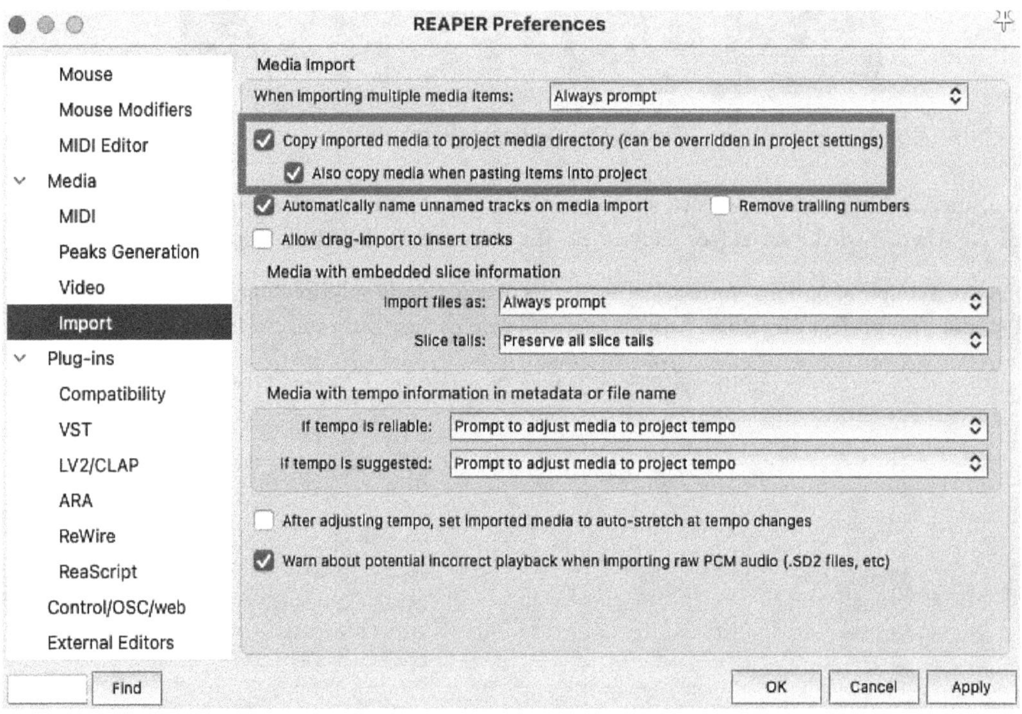

Figure 2.3 – Copying imported files to the project

The **Also copy media when pasting items into project** option should be active, too. This makes it possible to copy audio files when dropping files into REAPER. Activating these options is very important when we want to move or store projects because, if they are disabled, we can import and work with audio files in our project but the files will remain in their original location and not in the `Media` subfolder.

So far, we have seen the importance of knowing how to import audio files, as well as saving projects and activating options to keep our imported files organized. Now, we will explore how to use REAPER's **Media Explorer** to import files.

Delving into Media Explorer

The most convenient way to import media files into our project is through **Media Explorer**, which is a window within REAPER that lets us navigate through our computer's filesystem efficiently. With **Media Explorer**, we can preview files or choose how to import them into a project, as we will see next.

To access it, go to the **View | Media Explorer** menu. By default, **Media Explorer** opens at the bottom of the REAPER window, as seen in *Figure 2.4*:

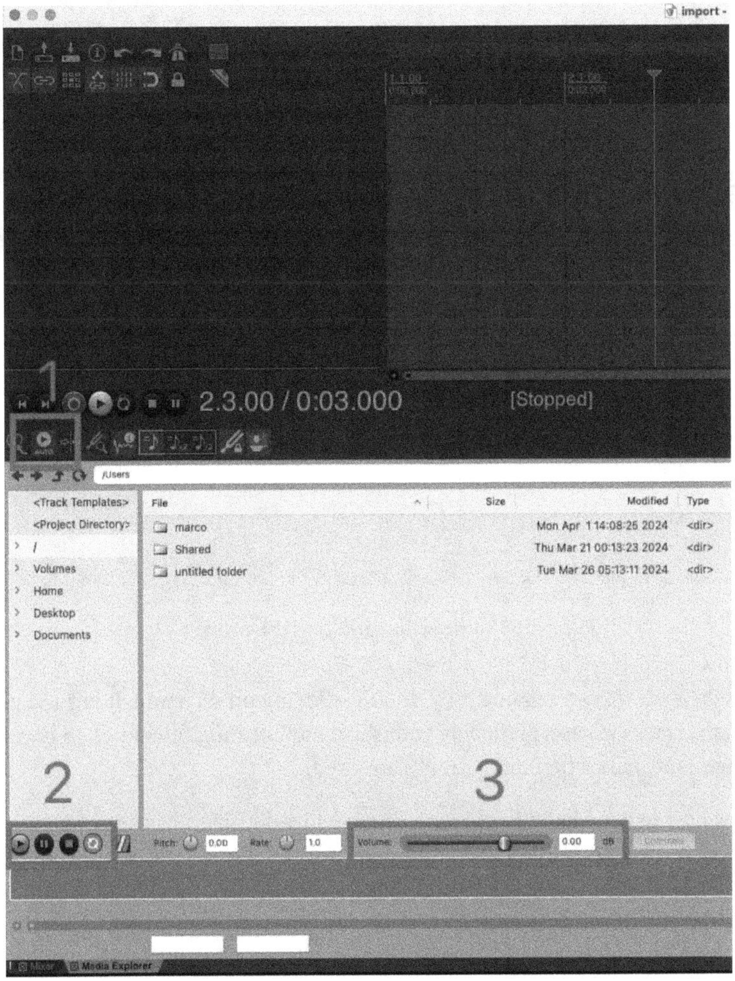

Figure 2.4 – Media Explorer

Within **Media Explorer**, we can navigate our system through folders and files.

One of the advantages of working with **Media Explorer** is that we can preview the files before importing them, either using the Transport buttons (labeled as **2**) or by leaving the **AUTO play** option activated (labeled as **1**), as seen in *Figure 2.4*. This window also has a **Volume** control for previewing the audio file (labeled as **3**).

Once we select a file to import, we can simply drag it to the Arrange area at the top or press the **Insert** button, as seen in *Figure 2.5*. This way, REAPER will create a new track with our file:

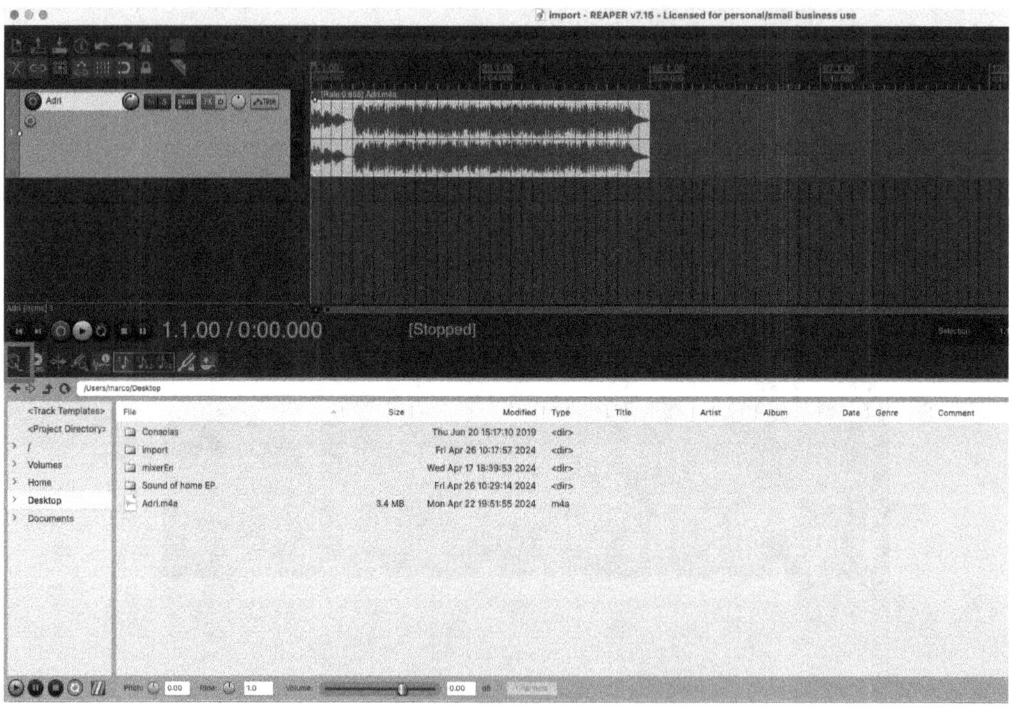

Figure 2.5 – Importing audio to the project

Once the track is created, we can rename it by double-clicking on its name. It is good practice to get used to renaming the tracks we use, preferably with short and meaningful names, to have good control of our session later, especially when many tracks are used.

Now that we know how to use **Media Explorer** to import files, let's learn about the arrange area, which is the main window of REAPER.

The arrangement window

Now, let's look at the main parts of the REAPER **arrangement window** (see *Figure 2.6*), where we can manipulate our audio files. In the top-left corner, we have the *toolbar* (labeled as **1**), which we'll detail in *Chapter 3*.

In the bottom-left corner is the *transport bar* (labeled as **2**), where the playback, record, stop, rewind buttons, and so on are located. Each one has a shortcut that we can see by hovering the mouse on each button.

In the bottom-right corner, we have several *controls* (labeled as **3**), including the project tempo. Here, we can adjust the **beats per minute** (**BPM**) of our project if it involves music. We also see horizontal and vertical zoom buttons (+ and -) (labeled as **4**), which are very useful for better visualizing our files.

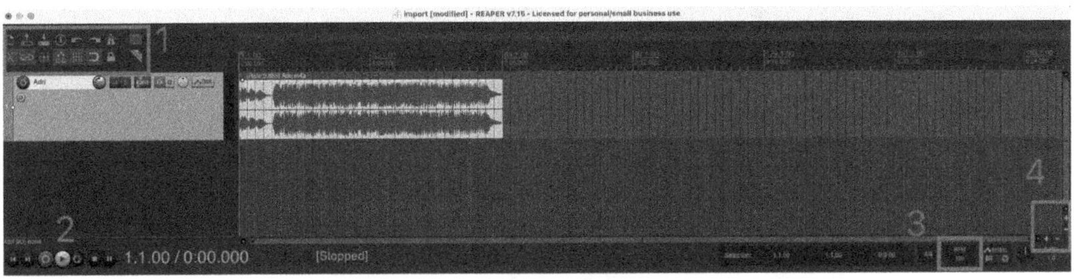

Figure 2.6 – Arrangement window

We also have other controls, such as global automation, time signature, and rate, but we will cover those in *Chapter 4*.

Using loops

A very common resource is called an **audio loop**. A **loop** is an audio file that contains a musical phrase or basic rhythm. The main characteristic of a loop is that it is edited so that we can paste several loops one after another and, thus, form a continuous section of music.

Using loops in a music production allows us to create music without having to record each instrument individually. Instead, we can use musical phrases that may have been created by us previously or by someone else. For example, we can use a drum loop to give rhythm to a song without needing to record the drums ourselves.

Loops are a fundamental part of many contemporary music styles, such as hip-hop, EDM, pop, and so on. In REAPER, we can import loops with the advantage of being able to change their pitch or tempo to fit the project's tempo.

In **Media Explorer**, we have several tools for importing loops, as seen in *Figure 2.7*:

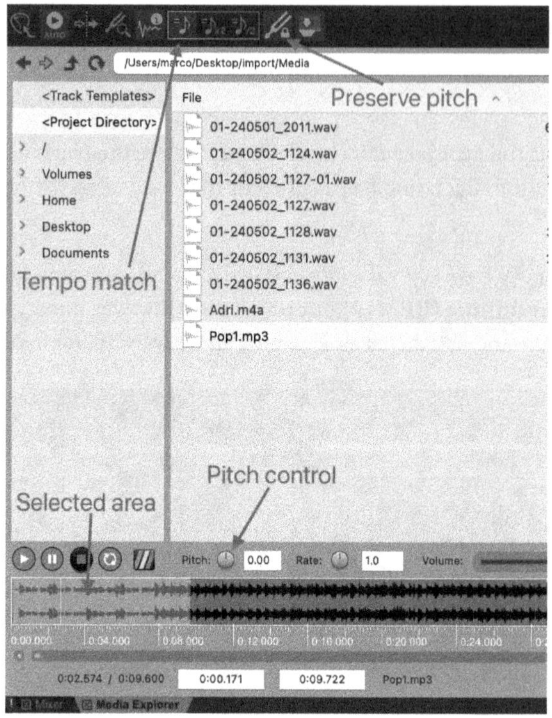

Figure 2.7 – Media Explorer tools

If we want REAPER to match the tempo of the file to that of the project, we must activate the **Tempo match** option. There, we also have the option to double the speed of the file or reduce it by half. This allows us to use loops of various tempos and have REAPER adjust them according to the project or work creatively.

We can make REAPER change the tempo of a file but preserve its pitch by activating the **Preserve pitch** button. If we deactivate this option, we will make the file higher pitched at faster tempos and lower pitched at slower tempos. This preference will depend entirely on the effect you are looking for.

We can also change the pitch of the file to our liking with the **Pitch** option at the bottom of the screen. Here, we can increase or decrease the pitch by semitones or fractions of a semitone. This option is usually useful when using files of a melodic instrument (bass, flute, saxophone, etc.) and we need it to fit a different key.

When importing an audio file from **Media Explorer**, it is not necessary to import the entire file. We can select only a part with the mouse and then drag it to the arrangement window or use the **Insert** button, as mentioned before.

Although we can also import audio simply by dragging a file from the computer desktop to the REAPER window, working with **Media Explorer** offers many advantages, as mentioned in the preceding paragraphs, so it is the recommended way to import audio.

We have seen how to import loops into REAPER, as well as how to adapt them to the tempo of our project, change or preserve their pitch, and even select only a part of the audio file if we want. Now, let's look at the procedure for making audio recordings in REAPER.

Recording audio files

Recording audio files is one of the most important tasks in any DAW. Through the recording process, we can capture vocals or musical instruments for a project, giving us extensive creative freedom. In REAPER, the recording process is quite straightforward, as we will see in the steps that follow:

1. The first thing we need to do is create a new empty audio track. We can do this with the **Track | Insert new track** menu or using the shortcut *Ctrl* + *T* (*Cmd* + *T* on Mac).
2. Once the track is created, we need to select the input of our interface where the microphone or audio source we want to record is connected. We can do this from the **Mixer** window, which we can show using the tab at the bottom, as seen in *Figure 2.8*:

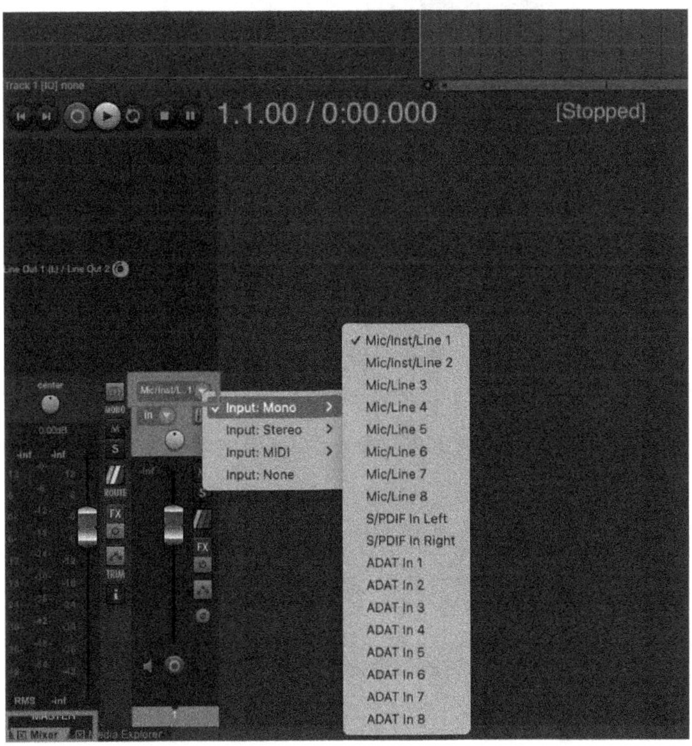

Figure 2.8 – Assigning recording input

In *Figure 2.8*, we can also see the menu of available inputs that appear at the top of the track. This menu will depend on the audio device we have selected in the REAPER settings. For example, if your interface only has two inputs, then only those will appear in the list.

Generally, we will have the option to choose mono or stereo inputs. Most of the time, we will use **mono inputs** because these are used to record individual microphones. **Stereo inputs** can be used to record stereo sources, such as synthesizers, effects processors, or music players that use two channels of the interface simultaneously (i.e., Left and Right channels).

Recording level

Once the appropriate input is selected, we must arm the track to record on it. **Arming a track** is the action of preparing a track for recording. It acts as a sort of safeguard that helps us control which tracks we can record on and which ones we cannot. We do this with the *red* button at the bottom of the track. This is a kind of safety feature that allows us to record only on tracks that are armed, as seen in *Figure 2.9*:

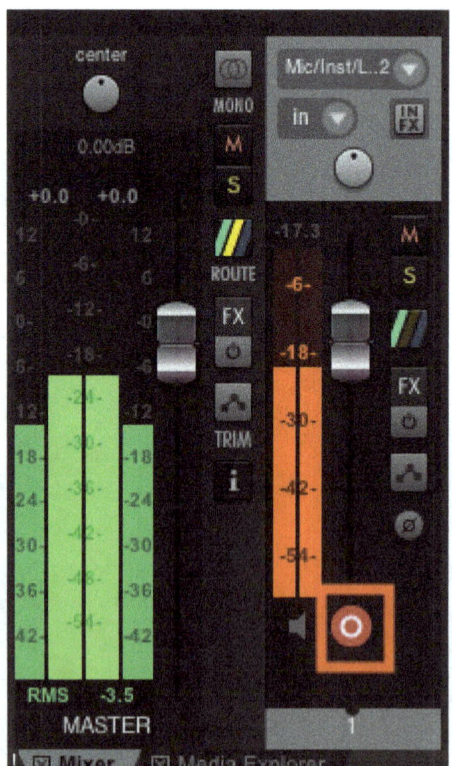

Figure 2.9 – Arming a track for recording

When we arm a track for recording, we can see the input signal level on the red meters. Here comes a very important part for recording properly: *we must adjust the signal level so that it hovers around -18 dBFS*, as seen in *Figure 2.9*.

Decibels (dB) are values used in audio to show the level of a signal. In the case of digital systems (such as DAWs), the most common decibels are called **decibels full-scale (dBFS)**. In a dBFS scale, the maximum value is 0 dB, and the entire scale is negative. A signal exceeding 0 dBFS will generate distortion, so we must avoid this when recording. In the REAPER **Mixer** window, the numbers on the recording meters indicate dBFS.

Adjusting the recording level depends on several factors. Let's examine some of the key factors:

- The first is the *gain knob* on our interface. We must identify the gain knob of the input we are using and adjust the level while speaking, singing, or playing the instrument to be recorded.
- The second factor is the *intensity of the performer*. If someone sings or plays very loudly, we can use less gain, but if they sing or play softly, we will need to use more gain. The important thing is to ask the musician to perform with the intensity they intend to record, so we can adjust the gain in a more realistic way.
- The third factor is the *type of microphone* being used. There is a wide variety of microphones, types, and models. Each of them has a different sensitivity, which is the amount of voltage they generate when used. Thus, a microphone with higher sensitivity will require less gain than one with low sensitivity. For this reason, it is normal to use different amounts of gain with each type of microphone.
- The fourth factor is the *instrument or source* being recorded. With electronic instruments, we can use their volume, in conjunction with the interface gain, to adjust the recording level. With acoustic instruments or vocals, the level depends on the performance volume and the distance between the source and the microphone. Ideally, we should not change this distance once the gain has been set, as moving the microphone closer or farther away will result in significant changes in the input level.

As we can see, several factors are involved when adjusting the recording level. They are all related to each other and will determine how much gain to use for a clean recording. If any of these factors change, we must ensure that the signal remains at the appropriate level.

The goal is always to leave the signal at an average of approximately **-18 dBFS**, regardless of whether the gain knob is very low or very high. This way, we will have 18 dB of **headroom**, which is the space reserved to capture the loudest parts of a recording without distortion. It is normal for the signal to be below -18 dBFS in some parts or to rise and reach near the maximum point; however, we must avoid it reaching 0 dBFS.

The headroom of 18 dB is usually sufficient in most cases, but if at any time the signal reaches 0 dBFS, a *red* indicator will light up at the top of the track, as seen in *Figure 2.10*. This means that the signal may begin clipping or distorting.

Figure 2.10 – Clipping indicator

In these cases, we can click on the indicator to reset it, and then we will have to reduce the gain to avoid distortion in the recording. Correct adjustment of the recording level is one of the critical points to obtain good quality results in audio production, so we must pay proper attention at the beginning of a recording.

To record properly, we must also be able to hear ourselves clearly. This is called **monitoring**. Let's see how to adjust our monitoring in REAPER.

Monitoring options

The type of monitoring we use depends a lot on the interface we have. Simpler interfaces usually have an output for headphones and studio monitors (speakers), as well as a knob to adjust their volume. Any of these options will be our main monitor. Larger interfaces often have more headphone outputs or additional monitor outputs.

If we do not have an interface, monitoring will be done through the computer's sound card, which has an output for headphones, and its volume must be controlled by software, from some menu or setting in the operating system.

When we arm a track for recording in REAPER and adjust its input level to -18 dBFS, we should be able to hear the audio that is coming in. The volume of this monitoring should be adjusted with the volume knob of the interface (or the volume of the sound card), not with the input gain.

That is, *we should no longer adjust the gain* to hear louder but adjust the volume of the interface, speakers, or sound card to listen at a comfortable volume. It is important to mention that the REAPER channel fader does not affect the recording level but does affect the monitoring volume, so we can also move this fader if we need an adjustment to our monitoring, as seen in *Figure 2.11*:

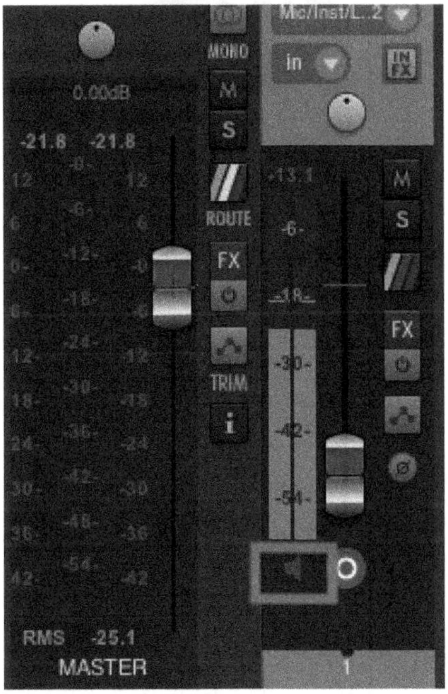

Figure 2.11 – Fader at the bottom

In the preceding screenshot, we see that the signal continues to enter the channel even though the fader is at the minimum. Unlike in *Figure 2.9*, on the left side of **MASTER**, there is no signal appearing. This indicates that no signal is being sent to the main outputs; therefore, we will not hear anything in the monitoring.

Below the channel meter, we can see a small *speaker* icon; this indicates the monitoring mode that is active. The initial mode is the Auto mode, which shows a *red speaker* icon, as seen in *Figure 2.11*. In this mode, we will hear the audio input while recording, but if we are not recording, we will hear the audio already recorded on the track. This is generally the most common and practical mode to use.

If we click on the *speaker* icon, it will change to a colorless state. Here, the monitoring will be turned off and we will not hear the incoming audio, only what is recorded on the track. Clicking the *speaker* icon again will change it to a *gray* color, as seen in *Figure 2.12*:

Figure 2.12 – Input monitoring

This is the **input monitoring mode**. Here, we can hear what is coming into the channel, but we will not be able to hear what is already on the track. As we can see, each mode serves a specific function, and we can select the one that works best for each situation.

Now that we know the channel monitoring options available in REAPER, we are ready to learn about the recording process.

Basic recording

Once we have an appropriate recording level and our monitoring is comfortable, we can start recording:

1. For this, we can use the **Record** button on the transport bar, as seen in *Figure 2.13*, or by using the keyboard shortcut *Ctrl* + *R* (*Cmf* + *R* on Mac).

Figure 2.13 – Record button

2. Then, we can see how a new audio item with the waveform in it is created on the track as we record.
3. We have two ways to stop recording. The first is by using the **Stop** button on the transport bar or by pressing the *spacebar*:

    I. REAPER will show us a window asking whether we want to save the recorded files or whether we want to delete or rename them. In this window, we can also deactivate the **on stop** option, so that REAPER always saves the new recorded files, as seen in *Figure 2.14*:

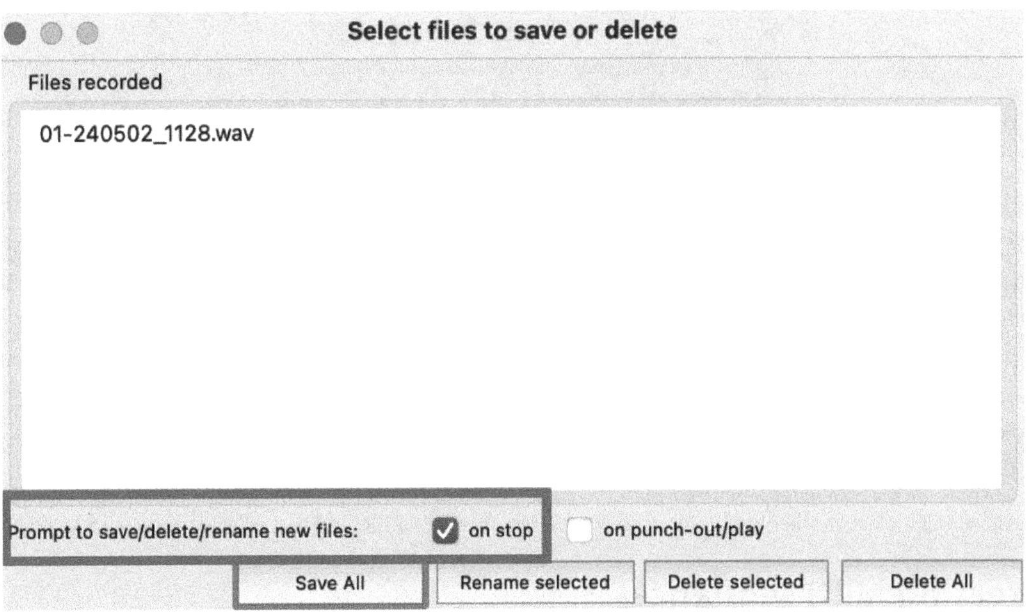

Figure 2.14 – Recording prompt

    II. In REAPER's settings, in the **Audio** | **Recording** section, we can also enable or disable this prompt each time we record something.

4. The second way to stop recording is by pressing the **Record** button or using the *Ctrl* + *R* shortcut again. This way, REAPER will not ask us what to do but will always save the take we just made.
5. In any case, if we don't like what we just recorded, we can undo the action with the **Edit** | **Undo** menu. In **REAPER Preferences**, within the **General** section, we can set the amount of memory to store the actions that we can undo, as well as some other related options, as seen in *Figure 2.15*. These options allow us to decide whether the selection of items, tracks, or time ranges will be included in the undo action list.

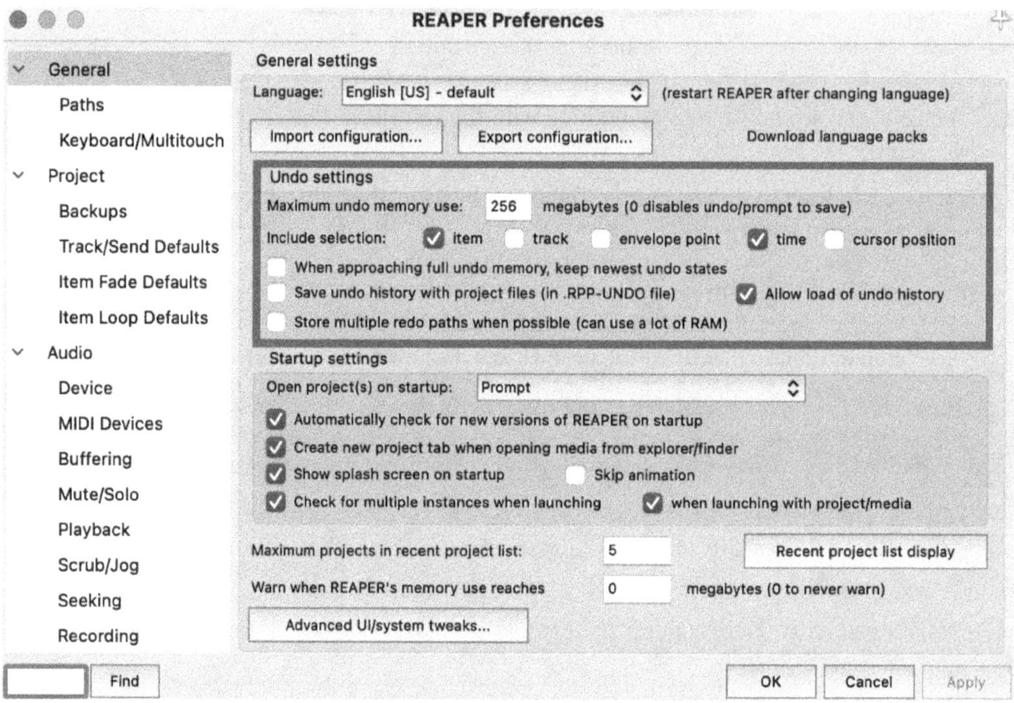

Figure 2.15 – Undo settings

As we've seen, the audio recording process in REAPER is straightforward but involves careful selection of the appropriate inputs and adjusting the recording level properly.

Next, we will look at another way to input sound content into REAPER, and that is by working with MIDI.

Creating MIDI sequences

In DAWs, there are primarily two types of content that we can record and edit: one is digital audio, as we've seen so far, and the other is MIDI information. Let's see what the latter entails.

What is MIDI?

MIDI (Musical Instruments Digital Interface) is a communication protocol developed in the early 1980s to establish communication between electronic musical instruments from different brands and models.

The original idea was to be able to play a synthesizer and have other interconnected keyboards sound at the same time. The communication principles of this protocol are so robust that, even though more than 40 years have passed since its creation, MIDI is still relevant and very important in today's music production. It is a very effective way to send musical information from one instrument (virtual or physical) to another, or from one software to another.

The basis of MIDI communication is through messages sent on channels. *MIDI handles 16 channels*, and the original idea was to use one channel for each different instrument. Among the most common messages, we have **Note On messages**, which indicate which note to play, with what intensity, and on which channel.

Example of MIDI communication

Let's see an example of MIDI communication. Suppose we connect a MIDI keyboard to a sound generator, as shown in *Figure 2.16*:

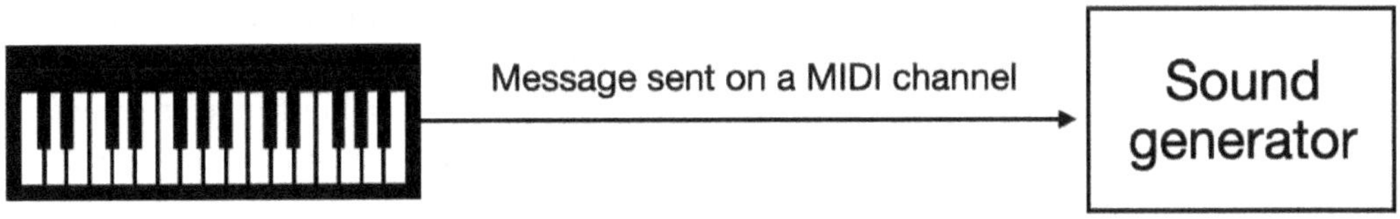

Figure 2.16 – Basic MIDI communication

If we press *note C4* on the keyboard, it will send a *Note On message* with *note C4* and a certain intensity to the sound generator on *channel 1*. Then, the sound generator receives the message and emits that note. When releasing the key, the keyboard now sends a **Note Off message** for *note C4*, which stops the note from sounding when received by the sound generator.

This process is repeated for each note played. It might seem like a lot of digital information; however, the data for an entire MIDI symphony weighs only a few **kB (kilobytes)**, which is very little compared to digital audio.

We can see that MIDI information is not audio, that is, it does not sound unless it reaches a sound generator (e.g., a synthesizer). Although it is also digital and uses bits, MIDI data indicates which notes to play or stop playing, with what sound and intensity, duration, and tempo, as well as some other parameters related to the performance.

We could think of MIDI data as a kind of *digital* score. A **musical score** is a sheet with information about musical performance, notes, timings, intensity, and so on but it has no sound. Similarly, MIDI is only digital information on how the notes should be played, but the sound must be generated by another element.

Now that we are familiar with basic MIDI communication, let's see the most common types of messages that we can encounter in a DAW such as REAPER.

MIDI messages

As mentioned earlier, messages are the basis of MIDI communication. In this section, we will explore some of the most common MIDI messages in music production.

Note On messages

One of the main MIDI messages is the **Note On message**. These messages must indicate which note to play. In MIDI, notes are assigned a number ranging from **0 to 127**. For example, the middle C note or C4 is assigned the number 60. The C#4 note is assigned number 61, D4 is 62, and so on. Unfortunately, this nomenclature is not standardized, so it is common to find instruments or music software where note 60 is called C3. In REAPER, note 60 is called C4, and the names of all other notes are derived from this.

The MIDI protocol handles more notes than is even possible with an instrument as extensive as the piano. A grand piano has 88 keys, ranging from note 21 (A0) to 108 (C8). As we can see, MIDI is much broader than any acoustic instrument in this respect.

The intensity of each note is determined by a parameter called **velocity**. This refers to the speed at which a note is played on a keyboard, so a higher velocity will generate a louder note. Its range also goes from **0 to 127**. For example, a velocity of **30** will produce a very *soft note (pianissimo)*, a velocity of **90** will produce a *loud note (forte)*, and the *loudest note (fortissimo)* will have a value of **127**. In REAPER, we can record MIDI notes and precisely control their duration and velocity according to our needs.

Control change messages

Another important type of message is the **Control Change (CC) message**. These messages are not musical notes but data that allow us to control many characteristics of the sound or performance. There are 128 types of control change ranging from **0 to 127**. Some of the most common ones are shown in *Figure 2.17*:

CC number	Name
1	Modulation wheel
7	Volume
10	Pan
11	Expression
64	Sustain pedal

Figure 2.17 – Common CC messages

Each of these controls has a range of variation from 0 to 127. For example, CC 7 is a message indicating the overall volume of the sound generator we are using. A value of 0 indicates zero volume, while 127 will be the maximum volume. Similarly, the other CC messages can help us generate expression and dynamics in a performance.

In REAPER, we can create and manipulate MIDI messages, both notes and controls, which gives us many creative possibilities in music production, as we will see in *Chapter 9* later in this book.

Using a virtual instrument

As we have seen when using MIDI data, we need a sound generator that receives this data and converts it into audio; we can do this with a synthesizer. Originally, MIDI was used with physical synthesizers, but currently, the most common practice is to use **virtual synthesizers**, which are plugins that serve the same function but within the computer.

Let's see how to use a virtual instrument in REAPER:

1. To do this, we will create a new track from **Track | Virtual instrument** on the **Track** menu. A window will appear with a list of all the plugins installed on the computer, as seen in *Figure 2.18*:

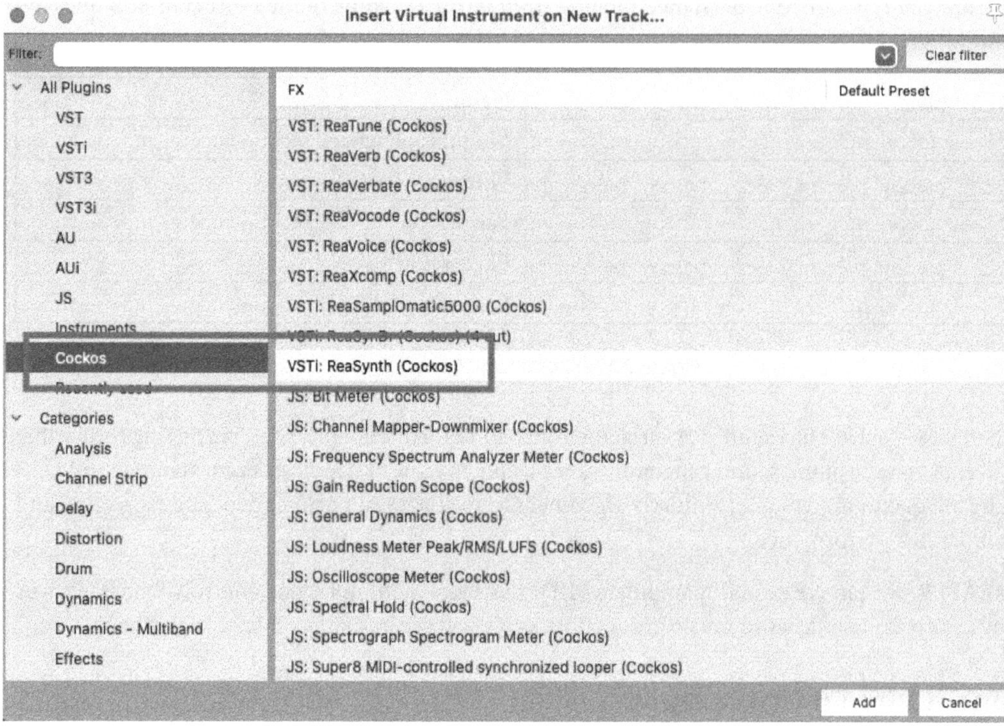

Figure 2.18 – Plugins window

2. For this example, we will use a synthesizer that comes installed by default with REAPER. In the left menu, navigate to the **Cockos** section and look for the **ReaSynth (Cockos)** synthesizer option, as seen in *Figure 2.18*.
3. All plugins in the **Cockos** category are included with REAPER. We can see three types of plugins: **VST**, **VSTi**, and **JS**. Let's look at each of them:
   - **VST**: These are the most common and popular plugins. **VST** (**Virtual Studio Technology**) was created by the company Steinberg several years ago and they were pioneers in creating plugins to process audio within the computer. In this category, we find effects and processors such as equalizers, reverbs, compressors, and so on.
   - **VSTi**: These are virtual instruments that use VST technology. This is where we find **ReaSynth** and other instruments.
   - **JS**: This refers to **JSFX** plugins. These plugins are exclusive to REAPER and are plugins that

the user can create or modify. They use the EEL2 (Extensible Embeddable Language 2) programming language and are part of REAPER's unique features because, thanks to them, a user with programming knowledge can modify or create their own plugins according to their needs.

In addition to the plugins created by Cockos, we can find on the internet an infinity of VST and VSTi plugins, both free and paid, with all kinds of features. If we want to install a new plugin, it is recommended to close REAPER first, follow the installation instructions of the developer, and then relaunch REAPER. Then, the list in *Figure 2.18* will be updated with the new plugin in the corresponding category.

4. Once we select and add the **ReaSynth** plugin with the **Add** button, the plugin window will open, and we will see the plugin in the **Inserts** section of **Mixer**, as shown in *Figure 2.19*:

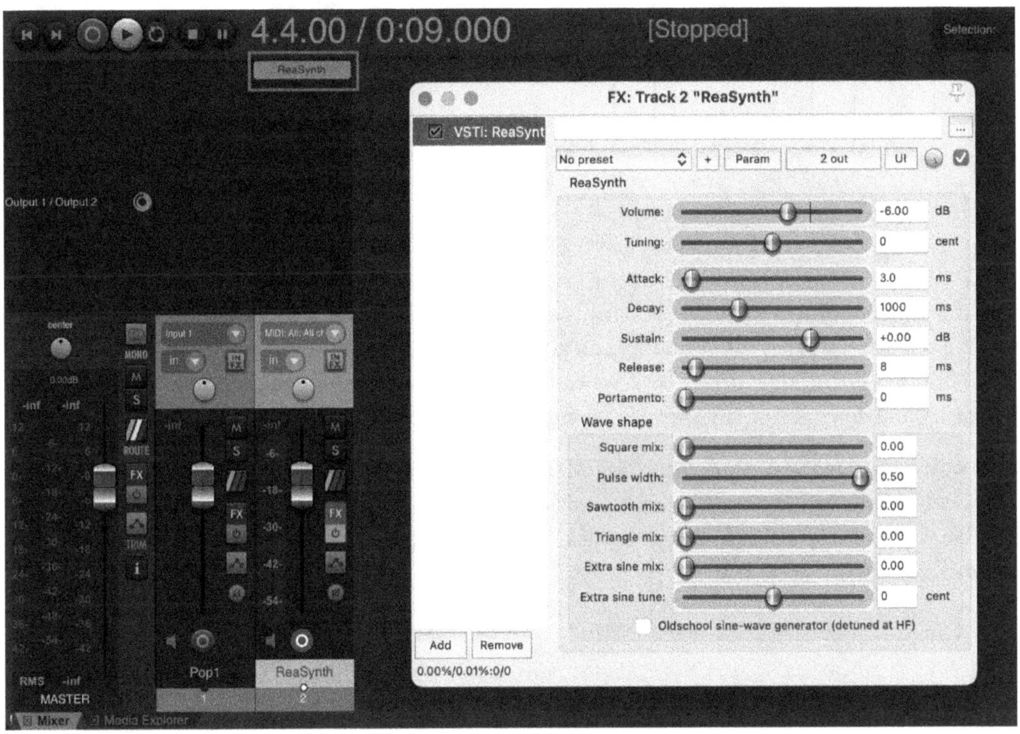

Figure 2.19 – ReaSynth plugin

Here, we can adjust the parameters of the sound generated by this synthesizer. For now, we will use the default loaded sound.

In this section, we've learned how to add a virtual instrument in REAPER and the types of plugins that can be used. Now, let's see how to add the MIDI notes that will make the instrument sound.

Creating MIDI notes

Once we have a sound generator, we can generate MIDI notes in various ways: using the virtual MIDI keyboard, using the mouse, or using a hardware MIDI controller.

Using the virtual MIDI keyboard

The first is by using a **Virtual MIDI keyboard**, which we can display from the **View | Virtual MIDI keyboard** menu. This virtual keyboard adapts our computer keyboard as if it were a small piano, as seen in *Figure 2.20*:

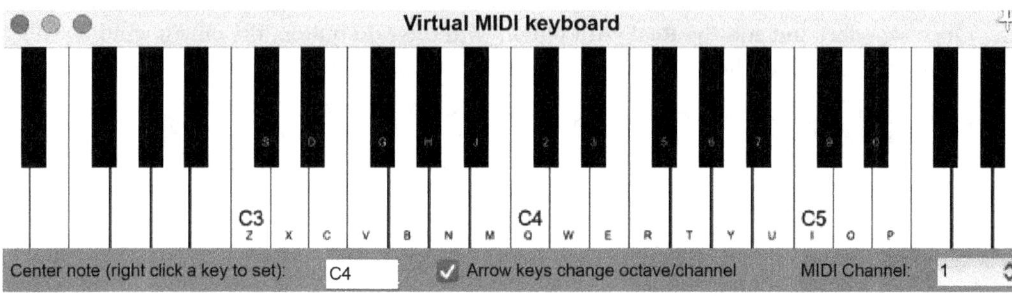

Figure 2.20 – Virtual MIDI keyboard

While the window of this virtual keyboard is active, we can use the indicated keys to play music notes. We see that the **Z** key is **C3**, and we can also play the black keys of the piano with **S**, **D**, **G**, and so on. With the *left* and *right arrow* keys, we can change octaves, making the sound lower or higher. With the *up* and *down arrow* keys, we can change the MIDI channel; for now, we will use channel 1.

In this way, we are ready to start recording MIDI or, as it is also known, create a **MIDI sequence**. Simply press the **Record** button or its keyboard shortcut, and we can start playing and recording MIDI notes. We will see a region appear on the track, but this time, it shows rectangular lines instead of a waveform, as seen in *Figure 2.21*:

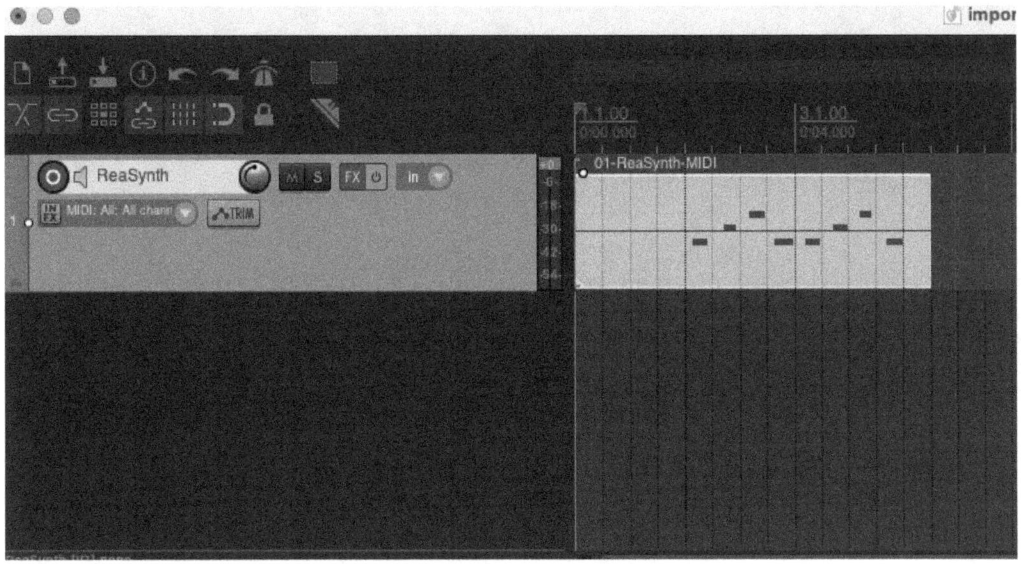

Figure 2.21 – MIDI region

These are the MIDI notes we have recorded, and, as we will see in the next chapter, we can edit these notes in many ways.

Using the New MIDI item menu

Another way to create MIDI notes from an empty track is by using the **Insert** | **New MIDI item** menu. This will create an empty region, and if we double-click on it, we will enter the **MIDI editor**, as shown in *Figure 2.22*:

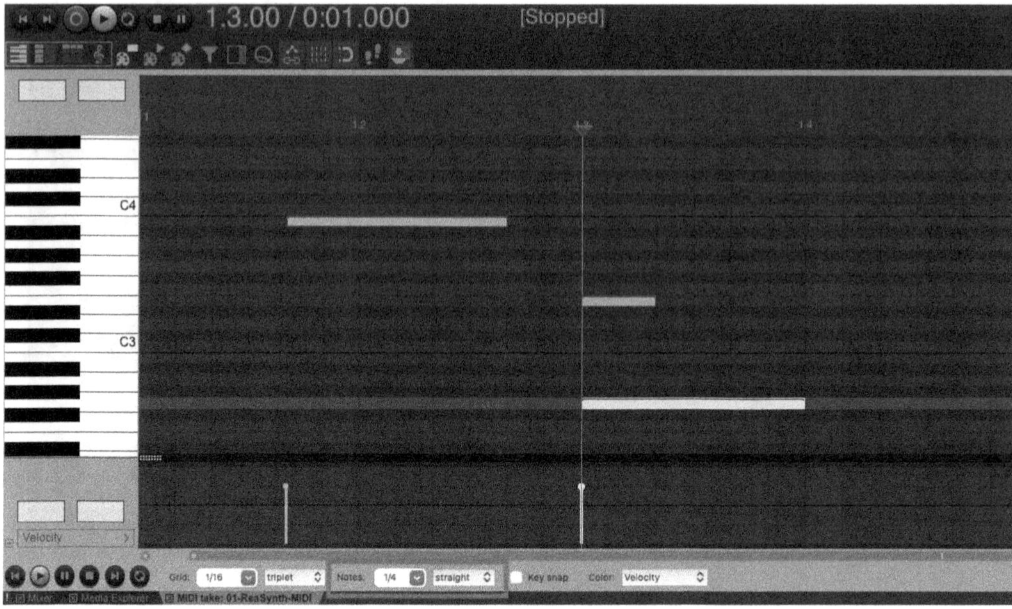

Figure 2.22 – MIDI editor

Inside the **MIDI editor**, we can use the mouse to draw musical notes. Also, by double-clicking at some point in the editor, we can create or delete notes. If we use double-clicking to input notes, we can select the duration of the note in the bottom menu, as shown in *Figure 2.22*.

Using a MIDI controller

REAPER can also record data using MIDI controllers. A **MIDI controller** is a device that generates MIDI data. There are many types of MIDI controllers, the most common being a musical keyboard, but there are also guitar-type controllers, wind controllers, percussion pads, knobs, sliders, and so on. Most of them connect directly to the computer via USB, although some of them can also be connected to an audio interface using MIDI inputs, if the interface has this kind of input available.

If we want to record using a MIDI controller, we just need to make sure that REAPER has recognized the controller in the REAPER settings, in the **Audio | MIDI Devices** section, as seen in *Figure 2.23*:

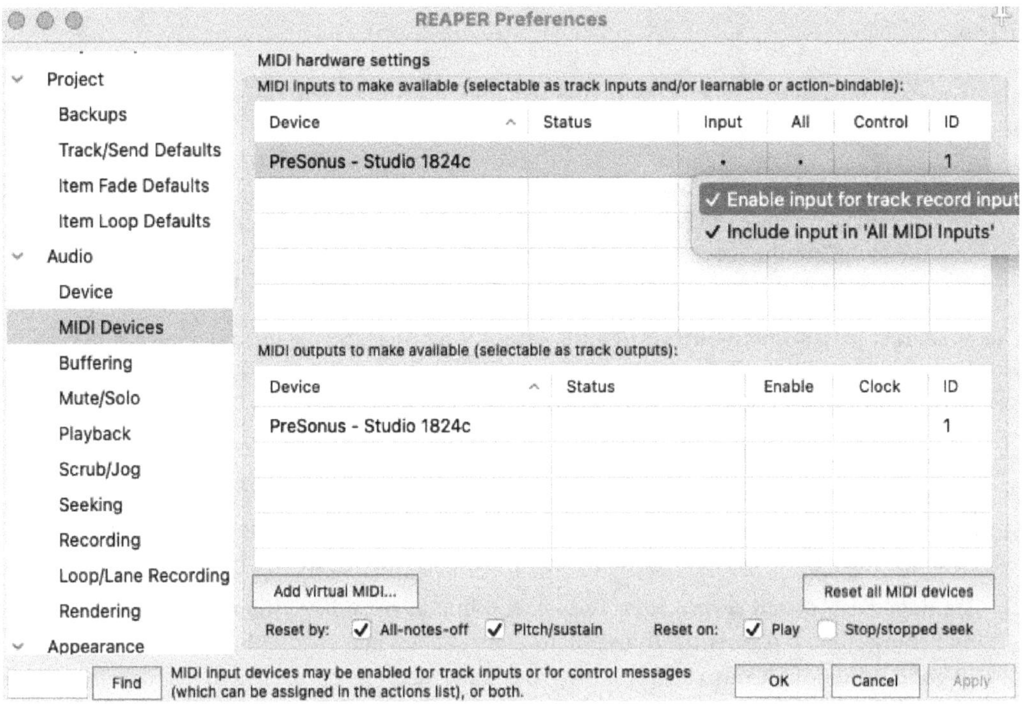

Figure 2.23 – MIDI Devices settings

In this window, we will click on the **Input** section that shows our controller or right-click on that section and select **Enable input for track record input**, as shown in *Figure 2.23*. Then, we can use our controller to record MIDI data on the track similarly to when using the virtual MIDI keyboard.

Troubleshooting

When we attempt to make audio recordings, it's common for something to go wrong. Although REAPER is a very stable DAW and generally doesn't present operational issues, we may encounter some common problems during the recording process. Here, we mention the most common ones, along with the most frequent solutions.

Noise

Noise is an unwanted signal. When conducting an audio recording, there can be several factors that generate noise. These are the most common:

- **Poor microphone quality**: Microphones generate noise on their own. The best microphones produce very low noise levels, so noise is usually not an issue. However, there are medium and low-quality microphones that can generate noise levels high enough to be heard. If this is the case, the only solution is to switch to a better brand or model of microphone.
- **Incorrect gain adjustment**: **Gain adjustment** is a crucial factor in achieving a noise-free recording. It's very important to adjust the gain level correctly (as discussed in this chapter) to ensure the recorded signal has the lowest possible noise level.
- **Quality of the audio interface or sound card**: This is a very common factor. Using generic sound cards is usually the main cause of high noise levels, both when recording and playing back audio. For this reason, it is highly recommended to use a high-quality audio interface to ensure low noise levels.
- **Damaged cables and connectors**: The weakest link in an audio system is usually the cables and connectors. It is essential to use high-quality cables and ensure that the connectors are in good condition. It's also advisable to avoid using adapters or extensions, as they are often sources of noise.
- **Ambient noise**: If the ambient noise level is high, this noise will be recorded, so it's important to have a quiet space to achieve recordings with low ambient noise levels.

If we consider the preceded points while recording, we will reduce the risk of getting noise in our audio.

Distortion

Distortion is a deformation that occurs in the audio signal when the signal level is too high for a system. In the recording process explained in this chapter, the main source of distortion would be an excess of gain. By keeping the recording level at **-18** dBFS, we avoid any possible distortion during the recording process.

Another possible cause of distortion could be recording an extremely loud sound that causes distortion in the microphone itself. The way to correct this is by reducing the level of the sound source (voice or musical instrument) or by moving the microphone away from the source.

Latency

Latency is a delay in sound that can distract the person recording or even make music recording impossible. Latency adjustment is achieved by changing the buffer size, as explained in *Chapter 1*. If it's not possible to reduce the buffer size to achieve sufficiently low latency, it's necessary to use a different driver, a higher-quality audio interface, or a computer with a more powerful CPU.

Summary

In this chapter, we have seen the options we have in REAPER for importing audio files, either with their original tempo and pitch or changing them according to the project's needs. We have also seen the considerations and settings necessary to record audio on a track, considering the input level to obtain a clean recording, without distortion and minimal noise.

We saw an introduction to MIDI so that we could differentiate it from audio and saw different options for making MIDI recordings or *sequences*, using either a virtual or physical controller or entering notes manually with the mouse.

Finally, we explained some common problems encountered while recording and how to solve them to get cleaner recordings. In the next chapter, we will see different techniques and tools for editing our audio and MIDI recordings.

3
Editing and Arranging

Now that we know how to input audio or MIDI into a project, let's see how we can edit the regions that we create. This is a fundamental part of audio production, where we adjust details and correct imperfections to achieve a high-quality project.

When we talk about arranging, we refer to the action of deciding which elements should sound and in which parts of the project. For example, in a musical project, the arrangement determines which instruments should sound in which sections. In a podcast project, we have something similar when it is determined at what moments there should be music or some sound effect.

Knowing how to edit and arrange audio files in a project will help you perfect the sounds you use in it.

In this chapter, we will cover the following topics:

- **Navigating around your projects**: This will teach you commands and techniques to navigate through a project efficiently
- **Audio editing tools**: Here you will learn various basic tools to manipulate an audio file
- **MIDI editing tools**: You will learn how to manipulate the MIDI data you have entered when creating sequences

By the end of this chapter, you will be able to navigate through your project efficiently. You will learn the techniques and professional tools required to achieve high-quality audio work. You will also learn techniques for editing MIDI information to perfect a musical performance. You will learn how to use tools to copy, duplicate, adjust, or delete audio files and MIDI sequences. You will learn about concepts such as quantization, the use of markers, and various zoom options.

We will start by learning how to navigate through our project, which is common in any type of work.

Technical requirements

To practice with the tools shown in this chapter, it is recommended that you create a new project (or use the project created in the previous chapter) and record or import some audio files, such as those that come with this book.

If you already have a personal project in which you have recorded or imported audio files, you can use it to put into practice what we will cover in this chapter.

Navigating around your projects

When working on an audio project, it is important to know how to navigate efficiently through the project. This will allow us to work faster and more intuitively, thus focusing better on the creative part of the work. In this sense, REAPER has various options that we will see in subsequent sections.

Transport functions

Transport functions allow us to play, record, and stop the project in different ways. Although we can use the *transport bar* with the mouse, it is more advisable to use keyboard shortcuts.

Using keyboard shortcuts makes the use of any software much more efficient, and REAPER is no exception. It is advisable to use keyboard shortcuts from the beginning to learn them gradually and develop our muscle memory, which is when our fingers learn automatically where a function is located.

Figure 3.1 shows the keyboard shortcuts for the transport functions (on a Mac, use the *Command* key instead of *Control*):

Function	Keyboard shortcut
Go to start	*Home, W*
Go to end	*End*
Record	*Ctrl + R*
Play/stop	*Spacebar*
Repeat	*R*
Play/pause	*Enter*

Figure 3.1 – Transport shortcuts

Most of the commands shown in *Figure 3.1* are self-explanatory; however, to understand the **Repeat** function, we first need to understand how REAPER handles time selection.

The **Repeat** function allows us to play a section of the project in loop mode. To do this, we must first mark the section we want at the top of the arrangement area with the mouse, as shown in *Figure 3.2*:

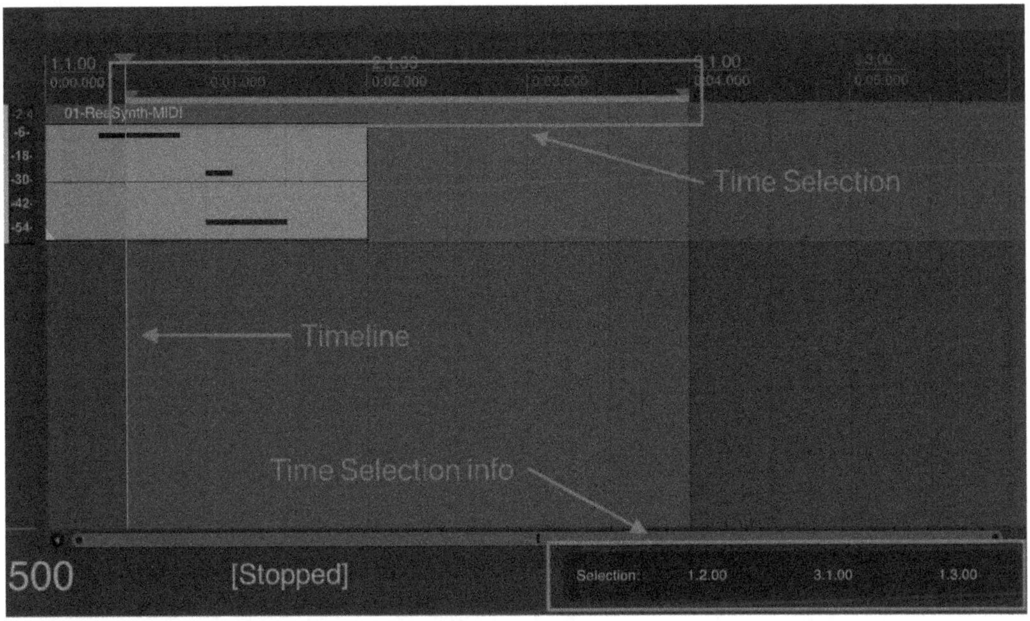

Figure 3.2 – Time selection and Repeat markers

At the bottom of the screenshot in *Figure 3.2*, the **Time Selection** range is displayed, showing the *start point*, *end point*, and the *length of the selection*. If the **Repeat** function is activated, playback will continue repeating within the selected zone until we stop it. This function is particularly useful, for example, during the mixing stage, where we need to listen to the same section multiple times without interruption.

In REAPER, playback starts from the point at which we place the **Timeline**, which is the line that vertically crosses the arrangement area. Every time we press **Play** and **Stop**, playback will start from the same selected point. However, if we stop playback using the **Pause** button, then the starting point will shift to the right. This is the difference between using **Stop** and **Pause**.

As we can observe, the time selection range is the same as the loop range. This remains true if the **Loop points linked to time selection** option is activated in the **Options** menu. If we deactivate this option, we can adjust the loop points independently of the selection zone, as seen in *Figure 3.3*:

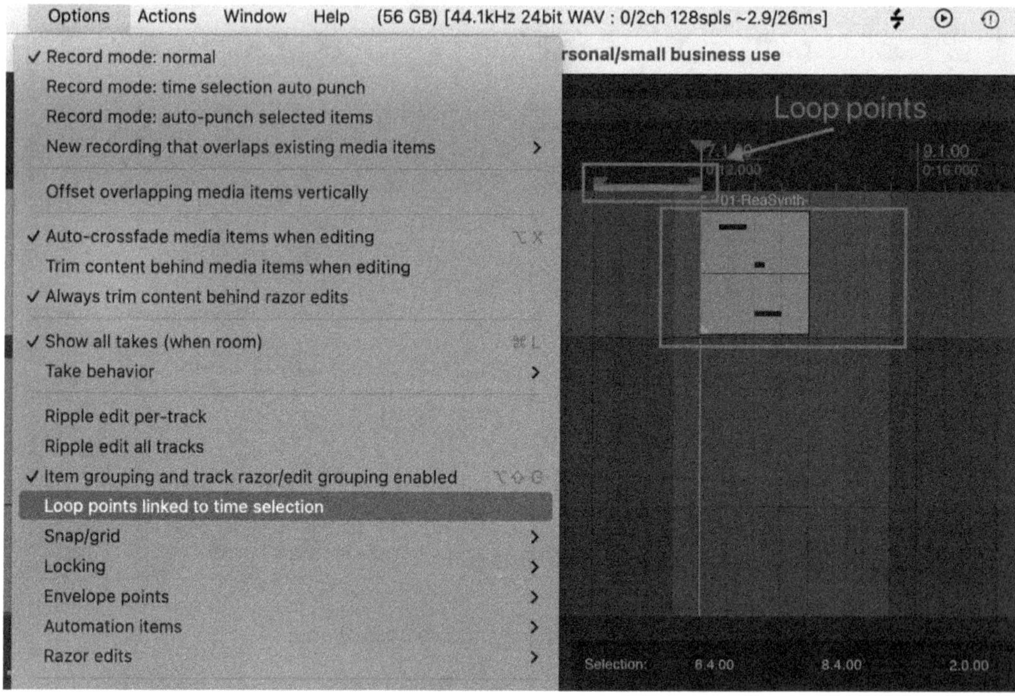

Figure 3.3 – Loop points unlinked to time selection

In *Figure 3.3*, loop points are displayed at the top, and below, the selected area is shown in a lighter color. This functionality can be useful in cases where we want to keep a section playing repeatedly while selecting or editing regions elsewhere.

If we want to move the timeline left or right, we can use the *left* and *right arrow* keys. The timeline will move in small steps depending on the zoom level we are using. The more zoomed in we are, the smaller the steps will be. We can also move the timeline in three-second increments using the *Ctrl* key with the *left* or *right arrow* keys.

Additionally, we can jump to any point in the project with the **View** | **Go to** | **Jump to...** menu, which uses the *Ctrl* + *J* command. With this command, we can specify the point we want to jump to, whether this is in seconds, minutes, measures, etc. Consider that to select hours, minutes, and seconds, you must use *:* as a separator, while to select bars or beats, . is used.

Another very practical way to navigate through a project is by using markers, which we will discuss next.

Using markers

Markers are a very useful tool that allows us to mark sections in a project and quickly navigate between them. Common examples of this can be markers in a musical project, where we can indicate verses, choruses, or endings. In the case of video projects, markers can indicate cue points to synchronize sound or voice.

Inserting a new marker

We can insert new markers with the **Insert | Marker** menu or by pressing the *M* key. The marker will be inserted at the point where the timeline is, whether it is stopped or playing. The markers will appear at the top of the arrangement area as small numbers, as shown in *Figure 3.4*:

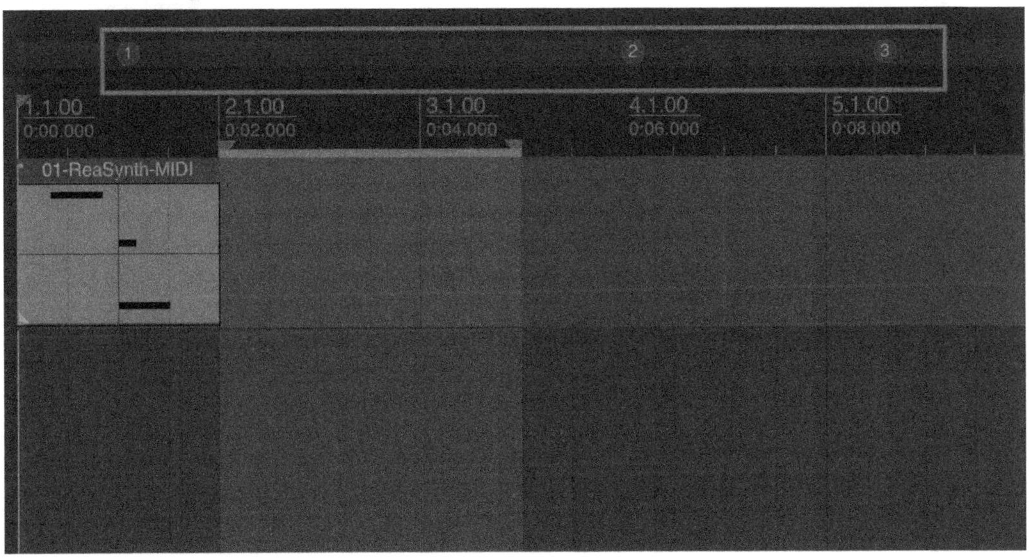

Figure 3.4 – Markers

To navigate to a marker, we only need to press the numbers *1* through to *0* at the top of the keyboard. We can also go to the previous or next marker using the *[* and *]* keys.

We can use more than 10 markers, but to navigate to marker 11 and beyond, we must press *Ctrl* + *J*, then the *M* key, followed by the marker number and *Enter*. For example, to go to marker 12, we press *Ctrl* + *J*, then *M*, *12*, and *Enter*. The number of markers used is entirely a personal preference, so there may be projects with few or many markers, depending on each person's needs.

Moving the markers

Once the markers are created, we can move them by dragging them with the mouse. If we want to delete them, we can *right-click* on a marker and select the **Remove marker** option or click on it while holding the *Alt* key (*Option* key on a Mac).

Right-clicking on a marker also gives us the option to edit it by selecting the **Edit marker...** option. A window will appear where we can give the marker a name to appear in the arrangement area and change its number or color if desired, as shown in *Figure 3.5*:

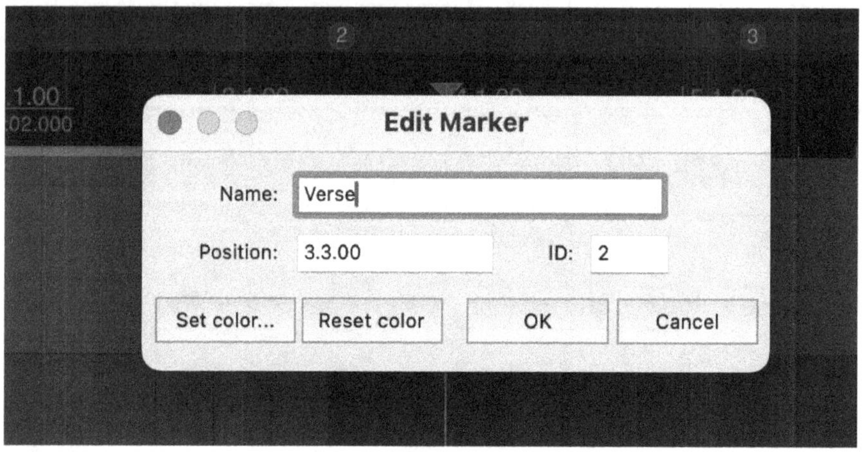

Figure 3.5 – Edit Marker window

Markers provide us with a lot of flexibility to work quickly on any project, so it is highly recommended to use markers when navigating through the session.

Now let's see some more options to adjust the zoom and navigate through a project.

Zoom and scrolling options

Among the most common functions when working on an audio project are zoom and navigation. As we saw in *Chapter 1*, we can use the small +/- buttons to adjust the horizontal and vertical zoom of the arrangement area. However, it is much more practical to use the *up* and *down arrow* keys to adjust the horizontal zoom.

Figure 3.6 shows several useful shortcuts for project navigation and zoom. It is advisable to use these shortcuts regularly to learn them more easily.

> **Tip**
>
> Remember that *Command* is used instead of *Control* on a Mac, and *Option* is used instead of *Alt*.

Function	**Shortcut**
Zoom in	*Up arrow*, +
Zoom out	*Down arrow*, -
Track size up	*Page up*
Track size down	*Page down*
Expand selected track	*!*
Minimize all tracks	@
Scroll up	*Alt up arrow*
Scroll down	*Alt down arrow*
Scroll left	*Alt left arrow*
Scroll right	*Alt right arrow*
Select track above	*Ctrl Alt up arrow*
Select track below	*Ctrl Alt down arrow*

Figure 3.6 – Zoom and scrolling shortcuts

Also, with the *mouse wheel*, we can perform the following different zoom shortcuts:

- If we use the mouse wheel alone, we will perform **horizontal zoom**
- With the *Ctrl* key, we perform **vertical zoom**
- With the *Alt* key, we have **horizontal scrolling**
- Combining *Ctrl* and *Alt* will give us **vertical scrolling**

Now that you know the various shortcuts for performing various types of zoom and scrolling, let's explore the **Zoom selection** option in the next section.

Using the Zoom selection option

Another very useful zoom function is right-clicking on a selection and activating **Zoom selection**, as shown in *Figure 3.7*:

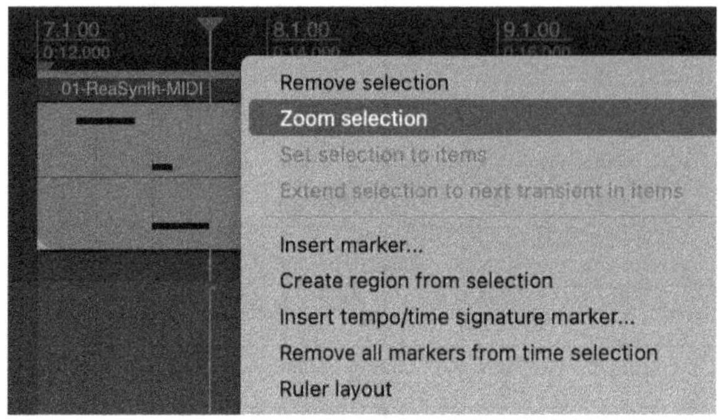

Figure 3.7 – Zoom selection

When we use this function, zoom will be applied along the selected portion, which is often useful during editing, as it saves us time.

In **REAPER Preferences**, in the **Appearance | Zoom/Scroll/Offset** section, we can adjust various zoom and scrolling values according to our preference or need, as seen in *Figure 3.8*:

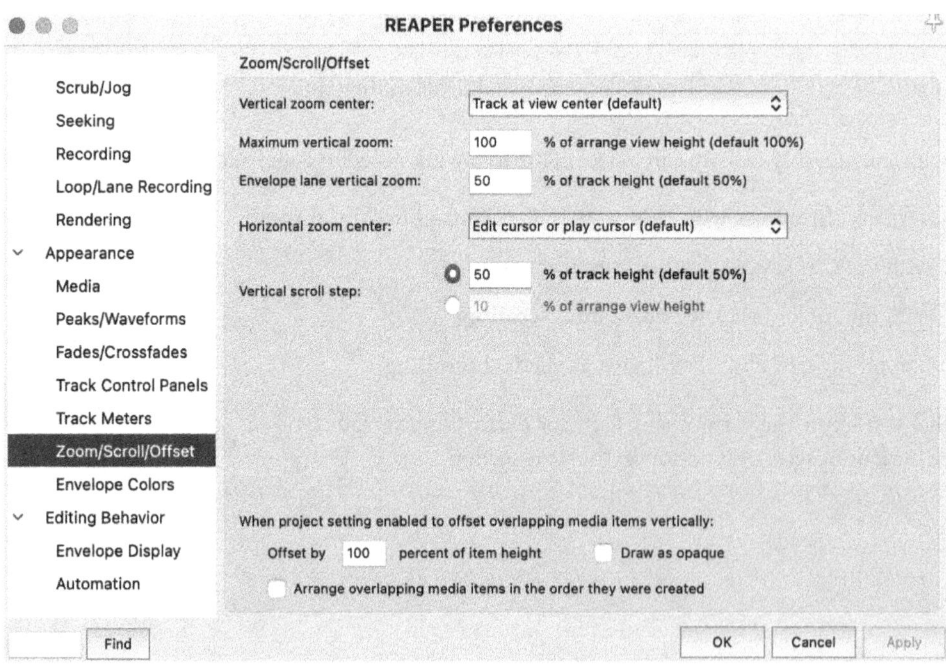

Figure 3.8 – Zoom preferences

For example, in this window, we can set the maximum zoom values or the reference points that will be taken when zooming. These preferences usually work well with the default values, but they can be changed according to the user's preferences.

Now that we have seen the different zoom options that we can use in REAPER, let's look at the tools we can use to edit audio.

Exploring audio editing tools

Once we have imported audio or recorded audio in REAPER, a crucial activity in the production process begins: editing. **Audio editing** is the stage where we adjust and modify the takes and files we have in the project so that we achieve the desired result.

For example, during the editing process, we will clean up takes or remove any noises that may be audible. We will also select the best parts of the recordings we have made, leaving only those that work properly in the project. In editing, we also move, copy, and arrange recordings at different points in the project, for example, to create sections in a song or repeat parts that were only recorded once.

In *Chapter 8* through to *Chapter 11*, we will explore editing techniques and tools suitable for various applications, such as music production and podcast creation. For now, let's look at the basic audio editing tools used in all kinds of projects.

Adjusting media items

Every time we import or record audio in REAPER, a **media item** is created, representing the region that displays the waveform of the recording. Generally, we can have two types of items with audio: mono and stereo. A mono item will display only one waveform, as shown on the *left side* of *Figure 3.9*, while a stereo item will display two waveforms, as seen on the *right side* of the figure:

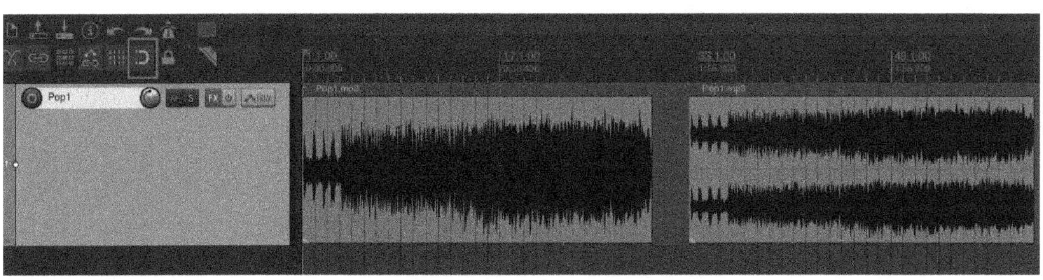

Figure 3.9 – Mono (left) and stereo (right) items

A **mono item** represents audio that has only one channel, so we'll hear the same information through the left and right speakers or headphones. A **stereo item** has two channels, so we'll hear different information in the left and right channels.

The first basic edit we can make to an item is to move it; we just need to drag it with the mouse and position it where we want it. We can also delete it by selecting it with a click and pressing the *backspace* key. If we accidentally delete something, we can simply undo the action with *Ctrl* + *Z* (or *Cmd* + *Z*).

Snap and Grid

When we move an item, the new position will be limited by **Snap**, which is a button with a magnet image, as marked in *Figure 3.9*. **Snap** allows us to place items at precise points, making it easier to arrange and synchronize them. However, if we need to move an item freely, we can disable **Snap** at any time.

The points where we can move an item to when **Snap** is active appear as lines called the **grid**. We can activate or deactivate the **grid** with the button to the left of **Snap**, as seen in *Figure 3.10*:

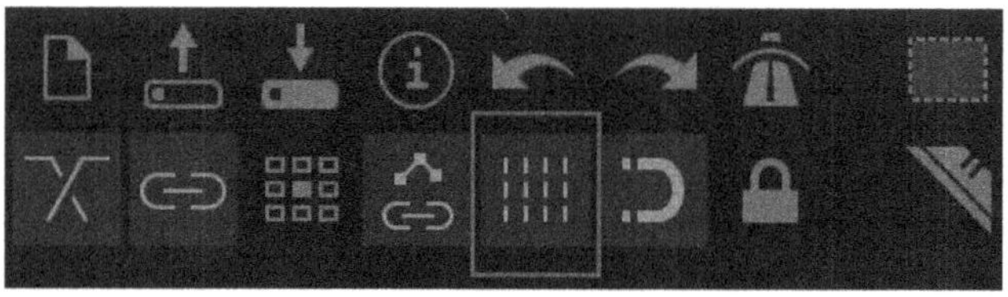

Figure 3.10 – Grid button

We can adjust the values of **Grid** and **Snap** according to our editing requirements. For this, we can right-click on the **Grid** or **Snap** button, and a window of options will appear, as seen in *Figure 3.11*:

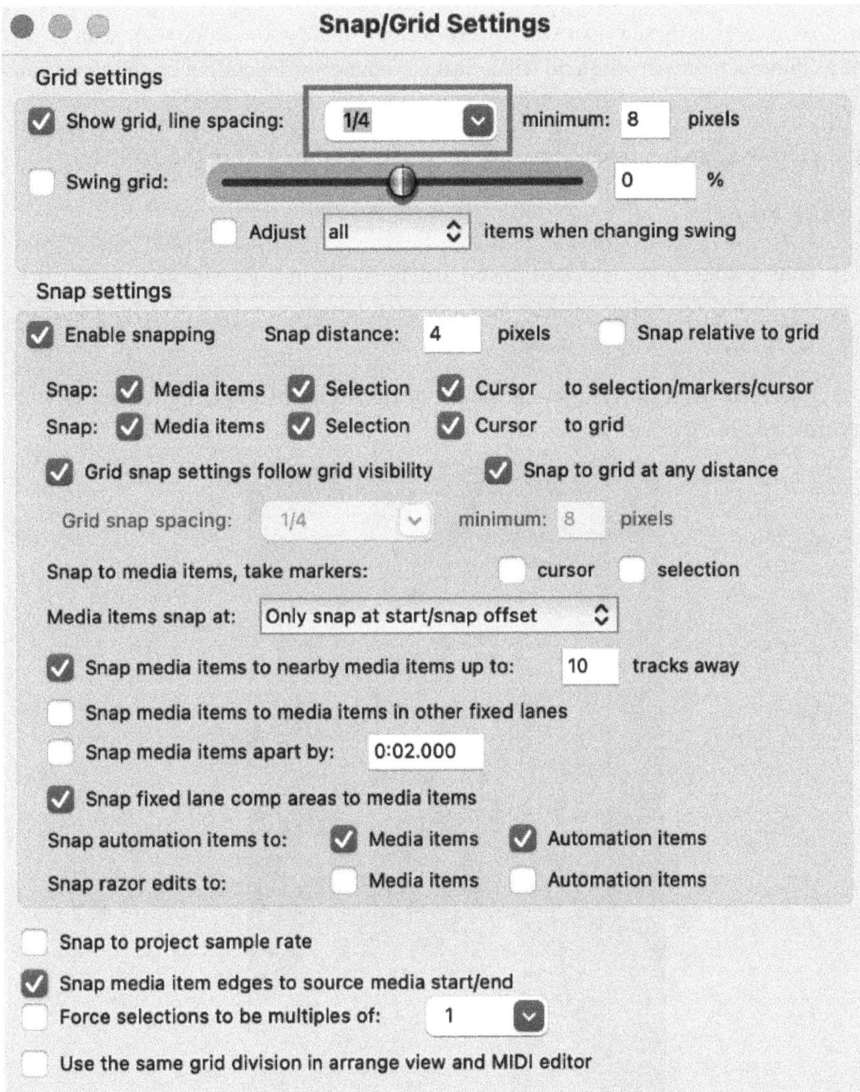

Figure 3.11 – Snap/Grid Settings

Of all these options, the most important is marked in *Figure 3.11*. In this menu, we can adjust **Grid** to different musical values. For example, **1/4** means musical notes with a quarter-note value. This means that the points for moving an item will be restricted to quarter notes in each bar. Thus, we can change the setting to eighth notes, sixteenth notes, etc., according to the resolution we need.

It's important to clarify that these values will be possible only if the zoom value we're using allows us to visualize the gridlines. Otherwise, the **grid** will adjust automatically depending on the zoom value used.

To temporarily bypass the effect of the **grid**, we can press the *Shift* key while moving an item to the left or right. In this way, we can freely move any item without the effect of the **grid**.

Adjusting the edge

Another basic editing adjustment is that of the **edge** item. With this tool, we can isolate or select only a portion of an audio file, removing parts that are not useful, such as noises, breathing sounds, or any other sound, before or after the audio we're interested in.

To adjust the edge, if we place the pointer on the left or right edge of an item, the pointer will change its shape, as indicated in *Figure 3.12*:

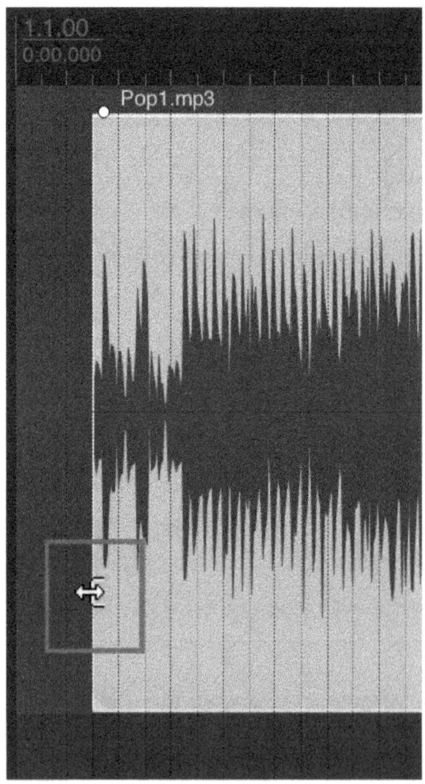

Figure 3.12 – Item's edge

Then, we can adjust the size of an item by moving the mouse to the left or right, *covering* parts of the audio we don't want to hear. At any time, we can *uncover* parts of the audio by extending the edges of an item again.

Our movements to show or hide parts of an item are also restricted by the **grid**. If needed, we can temporarily disable the **Grid** effect by pressing the *Shift* key while making the necessary adjustments.

Splitting an item

Another very useful function is **splitting** an item. Splitting items is a great way to move, copy, or delete portions of audio. For example, we might want to copy just a word or phrase and then paste it into another part of the project, or split a musical line into smaller sections to rearrange them creatively.

To split an item, we just need to position the timeline at the point where we want to split the item and select **Item | Split items at cursor**, or use the *S* key, as shown in *Figure 3.13*. It is important to mention that only the desired track or tracks should be selected; otherwise, all tracks will be split.

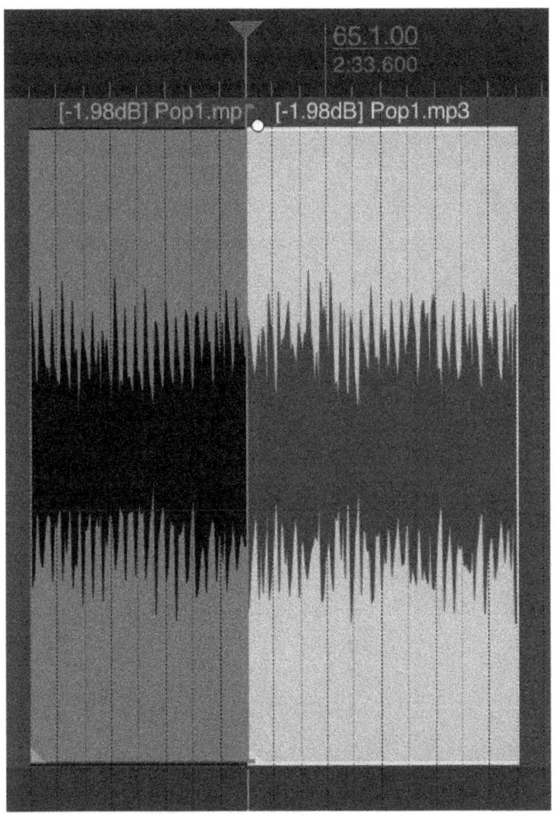

Figure 3.13 – Splitting an item

Then we will see how the item splits into two. Each of these items will now be independent, and we can perform any type of editing on each of them.

In addition to adjusting the edges of an item, as seen earlier, we can use a fade to make the transition between items smoother, as we'll see next.

Fade in and out

The use of **fades** is a common technique in audio editing because it helps avoid abrupt changes in volume. It's also a technique that can be used to gradually fade out the end of a musical piece.

To introduce fades, if we position the pointer at the upper-right or upper-left corner of an item, the pointer will change to a **Fade** tool shape, as seen in *Figure 3.14*. Then, we can create gradual volume fades, either at the beginning of the item, which is known as a **fade in**, or at the end, which is known as a **fade out**.

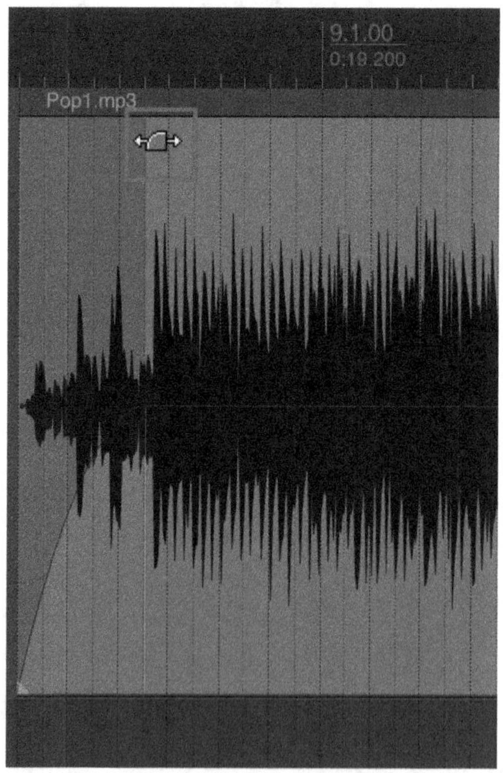

Figure 3.14 – Fade tool

If we double-click on an audio item, the **Media Item Properties** window will open. In this window, we can adjust many parameters of the item, such as its **Position**, **Length**, **Take name**, and much more, as seen in *Figure 3.15*:

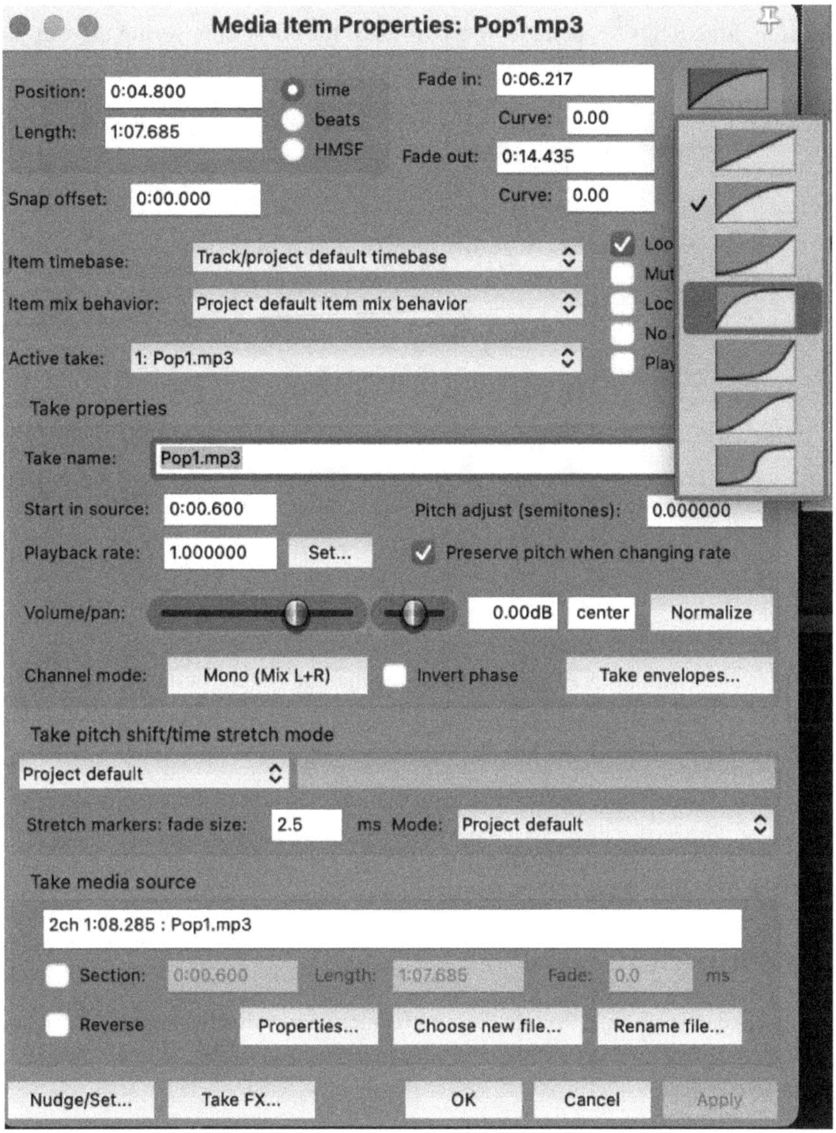

Figure 3.15 – Media item properties

Among the possible settings, we have the type of **curve** for fades, as marked in *Figure 3.15*. This choice depends entirely on the desired effect, and it is advisable to experiment a bit to decide which one works best in each case. For example, some curves are more linear than others, which makes the volume change sound different. There is no correct or suitable curve for all cases.

Another important function is a crossfade. A **crossfade** is the effect of lowering the volume of one audio while raising the volume of another when they both coincide, as seen in *Figure 3.16*:

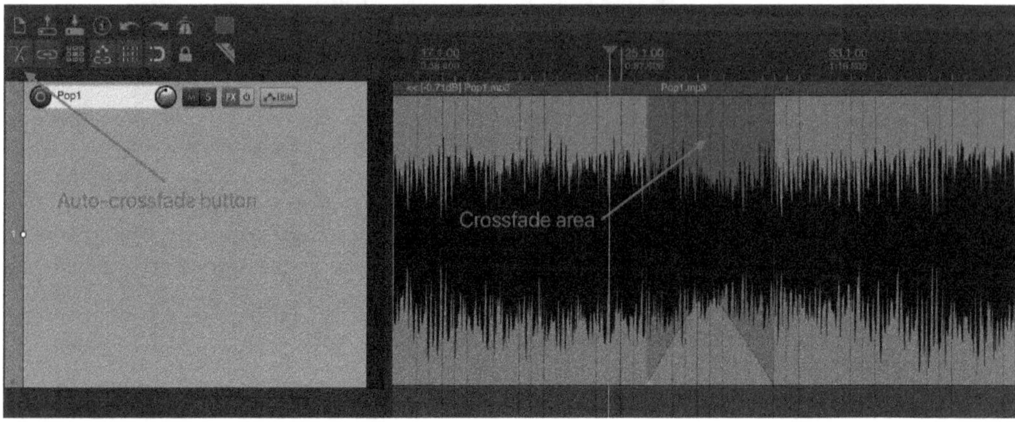

Figure 3.16 – Crossfade function

As we can see in the preceding screenshot, the area where both items coincide shows a different color, and the volume of the first item decreases at the same time that the volume of the second item increases. This allows for a smooth and very effective transition when combining audio files. An example of this could be song mixing by a DJ.

It is important to make sure that the **Auto-crossfade** function is enabled to have this functionality, as shown in *Figure 3.16*. Otherwise, the crossfade will not be created automatically.

Now, let's see one of the most important properties of an item: its volume.

Volume adjustments

Along each item, we can see a thin line that allows us to adjust the **volume** of the item. When we position the mouse over this line, the pointer will change shape, and we can raise or lower the volume of the item, as shown in *Figure 3.17*:

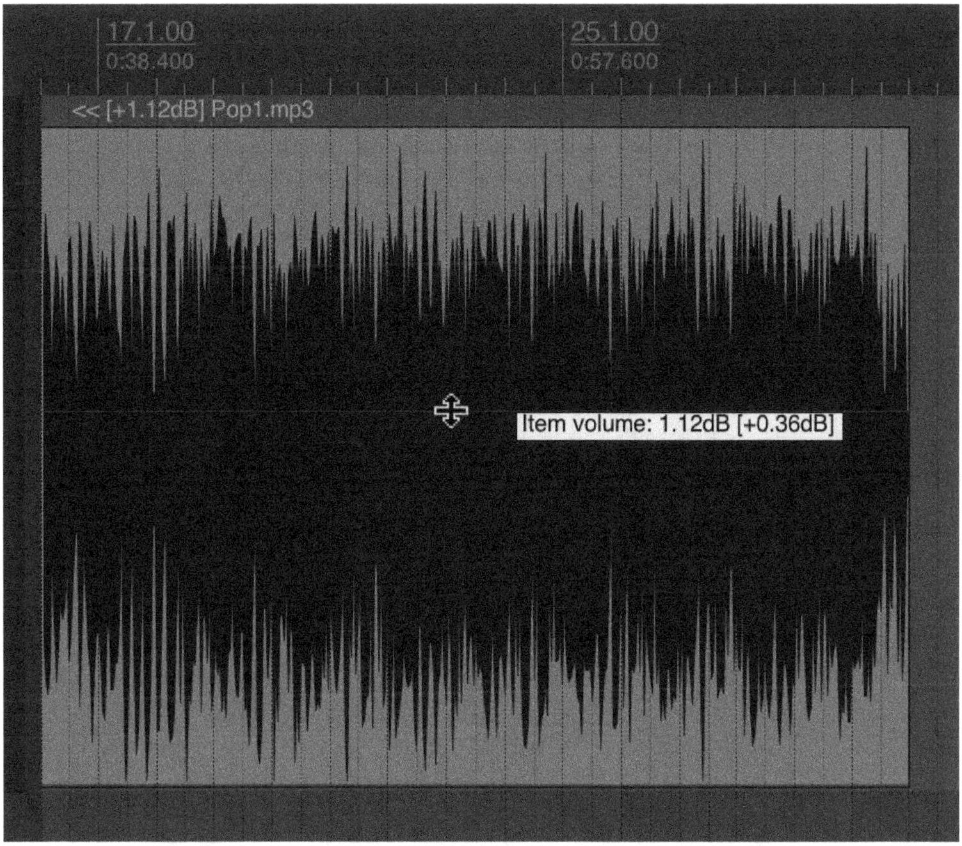

Figure 3.17 – Item volume

A small label will indicate the number of dB (decibels) by which we are increasing or decreasing the volume. In this sense, **0 dB** means *zero changes*. In other words, if the line is at 0 dB, we will get the original volume of the item. If we want to make more precise changes, we can press the *Ctrl* key while moving the line up or down.

We can also display a small volume knob on each item by activating this option: **Settings** | **Appearance** | **Media** | **Volume knob**.

In general, it is recommended not to raise the volume of an item too much, as we could generate distortion in the audio. Therefore, we must monitor the channel level (as seen in *Chapter 2*) every time we increase the volume of an item to ensure that the level does not exceed *-3 dBFS maximum*. However, when attenuating the volume of an item, there are no restrictions.

Now we know how to manipulate audio with great flexibility; however, there are still other common editing commands that we need to cover: copy and paste.

Copy and paste

The copy and paste commands are practically universal in any software, and REAPER is no exception.

Once an item is selected, we can copy it with the **Edit | Copy** menu or the *Ctrl* + *C* shortcut. Then we can position the timeline where we want to paste the item and apply **Edit | Paste** or *Ctrl* + *V*.

We can also cut an item instead of copying it. We do this with the **Edit | Cut** menu. A different way to copy items is to drag them while holding down the *Ctrl* key.

We can also select multiple items to copy, move them, adjust their edges, etc. To do this, we press the *Ctrl* key while clicking on the items we want to select.

Another very useful function when editing items is **duplicating**. Duplicating items is very practical when we want to repeat an item quickly, such as repeating a drum loop or bassline for several measures in music production.

If we select one or more items and press the *Ctrl* + *D* shortcut, the selected items will be duplicated, and the timeline will be positioned at the end of the last item, as seen in *Figure 3.18*:

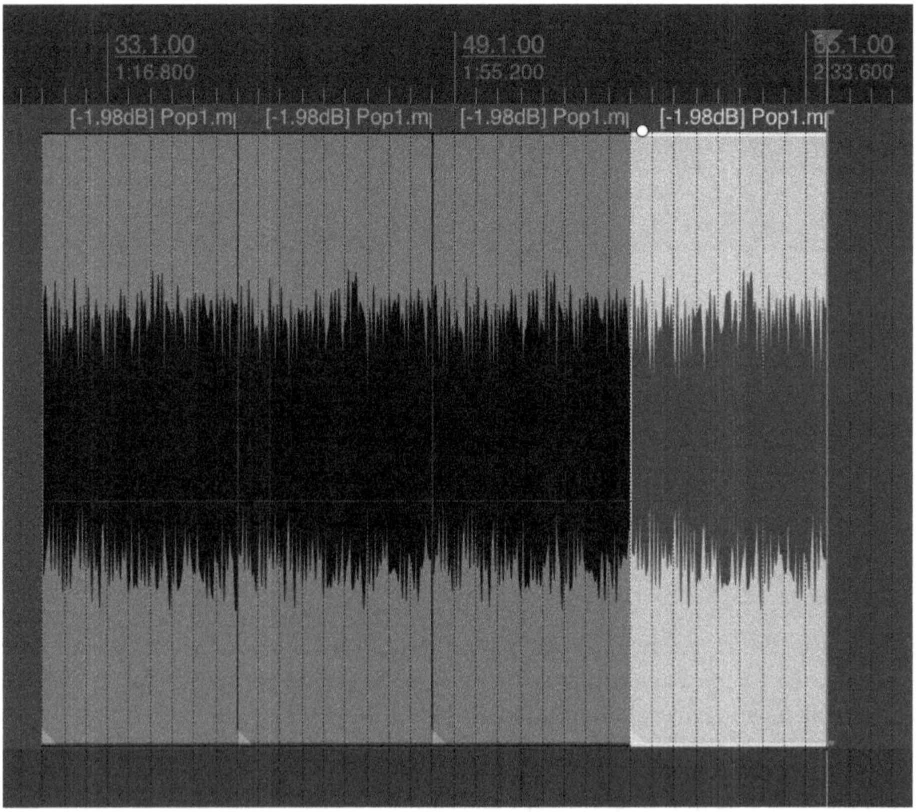

Figure 3.18 – Duplicating items

In pop or electronic music production, it is common to duplicate entire sections, such as the choruses or verses of a song, so this command can be very handy in those situations. We can also copy a portion of an item to paste it elsewhere in the project. For this, first, we must select the portion we want to copy, marking a time selection from the top of the arrangement area, as marked in *Figure 3.19*:

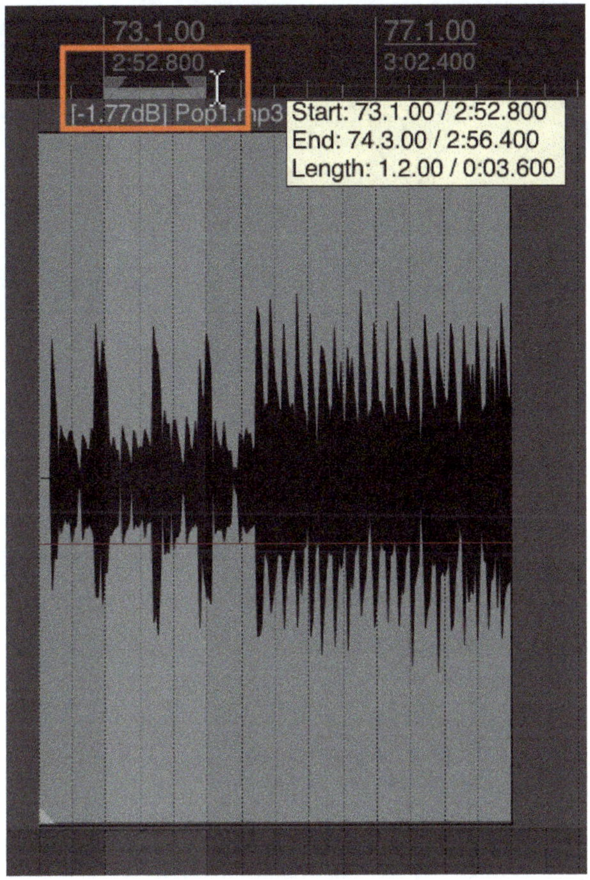

Figure 3.19 – Time selection

In the screenshot in *Figure 3.19*, the time selection appears in a lighter tone. Then we click on the desired item and use the **Edit** | **Copy within time selection** menu. Then that section will be copied and ready to be pasted, as seen in *Figure 3.20*:

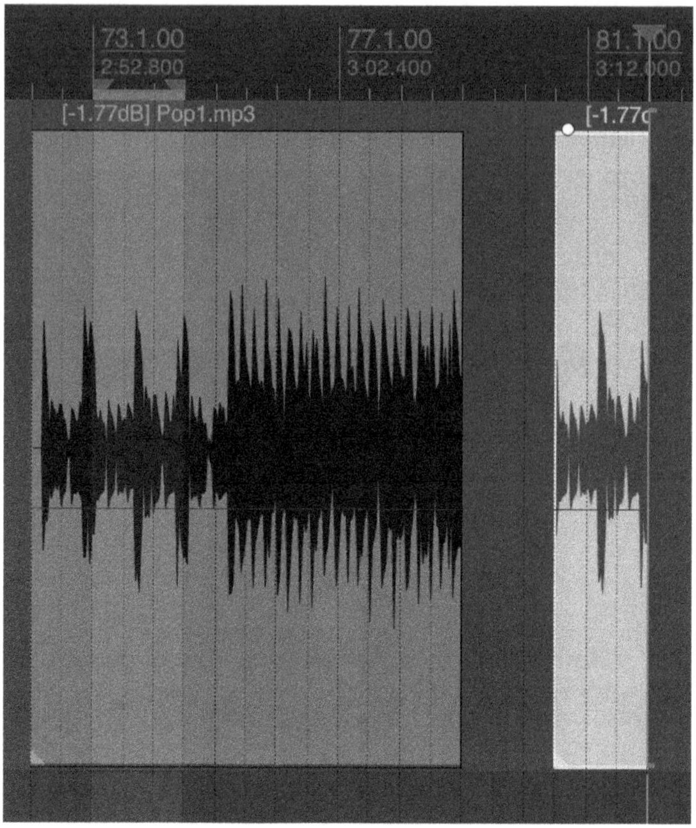

Figure 3.20 – Copying a time selection

This function allows us to take parts of an item, without the need to split it, to then paste them somewhere else.

It is common that, as we make many edits, our project becomes filled with many items that are difficult to manage. In these cases, it may be a good idea to join several items to create a new unified audio file. Let's see how to do this in the next section.

Joining items

All the functions discussed in the previous section allow us to copy and place items in different places, but it's also possible to join items together to edit them more easily.

There are two ways in which we can join items, as follows:

- By using the glue command
- By grouping the items

Let's explore these options in the subsequent sections.

Using the glue command

The first option is to join the items together by using the **glue** command to create a new audio file. To do this, you can follow these steps:

1. Select the items you want, either by using the *Ctrl* key and clicking on the items or by pressing the *Shift* key and clicking on the first and last desired item.
2. Select the **Item** | **Glue items** menu.

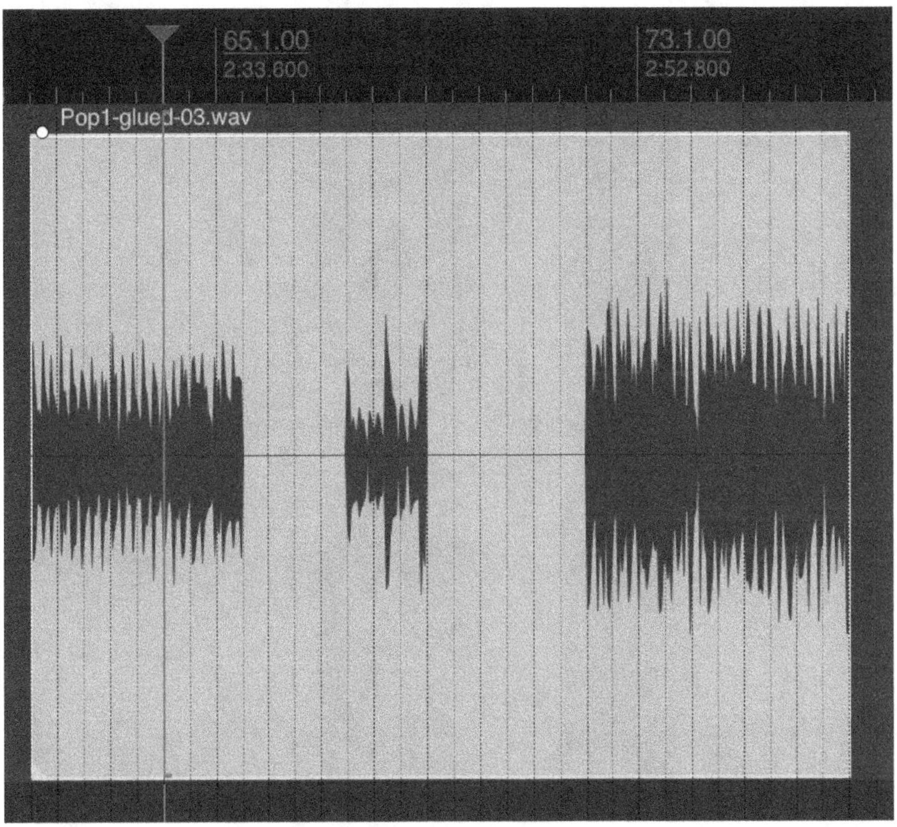

Figure 3.21 – Glued items

A new audio file will be created that encompasses all the selected items, including any empty spaces between them, as shown in *Figure 3.21*.

Grouping the items

Another way to join items is by grouping them. **Groups** are a temporary union of items, meaning they are joined so that we can edit them together, but we can ungroup them later if we need to make individual adjustments.

The selection process is the same as gluing them, but now you will use the **Item | Group | Group items** menu or the *G* key. Then the grouped items will display a different border and a *chain* icon, as seen in *Figure 3.22*:

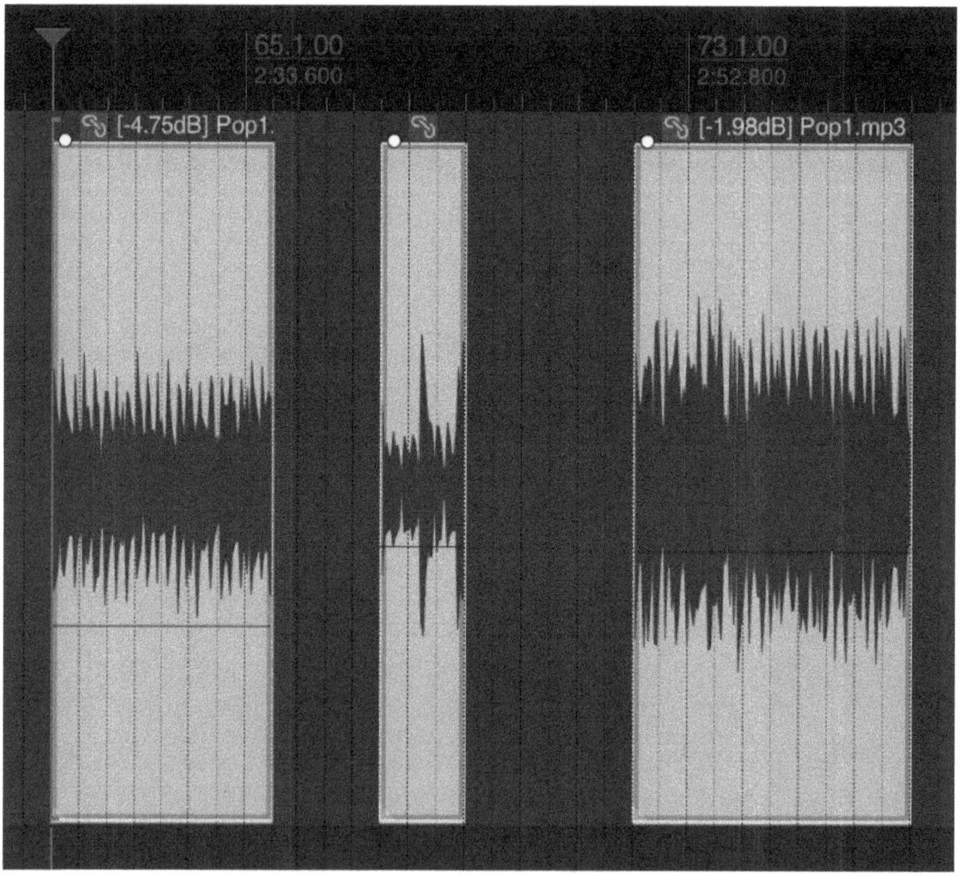

Figure 3.22 – Items group

This group of items can be moved, copied, and pasted as if it were a single item. The advantage of using item groups is that we can ungroup them at any time by selecting them and using the **Item | Group | Remove items from group** menu or the *U* key. Once ungrouped, the items can be manipulated individually as usual or regrouped when necessary.

As we have seen, the basic editing functions of REAPER are simple and very practical, as we can adjust the size of the items, their start or end points, their fades, and volumes individually or in groups. We also learned different ways to copy, paste, and split items in the editing process.

Now we will see tools that we can use to edit MIDI items. Several of the functions are the same as those of an audio item, as we will see next; however, there are also other unique functions for MIDI.

MIDI editing tools

As we saw in *Chapter 2*, MIDI is a different form of data compared to audio, as it is focused on music production. Therefore, unlike an audio file, with MIDI, we have much more control over each musical note and its sound.

When we create an item with MIDI data (as seen in *Chapter 2*), we can perform various edits similar to an audio item, such as selecting, copying, splitting, duplicating, and adjusting the edges of the item. However, the fade and crossfade functions, as well as volume changes, are not applicable to a MIDI item.

Exploring the Midi Editor

When we double-click on a MIDI item, we enter the **MIDI Editor**. Inside **MIDI Editor**, we find **Grid** and **Snap** functions that work similarly to the **Grid** and **Snap** in the arrangement area, as shown in *Figure 3.23*:

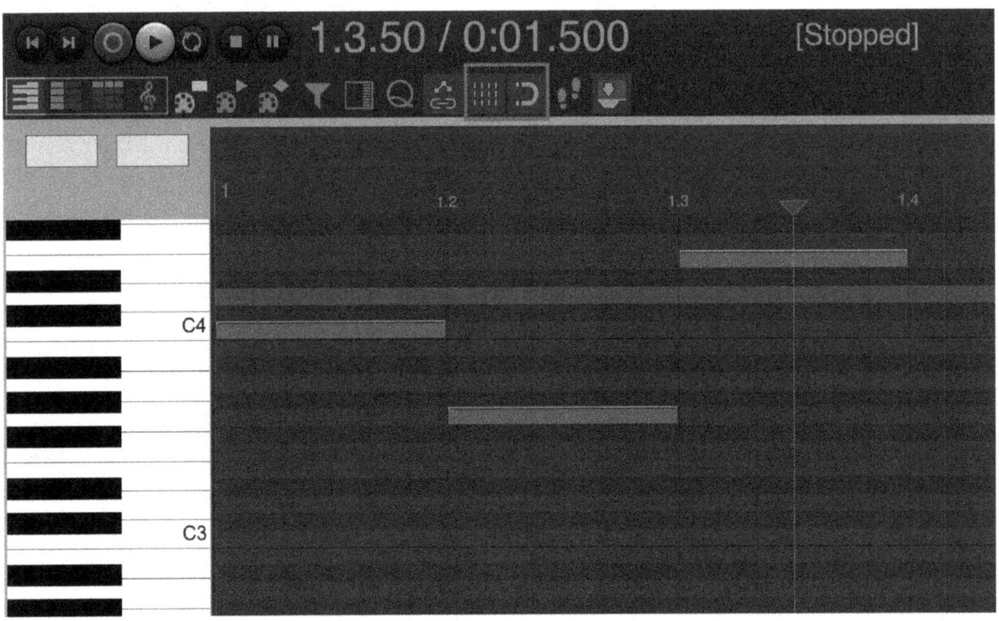

Figure 3.23 – Grid and Snap buttons

Within **Midi Editor**, we can move, copy, or delete the displayed MIDI notes. We can raise or lower the notes to change them (for example, to go from C to D), based on the musical keyboard on the left side. It is also possible to change their length by dragging them from the edges of the bars.

We can select multiple notes at once by holding down the *Shift* key. In *Figure 3.24*, we see two selected notes, and at the bottom, the option to choose the grid resolution is marked:

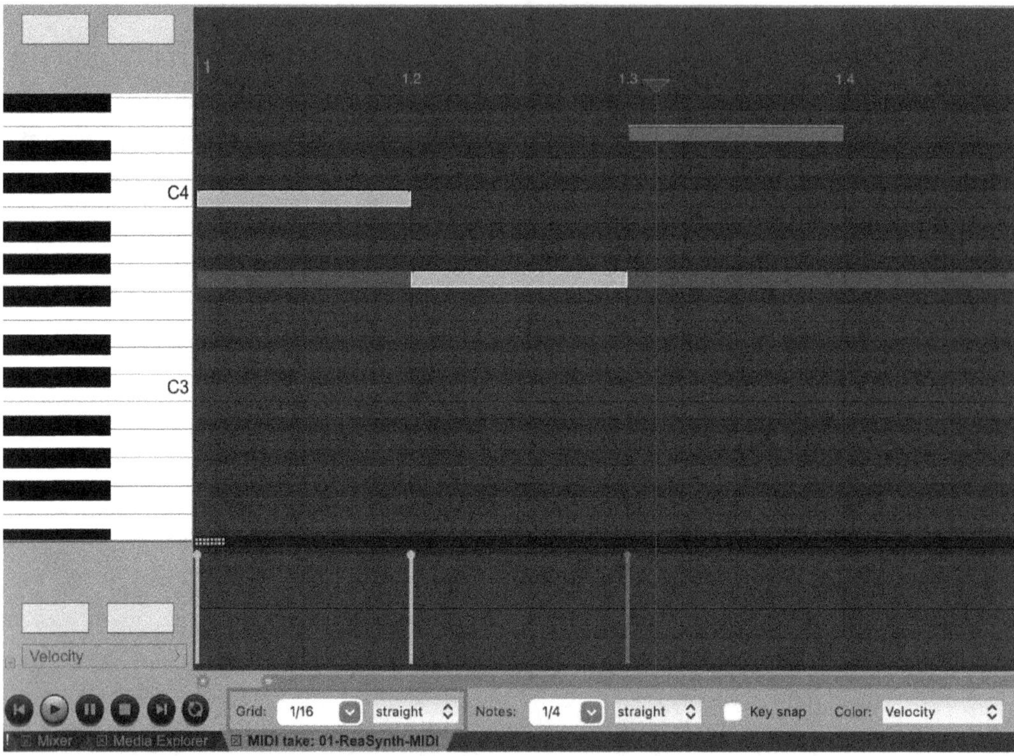

Figure 3.24 – Grid options

For example, *Figure 3.24* shows a **Grid** value of **1/16**, which means that editing movements will be restricted to sixteenth notes.

When editing MIDI notes, we can change their size or move them manually; however, there is a very practical tool that allows us to adjust the start points of MIDI notes: quantization.

Understanding quantization

One of the most common functions when editing MIDI is quantization. **Quantization** allows us to align MIDI notes with the grid. This is usually necessary when recording MIDI sequences in real time, either using the virtual MIDI keyboard or a hardware controller.

For example, *Figure 3.25* shows some MIDI notes recorded in real time, and if we look closely, their start points do not match the grid lines:

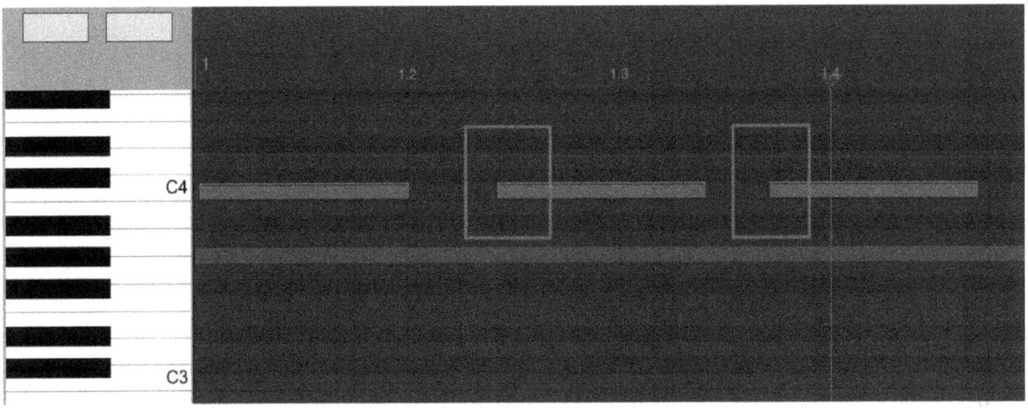

Figure 3.25 – Non-quantized MIDI notes

The goal of MIDI quantization is to align the start of the notes perfectly with the grid lines we are using. If we select the notes and then click the **Quantize** button (see *Figure 3.26*) or the letter Q, the **Quantize Events** window will appear.

We will see the selected notes move left or right to the nearest grid line (depending on the grid resolution). We can then press *Enter* to accept the quantization, and the notes will be in precise positions on the grid, as shown in *Figure 3.26*:

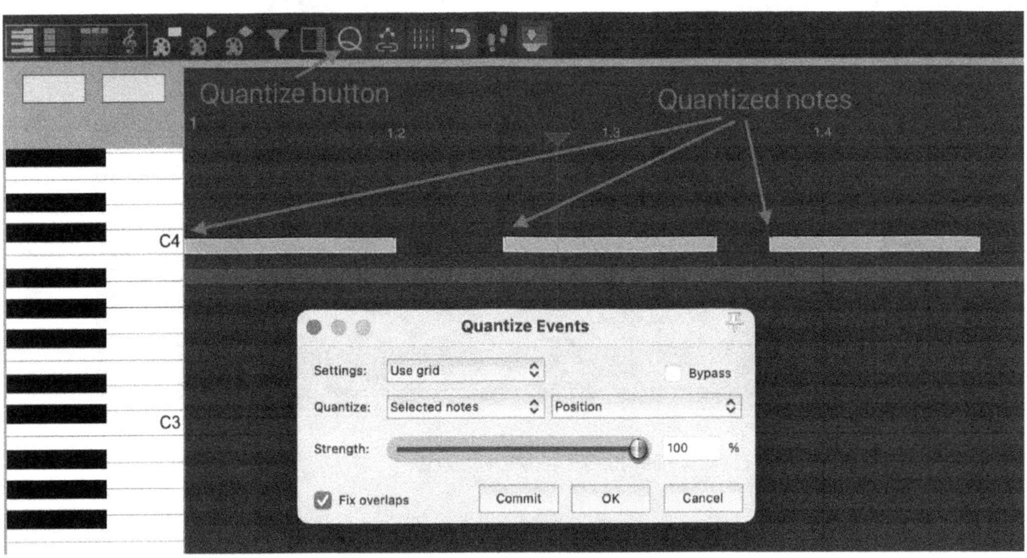

Figure 3.26 – Quantize Events window

In the **Quantize Events** window, we see the **Strength** slider set to **100%**. This indicates that the quantization will have 100% strength, and the notes will be quantized exactly to the grid lines. While this setting is often useful, quantizing notes 100% will make them sound perfectly in time, removing human imprecision. This kind of setting is common for electronic music or hip-hop.

With some other genres or music styles, it may sound more natural to reduce the quantization strength to 70% or 80%. This way, the notes will move closer to the grid but retain some degree of imprecision, making the final sound more *human*.

Working with MIDI velocity

At the bottom of **MIDI Editor**, we can see a section with vertical lines below each MIDI note. These lines represent **MIDI velocity**. As we know, velocity is related to the intensity of the notes. We can adjust the velocity by raising or lowering the vertical lines marked in *Figure 3.27* with the mouse, thus controlling the dynamics of each note, which is very important in a musical performance.

In *Figure 3.27*, we see three notes with different velocities:

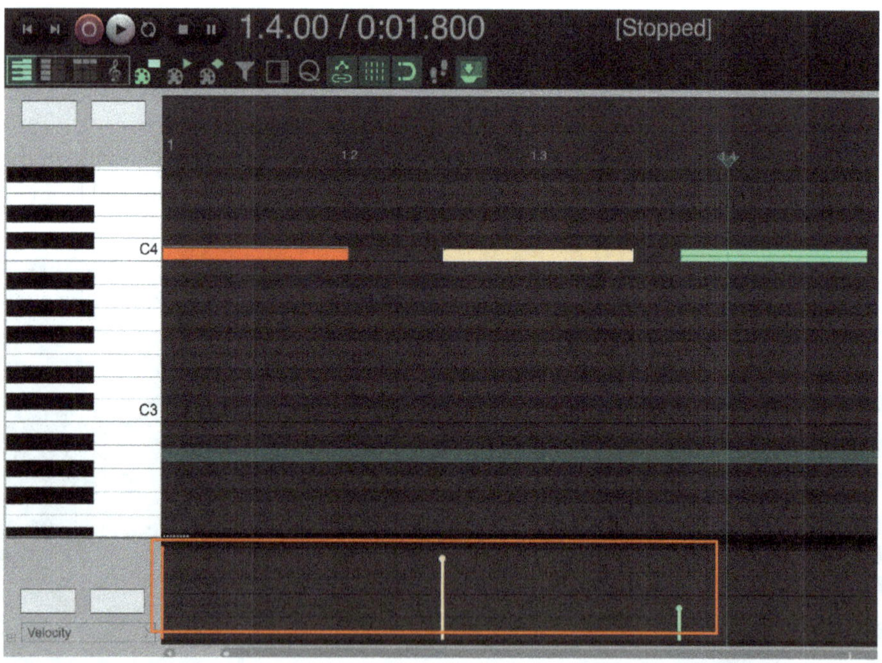

Figure 3.27 – MIDI velocity

On the left side of the velocity area, clicking where it says **Velocity**, we can open a menu to select any other **Control Change (CC)** that can be edited, as shown in *Figure 3.28*:

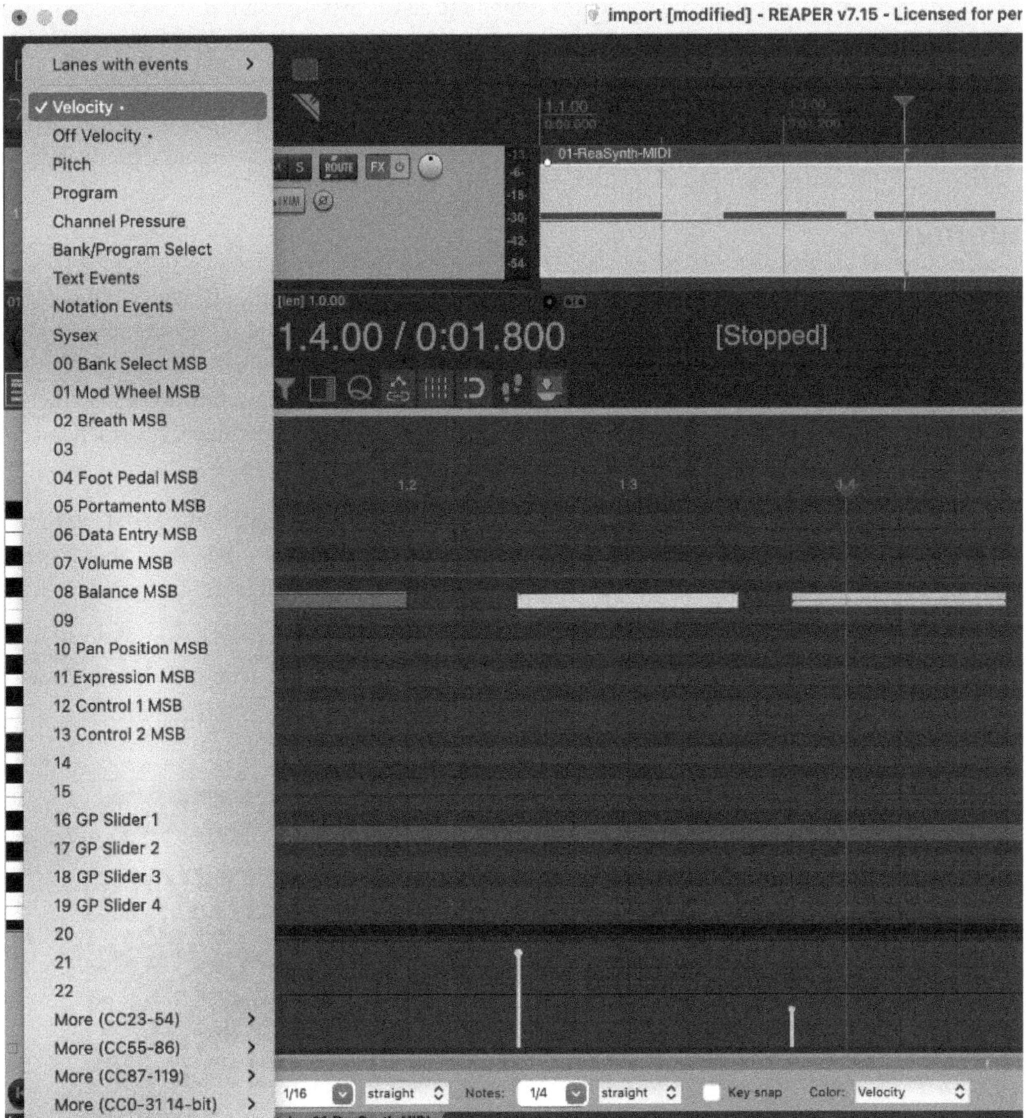

Figure 3.28 – Control Change menu

This function allows us to modify any CC individually for each note if desired, providing great flexibility in MIDI editing, which is something not possible with audio editing.

> **Important note**
>
> It's important to note that the response of each CC depends on the synthesizer and the sound used. In other words, not all sound generators respond to all CC messages, nor do they respond in the same way.

MIDI editing is very powerful and practical, yet it is simple to use. Perhaps this is why it's been more than 40 years since its conception, and it still is a very useful technology and the basis of music production.

Summary

In this chapter, we have seen a wide range of tools that allow us to start editing audio and MIDI items. We have also seen how we can navigate through the project using the scroll and zoom options to work more comfortably and accurately. You have learned how to use markers to identify and locate sections of your project more easily. You now know how to move, copy, or delete items, how to change their size, and how to adjust their volume. You have also learned how to edit MIDI sequences, which have the advantage of being adjustable in detail, even note by note.

All of this will help you refine the recordings you make, whether they are audio or MIDI, so that your project only uses the parts that work correctly. With the editing tools we've learned about, you will also be able to make corrections without noticing the difference between takes, along with using fades, crossfades, and volume adjustments to achieve a perfect result.

In the next chapter, we will look at what happens once you have edited and arranged all your items in a project: mixing.

4
Mixing Procedures in REAPER

In this chapter, you will learn about important procedures such as the use of audio processors and automation to achieve a good mix in REAPER.

Mixing is the stage of production that comes after editing. In the mixing stage, all the elements that make up the project are combined: vocals, instruments, effects, and more. It is a very artistic stage as it requires auditory sensitivity to make decisions. When we edit, we must ensure we select, clean, and arrange the audio and MIDI items into the necessary parts: verses, choruses, intros, endings, and so on. Once a project is edited, mixing will adjust the volume and effects of each element.

A good mix will allow us to hear all sonic elements clearly, without some standing out too much or getting lost. Knowing the processes and procedures used in mixing will help you achieve better results in the final sound of your productions.

Throughout this chapter, we will cover the following topics:

- **Volume and panning options**: You will learn about the criteria for adjusting the volume of the different sounds in a project and their positioning in a stereo mix
- **Using real-time audio processing**: You will learn how to apply processors that modify the original sound, whether to improve it or make it more interesting
- **Rendering audio processing**: You will learn how to apply effects permanently to your audio files
- **Creating dimension in the mix**: You will learn how to use the most important processors in audio mixing
- **Understanding automation**: You will learn how to create dynamics in your productions by automatically adjusting effects throughout the project

By the end of this chapter, you will know how to organize your project to carry out a good mix and understand how to apply important processors such as equalization and compression to your audio tracks, as well as other effects. You will also know how to record and edit your movements in the mix using automation.

Technical requirements

To carry out the different mixing techniques in this chapter, you'll need to edit a demo musical project.

In the supplementary files of this book on GitHub, you will find various loops of different instruments, such as drums, bass, guitar, and others. You can use these files to import them into a new project and arrange them to give them a musical shape.

On the other hand, if you have a personal project that you're already working on in REAPER, you can use it to practice the mixing techniques you'll be introduced to here.

The audio files for this chapter can be found in this book's GitHub repository: `https://github.com/PacktPublishing/Elevate-your-audio-production-with-Reaper`.

Volume and panning options

The most important task when mixing is adjusting the *volume*. In a REAPER project, we typically use a different track for each type of sound we use – for example, one track for each musical instrument, one for each type of voice, one for any sound effect, and so on. This technique allows us to have greater control over each type of sound, as well as to automate more easily, as we will see at the end of this chapter.

When we start working on the mix of a session, we must ensure that the session is organized so that we can work more quickly and without confusion.

Initial preparation

Before mixing, it's recommended to set up and organize the session. *Figure 4.1* shows a sample project with eight audio tracks. We can see that each track is named in a way that makes it easy to identify.

> **Tip**
>
> We must make it a habit to always name each track we use properly so that our session is understandable, even if we have many tracks.

To rename a track, we can double-click on its name, as shown in *Figure 4.1*:

Figure 4.1 – Naming tracks

It's also important to arrange the tracks conveniently. For example, we've arranged them by the type of sound or category. In this project, the percussion tracks are at the top, followed by the bass, guitar, synthesizers, and voice at the end; however, they can be arranged in any preferred order.

To reorder a track, you just need to drag and drop it where you want to place it, as shown in *Figure 4.2*:

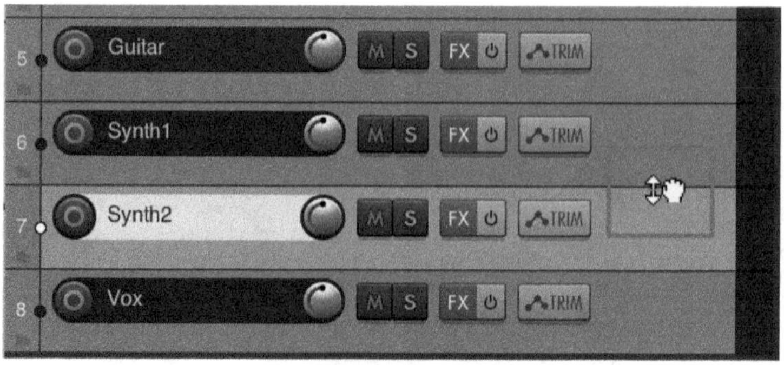

Figure 4.2 – Sorting tracks

Note the shape the mouse pointer takes when you're moving a track. We can also adjust the size of the mixer by placing the mouse below the *transport controls*, as shown in *Figure 4.3*:

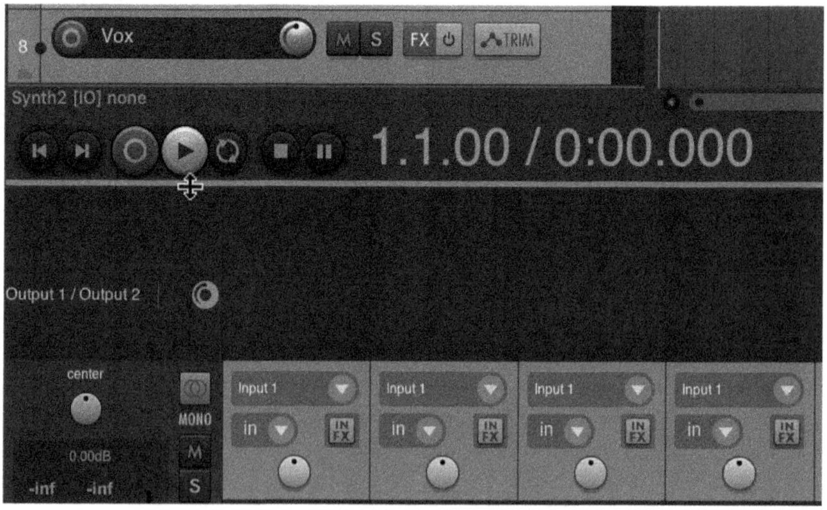

Figure 4.3 – Adjusting the mixer's size

The idea is to adjust the size of the mixer and the arrangement area so that we can work comfortably and see the channel information easily.

Another adjustment that can help us organize our project is the use of colors. We can apply a different color to each track, item, or group of tracks so that we have a visual order that allows us to work more quickly.

To do this, just right-click on the desired track and select **Track color**, as shown in *Figure 4.4*:

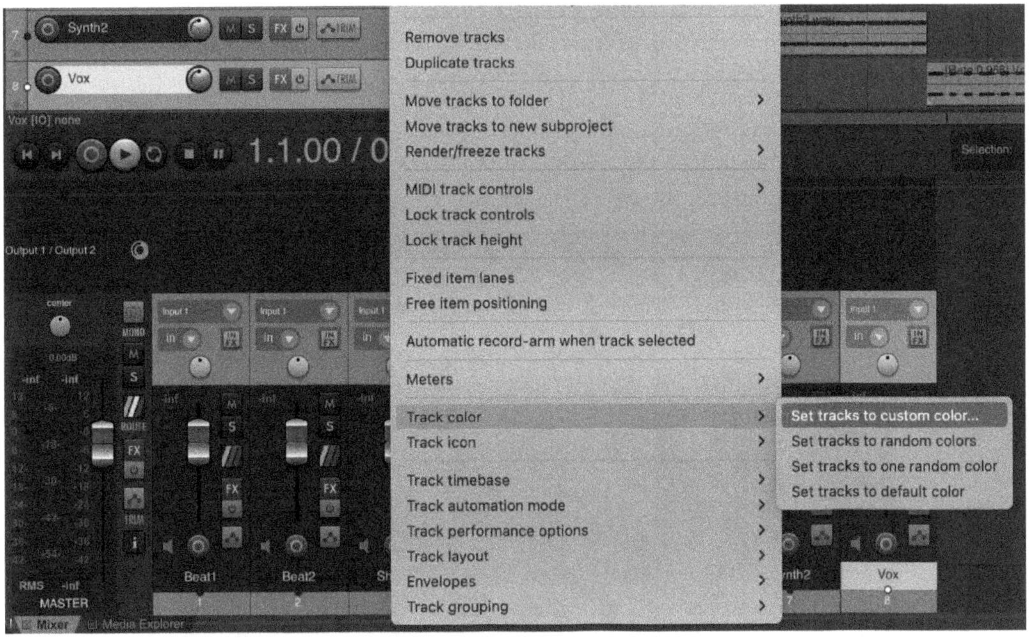

Figure 4.4 – Track color

As we can see, we have several options to select a particular color or use random colors. If you want to select multiple tracks, you can press the *Shift* key while clicking on the desired tracks.

We also have the option to add an icon to the track if desired. We can do this by using the **Track icon** command, which can be found next to the **Track color**.

Once our session is organized, we can begin adjusting the volume, as we will see in the next section.

Adjusting volume

Adjusting the **volume** of each track is perhaps the most important task in mixing. We can do this by moving the **channel fader** up or down. However, there are no strict rules on how it should be adjusted. In the end, this is a purely subjective decision that will depend on the type of project, trends, and personal taste.

In general, the idea is to adjust the volume of each track so that each element sounds appropriate and its volume sounds *natural* to our ears. To develop our ability to adjust the volume, it is very important to try to listen to references. A **reference** is an audio production with characteristics similar to ours and that we consider to be of great quality. For example, in a musical production, references can be songs of a similar genre and from a well-known artist.

When listening to a reference, it is important to pay attention to the volume of each instrument or element – that is, how loud the voice sounds compared to the drums, the volume of the guitars, and so on. This is an auditory training process that takes time, but it is very important to do if we want to achieve an appropriate mix.

Considering what was just mentioned, we can start adjusting the volume with the faders of each channel. The general recommendation is to adjust the volume of the tracks so that the signal on the **MASTER** meter stays peaking around **-6** dBFS, as shown in *Figure 4.5*:

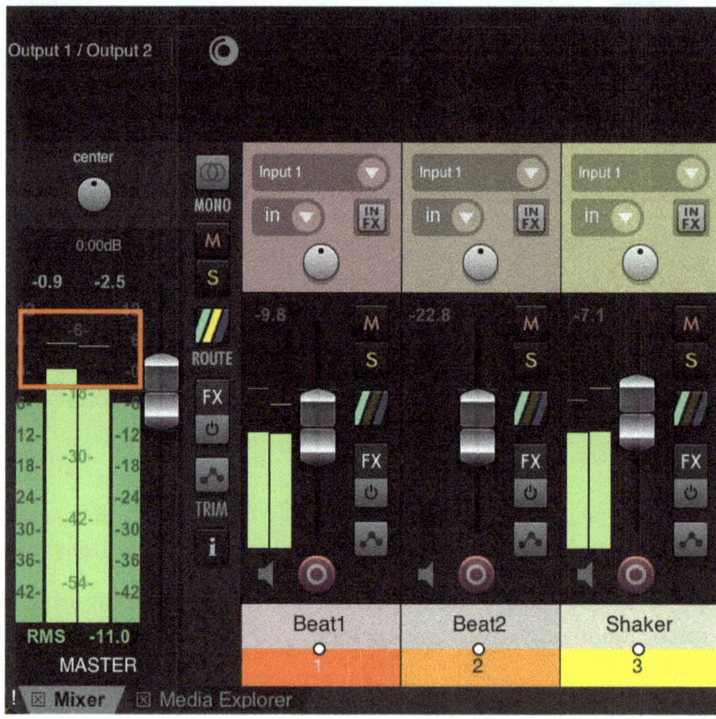

Figure 4.5 – MASTER peak level

As shown in *Figure 4.5*, the peak values are kept on the **MASTER** meter for our reference. Keeping the **MASTER** meter values around **-6** dBFS will allow us to maintain headroom in our project and thus avoid distortion. Notice that we keep the **MASTER** fader at **0** dB. In other words, you don't need to move the **MASTER** fader.

If we want to move several faders at the same time, we can select them by clicking on their name while pressing the *Shift* or *Control* key (*Command* on Mac), and then raise or lower them together. After this, we can select just one track to return to normal, individual mode.

If we want to reset the faders to **0** dB, we can just double-click on them.

Working with mute and solo

Now, let's look at two functions that are very useful when mixing: mute and solo, as indicated in *Figure 4.6*:

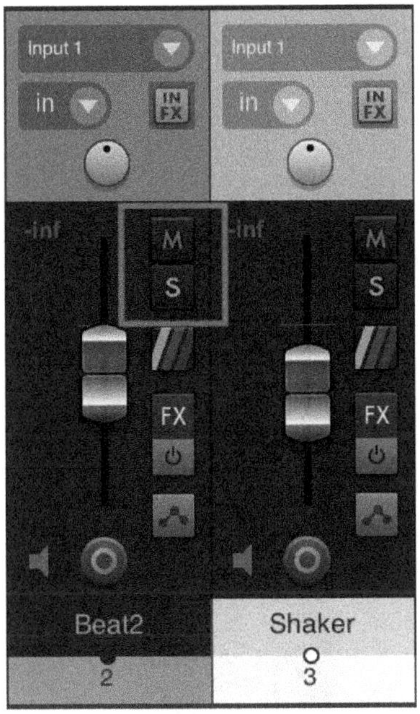

Figure 4.6 – The mute and solo buttons

The **mute** button (**M**) will silence the channel, while the **solo** button (**S**) will silence all other channels. When mixing, it may be necessary to solo a channel to hear only that channel more clearly. After doing this, we must deactivate the solo to hear all the channels again.

Once we have adjusted the volume of the channels, aiming for a proper balance according to our ears, it is recommended to adjust the panning, as we will see in the next section.

Panning

Panning or **pan** (which comes from *panoramic*) is the option we have to make the sound of each channel come from the left (L) or right (R) side of our monitoring (headphones, speakers). The use of panning is also subjective as there are no strict rules about which instrument or element should go to one side or the other.

In general terms, the main sounds are usually panned to the center, such as lead vocals or solo instruments. It is also common for instruments such as the kick drum, bass, and snare drum to be centered; however, for the rest of the instruments, the panning can be varied. In this respect, it is a good idea to listen carefully to our references as we can find panning criteria according to the type of music or audio production we are doing.

Other common criteria for deciding the panning of instruments include the position of the instruments on a stage or, for example, their position in an orchestra. This practice is quite common, especially in orchestral music.

To adjust the panning of a channel in REAPER, we simply need to drag the *pan* knob of the channel to the left or right, as shown in *Figure 4.7*:

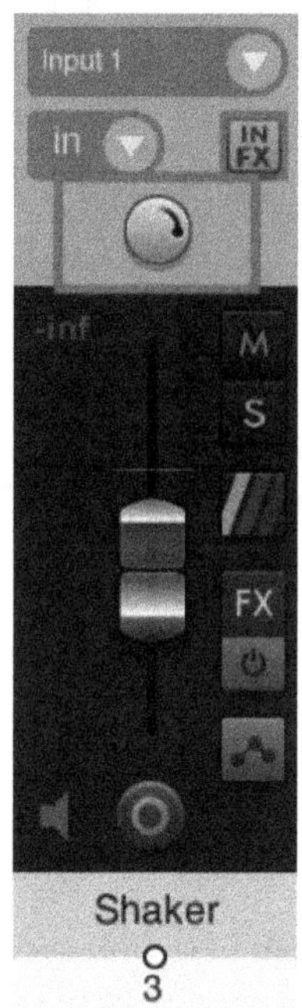

Figure 4.7 – Channel pan knob

If we want to quickly reset the pan to the center, we can double-click the *pan* knob.

So far, we have seen options that allow us to have better organization of our session before we start mixing. We have also seen the criteria and considerations for adjusting the volume and panning of the channels. Now, we will learn how to use real-time processors, which aid in our mixing work.

Using real-time audio processing

Real-time processors are plugins that modify the audio of a channel while the project is playing. This can be done through effect inserts. The **effect insert** area of the mixer is shown in *Figure 4.8*:

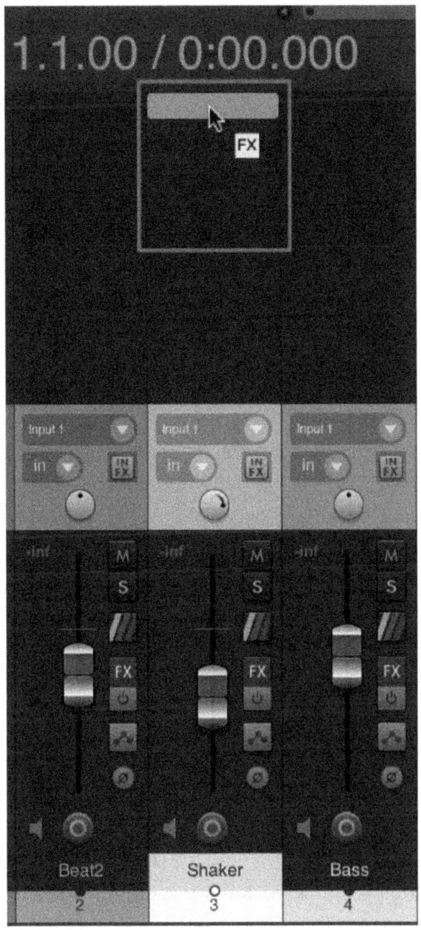

Figure 4.8 – Effects area

To add an effect, simply click on one of the slots in the effects area. Then, the effects window will appear, as shown in *Figure 4.9*:

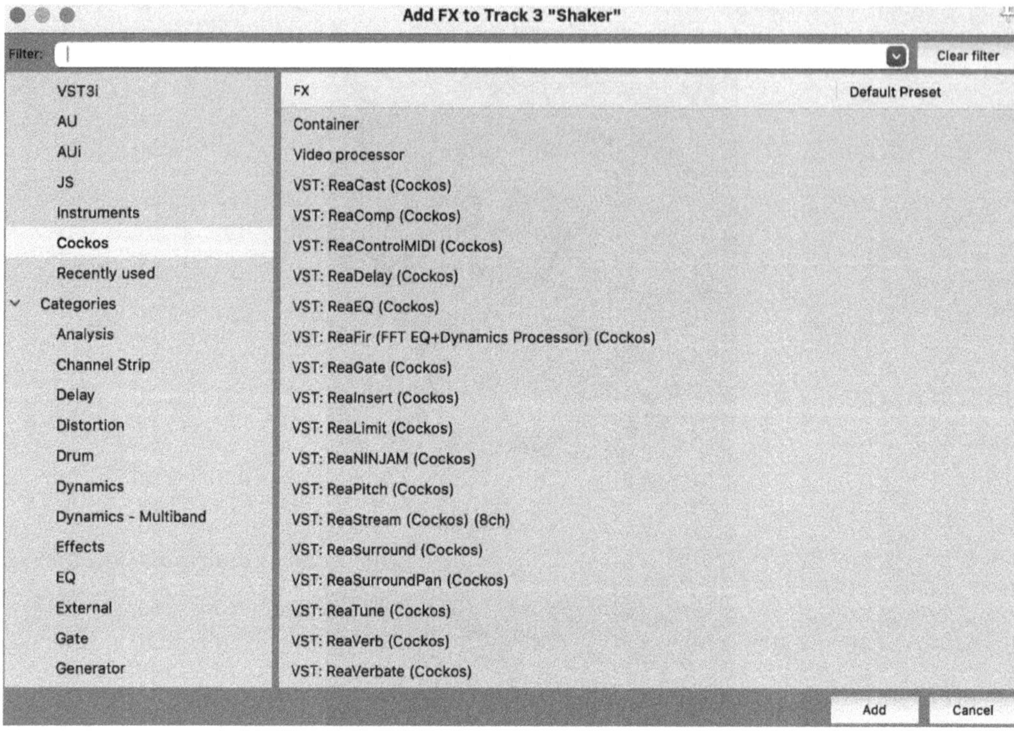

Figure 4.9 – Effects window

This window is similar to the one we saw in *Chapter 2*, where we chose a virtual synthesizer. Here, we can see a list of processor categories on the left-hand side, organized by type of effect or technology. This list will vary depending on the plugins you have installed on your computer. Throughout this book, we will rely solely on **Cockos** plugins, which are included with REAPER.

To add an effect to the channel, we just need to select it and press the **Add** button or the *Enter* key. For example, we will add an equalizer, which is one of the most important processors in audio, by selecting the **ReaEQ** plugin, as shown in *Figure 4.10*:

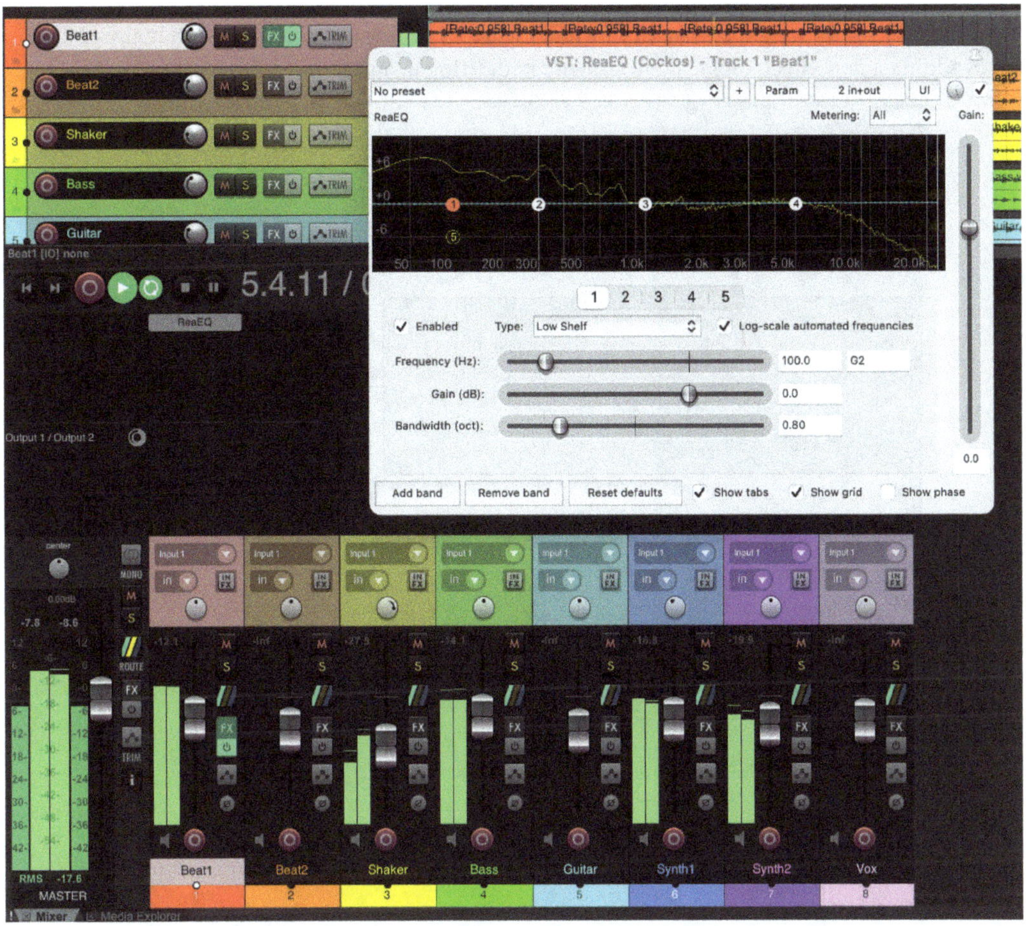

Figure 4.10 – ReaEQ plugin on channel 1

Here, we can see the **ReaEQ** plugin window, which is a multi-band equalizer. Each plugin will have a very particular window, depending on the type of effect it has. The native REAPER plugins (created by Cockos) have a very simple graphical interface; however, their audio processing quality is very good, and they can be used confidently in professional audio production.

If we play the project, then the audio of the channel will be processed in real time by the effect we have inserted. We can add multiple effects, one below another, creating **processing chains**.

> **Note**
>
> All these effects generate a load on the CPU, so the type of computer we have (kind of processor and amount of RAM) will allow the use of more or fewer effects.

If we right-click on the plugin insert, as shown in *Figure 4.11*, we will see a menu with many options, such as adding a new effect, replacing it, copying it, deleting it, and more:

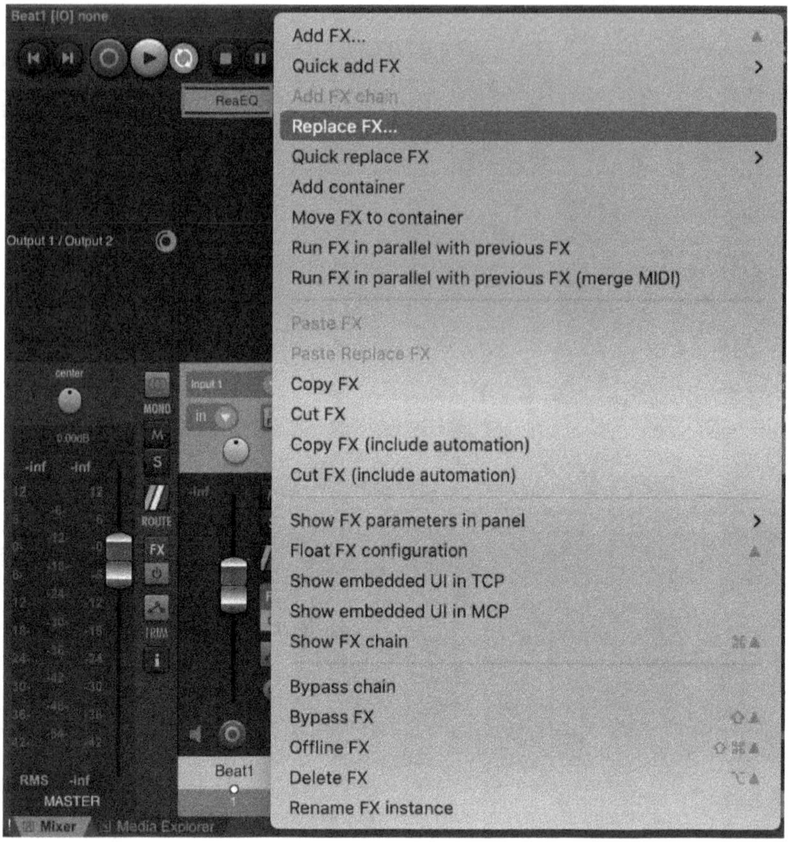

Figure 4.11 – Effects menu

On the other hand, if we left-click on the plugin insert, we can hide or show its window. If we want to quickly copy an effect to another channel, we just need to drag the plugin and drop it onto the new channel.

Sometimes, we may want to temporarily disable an effect so that we can hear the original unprocessed sound. To do this, we can use the **Bypass FX** command, which appears in the list shown in *Figure 4.11*, or disable the effect with the button in the upper corner of the plugin window, as shown in *Figure 4.12* (labeled as **1**):

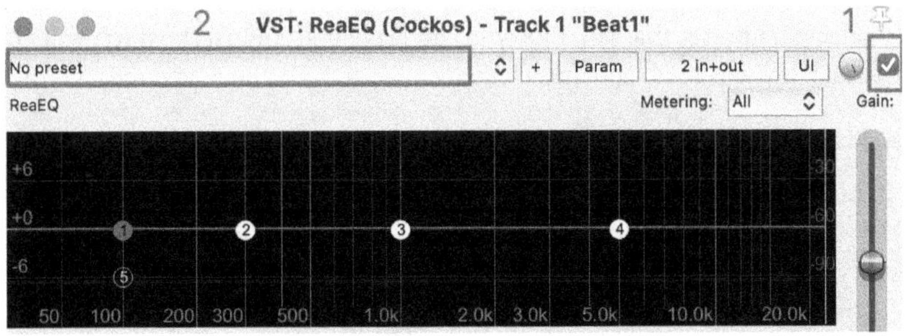

Figure 4.12 – Effect activation and presets

A convenient way to try out the sound of an effect is by using presets. To select a preset, we can press the presets menu shown in *Figure 4.12* (labeled as **2**). Each plugin will have a varying number of factory presets. These can serve as a basis for using an effect, after which we can modify it to our taste if needed.

You can also save custom settings in a new preset using the + button, as indicated in *Figure 4.13*:

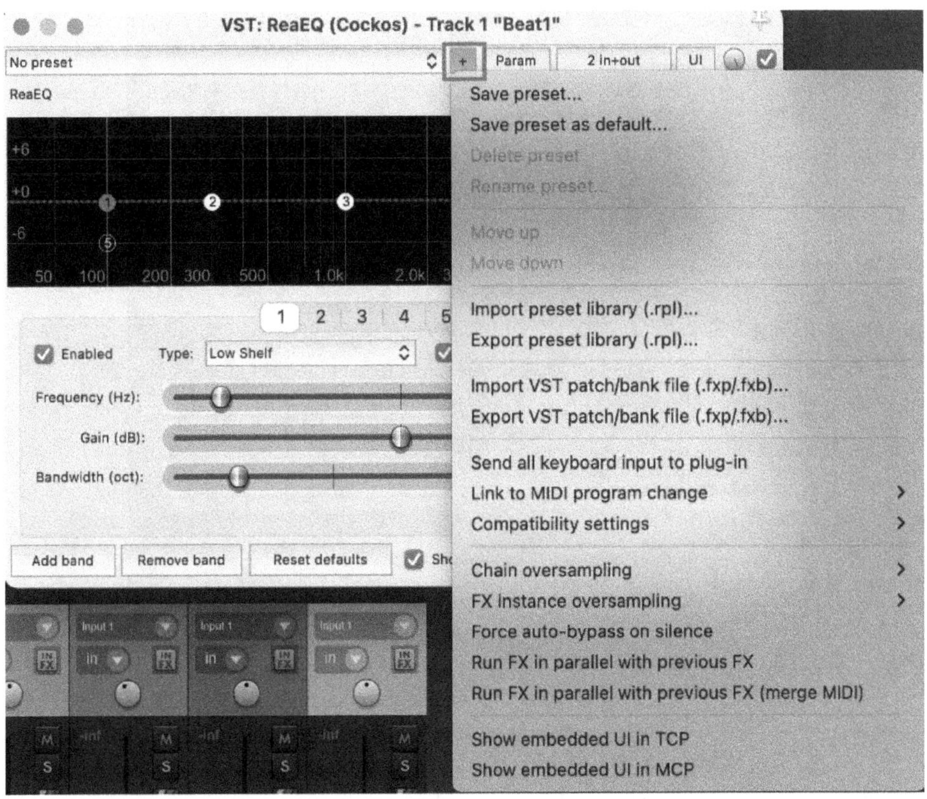

Figure 4.13 – Preset options

Once you have selected a preset that you like, you can leave it as an insert, which will affect all the items on that channel. If you want to add an effect only to a particular item, you must do the following:

1. Double-click on the item you want to process. The **Media Item Properties** screen will appear.
2. Click on the **Take FX...** button, as indicated in *Figure 4.14*:

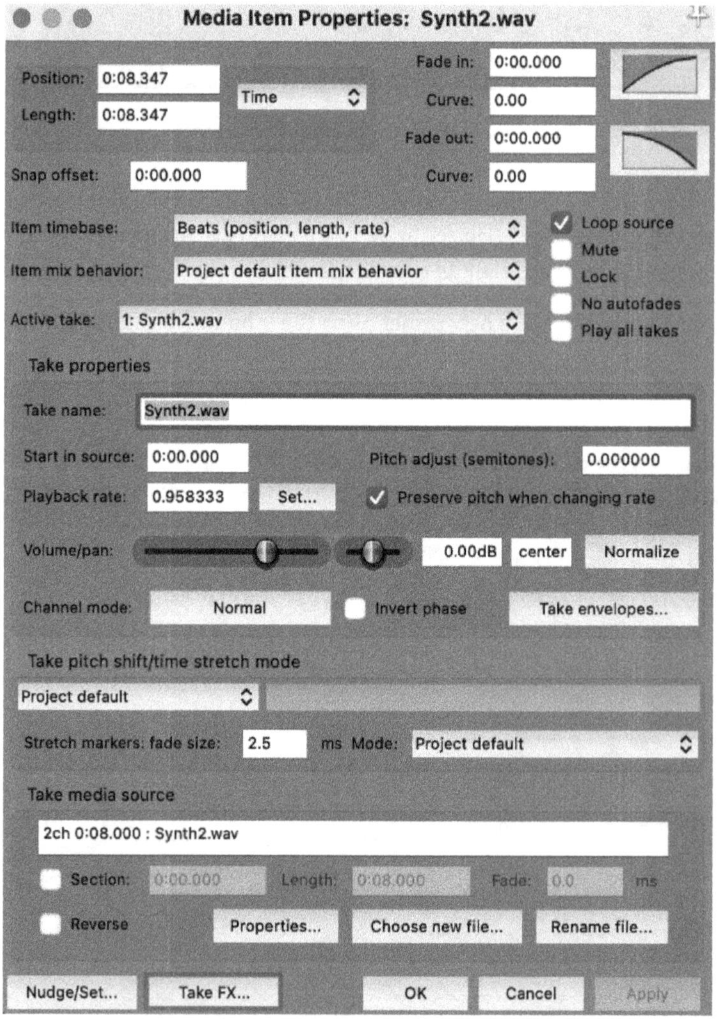

Figure 4.14 – Media Item Properties

3. REAPER will display the effects selection window, as shown in *Figure 4.9*. Select the plugin you want to use.
4. The effect window will be shown. Adjust the effect according to your needs.

When playing the project, you will hear the effect on the item. You can close the effect window and the **Media Item Properties** window.

To remove a real-time effect, go to the **Take FX** menu in the **Media Item Properties** window and, in the plugin window, press the **Remove** button, as shown in *Figure 4.15*:

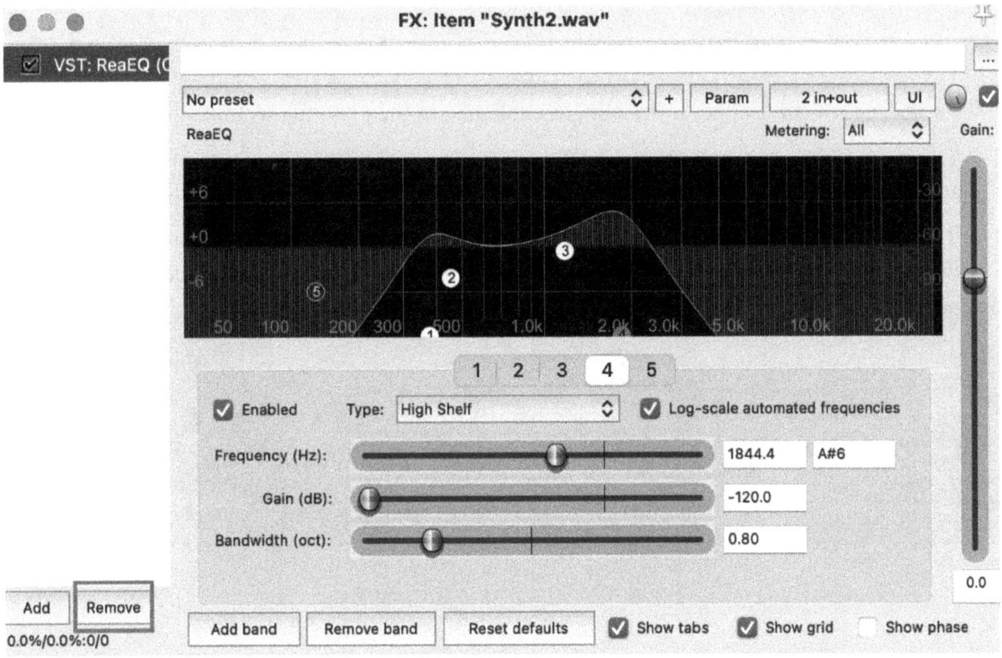

Figure 4.15 – Removing an effect

This way, you will hear the original audio again without any effect. It is also possible to create processing chains by adding several effects one after another. This can be done with the **Add** button, which is before the **Remove** button. The resulting sound will be a combination of all the active effects.

So far, we have seen different options for managing real-time effects. Each effect has particular characteristics and functions that we will start to see a little later. If we want to make the effect *fixed* on the item, we must use rendering, as we will see next.

Rendering audio processing

Using real-time effects allows us to hear what we are processing while the project is playing. The disadvantage of this form of processing is that the CPU must constantly work to generate the desired effect. As we add effects to multiple channels, we may reach the limits of what our CPU can handle.

In such cases, it is convenient to **render** the effects on items, which means creating new audio files that already have the effects included. This way, the CPU is relieved from processing in real time and only needs to read the new file.

How to render effects on an item

Here are the steps for rendering effects on an item:

1. Assign the real-time effect to an item, as explained in the previous section.
2. Select the **Item | Apply track/take FX to items as new take** menu. This menu can also be accessed by right-clicking on the item.
3. REAPER will create a new audio file, and two takes will appear on the track, as shown in *Figure 4.16*. The take shown in *Figure 4.16* is the new take with the effect already rendered:

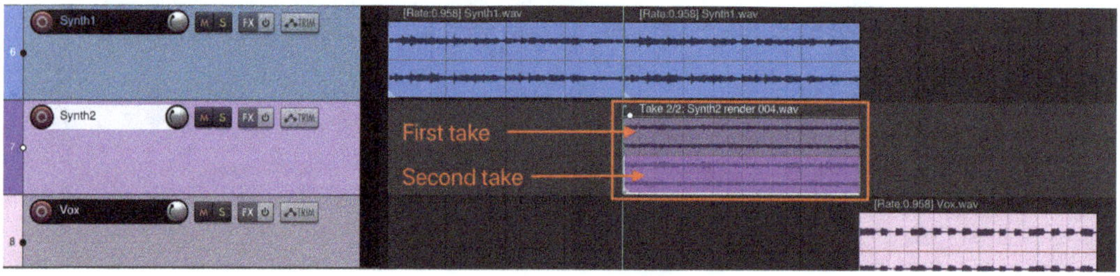

Figure 4.16 – Track with two takes

When we play the project, we will hear the effect as part of the item, without the CPU processing it in real time. The waveform will also change depending on how intense the applied effect is.

Managing multiple takes

Even though two takes are visible within the same track, only the selected take will be heard. If we click on the first take, it will be selected, and we will hear the original audio processed in real time. This way, we can modify the effect and create a new render with a new take, which means we now have three available takes.

This can be useful for comparing effects. For example, when applying an effect to a vocal, we can create several takes with different versions of the effect and listen to one version or another. We just need to select the take we want to hear.

We can also compare the original sound without effects and the sound with effects. We just need to remove the real-time effect from the original take (as mentioned in the previous section) and select the takes we want to hear, one at a time.

Even with multiple takes in an item, we can perform basic editing functions, such as trimming, creating fades, adjusting volume, copying, pasting, and more.

Printing effects into an audio file

An important characteristic of rendered effects is that they cannot be deactivated; the effects are permanently fixed in the newly created file. If we do not like the result of a rendered effect, we can use the **undo** function.

If we have decided which effect we want permanently on an item, we can remove the other takes from the track and keep only the active take. To do this, use the **Item | Take | Crop to active take** menu (also accessible by right-clicking on the item). This will delete the unselected takes and leave only the active take. This function can help keep our session cleaner; however, we should only do this if we are sure no further changes to the effect will be needed later.

Working with rendered and real-time effects

As we have seen, using rendered effects provides the advantage of saving CPU resources and allows us to manipulate audio files with integrated effects. In audio production, a combination of real-time and rendered processes is often used, depending on the needs of each sound.

For example, if an effect needs to be applied to all items in a track, it is better to use real-time effects on the channel. On the other hand, if the effect is only needed on one item, it is better to use real-time effects on that item only (using the **Media Item Properties** window). If we have decided that the effect should be permanent on the item, we can render it.

Projects such as audio post-production for video or podcast production often use item processing. On the other hand, in music production, it is more common to handle real-time processing for the entire track.

Now that we have seen the different ways we can apply processing to tracks or items and know how to activate or deactivate effects, it's time that we look at how to apply the most common and important effects in audio production.

Creating dimension in the mix

As we have seen, the most important actions in mixing are volume adjustment and panning. However, using effects to process tracks or items is crucial for making a mix sound complete and more polished. This helps create a mix with more *dimension*, making all elements sound clearer, more defined, and present.

In this section, we will look at the most important processors included in REAPER and how to use them.

> **Additional reading**
>
> For a more in-depth explanation of the processors included in REAPER, please refer to the REAPER Effects Guide: `https://dlz.reaper.fm/userguide/REAPEREffectsGuide2021.pdf`

Equalizer

An **equalizer** modifies the frequency spectrum of a signal. To better understand its function, we must first understand the spectrum of a signal.

Frequency and spectrum

Sounds have a property called **frequency**, which refers to how quickly a body vibrates. For example, a guitar string or a drumhead vibrates at a certain rate when played, which is called the frequency of vibration and is measured in **Hz (Hertz)**. The higher the frequency (more Hz), the higher the pitch of the sound. A low sound, on the other hand, has a lower frequency.

The human ear can perceive frequencies in a range of approximately 20 to 20,000 Hz (20 Hz to 20 kHz). Thus, within this range, we find all the sounds we can hear: lows, mids, and highs. *Figure 4.17* shows the approximate ranges of audible frequencies:

Frequency Range	Common Name
20 – 160 Hz	Low frequencies (bass)
160 – 400 Hz	Low-mid frequencies
400 – 1,500 Hz	Mid frequencies
2,000 – 6,000 Hz	High-mid frequencies
6,000 – 20,000 Hz	High frequencies (treble)

Figure 4.17 – Common frequency ranges

Each sound has a certain amount of energy in certain frequencies. For example, a kick drum has a lot of energy in low frequencies, while a shaker has more energy in high frequencies.

The graph that shows this energy distribution is called a **spectrum**, as shown in *Figure 4.18*.

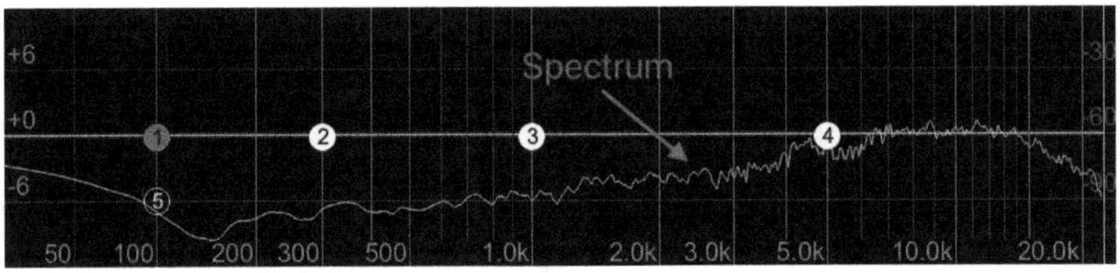

Figure 4.18 – Spectrum of a shaker

In *Figure 4.18*, the horizontal axis shows the frequencies from **20** to **20** kHz, and the vertical axis shows the amount of energy in dB. The spectrum shown is that of a shaker, which is a high-pitched percussion instrument. We can see that the line representing the spectrum has more energy in the **5** kHz to **18** kHz range, while it has little intensity in the **200** to **300** Hz range.

The spectrum of a signal allows us to visualize whether that signal mainly has high, mid, or low frequencies. Each sound generates a different spectrum, and it is interesting to observe and compare the spectrum of different types of sounds.

As mentioned earlier, equalizers are processors that allow us to alter the spectrum of a signal. For example, they can filter high or low frequencies or increase or decrease the energy in a certain frequency range.

In REAPER, we have a very comprehensive equalizer that also shows us the signal spectrum: **ReaEQ**. This is shown in *Figure 4.19*:

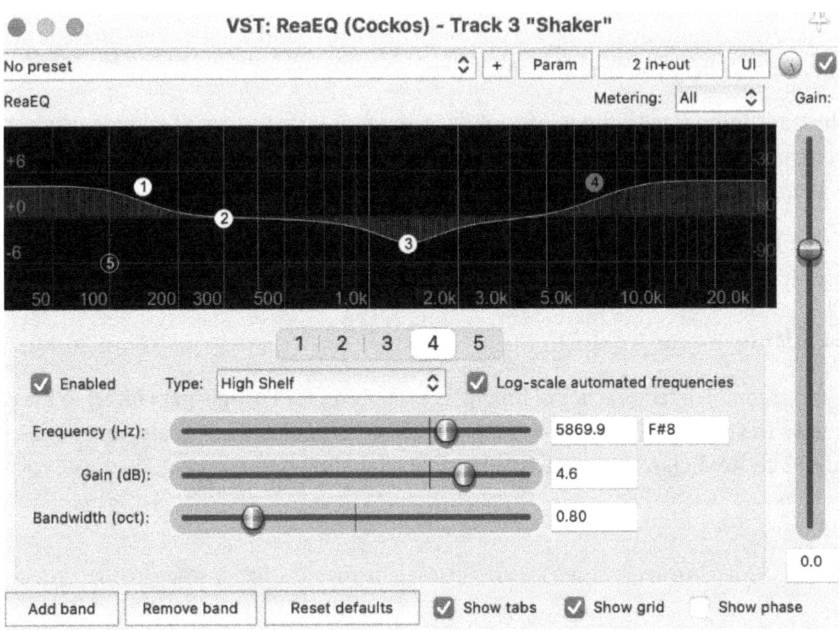

Figure 4.19 – ReaEQ plugin

With **ReaEQ**, we can perform any equalization work, and its user interface is very intuitive. Each small, numbered circle controls a band, and we can move it up or down to increase or decrease the intensity of the sound in that band. We can also move it left or right to change the frequency range it affects.

For example, in *Figure 4.19*, band **1** has been moved up (circle **1**), increasing the intensity of the lows. Band **4** has also been moved up, increasing the intensity of the highs. Band **3** has been moved down, reducing the intensity of the mids. In this way, we can *shape* any sound by altering its spectrum to our liking.

In general, we can summarize the effect of equalizing audio bands as follows:

- If we increase the high frequencies, we will have a brighter and clearer sound; if we attenuate them, we will have a duller sound
- If we increase the low frequencies, we will have a fatter sound; if we attenuate them, we will have a thinner sound
- If we increase the mid frequencies, the sound will become more present; if we attenuate them, it will become more distant

Equalization is a process that requires practice and ear training to make accurate decisions that improve the sound. One way to start training the ear is by boosting a band around 10 dB and listening carefully to the result. Then, move the band left and right to hear the difference in sound in each frequency range. This way, we will gradually identify the frequencies that help the sound and those that worsen it.

You can do this exercise also by cutting a band by 10 dB. The sound will be very different than when boosting, and this will help you hear the differences.

Try using these techniques with different sounds or musical instruments. If you are using the audio files provided for this chapter, try equalizing each of them in different ways. Don't be afraid to make mistakes; you are learning!

Remember that **ReaEQ** comes with several factory presets that we can use as a base for equalizing a sound. However, our ears should make the final decision.

High-pass filter

A common and recommended practice in mixing is to apply an **HPF (high-pass filter)** in the equalizer of each channel. The HPF is a filter that lets high frequencies pass and attenuates low frequencies. To activate the HPF in **ReaEQ**, select band **5** and enable it, as shown in *Figure 4.20*:

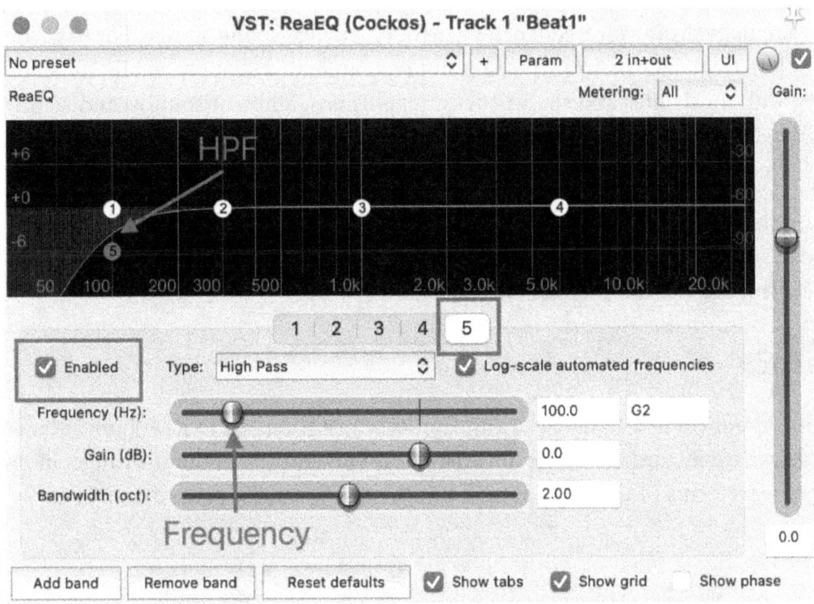

Figure 4.20 – HPF

Once activated, the HPF will attenuate the very low frequencies of the track, resulting in a cleaner sound without rumble. We must adjust the filter frequency with the control indicated in *Figure 4.20* so that the HPF does not excessively remove the lows. You can use the table shown in *Figure 4.21* as a guide to adjust the HPF frequency according to the type of sound:

Sound Source	**HPF Frequency**
Female vocals	180 Hz
Male vocals	90 Hz
Guitar (acoustic and electric)	80 Hz
Piano	60 Hz
Violin, trumpet, flute, treble instruments	180 Hz
Cello, trombone, bass instruments	60 Hz
Snare drum	100 Hz
Tom toms	70 Hz
Cymbals	300 Hz
Kick drum, bass guitar, tuba	Not necessary
Music, sound effects	Not necessary

Figure 4.21 – HPF frequencies

The idea is to attenuate the lowest frequencies generated by each sound source. For bass, kick drums, and other very low-frequency instruments, it is not recommended to apply an HPF most of the time. When dealing with music files and sound effects (explosions, ambient sounds, and so on), it is not recommended to use an HPF either. This recommendation is because all these sounds have important content in low frequencies, and that is part of their natural sound.

The equalizer is the most important processor in mixing because it allows us to adjust the frequencies of each sound to achieve a better balance. The next most important processor is the compressor, which allows us to control the volume changes of each sound.

Compressor

An important component of a signal is its **amplitude**, which is related to its volume. Sounds usually have amplitude variations, and this range of variations is known as the **dynamic range**. In *Figure 4.22*, we can see two waveforms of the same sound, but the top one has a more dynamic range than the bottom one:

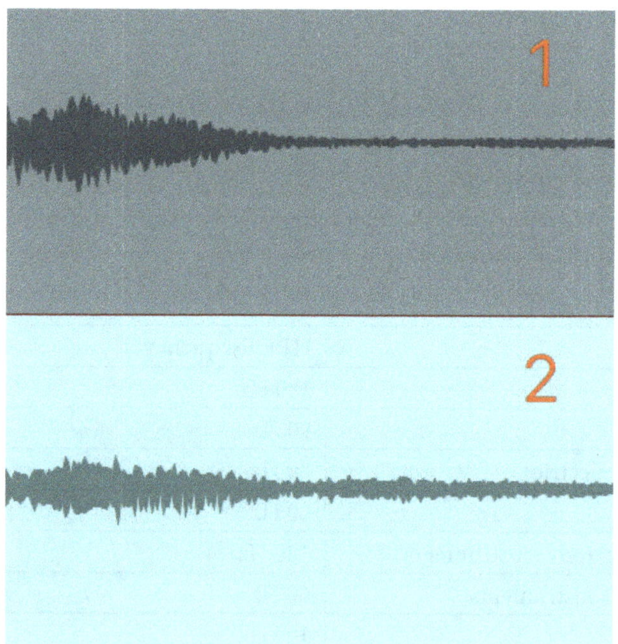

Figure 4.22 – Waveforms with different dynamic range

A greater dynamic range means it has more amplitude variations. We can see that the first figure has some higher peaks and that the end part of the sound is very small. On the other hand, the second figure has more constant amplitudes, and we can see that the final part has more amplitude than in the first image. This is because the second image is a compressed version of the first.

A **compressor** helps control the volume variations of a sound. This is very useful in mixing as it helps make sounds more consistent. For example, a vocal track naturally has volume variations, but sometimes, some words might sound a bit low. The compressor helps even out this volume, slightly reducing the louder parts and increasing the quieter parts.

REAPER has a very comprehensive compressor called **ReaComp**, as shown in *Figure 4.23*:

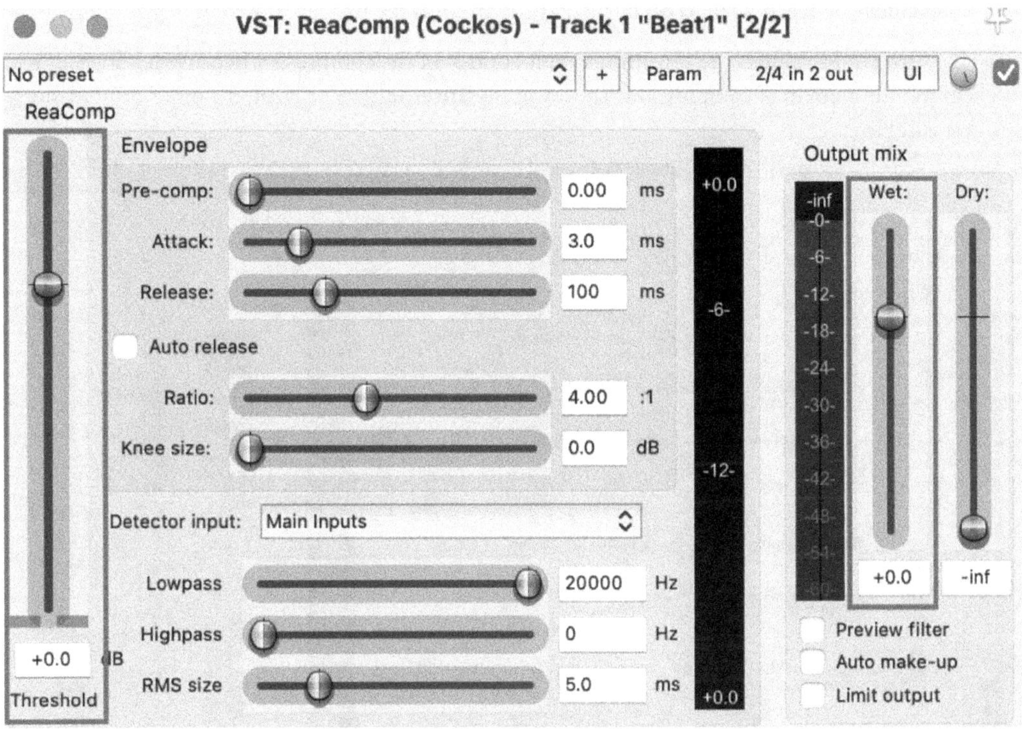

Figure 4.23 – ReaComp compressor

There are many types of compressors with different complexities and controls, as well as a wide variety of techniques to use them. Covering compression in detail is beyond the scope of this book, but let's look at a procedure that can help us apply moderate compression to various sounds, such as vocals and musical instruments, and is a good starting point for learning how to use compressors.

Steps to apply compression

Here are the steps you can follow to apply compression:

1. Insert the **ReaComp** plugin into the channel you want to compress.
2. Play the sound and lower the **Threshold** value of the compressor (marked in *Figure 4.23*) until you achieve between **4** and **6** dB in the **gain reduction** reading, as shown in *Figure 4.24*.

   The **Threshold** value is the most important control of the compressor because it allows us to control the amount of compression. The lower the **Threshold** value is set, the more compression we will have:

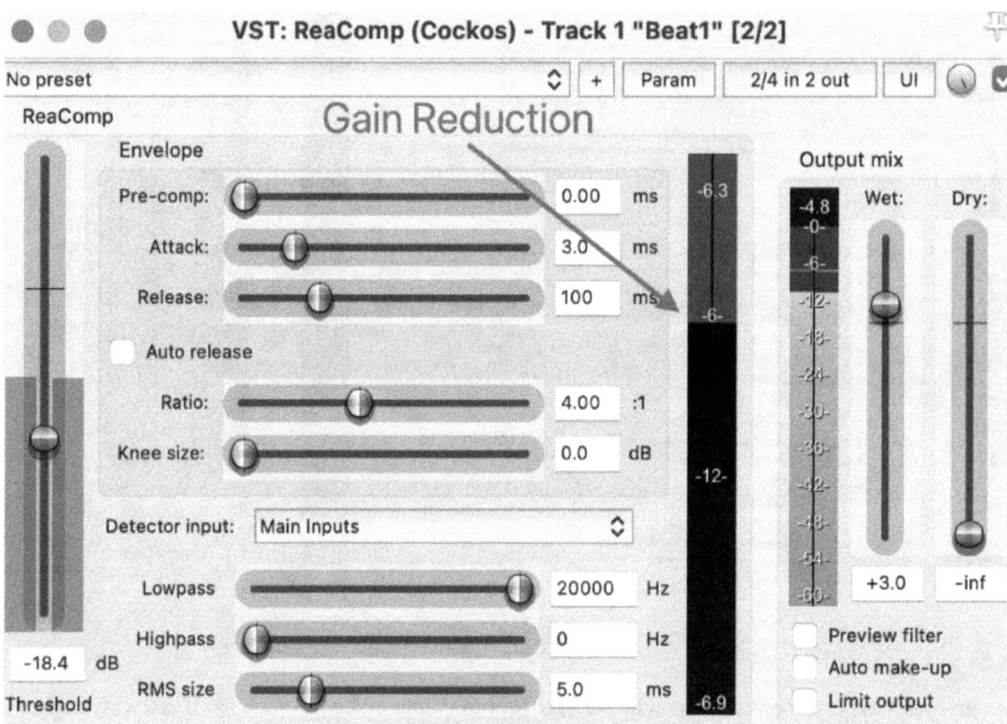

Figure 4.24 – Measuring gain reduction

3. Increase the **Wet** level (marked in *Figure 4.23*) by about **3** dB to compensate for the volume loss caused by the compressor. The idea is that the average volume of the uncompressed signal is similar to that of the compressed signal.
4. All other controls in **ReaComp** appear with appropriate values for working by default, so it is not necessary to change them initially. Using this procedure, we will achieve a sound with a more uniform and constant volume.

We can apply compression in this way to almost any type of sound. It is particularly important to use it on all vocal channels (spoken or sung) and on acoustic musical instruments, such as drums, guitar, bass, trumpet, flute, and others. Synthesized or digital instruments may not require compression or may only need 1 or 2 dB of gain reduction, depending on the experimentation with the resulting sound.

> **Important note**
>
> It is important to mention that the effect of the compressor is subtle and not always easy to identify audibly, but that does not mean it is not doing its job and that it is important to use it.

Now that we know how to control the spectrum and dynamic range of a sound, we can use an effect to add space to the mix. For this, we will use reverb.

Reverberation

Reverberation or **reverb** is an acoustic effect that's generated within an enclosed room or space. It results from hundreds of echoes bouncing quickly off the walls, floor, and ceiling. A classic example of reverberation can be heard inside a cathedral or cave, where surfaces reflect a lot of sound.

The larger the room, the more reverberation there will be. Conversely, if the room is small and filled with sound-absorbing materials such as curtains or carpets, reverberation will decrease. This explains why the sound changes when we remove furniture from a room; there's less absorption, resulting in more reverberation.

In REAPER, we have a couple of reverb plugins. Let's see how to use **ReaVerbate**, as shown in *Figure 4.25*. This effect simulates the reverberation of a room or hall:

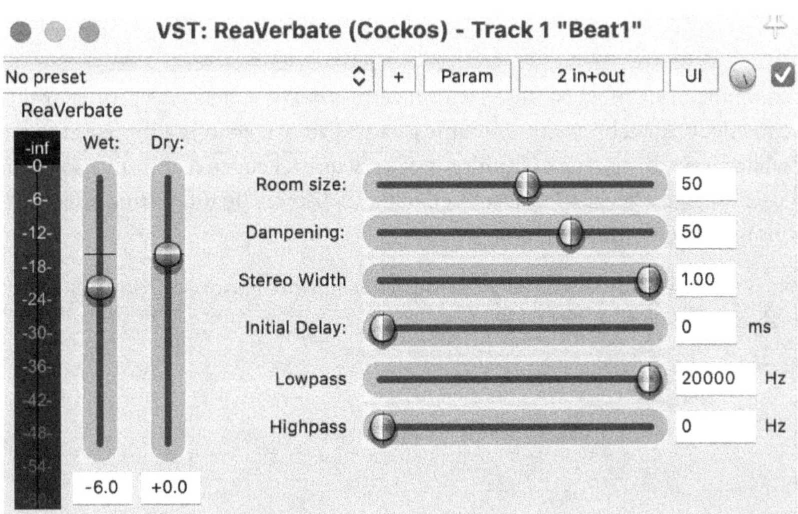

Figure 4.25 - ReaVerbate plugin

The main controls are **Wet** and **Dry**. In any plugin, the **Wet** signal is the signal with the effect, while the **Dry** signal is the original signal without the effect. If we insert a **ReaVerbate** plugin in a channel, we will hear the sound with a bit of reverb. Increasing the **Wet** level will increase the reverb.

The balance between **Dry** and **Wet** affects the final sound and is entirely a matter of personal preference, depending on the sound we are aiming for.

Let's see what the other controls of ReaVerbate do:

- **Room size**: Increasing this parameter will result in a longer reverb, simulating a larger room.
- **Dampening**: This simulates the absorption of high frequencies by materials in the room. Increasing this parameter will result in a less bright reverb.
- **Stereo width**: This controls how wide the panning of the reverb sounds. The most common setting is to leave it at the maximum value.
- **Initial delay**: This option controls the milliseconds that pass before the reverb starts. In a large space, it is normal to have a delay of 20 or 30 ms before hearing reverb, while in smaller spaces, it may only be 5 or 10 ms.
- **Lowpass/Highpass**: These are filters similar to those used in an equalizer. They help control the amount of high (using **Lowpass**) or low frequencies (using **Highpass**) in the reverb.

Not all parameters need to be adjusted all the time; it depends on the reverb effect we are aiming for. For example, we can use reverb to create the impression that someone is speaking inside a room or to create special effects to emulate that they are speaking in a cave. Therefore, we need to adjust the **ReaVerbate** parameters to create this illusion.

Delay

Another very common effect, often confused with reverb, is **delay**. A delay is a processor that typically gives us the echo effect. An echo is not the same as a reverb. An echo is a more defined repetition of the sound, while a reverb consists of hundreds of very quick echoes that form a sound field. Both effects can be used to give a sense of space, but delay can also create interesting effects in music by using repetitions to create rhythmic effects.

In REAPER, we have **ReaDelay**, a simple yet comprehensive processor. Let's look at the function of its controls, as shown in *Figure 4.26*:

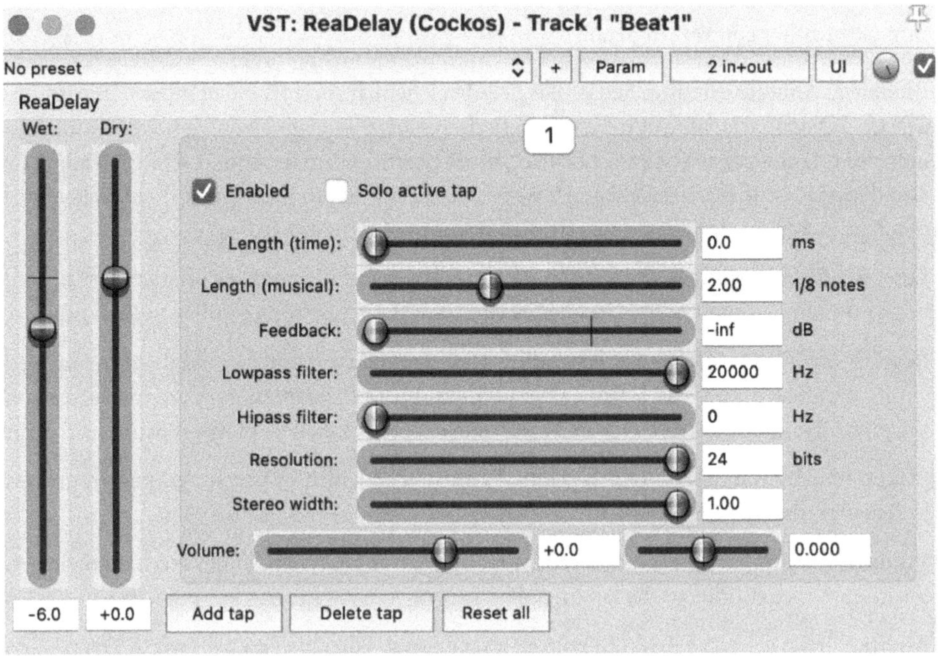

Figure 4.26 – ReaDelay plugin

On the left-hand side, we can see the **Dry** and **Wet** controls, which, as mentioned previously, control the balance between the signal with and without the effect. The main control in a delay is the **delay time**, indicated in this plugin as **Length (time)**. This control has two versions: the version with time in milliseconds and the version with musical values.

> **Tip**
>
> It is recommended to use only one of these controls (the version with time in milliseconds and the version with musical values) and leave the other at zero.

For example, if the **Length (time)** control is set to `500 ms`, you will hear a repetition of the sound every half second, and you can adjust this control as needed. On the other hand, the **Length (musical)** control is based on eighth-note repetitions; so, if it is set to a value of `1`, we will have eighth-note repetitions, if it is set to a value of `2`, we will have quarter-note repetitions (which are twice the length of eighth notes), and so on. The **Length (musical)** times depend on the BPM of the project.

Let's examine the other controls in detail:

- **Feedback**: Another important control is **Feedback**, which controls the number of repetitions or echoes. A **Feedback** value of minus infinity dB means there will be only one repetition. As we increase this control, we will start hearing more repetitions of the sound. The final adjustment also depends on the desired effect. However, be careful not to increase the feedback value too much as it could generate an uncontrolled number of repetitions.
- **Lowpass filter/Highpass**: Next, we have the **Highpass** and **Lowpass** filters. These affect the brightness and amount of low-frequency sound in the repetitions, similar to ReaVerbate.
- **Resolution**: The **Resolution** control allows us to reduce the number of bits in the processed audio, creating digital distortion, as explained in the *Principles of digital audio* section in *Chapter 1*. Normally, it can be left at 24 bits unless a distorted effect on the repetitions is desired.
- **Stereo width**: The **Stereo width** control adjusts the width of the stereo panning, similar to **ReaVerbate**.
- **Volume**: Finally, we have a **Volume** control and a panning control next to it, allowing us to position the repetitions to the left or right.
- **Add tap**: If we press the **Add tap** button, a second tab will appear, as shown in *Figure 4.27*:

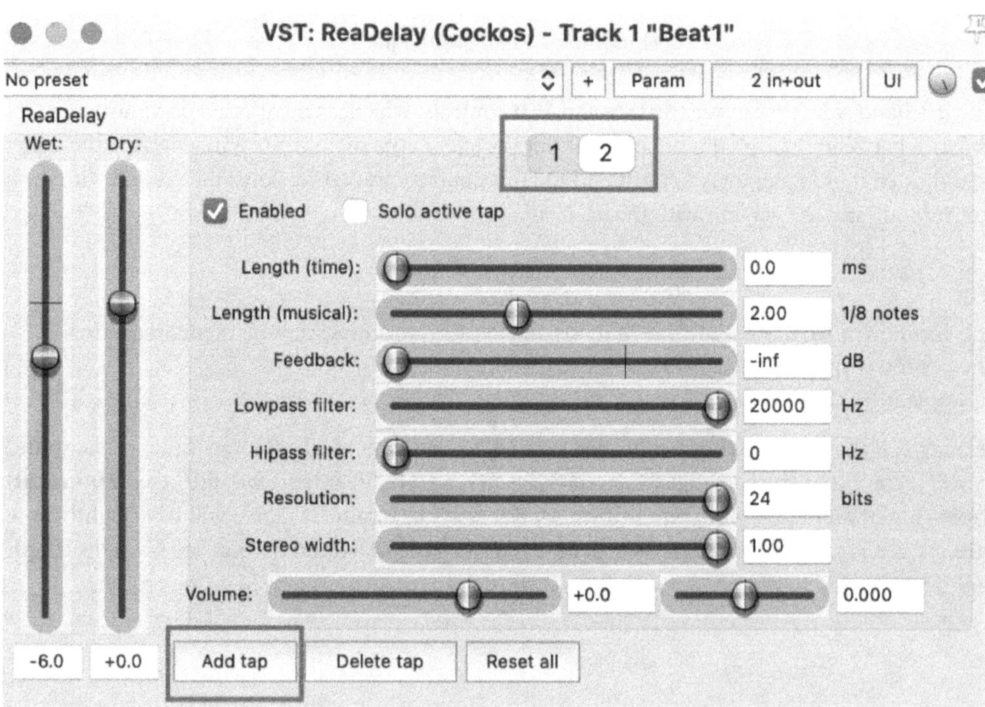

Figure 4.27 – ReaDelay with two taps

This allows us to have two delays with different settings each. For example, we can set the first delay (tap **1**) to a value of `500 ms` and panned to the left and set the second delay (tap **2**) to a value of `1000 ms` and panned to the right. The result will be echoes that sound from one side and then the other, creating an effect known as **ping-pong delay**.

In this way, we can add more taps if we want to experiment with multiple delays simultaneously.

As we have seen, by using equalization, compression, reverb, and delay, we can give more clarity, presence, and dimension to a mix. It is important to experiment and play with these effects to find settings that we like and expand our sonic creativity.

Next, let's look at the final and equally important step in the process of mixing a project: automation.

Understanding automation

Automation refers to programming automatic changes in the controls of a mix. For example, with automation, we can adjust a sound to change the volume at a certain moment, change its panning, activate an effect, or alter its intensity.

A typical case would be raising the volume of an instrument when its solo comes in or lowering the background music at certain moments in a podcast, video, or movie. We can automate panning to create the illusion of a sound moving from left to right. Automation offers many creative possibilities in production.

Automation is an important part of mixing any project nowadays as it allows us to adjust details that make the difference between a high-quality and a mediocre project.

Recording automation

REAPER has many automation functions; in fact, we can automate virtually any function or process. Let's look at a simple way we can start automating the volume of tracks in a project, which is one of the most common functions:

1. Right-click on the automation button of the track you want to automate, as indicated in *Figure 4.28*:

Figure 4.28 – Track automation button

2. A menu will appear, as shown in *Figure 4.29*. Select the **Latch (record fader movements after first movement)** option. This automation mode allows you to record any movements you make while playing the project:

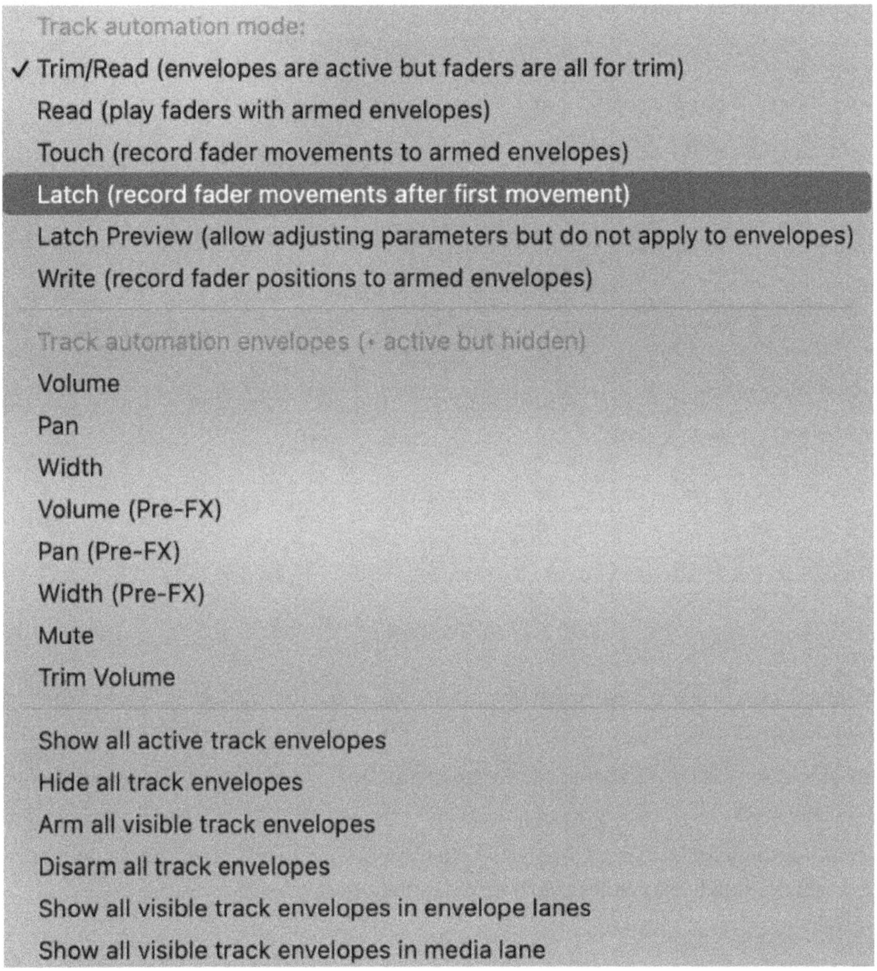

Figure 4.29 – Latch automation mode

3. Play the project and move the channel fader to raise or lower the volume in the parts where you need it. A special lane in the arrangement area will be generated, where the volume movements you make will be recorded as points, as shown in *Figure 4.30*. REAPER will continue to record volume movements until playback is stopped:

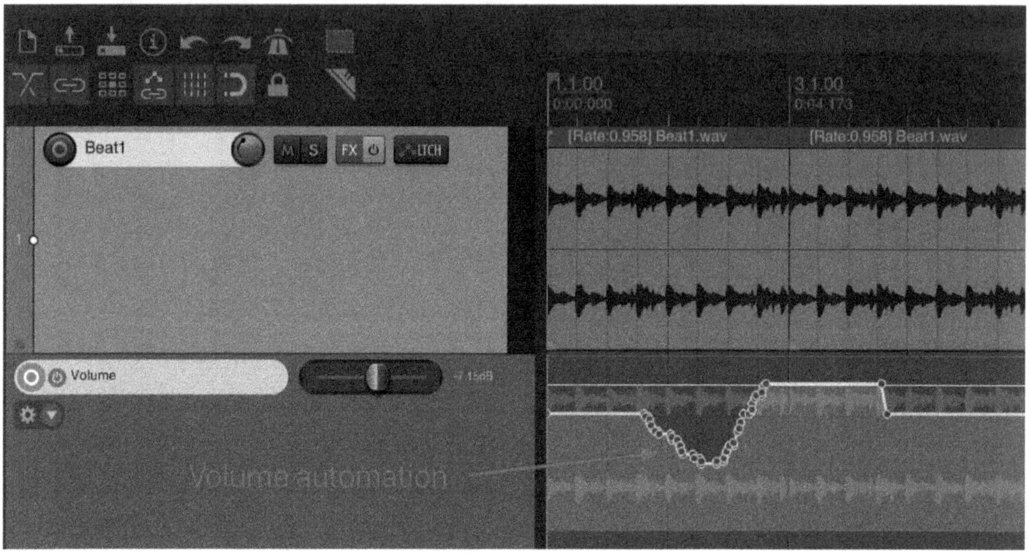

Figure 4.30 – Volume automation

4. Stop playback when you have finished automating. It is not necessary to let the whole project run to automate everything; you can automate it in parts or small sections.
5. If the automation is not right, you can undo it with the *Ctrl* + *Z* (*Cmd* + *Z*) keyboard command and re-automate.
6. Once the automation is correct, right-click on the automation button of the channel once more and select the **Read (play faders with armed envelopes)** option.
7. Play the project; you will see the fader move automatically following the previously programmed movements.

This procedure also allows us to automate any other track control, such as panning, mute, or any parameter of the effects on the track, such as the **Bypass** control of an effect, **Dry**, **Wet**, and so on. Each time you generate automation by moving a control or parameter, a new automation lane will appear, as shown in *Figure 4.31*:

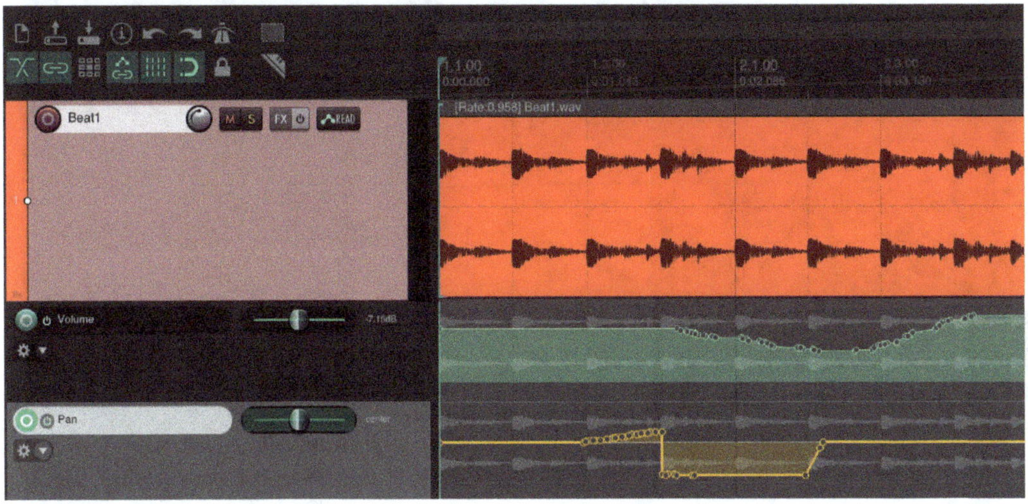

Figure 4.31 – Volume and pan automation lanes

If you like, you can adjust the size of the automation lanes similarly to the rest of the tracks to see the automation points more clearly.

As you can see, automation opens up many creative possibilities for activating or deactivating effects, modifying them in certain parts of a project, changing their intensity, and more Once we have recorded some automation, we can edit it to fine-tune details or make changes to it.

Editing automation

Once we have automation data, we can edit the points created in the automation lane. If we right-click in the automation lane, a menu with many options will appear, as shown in *Figure 4.32*:

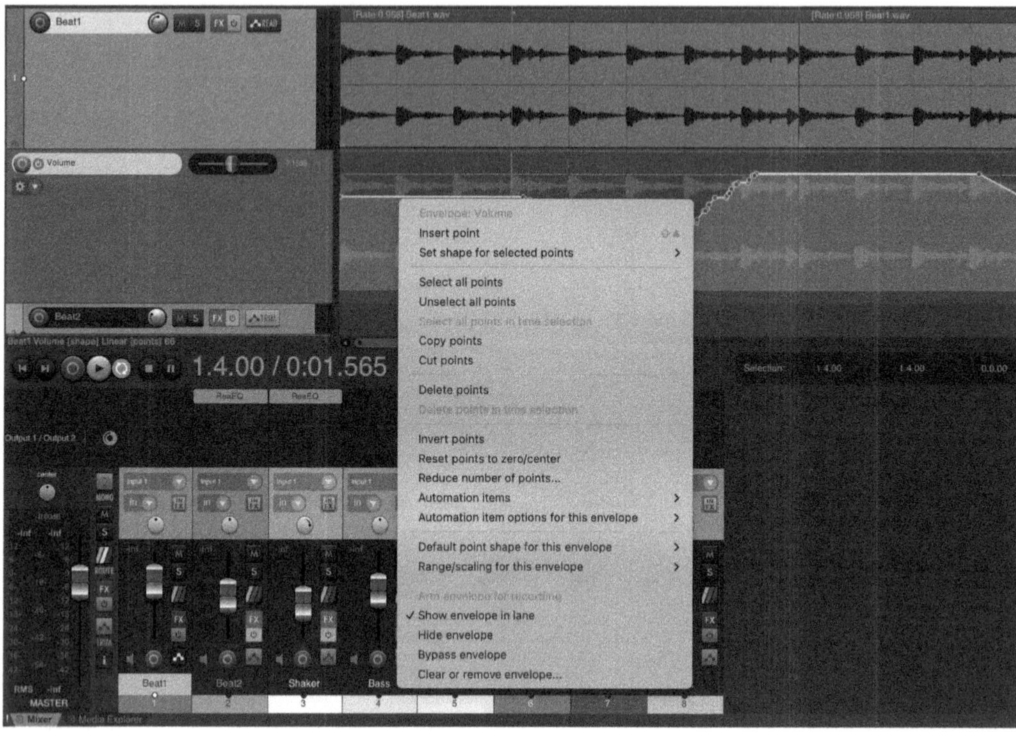

Figure 4.32 – Automation editing options

For example, we can select points, delete them, copy them, insert new points, and more. This means we can adjust the values of the automation very precisely according to what we need.

Each automation point can also be dragged and moved to change its value or position. If we press the *Shift* key while in the automation zone, the pointer will change to a *pencil shape*, allowing us to draw automation freehand.

As we can see, there are many other options for editing automation, but we will see several of them in the project application sections later in this book.

Automation requires some practice, but it is undoubtedly an important tool for perfecting the mix we make in REAPER.

Summary

In this chapter, you learned about many tools for mixing a project in REAPER. We saw how to organize tracks, name them, and change their colors for clarity. We also discussed considerations for adjusting the volume and panning of each channel.

Then, you learned how to use effects to process audio, either for an entire track or just for certain items. In this sense, you have learned the basic controls of the most important processors in the mix, which are the **ReaEQ** equalizer, the **ReaComp** compressor, the **ReaVerbate** reverb, and the **ReaDelay** delay.

Finally, you learned how to create and edit automation points to detail volume, panning, or effect changes in different parts of the project. As you have seen, the mixing stage allows you to manipulate the sounds you have recorded or imported in many ways, creating special effects and making fine adjustments to volume, panning, EQ, and more. We could say that the mix is where the "magic" happens, enabling you to create projects with dynamic sounds that change in different sections.

The next step is to master the project, where you will learn how to make the final preparations before you distribute your work.

5 Mastering and Exporting Projects

The final stage in the audio production process is mastering. Mastering is done once the mix is finished. Once all levels, panning, effects, and automation have been completed, the mix is considered finished. Mastering aims to optimize the mix and add the final touches of volume and sound to the production, making it ready for distribution.

In this chapter, you will learn the basic principles for mastering your projects and ensuring they meet the requirements for distribution on a streaming platform or physical medium. You will learn how to adjust the final volume of your production and about the other technical details you need to consider. All this will be done using REAPER's native processors, without the need for additional plugins.

Throughout this chapter, we will cover the following topics:

- **Principles of audio mastering**: You will understand what mastering involves and how it differs from mixing
- **Audio mastering processors**: You will learn how to apply the main audio processors in mastering
- **Exporting options**: You will explore the different ways REAPER offers to export files for use in other projects or to meet the needs of a client or distributor

With this chapter, we will complete the basic techniques to carry out an audio project in REAPER from start to finish.

Technical requirements

To apply the techniques explained in this chapter, you will need a fully edited and mixed audio project. This could be a musical project, as suggested in *Chapter 4*, or another type of project (podcast, audio recording, etc.) that no longer requires mixing or editing adjustments.

You can download a sample audio project from the book's GitHub repository at `https://github.com/PacktPublishing/Elevate-your-audio-production-with-Reaper`.

Principles of audio mastering

Audio mastering is the final stage of the production process. The goal of mastering is to prepare the final file that will be delivered, whether for distribution or to meet the project's requirements, such as audio for video, film, and video games, considering the type of audio file, format, duration, and so on.

To achieve the goal of mastering, several aspects must be considered:

- **Final quality control**: We must ensure that no noise or errors are heard in the final file. A well-mastered file should guarantee that everything sounds correct, as there are no further opportunities for correction later.
- **Definitive project duration**: Final adjustments to the duration of the final file are made during mastering.
- **Final volume**: One of the most noticeable aspects of mastering is the adjustment of the project's final volume. Depending on the type of project, a file with a specific volume must be delivered according to standards or technical norms.
- **Spectral balance**: **Spectral balance** refers to the balance between high, mid, and low frequencies. During mastering, slight adjustments to the project's overall equalization can be made, not to equalize a particular channel, as done in mixing, but to equalize the overall sound of everything together.
- **Track balance**: In the case of album production, mastering ensures a good balance between the volume and spectrum of all songs, so they sound as though they are part of the same album, not unrelated individual pieces.

As we can see, when mastering, we must pay attention to different details than those focused on during mixing. In *Figure 5.1*, we see a comparative table between important criteria in mixing versus mastering:

Mixing	**Mastering**
It works with individual tracks for each instrument or sound.	It works with a unified file, where everything is already mixed.
It focuses on the individual details of each sound to make necessary adjustments.	It focuses on the overall sound of the project.
The range of action is very broad. Each sound in the project can be worked on in detail.	The range of action is limited. Individual details cannot be corrected. Every action affects the entire project.
It's a creative stage where various effects can be experimented with to create impact or interest.	The creative part is reduced. It focuses more on quality control and standardized criteria.
It aims to achieve a correct balance between tracks for a unified sound.	It aims to achieve the correct volume and file format for adequate distribution.

Figure 5.1 – Mixing versus mastering

In the professional realm, it's common for the person mixing a project not to be the same person mastering it. This is because, during the mixing process, it's common to spend many hours repeatedly listening to a project, adjusting details, processing, adding effects, automating, and so on. This can cause ear fatigue, making it difficult to have good judgment for proper mastering afterward.

Fresh ears are very important during mastering, as they allow us to detect things that might have gone unnoticed during mixing.

Nonetheless, in current audio production, it is common for the same person to mix and master. In these cases, the recommendation is to try to rest the ears for at least a day between the mixing and mastering sessions. This way, we can have better judgment when evaluating the mix with rested ears.

Using sound references

During the mixing stage in *Chapter 4*, we mentioned it is important to have references on how a mix should sound according to the type of project, the genre, current trends, and so on.

In mastering, too, it is recommended to have reference works. This is because our ears quickly get used to a certain sound, and if we don't have a reference to remind us how a finished project should sound, we might find it difficult to achieve a good result.

Reference recordings can be productions we consider high quality, whose sound we like, and that are related to the type of production we are doing. During mastering, references will allow us to compare the volume, spectrum, and dynamics of our production with those of commercial productions.

With experience and practice, we gradually learn to recognize the qualities of a mastered production and sound references may be less necessary. But for those starting out in the world of mixing and mastering, having a good reference point is essential.

Types of mastering projects

In REAPER, we have two paths that we can take to master a project. Let's examine the pros and cons of both these approaches:

- The first way is creating a rendered file of the entire project and then importing this file into a new REAPER project. This method has the advantage of starting with a clean session, without all the processes used in mixing, and we can also import reference files into the project.

  This method should be used to master a music album, as it allows us to import all the tracks that make up the album into a new project and compare their sound. When using this method, plugins are inserted into each channel to process each song independently.

- The second way to master is by adding the mastering processes to the master track of the initial project, that is, to the master track of the mixing session. This method has the advantage of working directly from a single session and can be a bit faster. The disadvantage of this method is that the session can become confusing with all the mixing and mastering processors running in the same project.

  Another significant disadvantage of this second method is that the CPU must process all the plugins of the mixing and mastering channels at the same time. If the number of processes is larger than what the computer can handle, it might not even be possible to work this way.

Depending on the complexity of the project, one method may be more convenient than the other. In general, it's better to use the first method, but if the project is simple and doesn't require many plugins in the mix, it might be a bit more practical to use the second method.

In this chapter, we will use the second method, which involves inserting the processors into the project's master track. Now that we know the goals of mastering and its main differences from mixing, we can start looking at the processors typically used to master a project.

Audio mastering processors

As mentioned earlier, mastering is a stage where we must ensure the final quality of the production. To achieve this, it is necessary to process our audio file with some plugins, such as an equalizer, a compressor, and a limiter.

In the subsequent sections, we will explain how to use the most common processors in mastering. However, it is important to note that not all processes are always necessary, as it depends on how the original mix already sounds.

Equalization

One of the first points in mastering is to ensure that the spectral balance is appropriate. For this, we can use the **ReaEQ** plugin, inserting it into the master track, as shown in *Figure 5.2*:

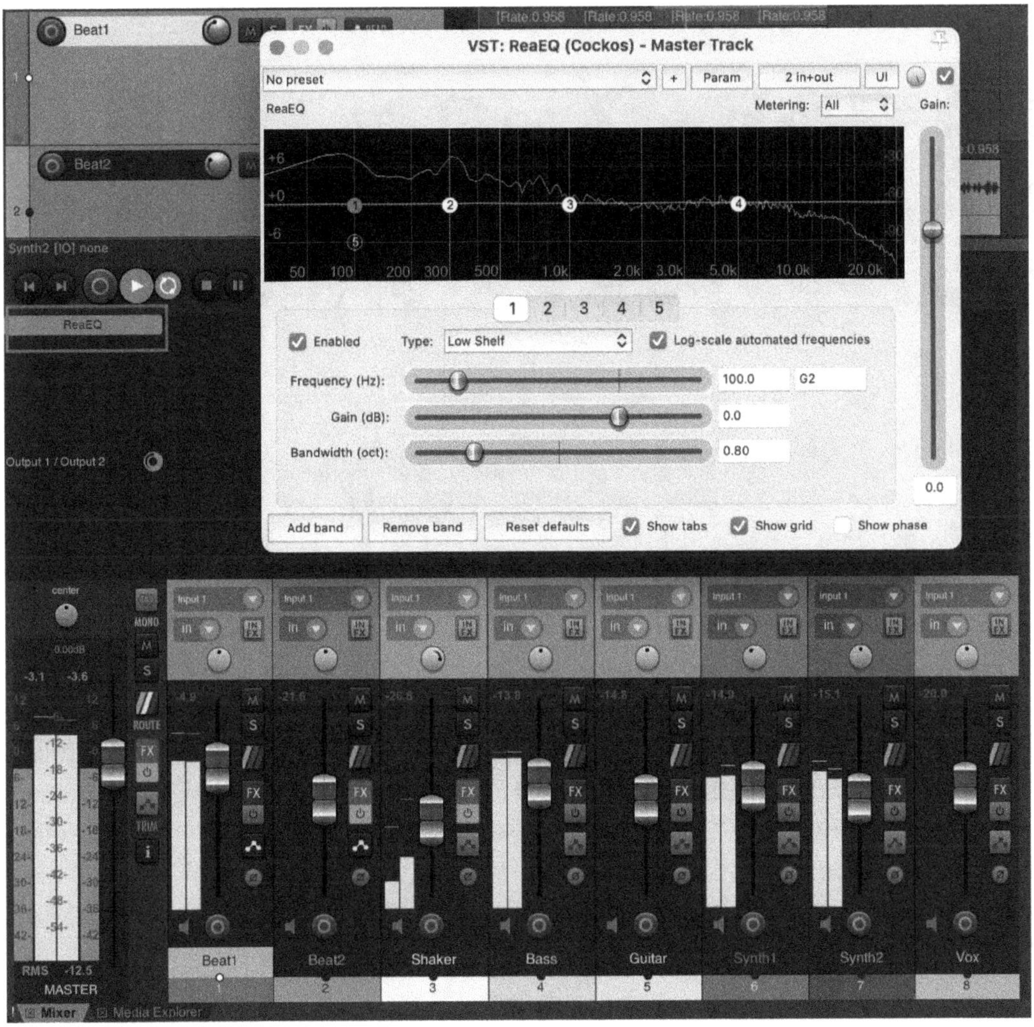

Figure 5.2 – Using ReaEQ for mastering

In the spectrum analyzer of **ReaEQ**, we can see that the curve is *higher* in the low frequencies (50–150 Hz) and *lower* in the high frequencies (10–20 kHz). This is normal and quite a common trend in many projects, especially in music. Thus, it is normal to have more energy in the bass than in the treble.

In projects where voice predominates, such as podcast or video projects, the curve will have less energy in the bass and more in the mid frequencies (300 Hz – 5 kHz), as shown in *Figure 5.3*:

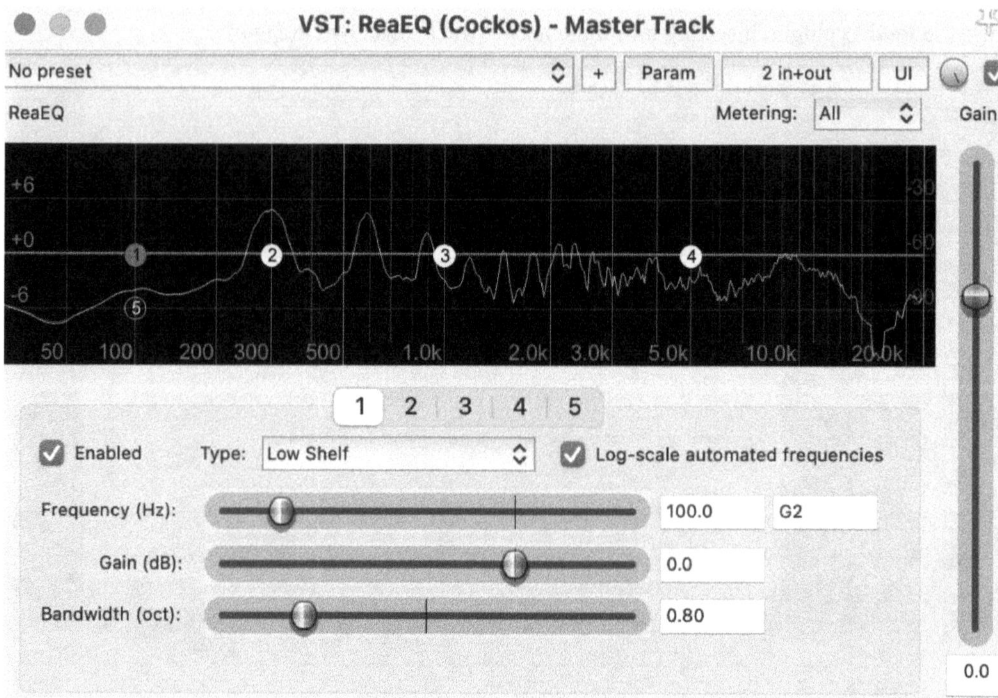

Figure 5.3 – Voice spectrum

This spectrum analysis can be very useful for determining whether there is an excess or lack of energy in any frequency band. For example, a well-mixed musical project will likely have a distribution similar to that in *Figure 5.2*. On the other hand, a voice project will have a distribution similar to that in *Figure 5.3*.

If we find an excess or lack of energy in any area, we can use the equalizer to compensate for this. For example, in *Figure 5.4*, we see that the spectrum has a *dip* around **2 kHz**:

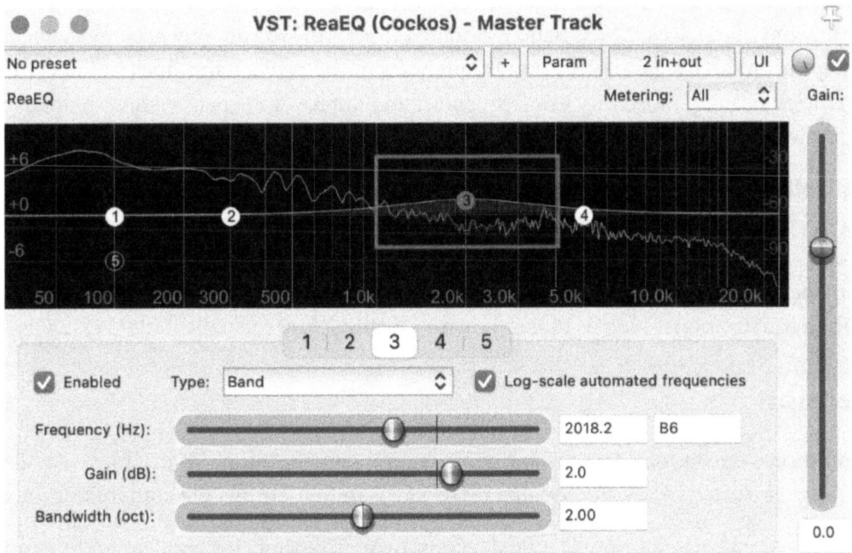

Figure 5.4 – Using EQ in mastering

In such cases, we can increase a couple of dB on that band with the equalizer to compensate for this lack of energy in that area, as shown in *Figure 5.4*, which uses band **3** to increase **2 dB** of gain at 2 kHz.

Using an HPF (High-Pass Filter)

Another common procedure in mastering is to use an **HPF** at **30** Hz, as shown in *Figure 5.5*:

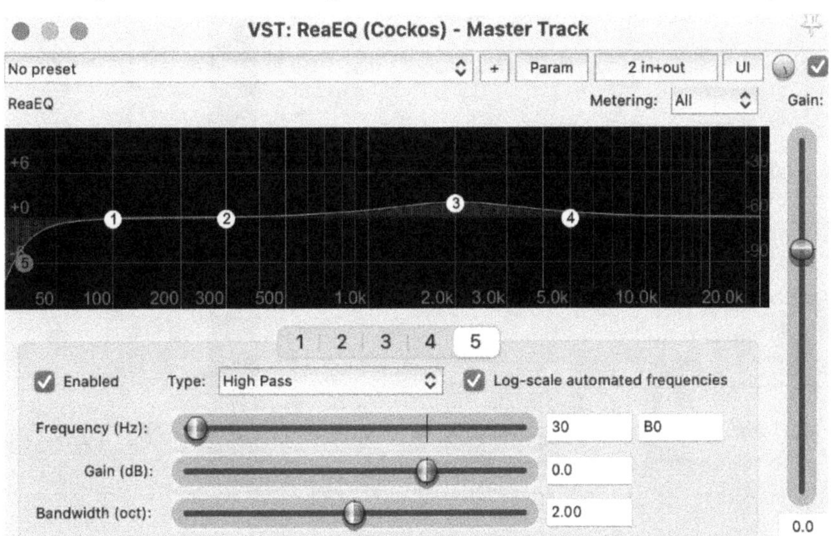

Figure 5.5 – Applying an HPF at 30 Hz

Remember that by default, **ReaEQ** has band **5** assigned to an HPF, so you only need to enable it. Using this HPF helps avoid an excess of very low frequencies in the project and does not affect the final sound, but it helps clean up those very low frequencies and improves the performance of loudspeakers, so using it is always recommended.

We can apply slight equalization in other bands if necessary. For this, it is recommended to listen to reference recordings and compare their sound with our project to make decisions. In some cases, it may be necessary to use an additional band. In general, it is recommended that in mastering, the equalization does not exceed + *or -2 dB per band*, as each adjustment can significantly change the mix balance. Subtle equalizations, such as those shown in *Figure 5.5*, are usually better.

Compression

Another common stage in mastering is applying general **compression**. To do this, we will use the **ReaComp** plugin inserted below the equalizer. The key is in the settings the compressor must have.

Figure 5.6 shows an example of how to adjust a compressor's settings for application to the project's master track:

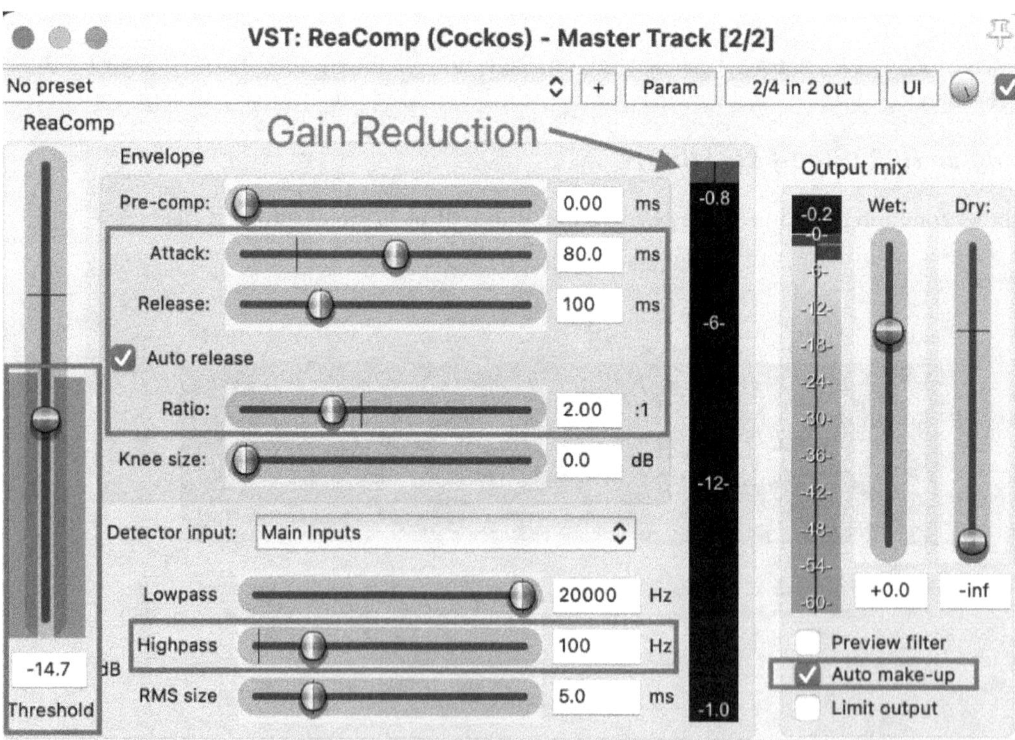

Figure 5.6 – Compression settings for mastering

Here is an explanation of each of the controls marked in *Figure 5.6* and the adjustment sequence:

1. Set the **Attack** time to `80.0 ms` or a nearby value. This parameter determines how quickly the compressor responds. This time allows the compressor to work at a medium speed, suitable for most mastering cases.
2. Set the **Release** time to automatic, using the **Auto release** selection. This ensures that the time it takes for the compressor to stop compressing adjusts automatically. In mastering, this automatic time usually works well for all types of projects.
3. Set the **Ratio** to `2:1`. This ratio indicates how aggressive the compression will be. In this case, a 2:1 ratio means that for every 2 dB of signal entering the compressor, only 1 dB will come out. It is important to use gentle compression in mastering, so a ratio similar to this is recommended.
4. Set the **Highpass** filter to `100 Hz`. This helps ensure that very low frequencies are not overly compressed, which improves the overall impact of the sound.
5. Enable **Auto make-up**. This function allows the compressor to automatically increase the signal volume when compressed.
6. Adjust **Threshold** to achieve a **GR** (**gain reduction**) of `1 dB`. This is the *most important* part. **Threshold** is the control that determines the amount of compression. To adjust the threshold, we should play the project and gradually lower the threshold so that the GR meter shows a maximum of about **1 dB**, as shown in *Figure 5.6*.

   The lower we set the threshold, the more compression there will be. This adjustment depends entirely on the type of signal we are compressing, so in some cases, the threshold may be lower or higher than in others.

By following the preceding steps, we will achieve light compression that affects the entire project. This type of compression is widely used professionally and is known as **glue compression**, as it has the effect of unifying all the sonic elements. If we disable and re-enable **ReaComp** while playing the project, we can hear the difference in sound quality before and after using the compressor.

Once we have used general equalization and compression, we need to make only the final volume adjustments before rendering our finished project.

Final volume adjustment

As mentioned at the beginning of this chapter, adjusting the final volume of the project is the most important task in mastering. General equalization and compression can help improve the final sound; however, there may be times when it is not necessary to use these tools in mastering. On the other hand, the final volume adjustment cannot be missed during mastering, making the process explained in this section mandatory in most cases.

Before we see how to process the volume of our project, let's understand a bit about the volume of an audio signal.

Understanding loudness

The subjective perception of the volume of a sound is known as **loudness**. Loudness is a subjective phenomenon because not everyone perceives the intensity of a sound in the same way.

Loudness perception is also a psychoacoustic phenomenon, as it refers to how our brains interpret different characteristics of sound to form an impression of volume. Among the characteristics that influence the perception of loudness are the following:

- **Intensity**: If a sound has more intensity, it is usually perceived as louder.
- **Frequency content**: Our ears are much more sensitive to mid frequencies (from 2 to 4 kHz) than to those in any other range. If a sound has more energy in this frequency range, it will be perceived as louder.
- **Duration**: The brain integrates the average energy of a sound to determine its loudness. Sounds that are too quick cannot be perceived as very loud. Generally, sounds must last longer than 300 ms for our brain to interpret them with greater loudness. A sound less than 300 ms long is not perceived as very loud, even if its intensity is high.

These characteristics of our auditory perception make a simple signal meter an inadequate parameter for determining the loudness of a sound. For example, in *Figure 5.7*, we see the mixer meters in REAPER:

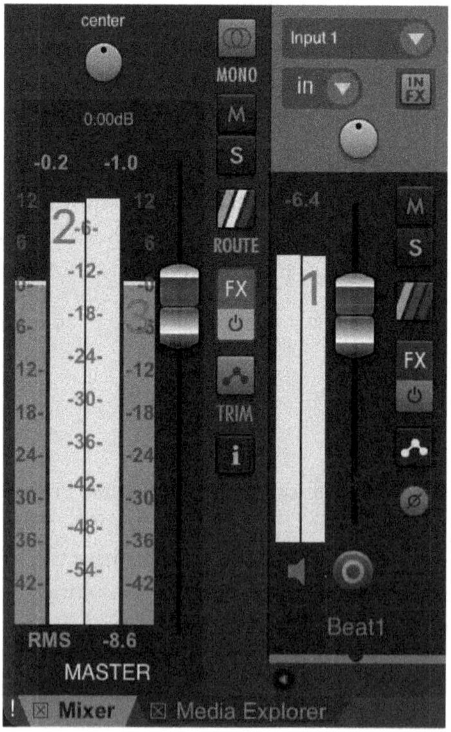

Figure 5.7 – REAPER mixer meters

Let's understand the significance of each of these meters:

- The meter marked as **1** is the **channel meter** and measures **peak values**, that is, the maximum instantaneous values of a signal. This was the meter we used to set the audio recording level in *Chapter 2*.
- The meter marked as **2** is the **master peak meter**. It works in the same way as the channel peak meter but measures the peak level of the entire project. We used this in the mix in *Chapter 4* to ensure we did not exceed levels while mixing.
- The meter marked as **3** is the **RMS** (**root mean square**) value meter for the master. The **RMS value** is the average value of a signal's energy. As shown in *Figure 5.7*, the master's peak value is higher than its **RMS** value. This is common for practically all signals.

  The **RMS** value has been useful for many years in the audio world because it approximates how our ears integrate the energy of a sound. Therefore, the **RMS** value gives us an approximation of perceived loudnessk.

  In other words, if we compare two signals with similar **RMS** values, we will perceive them as having similar loudness, regardless of whether their peak values are the same. Conversely, if we compare two signals with similar peak values but different **RMS** values, we will perceive the signal with the higher **RMS** value as being louder.

Since none of these meters considers the frequency content of the measured signal, none can indicate the level of a signal's loudness. For many years, audio engineers had to rely on measuring the **RMS** or peak values of a signal.

Introducing the LUFS (Loudness Units relative to Full Scale)

In 2011, the **ITU** (**International Communication Union**) established a recommendation with algorithms to measure the loudness of an audio program, the ITU-R BS.1770 recommendation (with some revisions years later). These algorithms consider not only the intensity and duration of a signal but also its frequency content, in a way similar to how our ears do. This allowed the establishment of a new way to measure loudness: the **LUFS (Loudness Units relative to Full Scale)**.

Currently, LUFS (also known as **LKFS** or (**Loudness K-weighted Full Scale**) allows us to measure the loudness of a signal or an audio program effectively, surpassing the results obtained using RMS or peak values. Therefore, LUFS is increasingly used in mastering to set the levels that a product must have when delivered for distribution.

Today, most streaming services and platforms such as YouTube use LUFS to normalize the volume of their content, ensuring that the user has a better experience by reducing the chances of some content sounding lower or louder than others.

In REAPER, we have a loudness meter that will be fundamental to our mastering work. It is the **JS: Loudness Meter Peak/RMS/LUFS** plugin, shown in *Figure 5.8*:

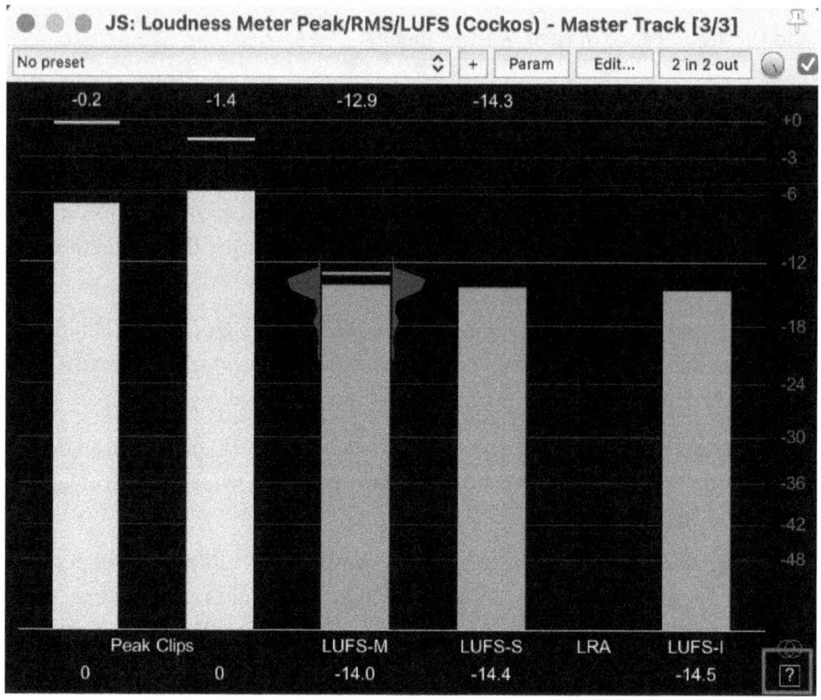

Figure 5.8 – JS: Loudness Meter Peak/RMS/LUFS plugin

This plugin is not in the **VST** plugin category but in the JS category, which, as explained in *Chapter 2*, means that it is a JSFX plugin native to REAPER, which can even be modified with programming knowledge. Let's look at its operation in more detail in the next section.

Using the Loudness Meter Peak/RMS/LUFS plugin

The **Loudness Meter Peak/RMS/LUFS** plugin allows us to measure the peak, RMS, and LUFS values of a signal. The most common way to use it in mastering is to insert it as an effect in the *master channel*, after all other processors (i.e., **ReaEQ**, **ReaComp**).

To see the meter's options, click the button marked **?** in *Figure 5.8*. Then, an options window will appear, as shown in *Figure 5.9*:

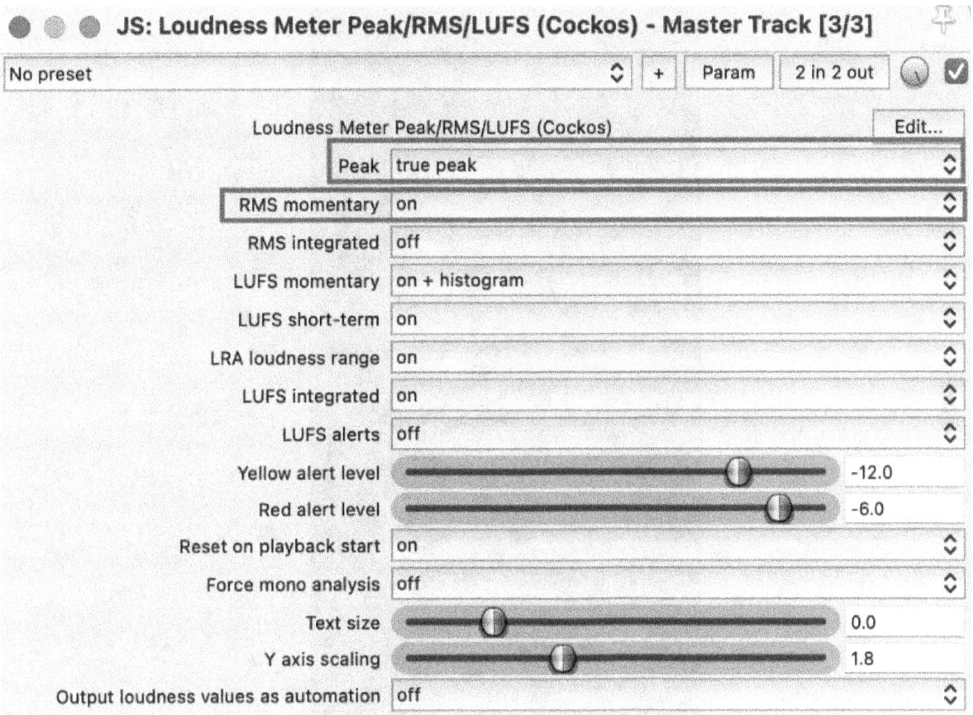

Figure 5.9 – Loudness Meter Peak/RMS/LUFS plugin options

In the options, change the **Peak** parameter value to **true peak**. Also, turn the **RMS momentary** option to **on**. These options let us better measure the signal's peak values during mastering and visualize the RMS value on the meter.

Once we have made the adjustments, we can close the options window by clicking the **?** button again. Then we can play the project and see the meter in action. If desired, we can adjust the meter window size by dragging from a corner.

With our meter ready, we can adjust the final volume of the project.

Adjusting the final volume

To adjust the volume of our project, we will insert an additional plugin in the master track, the **ReaLimit** limiter. This should be the last plugin in the processing chain, after the equalizer (**ReaEQ**) and compressor (**ReaComp**).

The idea is that the limiter is added just before the loudness meter so that we can measure its effect. Thus, our master track processing chain should look as shown in *Figure 5.10*:

Figure 5.10 – Master processing chain

The **limiter** is a processor that controls the peaks of the audio signal and adjusts the signal volume without causing saturation. The limiter is the only processor that must always be used in mastering to avoid saturation in the final audio. **ReaLimit** is a simple but very useful limiter, as shown in *Figure 5.11*:

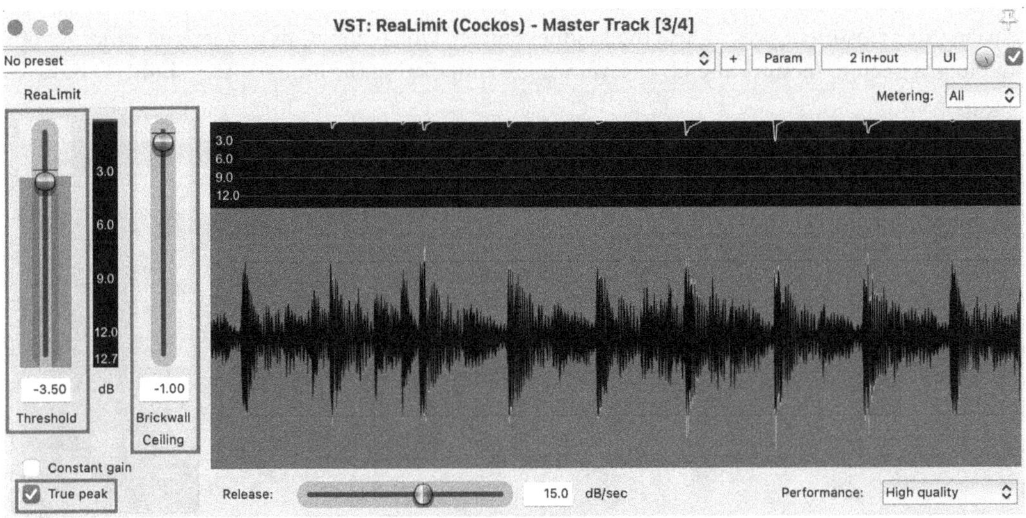

Figure 5.11 – ReaLimit plugin

When mastering, we will adjust the **ReaLimit** controls marked in *Figure 5.11*, as follows:

1. Set the **Brickwall Ceiling** to `-1.00 dB`. This is the maximum peak level that will come out of the limiter. In other words, our signal will never exceed this level. We set it to `-1 dB` as this is a very common standard value for practically any audio production.
2. Activate the **True peak** option. This option helps determine the true-peak values of the signal. True-peak values are the most used values today when measuring the peak of a signal.
3. Gradually lower the **Threshold** value. The more we lower the **Threshold**, the more volume the final audio will have.

The key is to adjust the **Threshold** level to achieve the desired volume. If we lower the **Threshold** too much, we will get more volume but start hearing distortion in the audio.

To make this adjustment, we can use the loudness meter, which allows us to keep the windows of both plugins open to monitor the LUFS level while manipulating the limiter's **Threshold**, as shown in *Figure 5.12*:

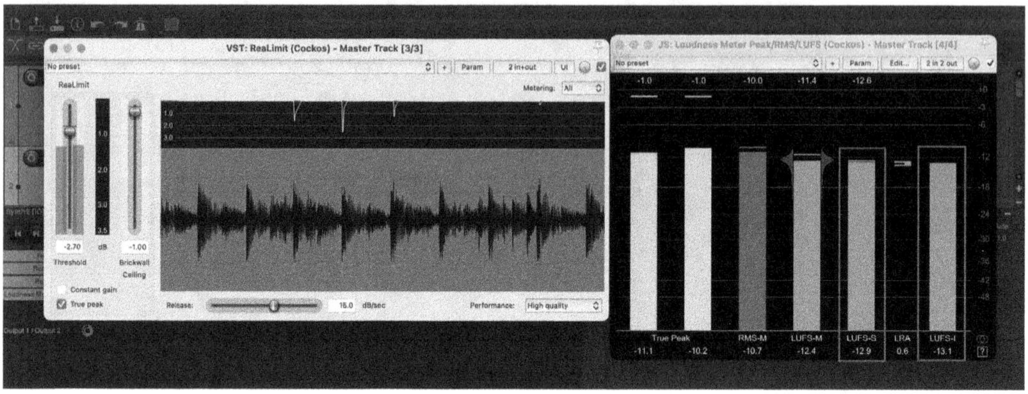

Figure 5.12 – Measuring loudness

The loudness meter has several bars indicating different signal values. The first two indicate the **True peak** value of the left (L) and right (R) channels. These values should reach a maximum of -1 dB. Then, there is a bar showing the mono **RMS-M** value (i.e., the sum of L and R). The **RMS-M** value is just a reference that gives us an idea of the average energy of the audio signal.

Then, we have several bars indicating the loudness value in LUFS:

- **LUFS-M**: This refers to the momentary LUFS value. This is a loudness value calculated in 400 ms intervals. It gives us an idea of the quick variations in loudness.
- **LUFS-S**: This refers to the short-term LUFS value. This is a loudness value calculated in three-second intervals. This value is marked in *Figure 5.12* because it is one of our main references for knowing the LUFS value of the program or production.
- **LRA**: This refers to the loudness range. This value gives us an idea of the volume variations throughout the program. A small LRA (3 to 6 dB) indicates the program has a constant volume. A large LRA (more than 6 dB) indicates that the program has greater volume variations.
- **LUFS-I**: This refers to the integrated LUFS value, which is a value that averages the loudness throughout the entire program. This value is marked in *Figure 5.12* because it is also one of the main values that enables us to determine the loudness of our production.

Now, the decision on what LUFS value to achieve in our production depends on several factors. For example, most music streaming services have normalized their content to -14 LUFS integrated. TV series and video content typically handle values of -24 LUFS. Depending on the type of production or client requirements, we can adjust the limiter to achieve the required loudness value.

Figure 5.13 shows some of the LUFS values used today for various purposes:

Usage	**LUFS-I (Loudness level)**
Audio CD	-9 LUFS
Music streaming	-14 LUFS
Dolby Atmos music	-18 LUFS
Streaming, TV series (dialogs)	-24 LUFS

Figure 5.13 – Loudness levels for different usages

In this way, it is possible to adjust the final volume of our production and have it ready for export, as we will see in the next section.

Exporting options

When we have finished our production, we need to generate a final file that we can distribute. To do this, we use the **File** | **Render...** command.

The **Render to File** window will appear, as shown in *Figure 5.14*, where we can make various adjustments to the final file we want to generate:

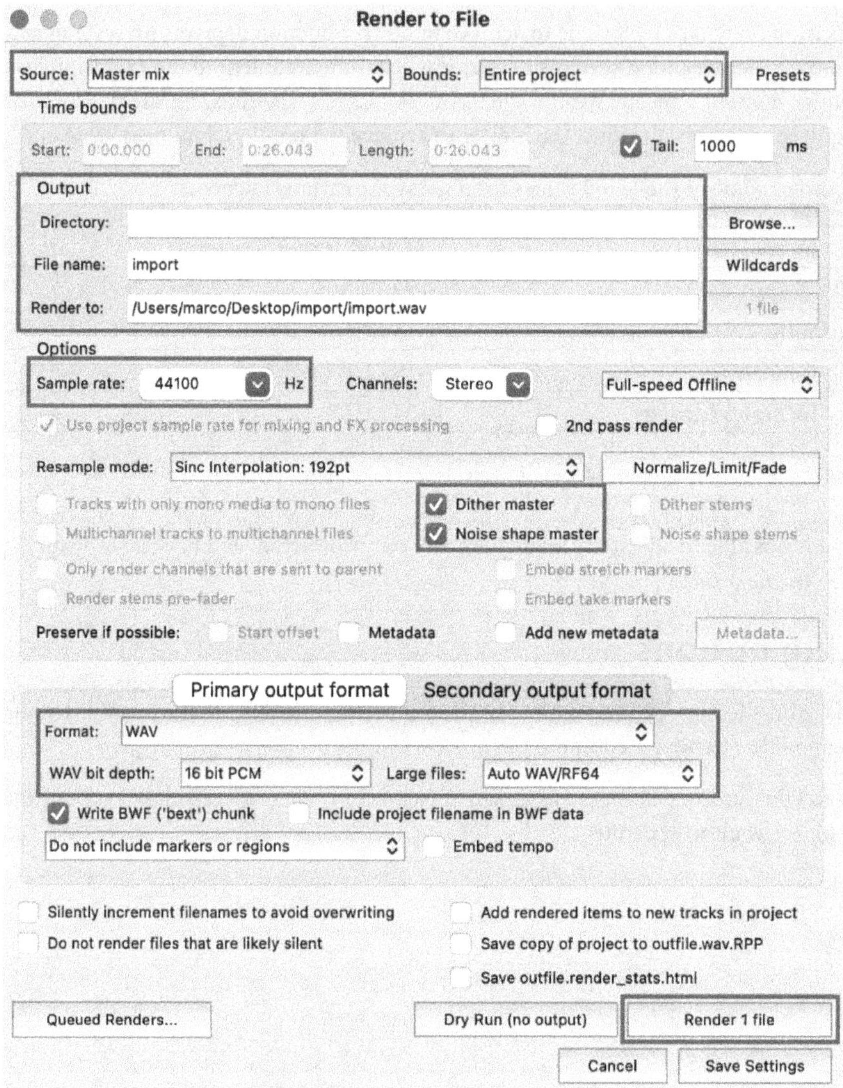

Figure 5.14 – Rendering options

The most important options we can adjust are marked in *Figure 5.14*, and they are as follows:

- **Source**: By default, this option is set to **Master mix**, which renders the entire project. However, other interesting options include **Selected tracks (stems)** and **Selected media items**. These options allow us to create a file from only certain tracks or items.

- **Bounds**: The default option is **Entire project**, which will create a file with the entire project's duration. However, another very useful function is **Time selection**, which will create a file with the duration of the selected area.
- **Output**: In this section, we indicate the folder where we want to save the new file and its name.
- **Sample rate**: In this section, we can change the sampling rate of the final file. For a music project for CD or streaming, and podcasts, we use `44100` Hz. For any other type of project (video, video game, movie, etc.), we use `48000` Hz or another specific frequency that the client requires.
- **Format**: In this section, we select the audio file format. The most commonly used file format is WAV, as WAV files are of the highest quality and the best option for any professional work.

  We can also choose **MP3** if we want a smaller file than WAV, albeit of lower quality. MP3 files are practical for testing or demos but are not recommended for final professional-level work.
- **WAV bit depth**: If we choose the **WAV** format, this option will appear. Here we can choose 24-bit PCM files, which are of the highest quality and recommended in most cases.

  Another common option is to use **16 bit PCM**, as it is the CD standard and is still in use for music streaming and podcasts. The choice will depend on the requirements of the client or the music/podcast distribution company.
- **Dither master | Noise shape master**: These options should only be selected if **16 bit PCM** files are generated, as explained in the previous point. These options help improve the quality of 16-bit files, so they do not lose sound information.

Once we have selected the desired options, we can press the **Render** button. The final audio file will then be generated, and ready to be distributed.

As we can see, there are several options for creating our final file. However, this guide can help you adjust the necessary points to create the correct file.

Make sure to check the requirements of your client or the distribution company for your project to deliver the correct type of file with the format, sampling rate, bit depth, and appropriate loudness levels as needed.

Summary

In this chapter, we have looked at the function of mastering, its importance, and its differences from mixing. We have also looked at the most common processors included in REAPER that can help us master any project.

We have also looked at the importance of loudness and how it can be measured using modern units such as LUFS. You now also know how to adjust a limiter at the end of your mastering process to establish the loudness level of your production. Finally, we have looked at the options that REAPER offers for exporting a final audio file, making it ready for distribution.

In the next chapter, we will explore one of the most important functions of REAPER, which can greatly accelerate your overall workflow: macros.

Part 2: Advanced Production Techniques

In this part, you will learn about more advanced techniques, commands, and functions that will allow you to work more comprehensively in REAPER. You will also be introduced to basic techniques for handling more complex projects, such as surround sound and audio for video.

This part has the following chapters:

- *Chapter 6, Exploring Custom Actions and Macros*
- *Chapter 7, Advanced Mixing and Processing*
- *Chapter 8, Working with Video*

6
Exploring Custom Actions and Macros

Now that you have a general idea of the audio production process in REAPER, it's a good time to learn how to use the many customization options REAPER offers.

Customization is one of REAPER's distinctive aspects. Unlike other DAWs, REAPER's customization capabilities make it a leader in this area. Among the options available to customize the work in REAPER, we have actions, menus, and toolbars.

In this chapter, we will address the topic of customization so that you can start making your work more efficient, achieving results more quickly, and with greater creative flow. You will also learn to use macros, which are sequences of repetitive actions that we can program to make our work more efficient.

We will cover the following main topics in this chapter:

- **Advanced shortcuts and toolbars**: You will learn to use keyboard shortcuts and customized toolbars according to your production needs
- **Using macros**: You will learn to use macros to perform repetitive tasks more quickly
- **Preferences and settings**: You will learn about various advanced adjustments in REAPER's preferences that will help you customize its operation according to your tastes or needs

With the knowledge you acquire in this chapter, you will be able to use REAPER in a more advanced way, allowing you to take advantage of its features to work more comfortably and efficiently.

Technical requirements

To carry out the examples included in this chapter, you should use any REAPER project. You can use one of the projects we have worked on in this book.

Advanced shortcuts and toolbars

Keyboard shortcuts are a vital tool for using any professional software. Extensive use of keyboard shortcuts is a common feature among people who master the use of any software. In this regard, it is highly recommended to practice using keyboard shortcuts and gradually increase your repertoire of shortcuts. Over time, we will learn more options that will give us greater mastery of the program.

A good starting point to learn new REAPER shortcuts is to go to the **Help | Key bindings and mouse modifiers** menu. This command will open a window in our internet browser and show us a comprehensive list of keyboard shortcuts and mouse modifiers. You can also check out this link for a list of shortcuts: `https://user.cockos.com/~glazfolk/ReaperKeyboardShortcuts.pdf`.

> Tip
>
> A good tactic for memorizing a new shortcut is to identify it and start using it from this point onward, avoiding the use of menus or toolbar buttons for that action. This way, we will gradually develop muscle memory in learning the shortcut.

It is important to be familiar with the shortcuts that REAPER includes; however, REAPER's capabilities do not end here. Let's see how we can perform various activities through the **Actions** function, which we explain next.

The action list

Actions are the core part of the workflow in REAPER. We can access the action list using the **Actions | Show action list** menu. The keyboard shortcut is the *?* key. A window will then appear, like the one shown in *Figure 6.1*:

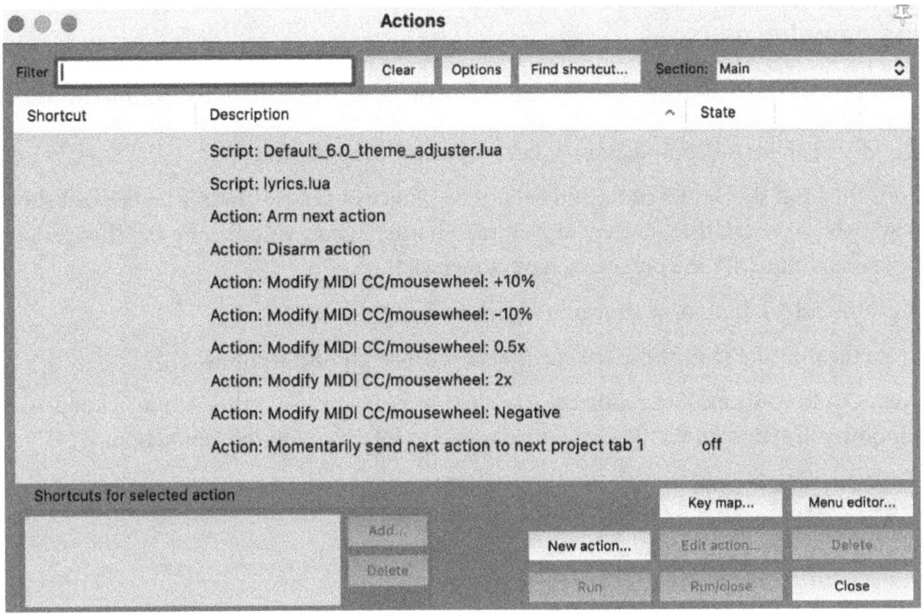

Figure 6.1 – The Actions list window

Let's look at the main options of this window:

- **Filter**: Here, we can type words that describe the action we are looking for, such as `cut`, `move`, `item`, `automation`, and `MIDI`.
- **Clear**: This clears the text from the **Filter** field.
- **Options**: This gives us options about the results shown in the **Filter** field.
- **Find shortcut**: This shows us shortcuts that are already assigned to an action.
- **Section**: This allows us to find actions for a specific section. For example, the same shortcut can work differently in the main window than in the **Media Explorer** window.
- **Run and Run/Close**: These options are used to execute an action or execute the action and close the window upon doing so, respectively. You can also execute the action by double-clicking on it in the list.

The number of possible actions within REAPER is vast, and we can find virtually any type of action we need. It is also worth mentioning that the **Actions** menu will display the most recently used actions, allowing you to call any recent action without needing to search for it again in the action list.

A recommended way to call actions is by using a **keyboard shortcut**. If an action has a keyboard shortcut assigned, it will appear in the **Shortcuts for selected action** section. If the desired action does not have shortcuts, we can assign the key combination that we want, as we will see next.

Creating new shortcuts

To assign a new shortcut to trigger an action, we can follow these steps within the **Actions** list window:

1. Decide which key or combination of keys to use for the shortcut.
2. Press the **Find shortcut** button, and enter your choice of keys to check whether that shortcut is available or not. If that shortcut already has another action assigned, we can choose another key or continue with the process to have it replaced.
3. Press the **Add...** button, as shown in *Figure 6.2*.
4. Enter the shortcut in the **Shortcut** section of the new pop-up window.
5. Press **OK** to confirm. If the shortcut was already assigned to another action, a confirmation window will appear to verify whether we want to replace it with the new action.

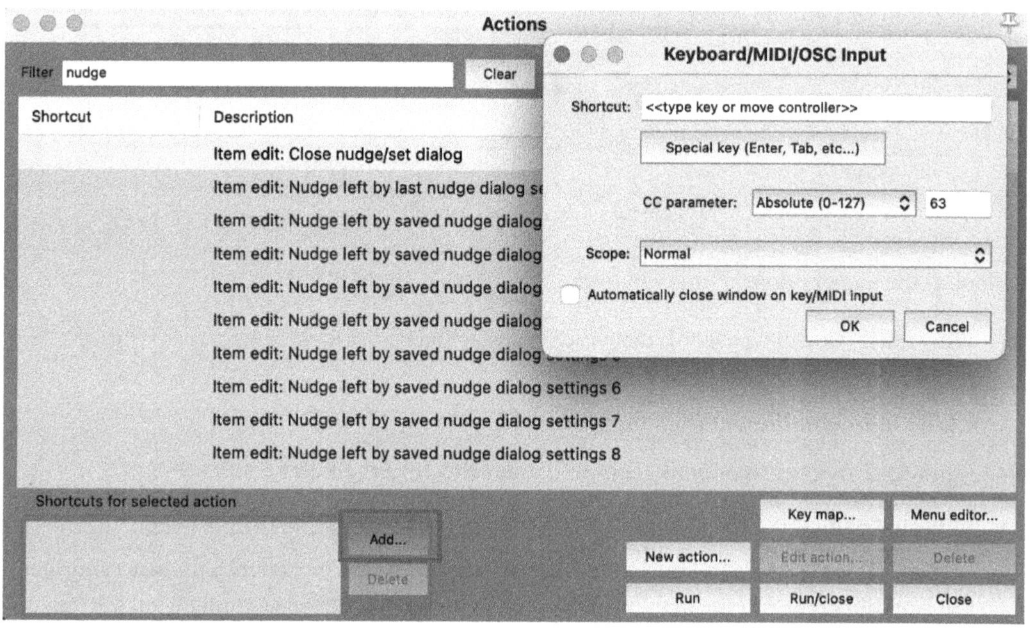

Figure 6.2 – Adding a new shortcut

This way, we can create or change shortcuts according to our preferences or needs.

Besides using keyboard shortcuts to trigger actions in REAPER, we can also use **MIDI messages** to execute actions, using either the keys, knobs, or buttons of a MIDI controller connected to the computer. To assign an action, we simply need to press the button or move the knob when the pop-up window shown in *Figure 6.2* appears. This way, we can use any MIDI controller to expand our action assignment possibilities.

Saving customizations

As we add or modify shortcuts, it is important to save all these changes and customizations so that we can load them later if we change computers or need to reinstall REAPER from scratch.

If we press the **Key map…** button in the **Actions** window, the menu shown in *Figure 6.3* will appear:

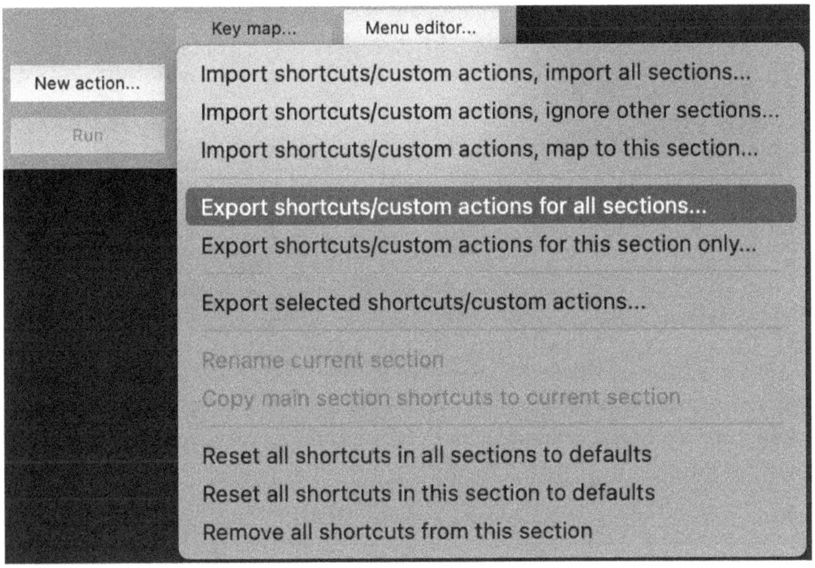

Figure 6.3 – Importing/exporting custom actions

Here, we have the option to export shortcuts and actions to be saved in a file. This same file can be imported at any other time using the **Import shortcuts/custom actions** option, which also appears in the same menu. As we can see in *Figure 6.3*, we have three options for importing shortcuts. You can use the one that best suits your needs – **Import shortcuts/custom actions, import all sections…**, **Import shortcuts/custom actions, ignore other sections…**, or **Import shortcuts/custom actions, map to this section…** if you only want to use the shortcuts in one section.

When considering the customization of keyboard shortcuts, as well as the use of MIDI controllers to trigger actions in REAPER, the work possibilities are only limited by our imagination. For example, we can assign actions to create or copy items with musical phrases or sound effects to the keys of a MIDI controller and trigger them in real-time, either in a recording studio or live performance. This will allow us to create music while generating new items, which enables us to develop the creative and spontaneous aspect of production.

Another option we can customize in REAPER is the toolbars, as we will see next.

Customizing toolbars

In addition to the main toolbar, REAPER has customizable **toolbars** that allow us to work efficiently. With these toolbars, we can add or remove buttons to execute different actions and commands.

If we right-click on an empty area of the main toolbar, the **Customize toolbar...** option will appear, as shown in *Figure 6.4*:

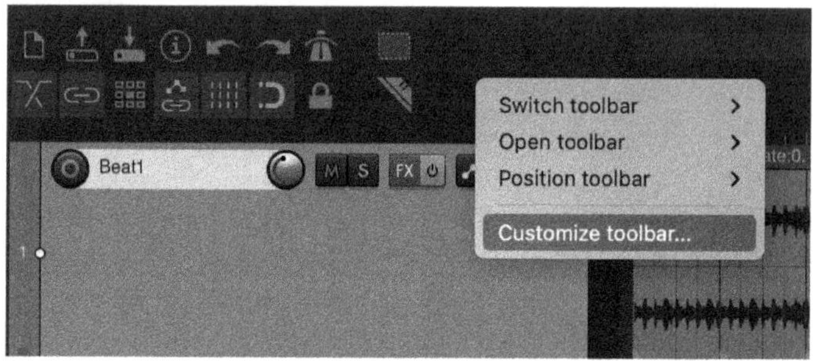

Figure 6.4 – Customizing the toolbar

When we click on the **Customize toolbar...** option, the **Customize menus/toolbars** window will appear, as shown in *Figure 6.5*:

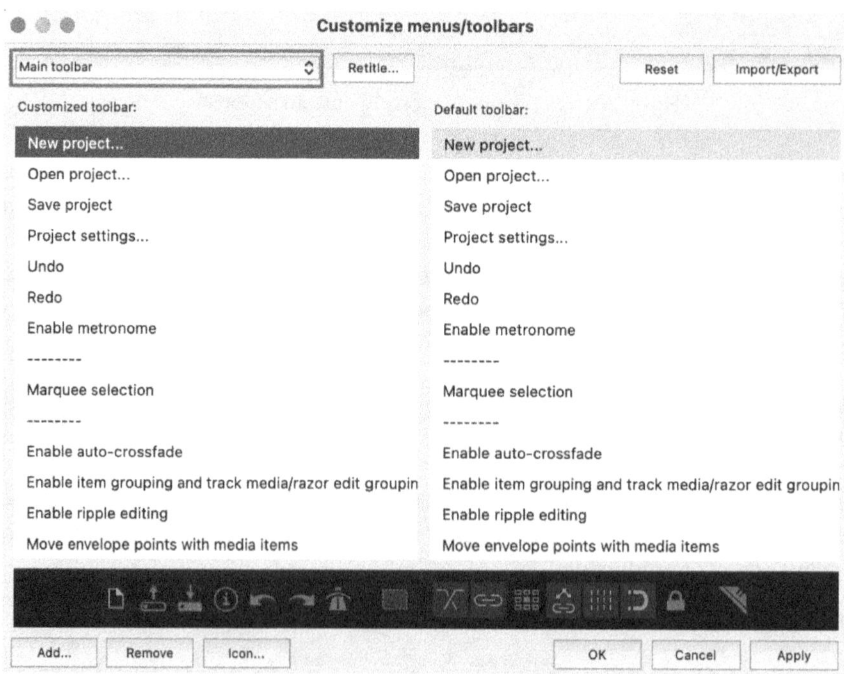

Figure 6.5 – The Customize menus/toolbars window

The functionality of this window is quite intuitive, but let's go through the steps to edit a toolbar:

1. **Select the toolbar**: Using the menu highlighted in *Figure 6.5*, select the toolbar you want to edit, whether it's the *main toolbar* or one of the available *floating toolbars*.
2. **Retitle**: Use the **Retitle** button to rename the toolbar. It is recommended to use names related to the toolbar's function, such as `Editing`, `MIDI`, or `Mixing`.
3. **Add actions**: Press the **Add** button. It will bring up the **Actions** list window, which we are already familiar with.
4. **Choose actions**: In the **Actions** list window, select one of the actions you want to add to the toolbar, and then press *Enter*.
5. **Customize buttons**: The action will appear in the toolbar, as shown in *Figure 6.6*. If you right-click on any of the toolbar actions, you will see a menu where you can change a button's text and its icon, or remove it (see *Figure 6.6*).
6. **Confirm changes**: Press the **OK** button to accept the adjustments.

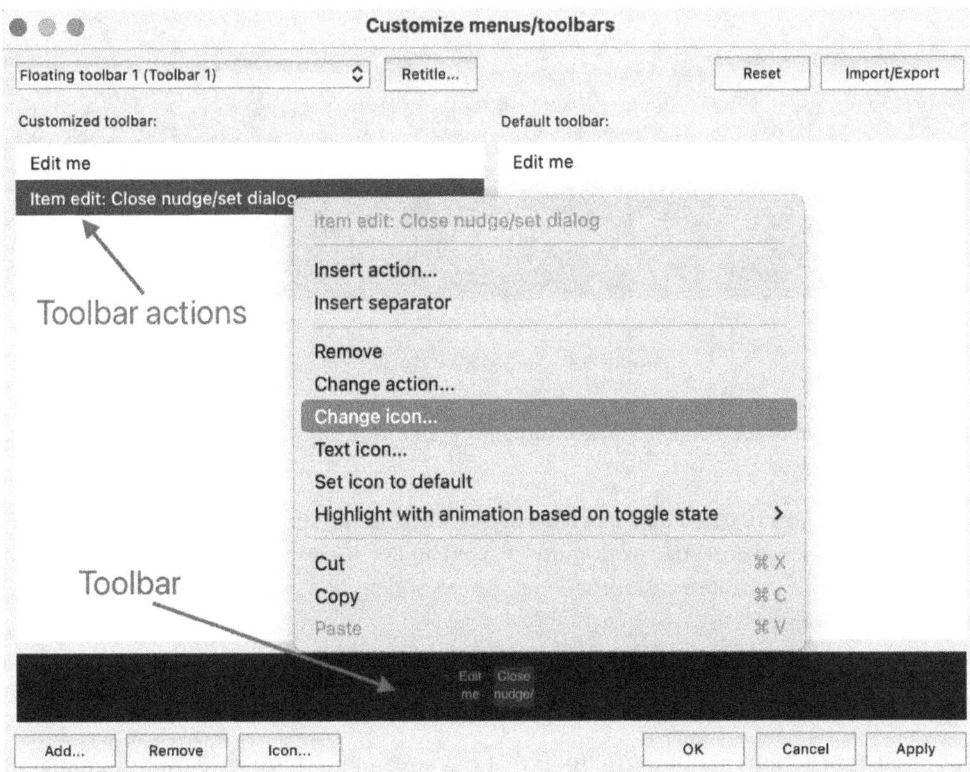

Figure 6.6 – Customizing a toolbar

This way, we can create multiple toolbars according to our needs. Once a toolbar is created, you can easily access it through the **View** | **Toolbar Docker** menu or by pressing the *F* key. The **Toolbar Docker** is a floating window that allows us to view and select the available toolbars, as shown in *Figure 6.7*:

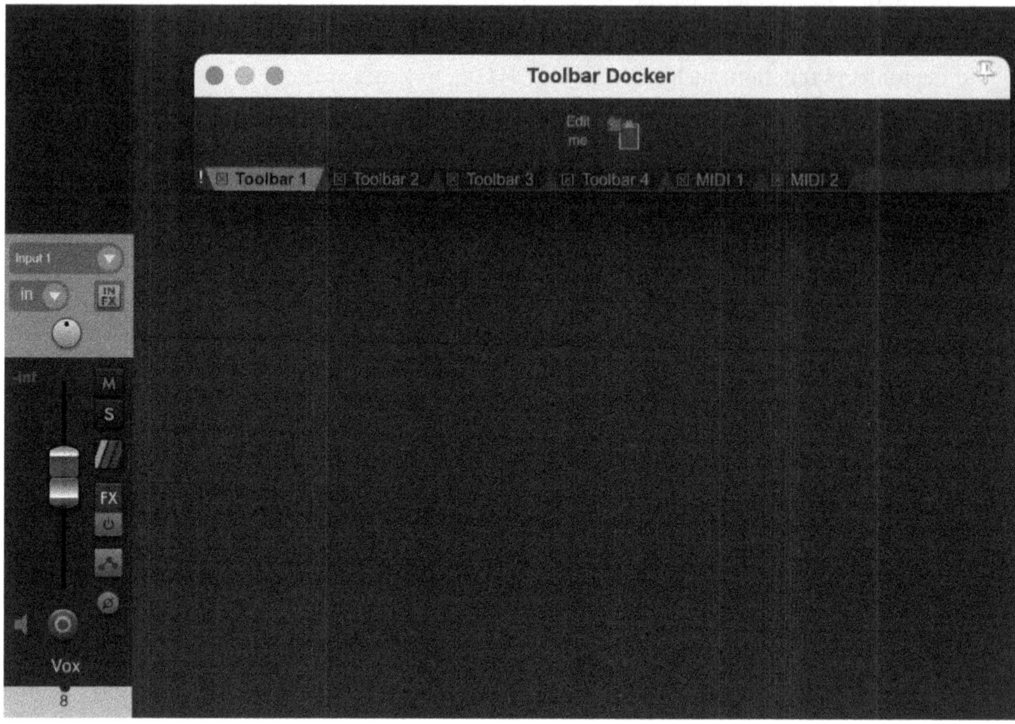

Figure 6.7 – The Toolbar Docker

You can adjust the size of the Toolbar Docker and place it in a location where it is useful and practical for you to have it.

So far, we have seen how to customize shortcuts and toolbars in REAPER to trigger various actions, which is very useful for making our work more efficient and comfortable. Now, we will see how we can link several actions to create a custom action or macro, which elevates REAPER's work capabilities to an even more advanced level.

Using macros

Macros or **custom actions** are powerful tools that can streamline your workflow by automating repetitive tasks, chaining multiple actions, and customizing your work environment to fit your specific needs. In this section, we will explore how to create and use macros in REAPER. We will also discuss the advantages of using macros and delve into some interesting applications.

A **macro** is a sequence of predefined actions that can be executed with a single command or keystroke. Macros allow you to automate repetitive tasks, saving time and reducing the risk of errors. By combining multiple actions into a single macro, you can create complex workflows that would otherwise require multiple steps.

Common uses of macros

Let's look at some of the common uses of macros:

- Macros can automate common editing tasks, such as splitting items at the cursor, deleting the left portion, and then trimming the right portion. This is especially useful for podcast editing or cutting up long recordings into smaller segments.
- Macros can be particularly useful for MIDI editing. For example, you might want to select all notes of a certain pitch and then transpose them up an octave.
- Macros can be used for batch processing, such as rendering multiple tracks or exporting multiple items.
- You can also use macros to apply a series of effects to a track or item. For example, you might want to add reverb, then EQ, and finally, a compressor to a track. The idea is to browse or search for different actions in the **Actions** window and experiment. Feel free to do this!

Now that we have seen the most common uses of macros in REAPER, let's look at the advantages of using macros in our workflow.

Advantages of using macros in REAPER

The advantages of using macros in REAPER include the following:

- **Efficiency**: Automate repetitive tasks to save time
- **Consistency**: Ensure the same steps are followed every time
- **Customization**: Tailor the DAW to fit your unique workflow
- **Complex tasks**: Execute complex sequences of actions with a single command
- **Error reduction**: Minimize human error by automating precise tasks

Macros can be tailored to perform virtually any sequence of actions within REAPER. They can be triggered via keyboard shortcuts, toolbar buttons, or MIDI controllers. REAPER allows you to record your actions and save them as macros.

Now that we know what a macro is, let's see how to create a new macro in REAPER.

How to create macros

To create a new macro or custom action, follow these steps:

1. Open the **Actions** list.
2. Press the **New action…** button and then **New custom action…**, as shown in *Figure 6.8*:

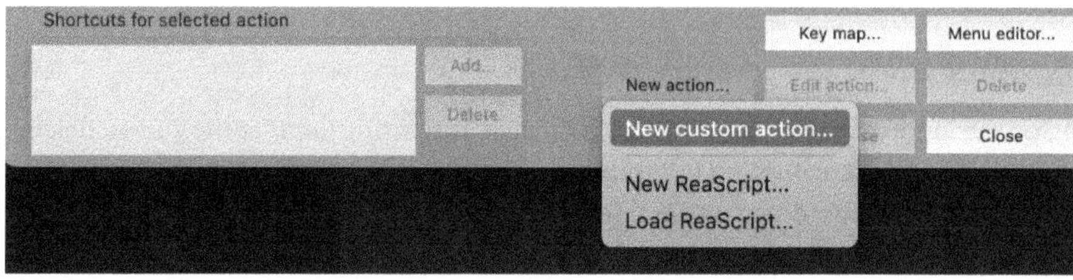

Figure 6.8 – Creating a new custom action

3. The **Create Custom Action** window will open, as shown in *Figure 6.9*. You can search for and add actions that you want to include in your macro by double-clicking on each.

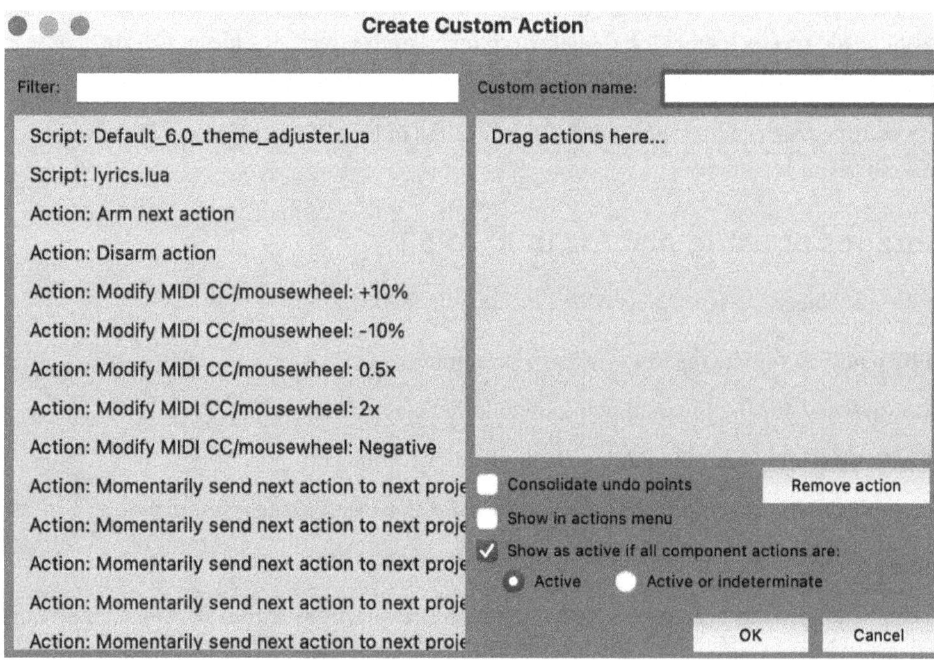

Figure 6.9 – Custom Action Editor

4. Name and save the macro. Once you've added all desired actions, give your macro a meaningful name by typing it in the **Custom action name** field. Click **OK** to save the macro.

To use a macro, you can trigger it from the **Actions** List, assign a keyboard shortcut to it, or add it to a toolbar.

Example: creating a simple macro

Now, let's see an example by creating a simple macro that performs the following sequence of actions:

1. Save the current project.
2. Select all tracks.
3. Mute all the selected tracks.

To perform this sequence of actions, follow these steps:

1. Open the **Actions** list window.
2. Create a **new custom action**.
3. Add these actions:
   - Search for `Save project`:
     - Double-click on **File: Save project**
   - Search for `Select all tracks`:
     - Double-click on **Track: Select all tracks**
   - Search for `Mute tracks`:
     - Double-click on **Track: Mute tracks**
4. Name the **custom action** and click **Save**.

Note that if you want to create a macro, it's recommended you do some planning:

- Before creating a macro, outline the sequence of actions you need
- Test your macro thoroughly and refine it as needed to ensure that it works correctly
- Give your macros descriptive names so that you can easily identify them
- Use REAPER's built-in actions to build your macros instead of trying to create everything from scratch

Macros in REAPER offer a powerful way to enhance your workflow. While there is a learning curve, the time invested in creating and fine-tuning macros can lead to significant efficiency gains. By understanding the advantages of using macros and exploring their various applications, you can tailor REAPER to fit your unique needs and take your audio production to the next level.

Experiment with creating your own macros, and you will quickly discover how much they can improve your productivity and streamline your audio production process. Whether you're editing MIDI, applying effects, or batch-processing tracks, macros can help you work smarter and faster in REAPER.

Now that you know how to create and use macros, let's explore some advanced preferences and settings in REAPER.

Exploring preferences and settings

REAPER is software that allows us to work without needing to adjust too many preferences. However, if you want to start customizing your experience with REAPER further, consider using some of the additional settings we will explore in this section.

Let's open the **REAPER Preferences** window, as shown in *Figure 6.10*, with the **Options** | **Settings** menu:

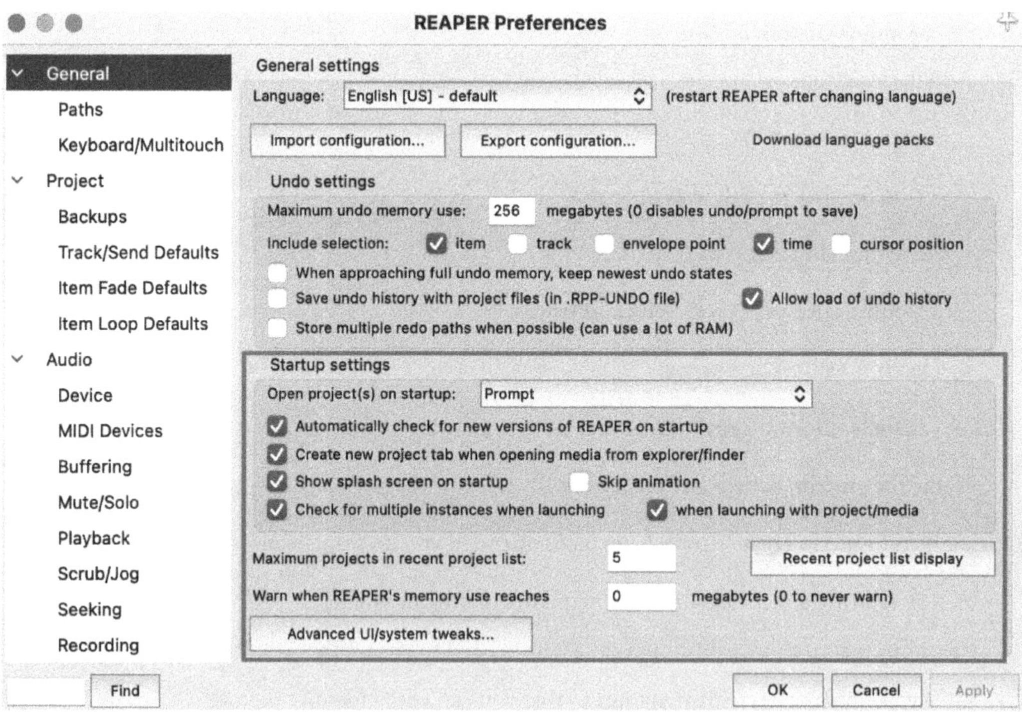

Figure 6.10 – REAPER General Preferences

Next, we will describe some of the main options found in the tabs of the **REAPER Preferences** window.

General

In *Chapter 1*, we saw that we can adjust the language and the behavior of the **Undo** function in the **General** tab. In this tab, we also have various options to start up REAPER, as highlighted in *Figure 6.10*. Among these options, we can choose to create a new project, open the last project, or ask what to do each time we open REAPER. Let's look at the options nested under the **General** option:

- In the **Paths** section, we can set the paths that REAPER will use to create new files or save the created renders. Generally, it is not necessary to change anything in this section, and REAPER will use the project folder to save files.
- In the **Keyboard/Multitouch** section, we can choose different options for how certain auxiliary keys on a keyboard will respond. In the **Multitouch** section, we can enable functions such as swipe, zoom, or rotate if we have a trackpad.

Project

The **Project** tab allows us to choose a REAPER file (`.RPP`) as a basic template. This can be very useful and practical once we have created projects with various plugins, colors, and so on and want to reuse the same structure in another project. Let's look at the options nested under the **Project** option:

- The **Backups** section is important because, here, we can determine how REAPER will handle the backup versions of a project, as well as adjust the **Auto-save** function, which makes REAPER automatically save the project at regular intervals.
- In the **Track/Send defaults** section, we can adjust the default levels of the faders and sends. We can also adjust the default size of each new track.
- In the **Item Fade Defaults** section, we can choose the shape that fades or crossfades will have by default. This can be useful if we find that we frequently use a particular type of curve when applying fades.

Audio

In the **Audio** tab, we can make various advanced adjustments regarding the use of the driver and audio processing. However, most of these settings can be left at their default values.

However, in the **Recording** section, we can assign a default structure to the names of files or items that are recorded in projects.

Appearance

In the **Appearance** tab, various visual parameters can be adjusted. For example, we have the option to adjust the space between tracks. We can also show or hide guidelines for item editing, as well as adjust the width of the cursor. Let's look at some of the options nested under the **Appearance** option:

- In the **Track Meters** section, we can adjust the minimum and maximum values (in dB) shown by each track's meters, as well as the meter decay time
- In the **Zoom/Scroll/Offset** section, we can specify how the cursor should be centered each time we apply a zoom

Editing Behavior

In this tab, we have options for the movement of the cursor while editing. There are also advanced options regarding REAPER's behavior during automation. The **Mouse** section shows different behaviors that the mouse can take while editing, such as the function of the mouse wheel, the use of double-clicking, or the use of modifier keys (e.g., *Shift* and *Ctrl*).

In the **MIDI Editor** section, we can adjust the behavior of the MIDI editor.

Media

In the **Media** tab, we have options for when we import or export MIDI items and video or audio files. Additionally, in the **Import** section, we can set whether we want REAPER to automatically adjust to the tempo of an imported audio file.

Plugins

In this tab, we can set the general behavior of plugin windows and indicate the paths to the **VST** and **LV2/CLAP** plugins. This can be useful if we want to organize our plugins in a different folder than the default ones. If this is the case, we must tell REAPER where the folders with our plugin files are located.

> **Additional reading**
>
> The options and settings in REAPER are extensive. You can find detailed information about each of them in the REAPER User Guide at `https://www.reaper.fm/userguide.php`.

Summary

In this chapter, we have seen how to use REAPER's actions, which are the core part of automating processes, to create new shortcuts, customize toolbars, and create macros. We have also seen some settings that allow us to customize the functionality and appearance of REAPER when performing various tasks. The information we have covered in this chapter will help you work faster, systematize actions in your production process, and make REAPER a much more personalized tool that meets your requirements.

In the next chapter, we will explore some advanced mixing and audio processing techniques that will allow you to achieve professional and interesting results in your audio projects.

7
Advanced Mixing and Processing

So far, we have seen many functions in REAPER for working on audio production. In this chapter, we will look at some more advanced functions used in professional mixing.

With the knowledge you acquire in this chapter, you will be able to handle groups of tracks in various ways, which will allow you to be more efficient when working with large sessions. You will also learn the basics for working on surround projects or systems with more channels than a stereo system.

In this chapter, we will cover the following main topics:

- **Using groups and VCAs**: This will allow you to manage projects with many channels more efficiently
- **Multi-channel projects**: You will learn techniques for creating projects with more than two output channels, such as a surround session
- **Using multi-channel processors**: You will learn about advanced processing techniques

Learning about all these tools will allow you to handle more complex mixing sessions, undertake more advanced projects, and take your effects processing to the next level.

Technical requirements

To carry out the examples in this chapter, you will need to use the finished project from *Chapter 5* or another mixed project that has more than four tracks.

Additionally, the *Multi-channel projects* section discusses how to set up a REAPER project to work in surround formats (i.e., 5.1). To work with this format, you need an audio interface with at least six output channels connected to five full-range speakers and a subwoofer.

Using groups and VCAs

When a project begins to have many tracks (let's say more than 10), controlling the mix becomes more difficult. It is common for a music or film production to use more than 50 or even 100 tracks! In these situations, it is necessary to group tracks to have better control of the session and work more efficiently.

In REAPER, we have several possible ways to group tracks: using folders, groups, and VCAs. Let's see how to use each of them.

Using folder tracks

Folders are a very practical tool that allows us to group several tracks and process them all together. They also allow us to control the volume, mute, or solo for that group of tracks. A typical use is to group tracks with similar instruments or functions, such as percussion, vocals, guitars, and so on. In the case of podcasts or video post-production, we can group effects, music tracks, or dialogues.

Folders also help us keep our session more organized, as we can *close* a folder track so that its contents do not take up as much screen space.

Let's see how we can create a folder track:

1. Select all the tracks you want to group in a folder, using the *Shift* or *Ctrl* key (*Cmd* on Mac). You can select them from the mixer or the arrangement area.
2. Select **Track** | **Move tracks to folder** | **New folder track**. A new folder track will appear with the selected tracks inside, as shown in *Figure 7.1*:

Figure 7.1 – Folder track

Once the folder track is created, it is recommended to assign it a name, just as we do with any other track. A **folder track** sums the audio of all the tracks it contains and combines them into a single track. If we move the folder track fader, the volume of the entire group of tracks will be affected. Similarly, we can mute or solo a folder track.

The folder track has a *small triangle* on the left side, as seen in *Figure 7.2*, marked **1**. Let's look at its functionality:

- We can press this triangle once to reduce the size of the contents of the folder track (see *Figure 7.2*)
- If we press the triangle again, we reduce the contents even more
- If we press the triangle a third time, we return to the original size of the tracks

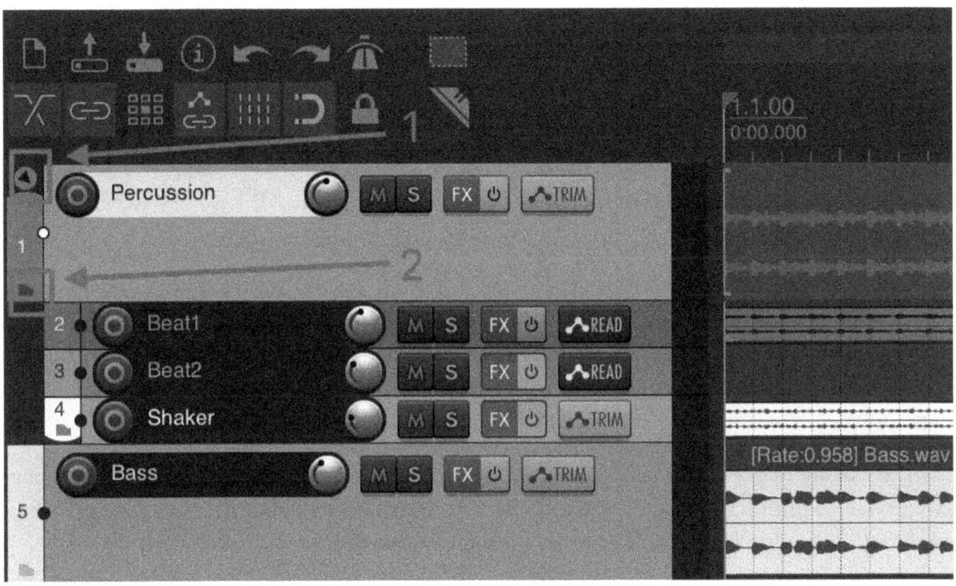

Figure 7.2 – Folder track views

If we want to convert a conventional track into a folder track, we can press the small folder marked as **2** in *Figure 7.2*. This also deactivates the function of a folder track and turns it into a conventional track, so be careful when using this button when you already have tracks assigned to a folder track.

When we convert a conventional track into a folder track, it will appear as a new option in **Track** | **Move tracks to folder**, as shown in *Figure 7.3*:

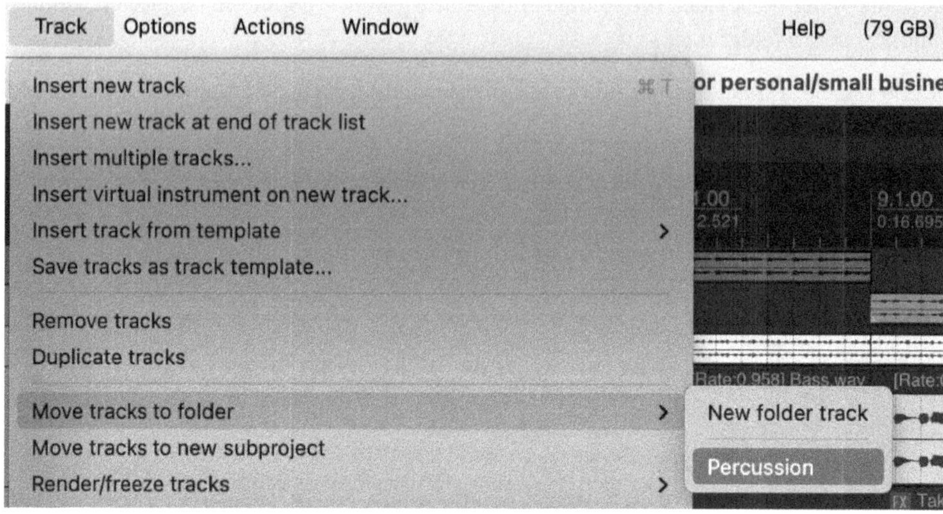

Figure 7.3 – Folder assignment

A folder track is very useful when we want to apply processing to an entire group of tracks, such as applying general equalization or compression to an entire drum kit or group of guitars, vocals, and so on. For this, we simply add a plugin as an insert in the same way we do with a conventional track and adjust the plugin to our liking. The effect will be applied to the sum of tracks.

As we can see, using folder tracks can allow us to have better project organization as the number of tracks increases. Additionally, we can use folder tracks to process or automate groups of tracks, as their operation is practically the same as that of a conventional track.

REAPER is a piece of software full of alternatives. Let's look at another way to group tracks using the Track Grouping Matrix.

Grouping channels

Another way to group tracks in REAPER is by using the **Track Grouping Matrix**. This function is quite powerful and allows us to create groups to control the parameters of different tracks simultaneously. Unlike a folder track, here, the signal of each channel is not combined or summed, but their controls are linked to be controlled together.

To activate the **Track Grouping Matrix**, select **Track** | **Track Grouping** | **Track Grouping Matrix**. This will show a new tab next to **Mixer** and **Media Explorer**, as shown in *Figure 7.4*:

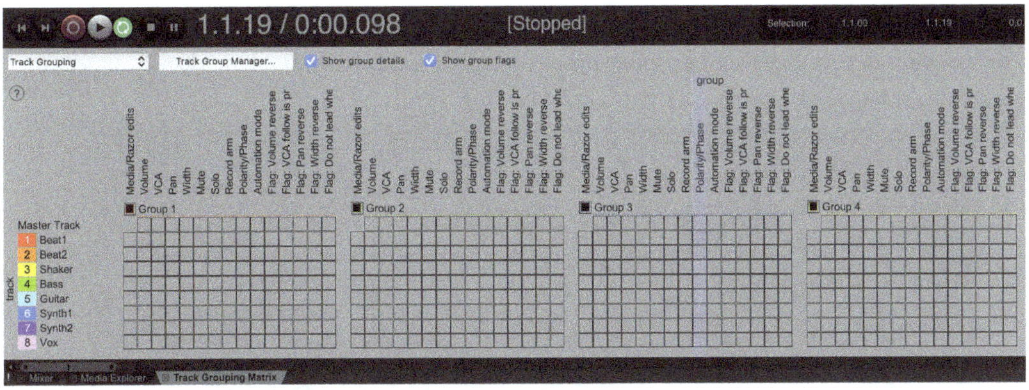

Figure 7.4 – Track Grouping Matrix

Although its appearance may look intimidating at first, this tool is easy to use. On the left side, we have the list of tracks in our project. On the right side, we see a series of matrices (grids) with the names **Group 1**, **Group 2**, and so on. These are the group controls we can create. Let's see an example.

Suppose we want to link the volume controls of the percussion tracks – that is, tracks 1, 2, and 3 – using **Group 1**. We simply click on the boxes where the **Volume** parameter intersects with the corresponding tracks, as shown in *Figure 7.5*:

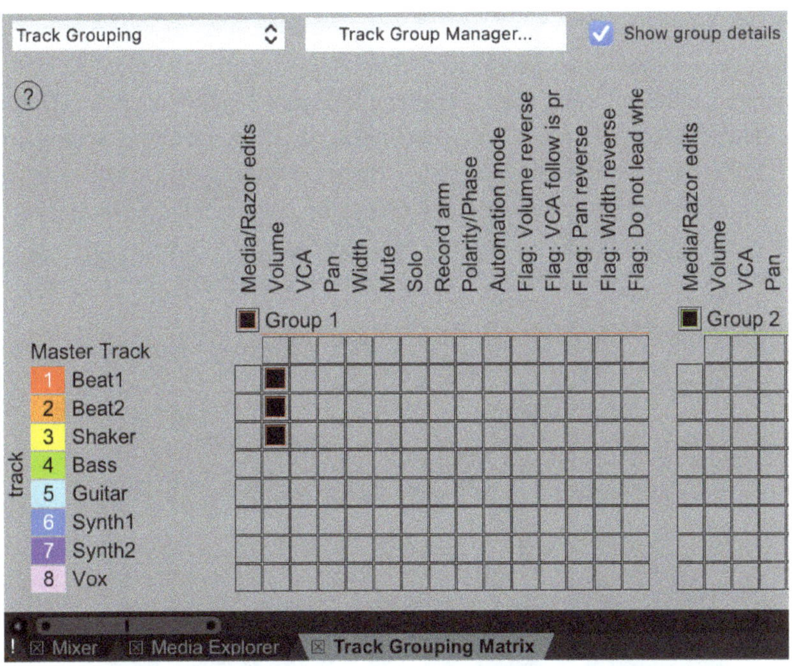

Figure 7.5 – Track Grouping Volume

Now, the volume controls of those tracks will be linked. If we move any of those three faders on the mixer, we will see how the other two move proportionally. Additionally, small marks will appear on the fader of each track, as shown in *Figure 7.6*, indicating that those faders are grouped:

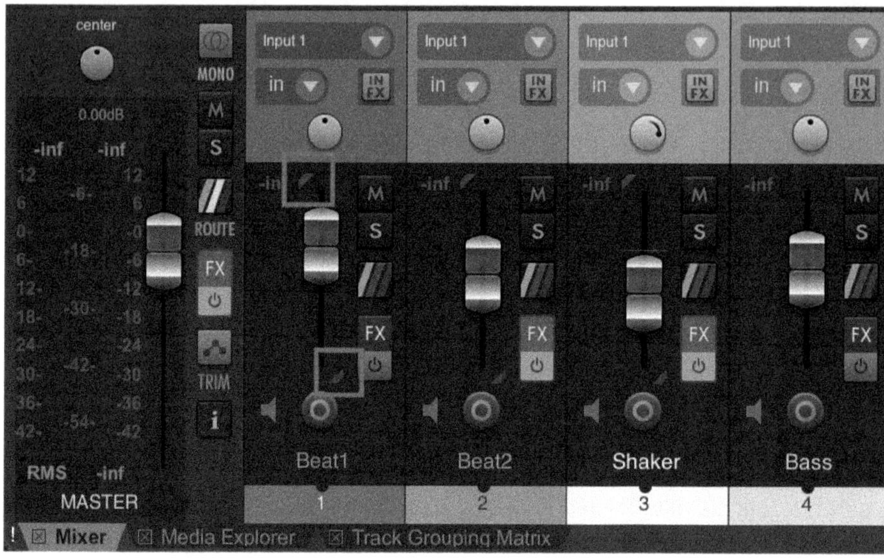

Figure 7.6 – Grouped tracks

In this way, we can activate any other parameter within the grouping matrix to link it within a group. We can link panning, mute, solo, and so on. For example, *Figure 7.7* shows that the volume of tracks **1**, **2**, and **3** are linked, the pan of tracks **1** and **2** are linked, and the mute of all tracks is also linked:

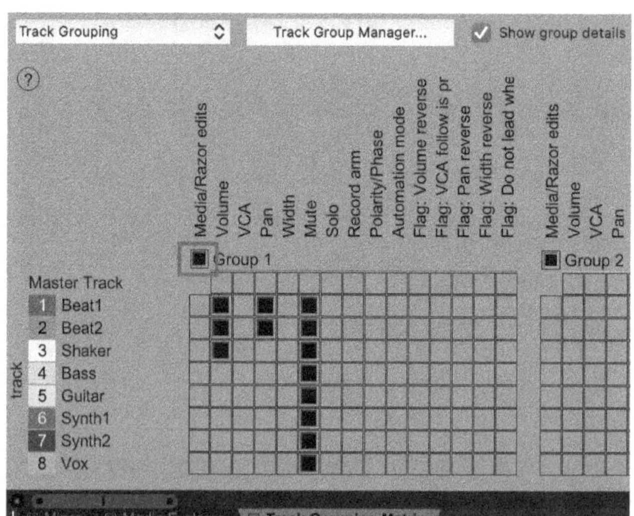

Figure 7.7 – Linking different parameters

As we can see, it is not necessary to group the same parameters of each track; we have the freedom to link or unlink channels as needed. REAPER gives us up to 64 different groups, so our options are vast.

If we want to deactivate a group, we simply click on the main control of the group, marked in *Figure 7.7*. With this same control, we can reactivate the group.

If we right-click on the group name (**Group 1**, in this case), the group properties window shown in *Figure 7.8* will appear:

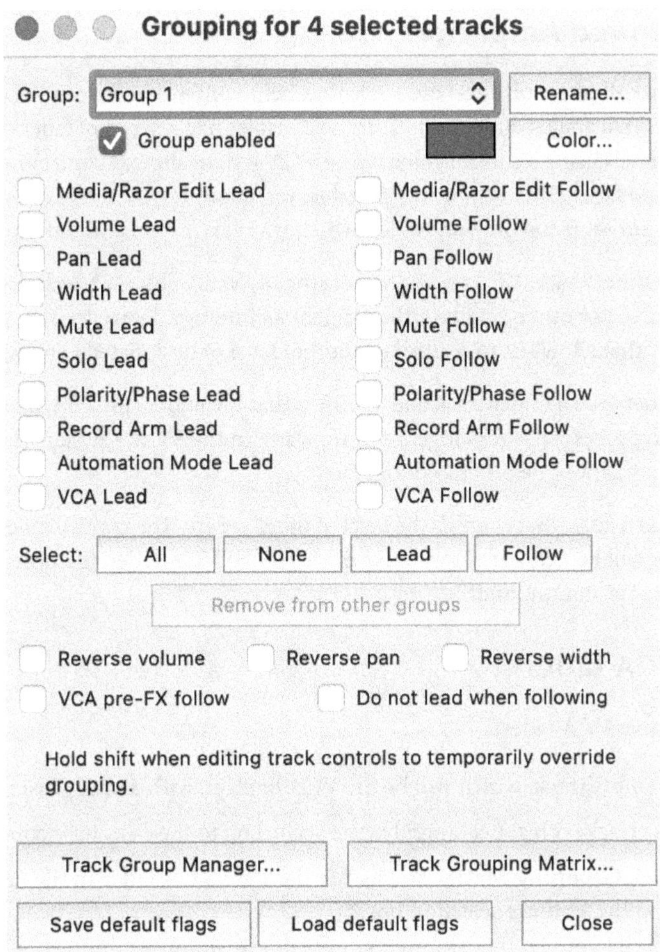

Figure 7.8 – Group properties window

From this window, we can rename the group, change its color, enable it, or activate different parameters we want to link.

We must be careful to maintain good organization in the groups we use so we don't get confused when mixing. If we focus on grouping the parameters we need to make our mix easier, we will see the great advantage of using groups in REAPER. Over time, experience and practice will help us decide which elements need to be linked and which do not.

Generally, using folders or groups can solve practically any grouping need in a complex mix. However, there is another way to control the volume of our channels, and that is by using VCAs.

Voltage Controlled Amplifiers (VCAs)

VCAs (Voltage-controlled amplifiers) are tools that help control the volume of channels. VCAs originated in large-format analog audio mixers. These consoles had a series of faders that could adjust the gain of other channels using a control voltage. The VCA system allowed controlling several console channels from a single fader. This way, it was possible, for example, to control the volume of all the microphones of a drum set using only one fader, which was very useful at the time.

In REAPER and any other DAW, VCAs remain conceptually valid, although technically, there are no control voltages involved or other details of the original technology. However, the use of VCA is the same: to have a fader that allows us to control the output level of designated channels.

The main difference between a folder track and a VCA is that the folder sums the signal of all assigned tracks, allowing us to process all tracks together if we want. In the VCA, the signals are not summed in any channel, so they cannot be processed together.

In REAPER, a VCA is a fader that *controls* the level of other faders. The control fader will be a *leader* fader, and the others will be *followers*. If we raise the level of a VCA fader, the other assigned faders will also rise by the same amount in dB.

Assigning a VCA fader

Let's see how to assign a VCA fader:

1. Create a new empty track, which will be the VCA control, with **Track | Insert new track**.
2. Name this new track with a meaningful name according to the case, for example, `Perc VCA`.
3. Open the **Track Grouping Matrix** and assign the **Perc VCA** fader to the *Lead* **(L)** mode by double-clicking the **Volume** selection box.
4. Assign the tracks you want to follow the VCA to the *Follow* **(F)** mode by triple-clicking their **Volume** selection boxes, as shown in *Figure 7.9*:

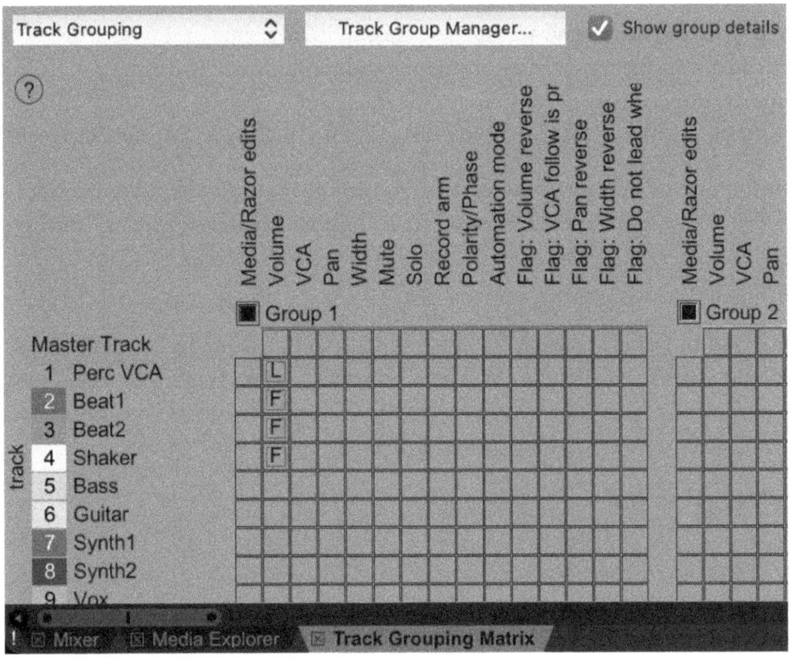

Figure 7.9 - VCA Assignment

If you move the VCA fader (**Perc VCA**) on the mixer, you will see that the other faders follow its movements. Unlike linking with groups, if you move any of the other faders, neither the VCA nor the other faders will move. This makes mixing with VCAs more intuitive, as we can adjust the relative volumes of a group of channels and have a *master* control (VCA) of that group.

In this example, we only assigned the **Volume** parameter to follow the VCA, but we can assign panning, mute, and all other parameters shown in the **Track Grouping Matrix** if desired.

As we can see, REAPER's options for grouping using folders, groups, or VCAs are extensive and complete. The choice of each option depends on personal preferences and the different needs we have in the mix: processing all signals together (*folder*), linking channels (*group*), or having some channels follow another (*VCA*).

Now, let's see how we can prepare REAPER for projects involving the use of multiple output channels.

Multi-channel projects

Most audio projects are stereo projects, which means that the project has two output channels: left and right. This solution is suitable for most applications because, in most cases, we listen to music or videos using headphones or a pair of speakers. Due to its simplicity and practicality, the stereo system has been the standard for many decades and remains in use today.

However, a stereo system is not the only way to reproduce audio content. For several decades, experiments have been conducted with the use of three, four, five, and more channels, attempting to create a more immersive sound experience. The quadraphonic system of the 1970s was one of the attempts of multi-channel systems that, due to the technical difficulties of the time, could not remain viable.

The 5.1 surround sound of the 1990s, thanks to digital audio, has remained the standard in the film industry, using five full-range channels and a subwoofer for very low frequencies. Thus, we can find a wide variety of multi-channel systems, where the idea is to have multiple speakers generating sound from different directions.

To use REAPER in multi-channel projects, it is necessary to have an audio interface with enough outputs to feed more speakers. The topic of surround sound is very broad and does not correspond to the objectives that this book aims to cover. In this section, we will focus on explaining how to configure REAPER to carry out 5.1 surround projects.

First, let's see what a 5.1 system is.

The 5.1 system

The **5.1 surround system** is a sound configuration used in home theater, cinema, and video games to create an immersive listening experience. This system is called 5.1 because it consists of six audio channels: five full-range channels and one low-frequency effects channel (the ".1"), which is played by a subwoofer.

The channels of a 5.1 system are as follows:

- **Center (C)**: Placed in front of the viewer, usually above or below the screen. It is responsible for dialogue and main voices, ensuring they are clear and precise.
- **Left and right front (L and R)**: Located on either side of the center channel. These speakers handle music, sound effects, and other main sounds that move from left to right.
- **Left and right surround (LS and RS)**: Placed to the sides or behind the viewer. They are used for ambient and background effects, creating the sensation that sounds are coming from all directions.
- **Low-frequency effects (LFE)**: Responsible for low frequencies, such as explosions, deep bass, and other low-frequency effects that add impact and depth to the sound experience.

Now, let's look at the benefits of using a 5.1 system in the next section.

Advantages of the 5.1 system

A 5.1 surround system has the following advantages compared to a conventional stereo system:

- **Immersion**: By distributing the sound across multiple speakers, the 5.1 system creates an enveloping listening experience, making the viewer feel like they are in the middle of the action
- **Clarity**: The separation of channels allows for greater clarity and precision in sound reproduction, especially in dialogue and effects
- **Versatility**: The 5.1 system is compatible with a wide range of media, including movies, music, and video games, and is one of the most common formats in the entertainment industry

As we can see, the 5.1 system presents significant advantages; however, it is not very common to find users who have a properly placed and calibrated 5.1 system. Nonetheless, being the most common system in today's movie theaters, it is worth exploring.

REAPER offers multi-channel options beyond 5.1 (i.e., 7.1, 9.1, 7.1.4, etc.); however, we will use the 5.1 system as an example since it is a good starting point, and the other larger systems use a similar configuration.

Configuring a 5.1 system in REAPER

Let's look at the steps to configure a 5.1 project:

1. Create a new project in REAPER. No special configuration is required in this regard.
2. Ensure that we are using an audio interface with at least six output channels. This can be verified in REAPER's preferences, through the **Options** | **Settings** menu, and by navigating to the **Audio** | **Device** tab, as explained in *Chapter 1*. Most 5.1 projects use a sampling rate of 48 kHz, so it is important to also adjust this value in this same tab.
3. Configure the **MASTER** track in REAPER. Right-click on its fader; this will bring up the master track outputs window, as shown in *Figure 7.10*. In this window, change the number of **Track channels** to `6` using the option marked in *Figure 7.10*:

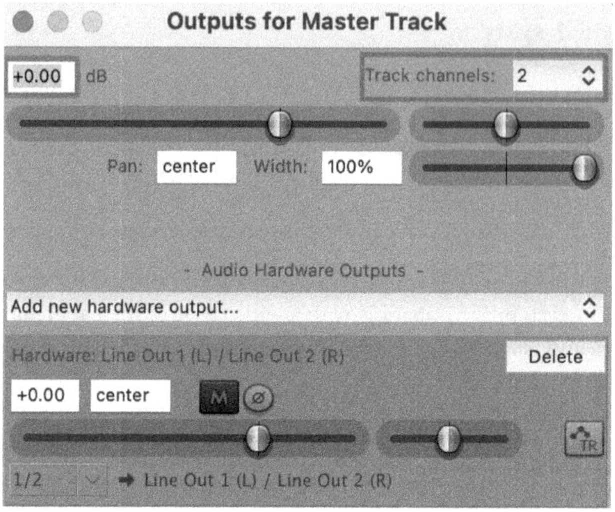

Figure 7.10 – Master Track channel settings

4. In the same window, change the output assignment to **Multichannel source | 6 channels** from the section marked in *Figure 7.11*. Then, we can close this window.

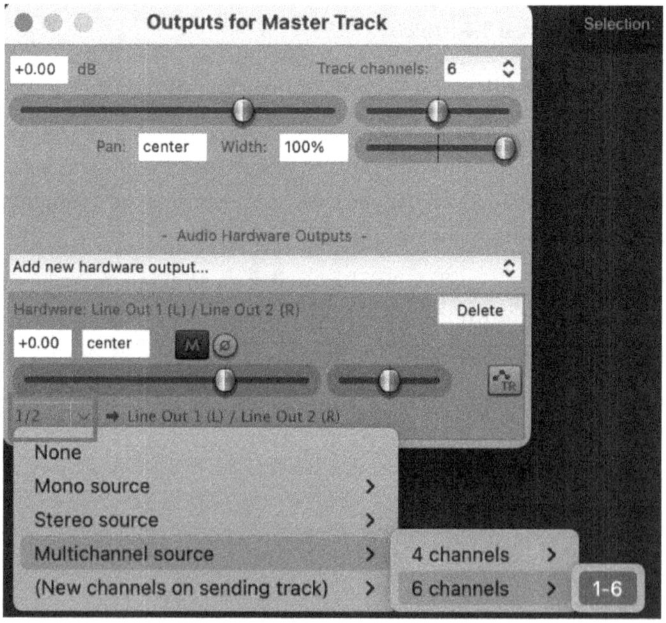

Figure 7.11 – Track source assignment

5. Import an audio file into the project or create a new track to record audio in it. This process is the same as previously seen, requiring no additional adjustment.
6. Open the **Routing** window for this new track by right-clicking on its fader, similarly to what we did with the master fader. In this window, change the track channels to `6` using the section marked in *Figure 7.12*. Then, we can close this window.

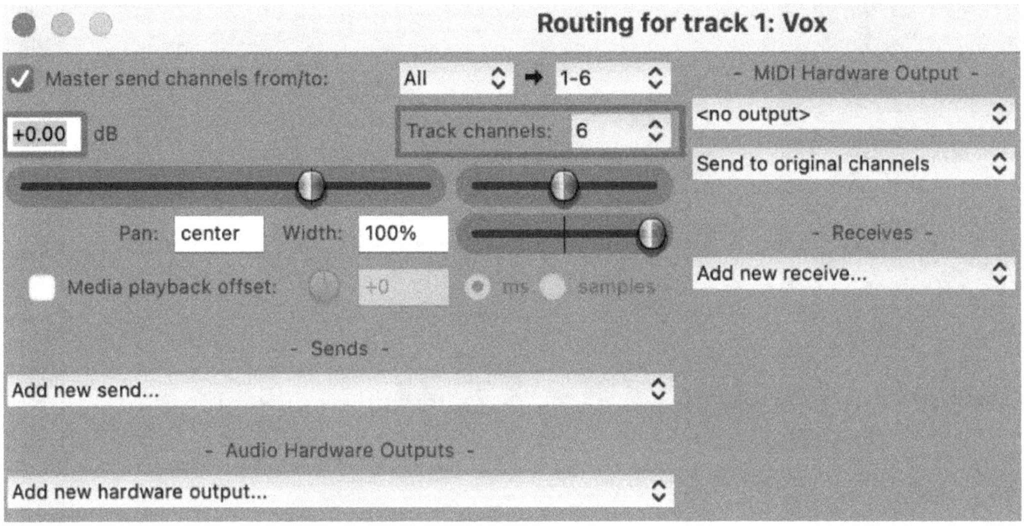

Figure 7.12 – Track channel assignment

7. Insert the **Cockos | VST: ReaSurroundPan (Cockos)** plugin on the audio channel, as shown in *Figure 7.13*. This plugin is not an effect but a **surround panning control** that will allow us to move and direct the audio from that channel to any of the available channels: L, C, R, LS, RS, or LFE.

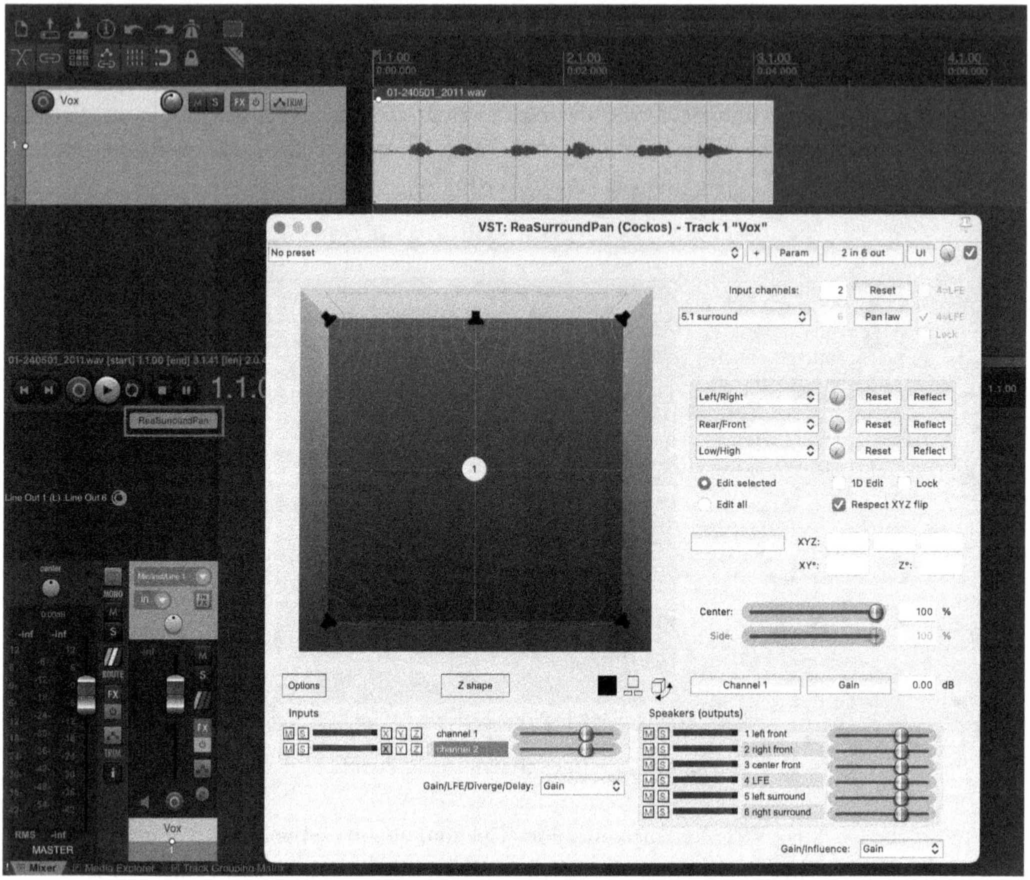

Figure 7.13 – ReaSurroundPan panner

This process should be done for the other tracks we add to the project. This way, we will be ready to perform a 5.1 mix, adjusting the **ReaSurroundPan** panner as we will see next.

Using the surround panner

The **ReaSurroundPan** plugin is the key part of surround work. It is precisely by using the panning that we can position sounds where we want: front, sides, or back. The first step in handling the panner is to set the input channels in the section marked **1** in *Figure 7.14*:

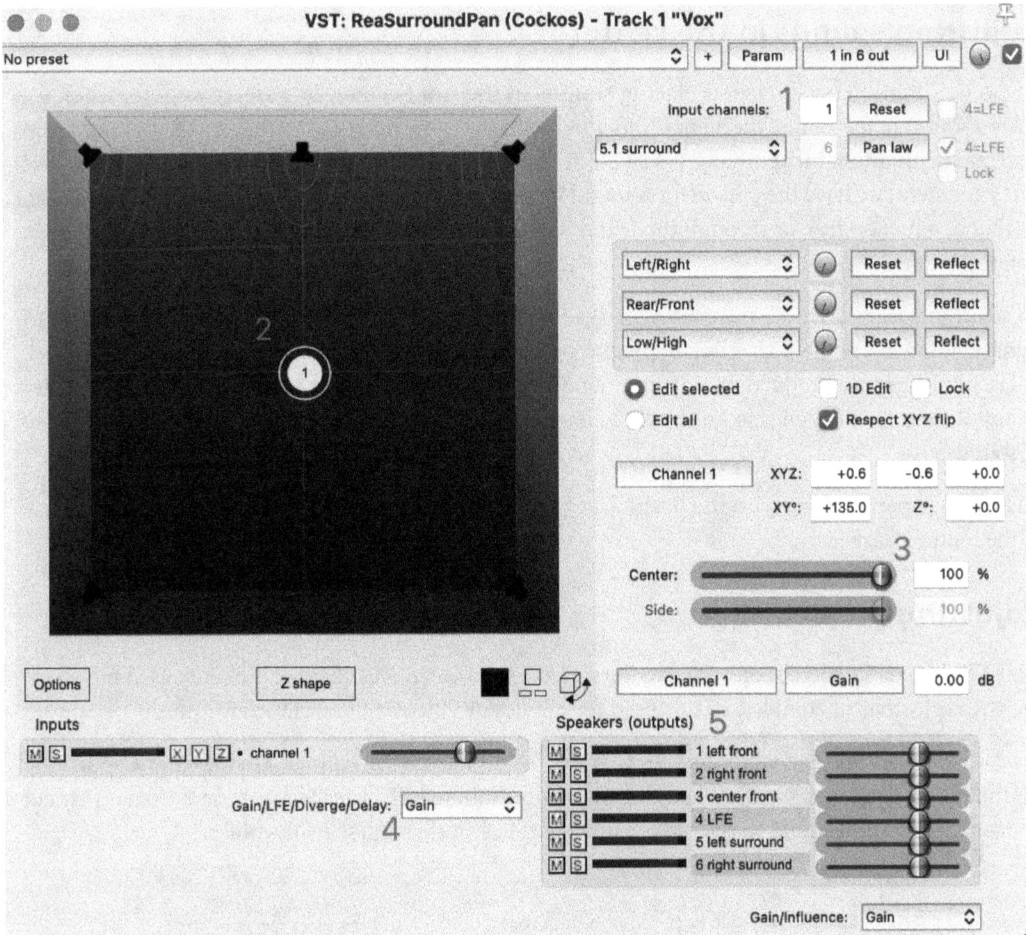

Figure 7.14 – Adjusting the surround panner

Generally, we will use only one input channel, as shown in *Figure 7.14*. If the channel audio is a stereo signal, such as a music file or audio loop, then we will use two channels in the **Input channels** section. Once this parameter is set, we can move the circle on the **XY pad**, marked as **2** in *Figure 7.14*. The idea is to move this circle while listening to the track's audio to experiment with different positions around the listening area.

The five loudspeakers must be connected to the first five outputs of our interface, so we can hear the audio move around us following the panner's position. The default speaker output order is indicated in the **Speakers (outputs)** area, marked as **5** in *Figure 7.14*.

Adjusting sounds in the center

A special situation occurs when placing sounds in the front center. In a stereo system, when we place a sound in the center, the signal comes out with the same intensity from L and R, but our brain generates a **phantom center** that gives us the sensation of sound coming from the center. In the case of a 5.1 system, we have the option for a sound in the center to come out through the center speaker, C (that is, a *real center*), or through the L and R speakers (that is, through the *phantom center*) as in a stereo system.

To adjust this feature, we use the control marked as **3** in *Figure 7.14*. This control adjusts the amount of signal coming out of the C channel. In practice, it is valid to use the phantom center or the C channel. For example, in post-production, it is common for the background music to go to the phantom center (L and R) and for dialogues to go to the C channel. This helps to have better separation and clarity of sounds.

It is worth experimenting with the positions of the different sounds in a mix, as well as with the use of the center channel.

Adjusting the LFE

The **LFE** channel should be connected to the system's subwoofer. This channel is mainly used for effects such as explosions or rumbles, so it is used for movies or videos, but not much for music.

If we want to send any signal to the LFE channel, we do it from the panner. First, we must adjust the control marked as **4** in *Figure 7.14* and change it from **Gain** to **LFE**. Then, we can use the fader marked in *Figure 7.15* to add sound to the LFE channel and hear it through the subwoofer:

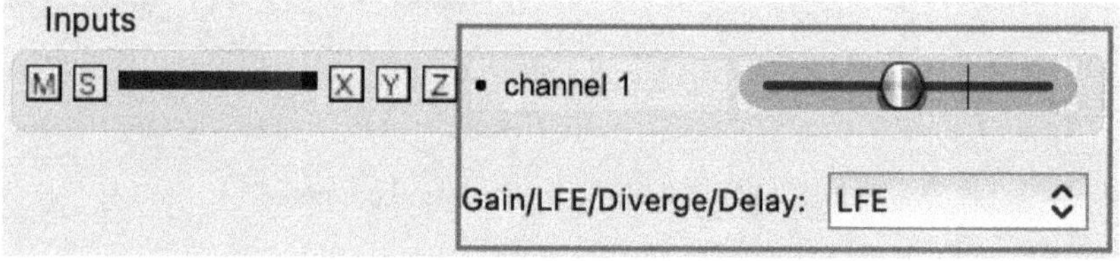

Figure 7.15 – Controlling the LFE channel

> **Tip**
>
> It is recommended to be moderate in the use of the LFE channel, as an excess of signal in this channel can generate a mix with exaggerated bass.

Up to this point, we have seen how to use the surround panner to control mono tracks. Next, let's see how to handle stereo tracks.

Handling stereo files

If the track we are panning has a stereo file, then the panner will show us two panning control circles, as shown in *Figure 7.16*:

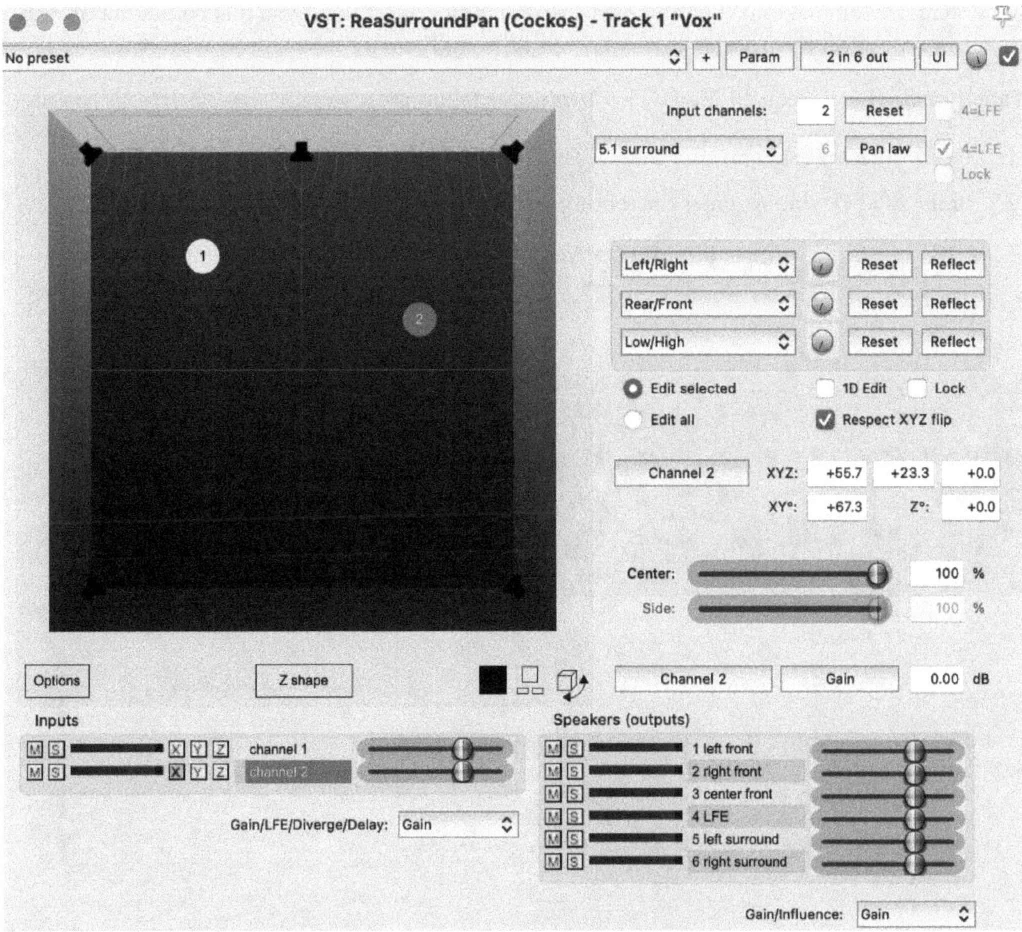

Figure 7.16 – Panning stereo sources

Circle **1** represents the L channel information of the stereo source and circle **2** represents the R channel. In 5.1 mixes, we can move and place these circles wherever we want, meaning it is not mandatory to place them in L and R, giving us many interesting options when mixing in surround.

As we have seen, a 5.1 project opens many possibilities for creating surround content. Using the **ReaSurroundPan** panner, we have great flexibility to position the sound of any track in the different 2D positions that the 5.1 system provides us. Now that we know how to create and manipulate a multi-channel project, let's see how we can use multi-channel processors in REAPER.

Using multi-channel processors

A **multi-channel processor** is a processor that can affect more than two channels simultaneously. In REAPER, we have different options to process multi-channel or surround tracks. For example, in a 5.1 system, we can make an equalizer on a surround track affect the signal that comes out of each speaker, or only affect the front speakers, rear speakers, and so on.

To apply multi-channel equalization on a 5.1 track, we follow these steps:

1. Insert the **ReaEQ** plugin after the 5.1 panner.
2. In the **ReaEQ** window, enter the routing options, marked in *Figure 7.17*:

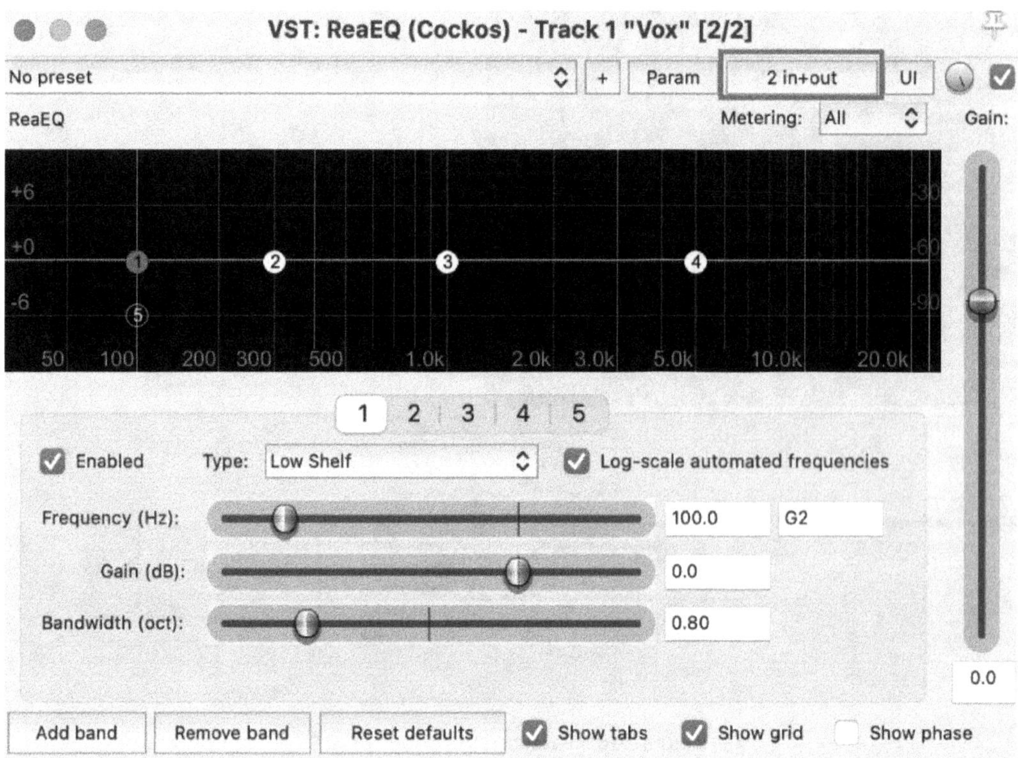

Figure 7.17 – Plugin routing options

3. A small plugin routing window will appear. In this window, change **Plug-in channels**, marked in *Figure 7.18*, from **2** to **6** channels:

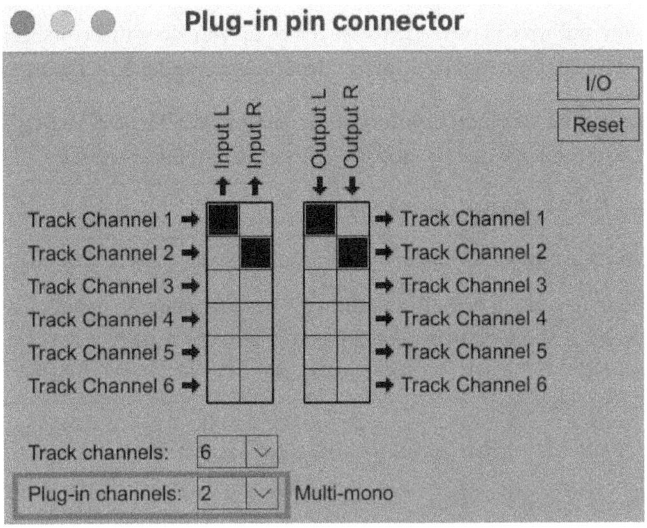

Figure 7.18 – Assigning plugin channels

4. Then, the routing window will change to a six-channel matrix, as seen in *Figure 7.19*:

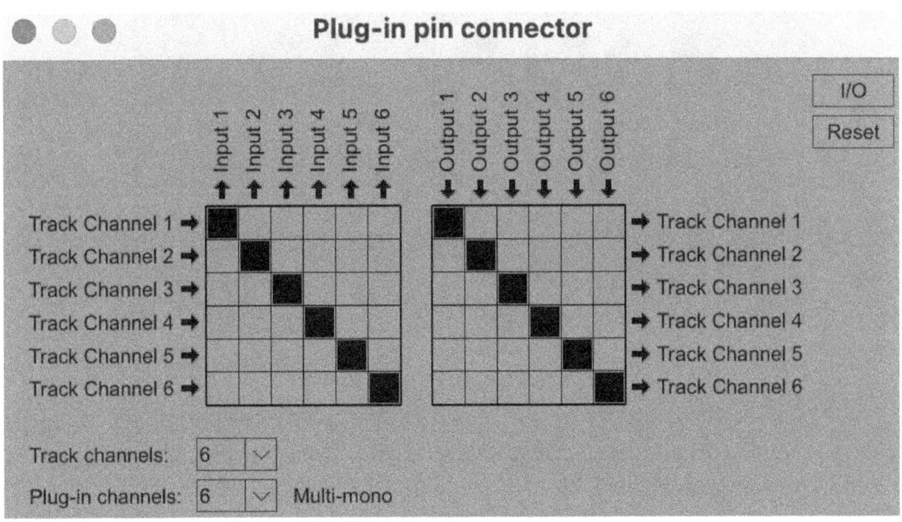

Figure 7.19 – Multi-channel plugin routing

We can close this window and we will be ready to use the equalizer. Now, this equalizer will process each of the six surround channels of our track, similarly to how a stereo equalizer works on a stereo track.

Some plugins may not handle so many inputs simultaneously, such as the **ReaDelay** delay. In these cases, we will need to add multiple instances of the plugin, as explained here:

1. Insert an instance of **ReaDelay** after **ReaEQ**.
2. Enter the routing window of **ReaDelay** in the same way as done with **ReaEQ**.
3. In this case, the plugin does not give us the option to change its number of channels, so we leave the plugin with the **6** channels of the track, as shown in *Figure 7.20*. This means that this plugin can only handle two channels at a time, so we will need to insert a new instance of **ReaDelay** below the first one.

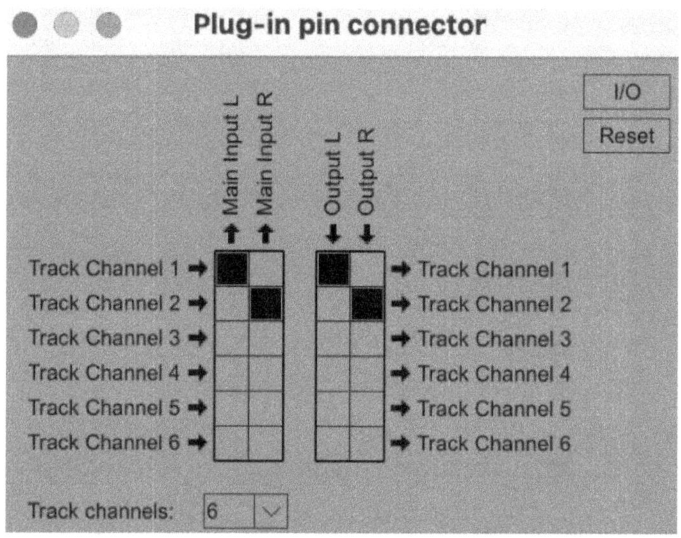

Figure 7.20 – Stereo plugin routing

4. Enter the routing options of the second **ReaDelay** and change the plugin's inputs and outputs to **3** and **4**, as shown in *Figure 7.21*:

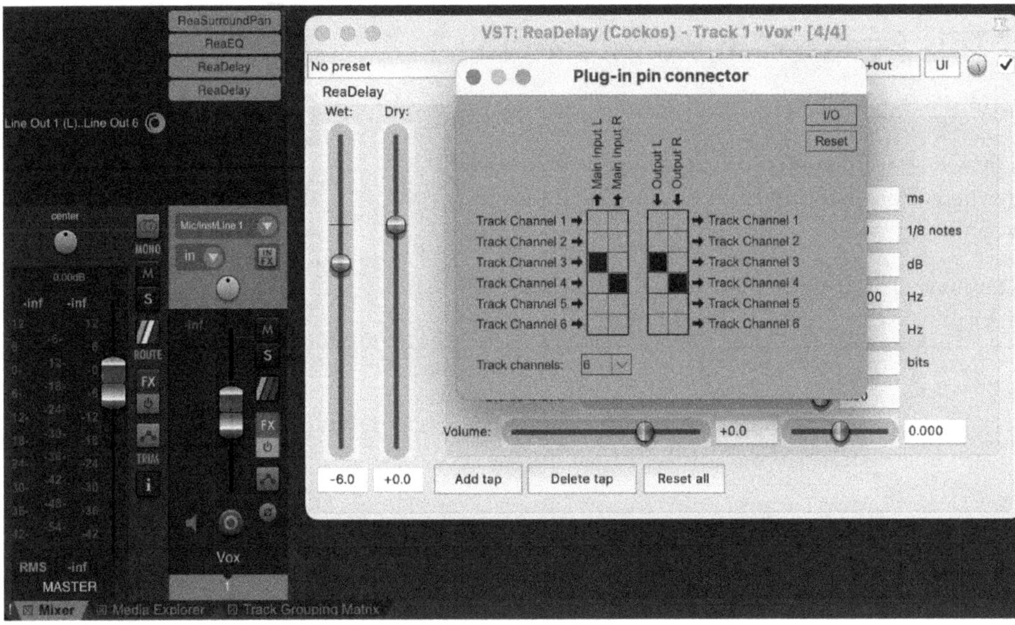

Figure 7.21 – Plugin routing for channels 3 and 4

5. Similarly, add a third instance of **ReaDelay** and make a similar adjustment in the routing, but this time, activate channels **5** and **6** and deactivate the others.

In this way, we will have the effect (in this case, delay) on each of the six channels of our surround track. Although this procedure is a bit more complicated, it gives us the flexibility to change the parameters of each instance of the plugin if we want to, such as setting a slower delay on the front channels and a faster delay on the surround channels, or any other combination.

By following either of the two procedures explained, we will have the tools to process our surround projects and let our creativity flow.

Summary

In this chapter, we have seen how to use advanced tools in REAPER, such as grouping tracks using folders, groups, or VCAs. We also saw how to configure multi-channel projects and tracks, using the example of 5.1 surround systems, as well as the principles for using REAPER's surround panner.

Finally, we saw how to process multiple audio channels within the same track by assigning multi-channel plugins or using multiple instances of stereo plugins. This will allow you to process your mono audio tracks up to the most complex multichannel configurations you might handle, such as 5.1, 7.1, and so on.

Now that we have enough tools for audio work in REAPER, let's see how we can work with video files in the next chapter.

8
Working with Video

Whether you are writing music for a short film, editing audio for a video podcast, or designing sound effects for a video game, chances are you will find yourself working with video in REAPER sooner rather than later.

The good news is REAPER has a powerful video engine and a comprehensive set of tools that make it highly capable in this area and allow you to perform essential video editing tasks that go beyond just adding audio.

This chapter will explore the ins and outs of working with video in REAPER so that you'll be able to tackle any sound-to-picture projects easily. You will learn about the following:

- **Editing video projects**: We will explore importing video files, configuring our project to match the video's specifications, and even learn some fundamentals for video editing in REAPER.
- **Working with dialog from editing to post-production**: We will learn how to sync, edit, clean up, and process dialog to achieve professional results.
- **Handling music post-production for video**: We will explore how to integrate and process pre-existing music into our video projects.
- **Spotting sound effects and processing them**: Additionally, we will explore how to integrate, edit, and process existing sound effects into our project to complete its soundtrack.
- **Rendering video files**: Finally, we will explore the ways in which we can export video files in REAPER to ensure the best possible quality for the task at hand.

By the end of the chapter, you will be able to work on a variety of audio-for-video projects and even be able to handle essential video editing tasks, all within this powerful DAW.

Technical requirements

To follow along with this chapter, it is recommended that you create a new REAPER project and have a few video files handy. These can be videos recorded using your phone, or even ones captured while playing video games.

Additionally, if you are curious about sound design, find a few appropriate sound effects on websites such as **Freesound** (`freesound.org`) and **Sonniss** (`https://sonniss.com/gameaudiogdc`). You will then be able to add these to your video using the methods explained in this chapter. If you are planning to create music alongside your video, refer to *Chapter 2* for recording MIDI and audio if you haven't done so yet.

Example audio and video files for this chapter can be found in the GitHub repository of this book at: `https://github.com/PacktPublishing/Elevate-your-audio-production-with-Reaper`.

Royalty-free music for use in personal and commercial projects can be found in the **YouTube Audio Library** (requires a YouTube account): `https://www.youtube.com/audiolibrary`.

Editing video projects

This section explores importing your first video into a REAPER project and getting everything set up for perfect sync, video editing techniques, and basic functions of the **Video Processor** plugin.

Importing video files

To import a video file, create a new REAPER project and locate the video files you intend on importing into it. Simply dragging them onto your empty timeline will create a new track (see *Figure 8.1*).

You'll find that the track looks just like the ones you've created before. This is because REAPER's tracks are agnostic to the type of media they contain and each track could simultaneously house audio, MIDI, photos, and videos all beside each other (if you so please). Despite this unique capability, it is generally wise, of course, to reserve video tracks purely for video.

You will notice that importing a video file doesn't automatically display it onscreen. To reveal the video, use the *Ctrl* + *Shift* + *V* (replace *Ctrl* with *cmd* on Mac) keyboard shortcut to display the video window, as shown in *Figure 8.1*. You can also find it under **View** | **Video Window**.

Figure 8.1 shows an example of what we'll see right after importing our first video into an empty REAPER project:

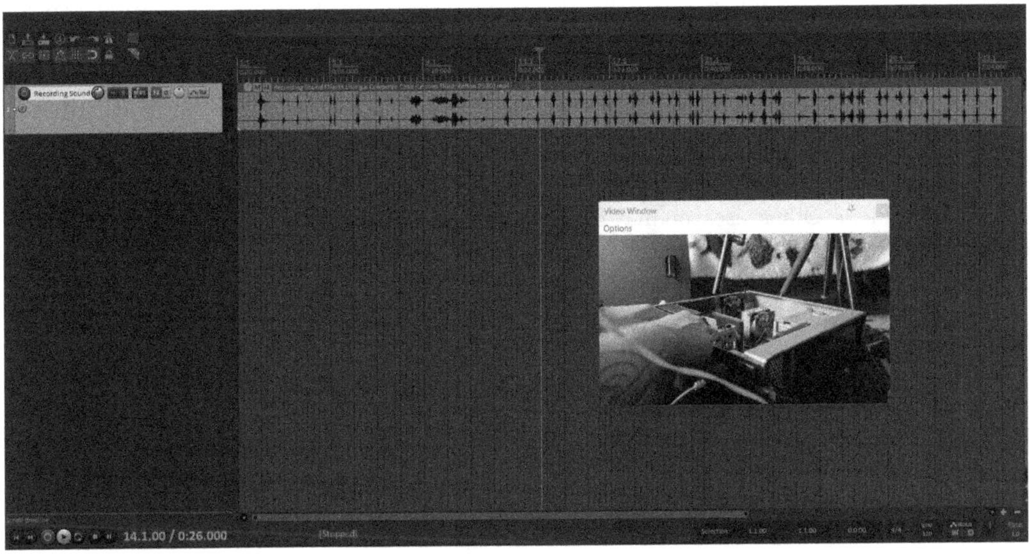

Figure 8.1 – After importing your video

If the video you are working with has audio, you will see its waveform just like with any regular audio file. If you will be adding to the existing audio rather than replacing it, you will be able to use all the same plugins and effects that you are already used to using on regular audio tracks. REAPER also offers a small selection of video processing and editing tools in the form of plugins that we will be in the section covering the Video Processor plugin.

> **Important note**
>
> **Muting** a video track will also stop it from outputting any video. If you don't intend on keeping the original audio, simply lower its volume to a minimum.

Next, we will learn how to set up our project to always maintain perfect sync with our video and ensure that playback remains smooth.

Adjusting your project settings

Video and audio are different types of media that use a fundamentally different timebase. While video consists of *frames*, audio consists of individual *samples*. The speed at which they are played back is thus defined as *framerate* and *sample rate* (see *Chapter 1*) respectively.

The central conundrum here is that it takes many more samples for a sound to reach our ears than it takes frames to create the impression of a moving image. While cinematic movies are presented in 24 or 25 frames per second, the audio that accompanies them usually has a sample rate of 48,000 Hz – or, as it's more commonly referred to, 48 kHz.

A sample rate this high is required in order to recreate the full spectrum of 20 Hz to 20 kHz that is audible by the human ear while our eyes can perceive 24 frames per second as smooth motion.

In order to achieve perfect sync with the picture, it is important to set up your project to match your video's specifications. Otherwise, you may find that your audio will slowly drift out of sync over the duration of the video once you export it. This might not be noticeable in a three-minute web video but will increasingly become so in longer-form content.

Displaying video properties

To view the specifications of our recently imported video file, double-click on the item to open the **Media Item Properties** window. Here, click the **Properties...** button near the bottom of the window, as shown in *Figure 8.2*:

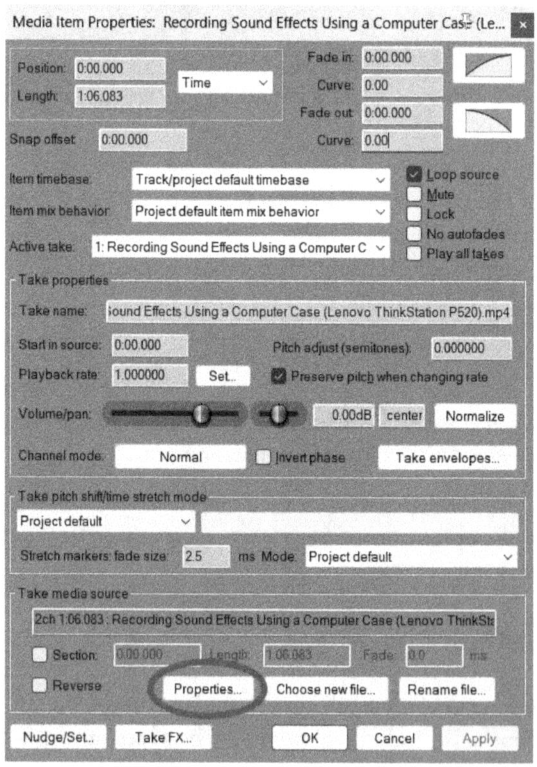

Figure 8.2 – The Media Item Properties window

This will open a window containing a wealth of technical information about our video. Luckily, we only need to be concerned with the first couple of lines where we'll find the video file's general specifications, including the *framerate* measured in **frames per second** (**fps**), as shown in *Figure 8.3*. Take note of your video's fps value.

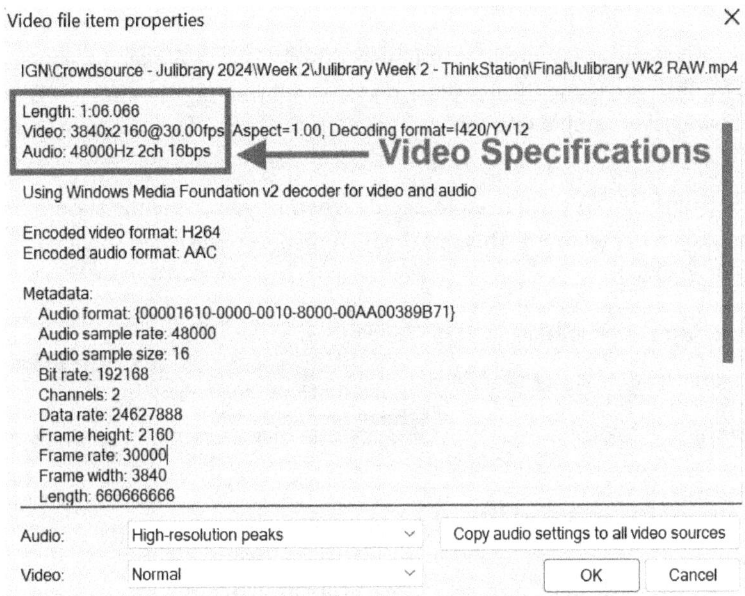

Figure 8.3 – The Video file item properties window

Another important factor can be the video's original **audio sample rate**. If we intend on keeping or even processing the video's original included audio, we should match our project settings to the sample rate in the video in order to maintain sync throughout.

Matching project settings

Armed with this knowledge, we will be heading to our project settings. You can find these within **File | Project Settings** or by pressing *Alt* + *Enter* on your keyboard, as shown in *Figure 8.4*:

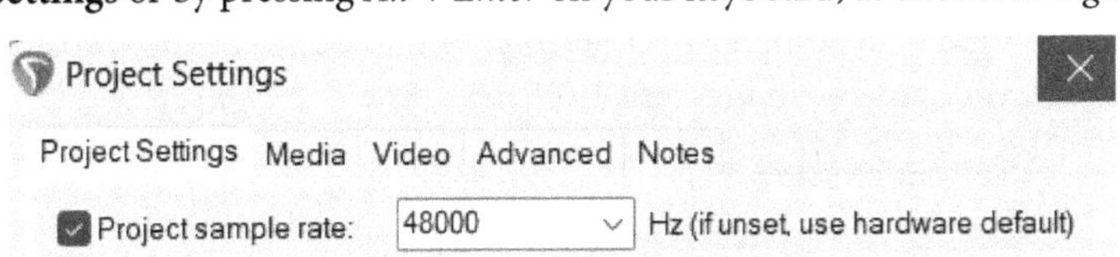

Figure 8.4 – Project Settings

On the first page, you will want to check **Project sample rate** in the **Project Settings** tab and set it to `48000` **Hz**. Regardless of the framerate, *48 kHz* is the recommended rate when working with video.

It is the sample rate at which most mobile devices and cameras operate when capturing or playing back video and has also become the international broadcast standard. As such, using this sample rate will ensure maximum compatibility with different endpoints.

> **Important note**
>
> Note that you *can* create audio for video at higher sample rates. *Chapter 11*, which explores sound design for film and games, will explore reasons why you might want to. It is important to ensure that whichever sample rate you use is a *multiple* of 48 kHz, such as 96 or 192 kHz.

On the **Project Settings** tab, you will need to decide whether your timeline should be divided by **Beats** or **Time**, as shown in *Figure 8.5*. This sets the increments events when snapped to if you move them with snapping enabled.

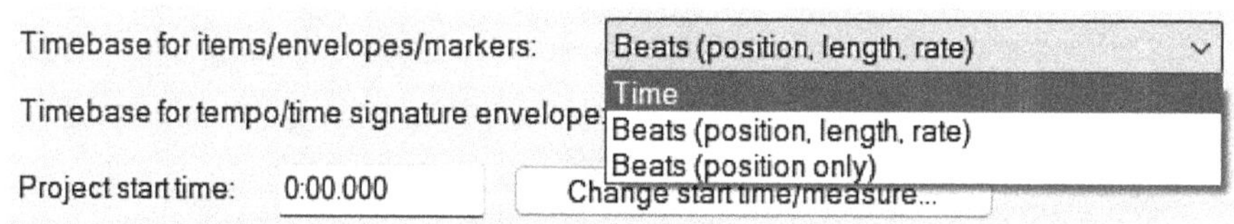

Figure 8.5 – Timebase selection dropdown

If you will be composing music to picture, select **Beats (position, length, rate)**. If your goal is to add sound effects, edit voiceover, or mix a podcast, **Time** is the preferable choice as it allows you to more precisely move items to sync with the picture.

> **Important note**
>
> While it may seem like your timebase decision is final, you will actually be able to change this setting anytime later without having to bring up your project settings each time. This allows you to work on musical content, sound effects, voiceover, and other elements side by side without having to utilize separate projects.

Finally, navigate to the **Video** tab of the **Project Settings** window and set your project's **Frame rate** setting to match that of your video – in this case, `30` fps, as shown in *Figure 8.6*:

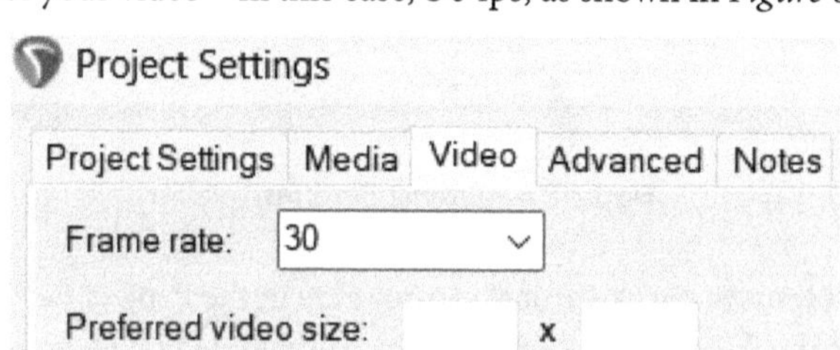

Figure 8.6 – Project Settings | Video

Now, we can close our **Project Settings** window. It's always a good practice to briefly watch your video after this change to make sure it is playing smoothly. Setting the framerate incorrectly can lead to jittery playback and can make syncing sound effects or voiceover more difficult and less precise.

Setting the timeline ruler grid

After exiting **Project Settings**, we can customize one more timebase-related setting, independently of how we previously set our overall project timebase.

Right-click the *timeline ruler* at the top. In the bottom section of the resulting drop-down menu, we will find options that define which units of time will be displayed in the top **Ruler** and **Transport clock**, as shown in *Figure 8.7*:

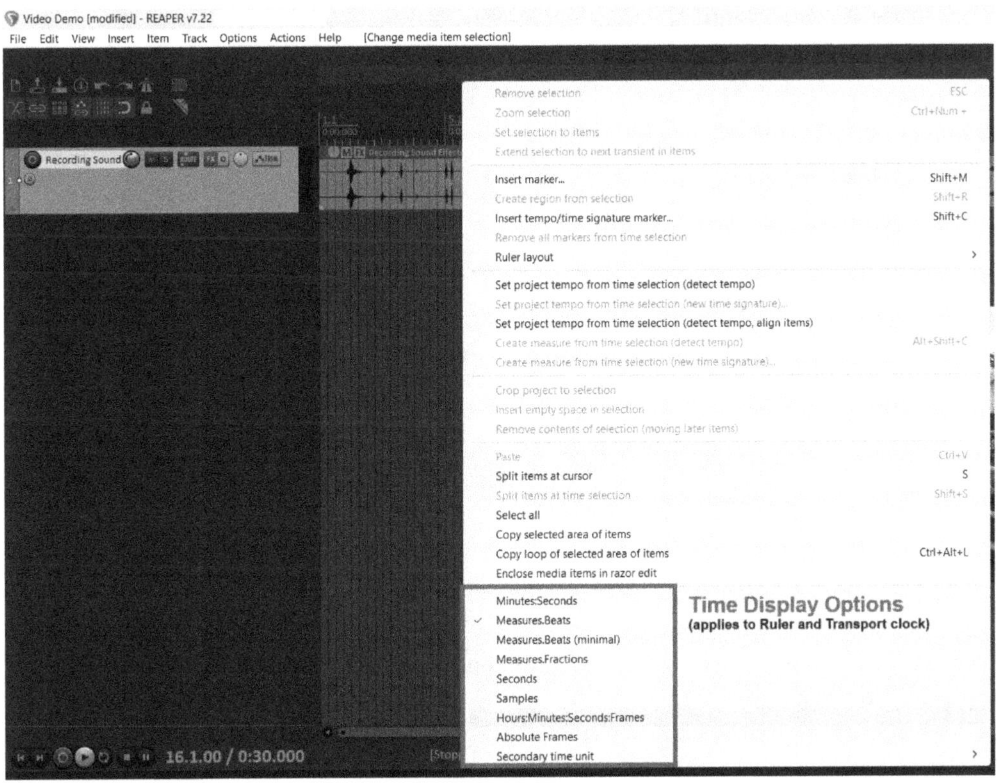

Figure 8.7 – Ruler settings dropdown

Now that we've set up our project for the use of video, we will explore how to edit video in REAPER. Later sections will also cover specific best practices for working with musical and non-musical content alongside video.

Disabling embedded audio

If we wish to not use the audio contained in our video file, we can set the track's volume to a minimum. Alternatively, we can disable the audio track entirely by entering our file's **Video file item properties** settings as described in the previous section, clicking the **Audio** drop-down menu toward the bottom of the window, and then selecting **Disable audio** (see *Figure 8.8*). This change can be reverted at any time should the audio track be needed after all.

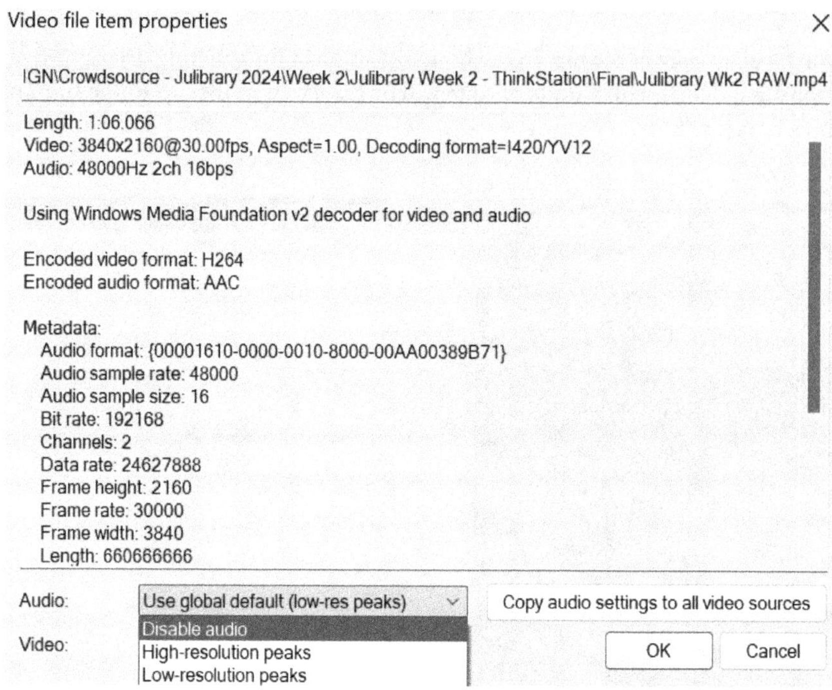

Figure 8.8 – Disabling the embedded audio track

We can exit this dialog by clicking **OK** and should now see that the waveform of our video has disappeared. Note that if we want to synchronize dialog to replace a camera's built-in microphone audio, we will need to keep the audio in place and simply turn it down later.

Video tracks and routing

While on the surface a track containing video looks exactly the same as one with audio, there are a few key differences. For one, besides outputting audio (should the video file contain it), video tracks also send their video signal through all routing connections made. Whichever video track is higher up in the track hierarchy will be the top layer in REAPER's video output, and other video tracks will have to be routed to the primary one for any compositing, such as transitions, and green screens to be possible. An introduction to this will be covered in the *Video Processor plugin* section.

Understanding ripple editing

An editing workflow that has not been touched on thus far but will prove incredibly handy for working with video, voiceover, and other continuous content is **ripple editing**. Simply put, enabling ripple editing means that edits made at one point on the timeline will affect objects that follow. It enables us to perform edits such as cutting out a scene while avoiding any gaps in our footage because the section after our cut will immediately snap to the end of the preceding one.

To enable the feature, click the *ripple editing* icon found in our default toolbar, as shown in *Figure 8.9*. Clicking it once will enable **Ripple editing per-track** and clicking again enables **Ripple editing on all tracks** while clicking a third time will disable it again.

The *Alt* + *P* (*option* + *P* on Mac) shortcut can also be used; however, we must then pay close attention to the *ripple editing* icon as it's our only way to tell which mode we're in.

Figure 8.9 – The ripple editing button and its two functions

Knowing the difference between these two modes is essential as ripple editing can be extremely powerful if used correctly yet highly disruptive to our project's integrity if the wrong mode is used for a given task. It is an essential feature to learn if we want to be able to edit long-form content, such as podcasts and dialog, quickly while avoiding common pitfalls.

> **Important note**
>
> Ripple editing only references an item's start point and initial length. Trimming an item will not affect others while in this mode.

Ripple editing per-track

The **Ripple editing per-track** mode is the one to use when you only want a single track to be affected by the ripple effect of your edits. Once enabled, it follows your selection and can be used across all your tracks without their edits affecting each other. With **Ripple editing per-track** enabled, whenever you move, delete, or insert an item on a given track, all other subsequent items will move. This is demonstrated in *Figure 8.10* as follows:

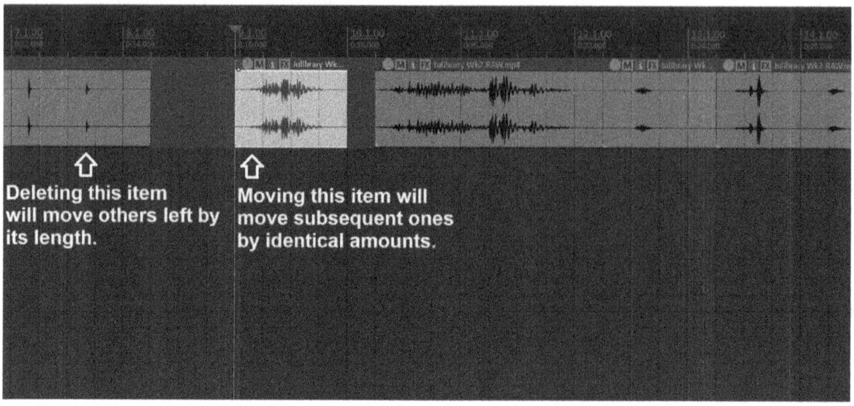

Figure 8.10 – Ripple editing per-track explained

Here is how **Ripple editing per-track** works:

- *Deleting* an item will move all following items left by the exact length of the item or segment that we deleted.
- *Moving* an item will move all subsequent items by the same amount as if they were held together by magnets. This also applied to any gaps between subsequent items. Essentially, all edits stay in place and are merely moved around in time.
- *Inserting* a new item between existing ones will move the ones to the right of the gap out of the way by the duration of the item inserted. Dropping a new item on top of an existing one will split the latter and widen the resulting gap to fit the new item.

Ripple editing on all tracks

The **Ripple editing all tracks** mode of ripple editing makes edits made anywhere in our project affect *all* overlapping and subsequent items regardless of which track is selected. It's a very useful tool for many use cases but should be used very consciously.

A common scenario would be cutting out sections of a video that we have already synchronized dialog and sound effects to. By enabling the **Ripple editing all tracks** mode, we can ensure that all dialog and sound effects after our edit will remain in sync with the subsequent footage.

Similarly, a common mistake is deleting or moving items while unknowingly having this feature enabled, resulting in all following items moving into different positions.

Figure 8.11 shows a basic overview of how editing and moving individual items affects others with this mode enabled:

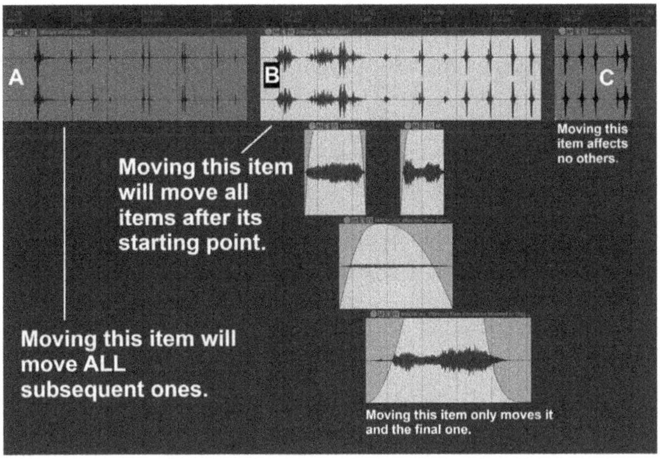

Figure 8.11 – Ripple editing on all tracks explained

Here are the ways in which the **Ripple editing all tracks** mode can be used:

- *Moving* an item will move all items that start later than its starting point, including overlapping ones. Overlapping items that start *earlier* than the selected one will not be moved.
- *Deleting* an item moves all following items left by the exact length of the item or segment that we deleted. Items that overlap and are *longer* than the selected one will only have the overlapping portion removed. If the selected item was *1 minute* and the overlapping one *1 minute and 30 seconds* in length, the final *30 seconds* of the latter would remain and be moved to the left.
- *Inserting* a new item between existing ones will move the ones to the right of the gap out of the way by the duration of the item inserted.

With ripple editing now a tool in our belt, we can start performing essential video editing tasks in REAPER comfortably. With the feature enabled, cutting out sections of the video or inserting other video files makes sure there are never any blank frames between segments and your footage retains its continuity.

> **Important note**
>
> Utilize **Ripple editing per-track** when just starting on a project, and **Ripple editing all tracks** when removing sections from or adding new ones to projects that already contain dialog, music, or sound effects alongside your video. For everything else, our basic editing techniques will suffice.

Video Processor plugin

Beyond basic trimming, moving, and cutting, REAPER also has a plugin that allows for all kinds of handy features, such as adding titles or timecodes to your video, transitioning between clips, color correction, and more. Since the **Video Processor plugin** could fill an entire chapter on its own, we will be looking at the basic necessities that will come in handy on our day-to-day projects involving video.

To use the Video Processor plugin, we just need to bring up the **FX chain** window for our video track and search for `video` to find the Video Processor plugin.

While its scripting-focused interface may look intimidating at first, it won't take much in the way of coding knowledge to use the features most essential to our work.

All of the plugin's capabilities are accessed via presets that can be found by clicking the drop-down menu at the top of the plugin window, as shown in *Figure 8.12*:

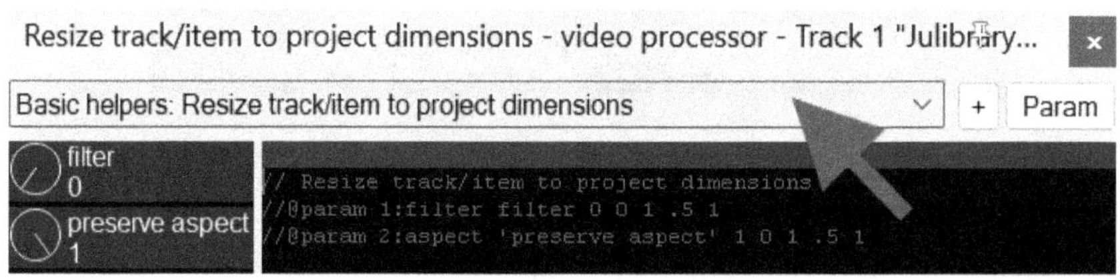

Figure 8.12 – Plugin presets menu

The Video Processor plugin contains a number of parameter dials on the left that change with each processing preset as well as a window showing the script making up the preset. This scripting area is also where we will insert any custom values, such as the titles we would like to add to our video.

Adding titles and timecodes

A common request we will receive when working in audio for video content professionally is adding timecodes or titling (such as a copyright notice) to our video files. Luckily, REAPER makes this easy to do right in the DAW without having to rely on a separate video editing app!

To get started, we'll click the preset drop-down menu and select the **Overlay: Text/Timecode** preset. This will result in the plugin window looking as follows:

Figure 8.13 – The Video Processor plugin (black sections inverted for legibility)

While there is a lot of code and plenty of controls onscreen now, we only need to concern ourselves with a few.

In order to add our own title to the video, we need to locate the first three lines of code, which will look like this by default:

```
// Text/timecode overlay
#text=""; // set to string to override
font="Arial";
```

To add our own title, we simply need to remove the # in *line 2* and write our title between the apostrophes. If we want to use a different font, the native Fonts (Windows) or Font Book (Mac) apps can help us find one we like.

To change the font of our title, we simply have to type in the full name of our desired one where it currently says `Arial`.

Putting it all together, our code should look something like this:

```
// Text/timecode overlay
text="This is a Test!"; // set to string to override
font="Times New Roman";
```

Once we've finished inputting our text and font name, we have to commit these changes by pressing *Ctrl/cmd + S*. The resulting title would then look like this:

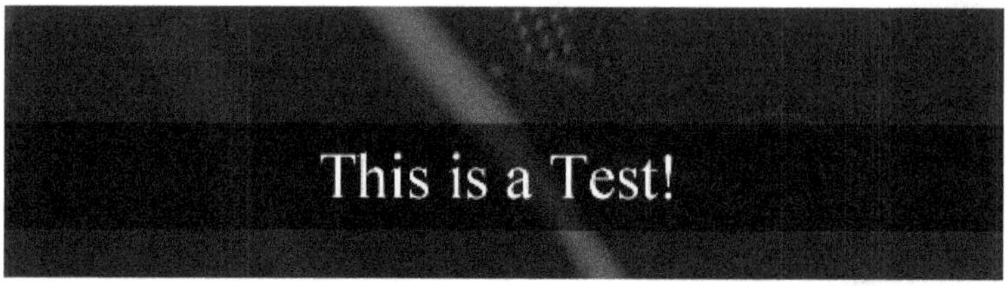

Figure 8.14 – Our first custom title

The background strip can be customized using the control dials labeled **BG**, allowing us to fit it to the width of the text, change brightness and opacity, and add padding to increase the space between the text and background borders.

When working on video projects for clients, it is a best practice to include the timecode in your exported video files to make sure that audio and video sync is maintained throughout the production process as different people may be using different apps to work on a project.

Timecode embedding is largely automated and only requires us to flip the **Show timecode** dial to `1`. This will display the project's timecode in the standard `Hours:Minutes:Seconds:Frames` format. The frame rate displayed will automatically match what we've previously set in the project settings.

The same background settings and our choice of font will also apply to our timecode.

Video transitions

Sometimes, a hard cut from one shot to another can be jarring or feel out of place. A smooth transition could help give our video better continuity. REAPER can do this, too. Unlike audio, however, this cannot be achieved with simple crossfades.

Instead, this is another use case for the Video Processor plugin. Here, we'll select any of the plugin presets labeled **Transition** and make sure our `wipe pos` dial on the left is turned to `1`.

We then need two video clips or split a single video clip into two pieces. To fade from one clip to another, we will have to move our second clip onto a new track and have it overlap the former one for the duration of our intended transition.

Next, we will have to create a send from **Track 2** back to **Track 1** so that the plugin *sees* both video feeds and can transition between them. To do so, simply click and drag the **Route** button from **Track 2** onto **Track 1**.

Now that the plugin is receiving both video feeds, we can show the `wipe pos` parameter envelope, which we will then use to create our transition. To do so, click the first track's **Trim** button and activate the parameter in the following list:

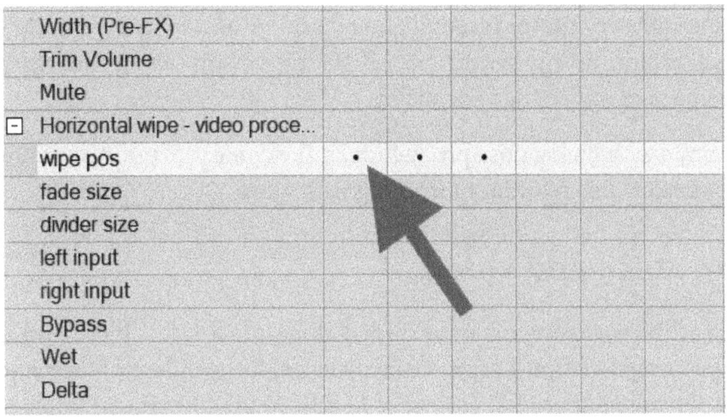

Figure 8.15 – Activating the wipe pos parameter envelope

Then, using what we learned in *Chapter 4*, we can draw our **automation** curve controlling the transition from `wipe pos 1` (**Video A**) to `0` (**Video B**), as shown in *Figure 8.16*:

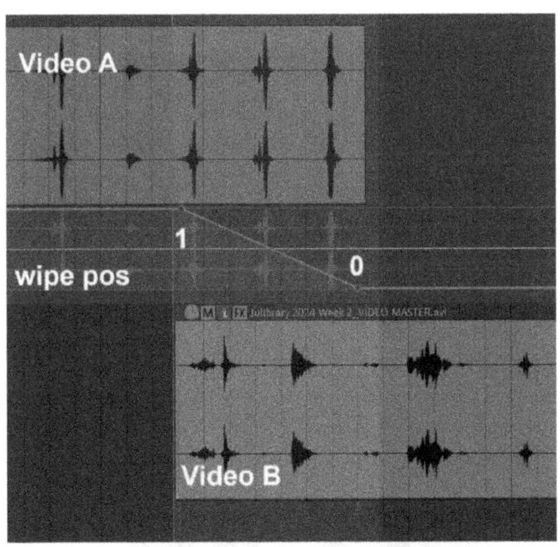

Figure 8.16 – A video transition on the timeline

A good way to add movement and dynamism to our transition is by trying out different curve shapes, which accelerate and decelerate transition speed in the process.

With these tools, we can handle most simple video editing tasks and will be ready to start working on audio-for-video projects.

Working with dialog from editing to post-production

Whether it's movies, podcasts, YouTube videos, or games – dialog is incredibly important and must be treated as such whenever we get to work with it. This section will introduce several concepts and approaches to working with spoken word recordings and explore how best to work with them alongside video. Further, we will explore how to synchronize direct microphone audio with raw camera footage, cleaning up, processing, and mastering your dialog.

Chapter 10 will continue with dialog post-production in the context of podcast production, so it will contain a lot of information also relevant to working with video.

Synchronizing voice and video

When we are tasked with processing dialog recorded alongside a video, it is commonplace to have the audio that has been captured on a separate recorder with the video footage captured onsite. If you haven't done so, download the audio and video files from the `Chapter 8` folder in the GitHub repository (see the *Technical requirements* section) of the book.

Here, we will find an audio and video file from the same take of a brief `talking head` video that we will now have to synchronize. Importing these two files into REAPER will reveal that they have slightly different lengths and starting points. This is to be expected if audio was recorded externally and is an easy enough fix for us:

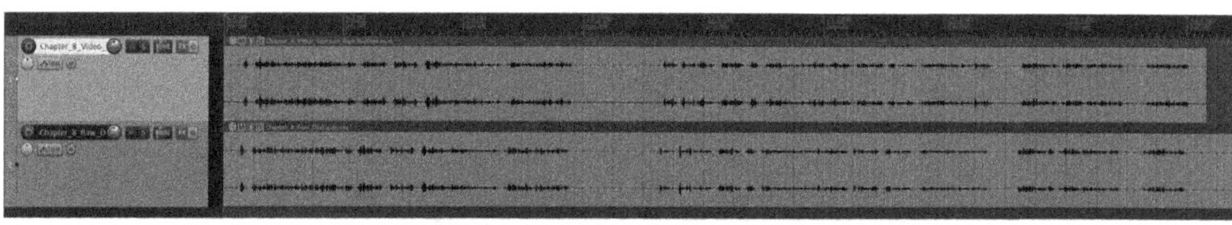

Figure 8.17 – Our video and audio are still out of sync

To avoid confusion, let's name our tracks `Video` and `Dialog` respectively.

Next, we will disable snapping by pressing *Alt/option* + *S* or clicking the *magnet* icon in our main toolbar, as shown in *Figure 8.18*. This gives us complete freedom of movement to align our audio recording precisely.

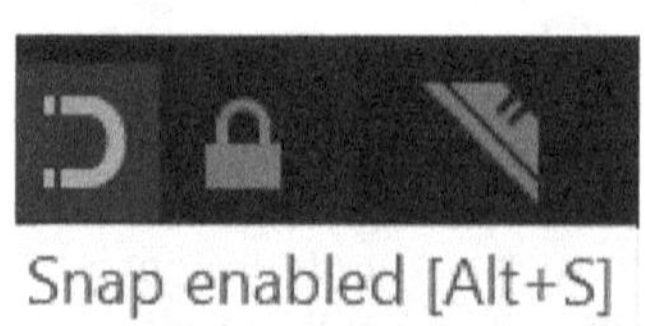

Figure 8.18 – The Snap button

Now, we will zoom in a decent amount and first try to line up the first couple of words *visually* by referencing their waveforms, as shown in *Figure 8.19*. It can be helpful to also increase the track height of the audio track by clicking and dragging the bottom of its track header.

Note that, depending on the camera's position, recording quality, and environmental noise, the waveform of the video file might look quite different. This is why most professional videographers and filmmakers like to start every take with a clap or the famous **clapperboard**, providing an impulse that is easy to align across microphones.

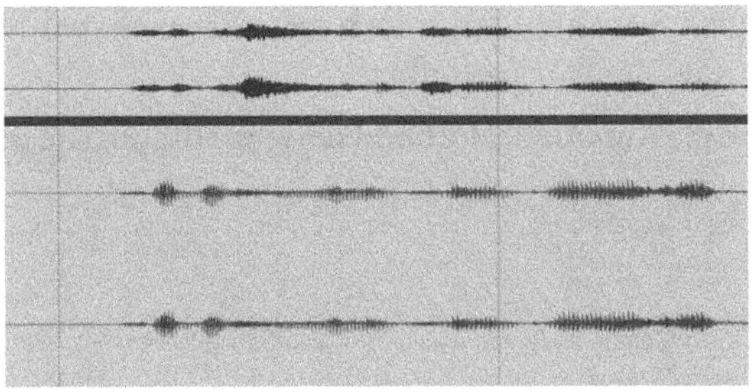

Figure 8.19 – Lining up audio (bottom) and video (top)

Since our video doesn't feature a loud clap, we will have to use both our eyes and ears to find the sweet spot of sync. Once we've roughly aligned the two items visually, we should now play back our project while fine-tuning the position of the audio clip.

While moving the item left and right, we will notice the tonality shifting from what sounds like a slapback echo, to phasing, to, eventually, both tracks sounding like *one source*.

What to do when audio is drifting out of sync

It is not uncommon to be sent video and audio recordings of the same take that will slowly drift out of sync over time. Most often, this is due to the camera operating at 48 kHz while audio has been recorded at 44.1 kHz, which is the default setting on many recorders. The easiest, albeit tedious, way to remedy this is to align the audio in chunks, separated whenever it starts to produce audible artifacts. To do so, we would separate our audio track into several shorter segments and gently nudge them to more closely sync with the audio contained in our video file.

Reducing static background noise using ReaFir

It is rarely the case that onsite or on-set dialog has been recorded in a perfectly quiet environment. The presence of air conditioning systems, city noise, wind, and other environmental factors as well as low-quality mics or recorders can mean that noise reduction will be necessary before our recordings can be processed further.

While most professionals rely on pricey tools, such as **Izotope RX** or **Cedar Studio**, REAPER offers a surprisingly capable, multi-functional plugin called **ReaFir** that can come in handy in these situations.

The **ReaFir** plugin can function as an EQ, a multi-band compressor, and, most importantly, a **denoiser** capable of learning a recording's **noise profile** and subtracting it, resulting in a drastically lowered noise floor.

To get started, let's follow these steps:

1. Add the **ReaFir** plugin to our audio track. Here, we will change our **Mode** to **Subtract** as we want to subtract the noise from our recording.
2. Now, we need to click the **Automatically build noise profile (enable during noise)** checkbox:

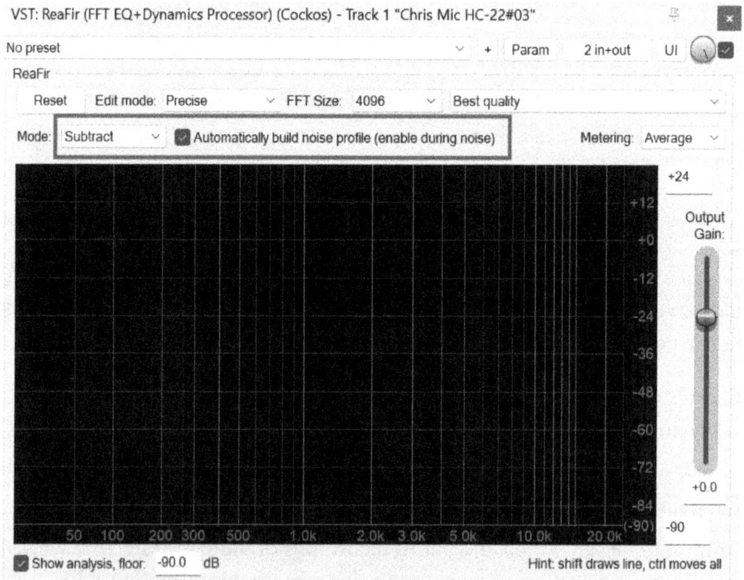

Figure 8.20 – Setting up ReaFir for noise reduction

3. With this checkbox enabled, **ReaFir** will automatically analyze the incoming signal during playback and create a *noise profile*. To capture it, we will have to select a portion of our audio that contains a longer stretch of silence and **no dialog**, as shown in *Figure 8.21*:

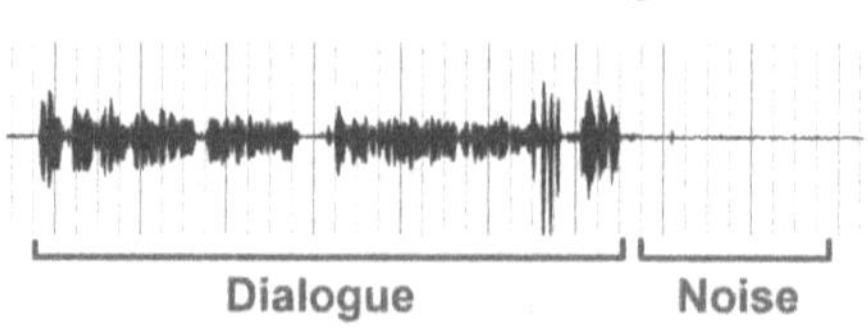

Figure 8.21 – Locating noise in dialog items

> **Note**
>
> The omnipresent background noise in a location is usually referred to as **room tone** by audio professionals. When filming interviews or recording dialog, it is a best practice to record and leave in at least a couple of seconds (ideally between 15 to 30 seconds) of room tone so that background noise can be removed more easily during post-production.

4. With this section selected and **Repeat** enabled, we can briefly play it and should see our spectrum in **ReaFir** look something like this:

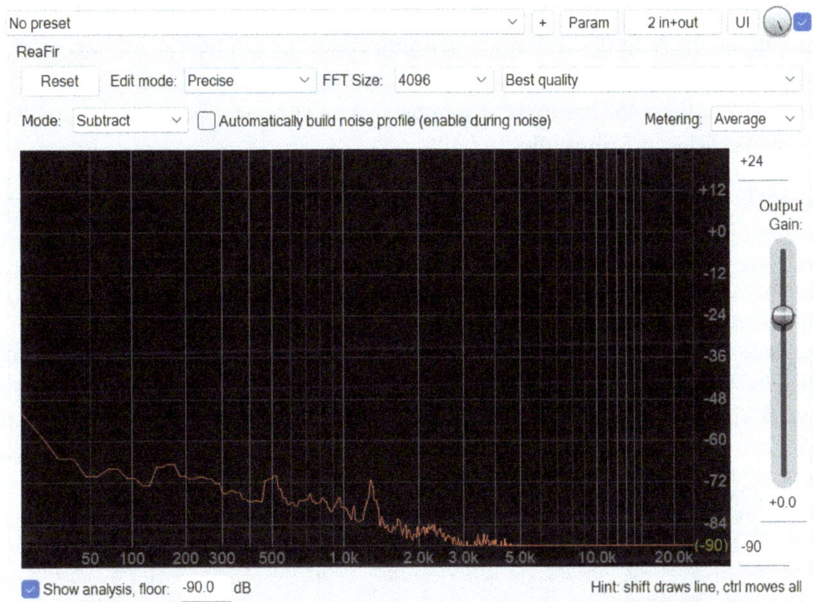

Figure 8.22 – ReaFir after learning a noise profile

The *red* graph represents the frequency distribution of our noise floor, which **ReaFir** just *learned* from us playing back a section with background noise. Before listening to the result, we will have to disable **Automatically build noise profile (enable during noise)** to enter noise reduction mode.

We should now have a recording with a noticeably reduced noise floor throughout. However, it is possible that some artifacts may occur if our background noise changes over time or the room tone snippet available to us is too short.

This side effect can be reduced by pressing *Ctrl/cmd* and dragging the *red noise profile* up or down to increase or decrease the noise threshold. More often than not, this will take manual adjusting until we're satisfied with the balance of signal and noise.

We can always try again by sampling different sections of room tone and seeing which makes for a more universal noise profile. To reset the profile, just click the **Reset** button in the top-right corner of the plugin.

Note that **ReaFir** is not as advanced as other paid noise reduction plugins or restoration apps. However, its subtle artifacts would be masked in any project that also features music, sound effects, or a combination of the two.

Cleaning up dialog with ReaGate

Beyond reducing the overall noise floor, using a gate enables us to now completely strip out any residual noise in between words and sentences. **Gates** are members of the dynamics family, but unlike a compressor, which reduces the loudness of sounds *above* a volume threshold, a gate will reduce or fully eliminate audio *below* the threshold.

ReaGate is a highly capable plugin included with REAPER, which we'll be using to further clean up our dialog.

> **Note**
>
> Not every piece of dialog needs noise reduction and gating and your approach should always be informed by what sounds best and most natural in the overall context of the project you are working on. Decisions about dialog cleanup should always be made *after* an initial listen-through.

Let's bring in **ReaGate** after **ReaFir** in our signal chain and take a look at its parameters:

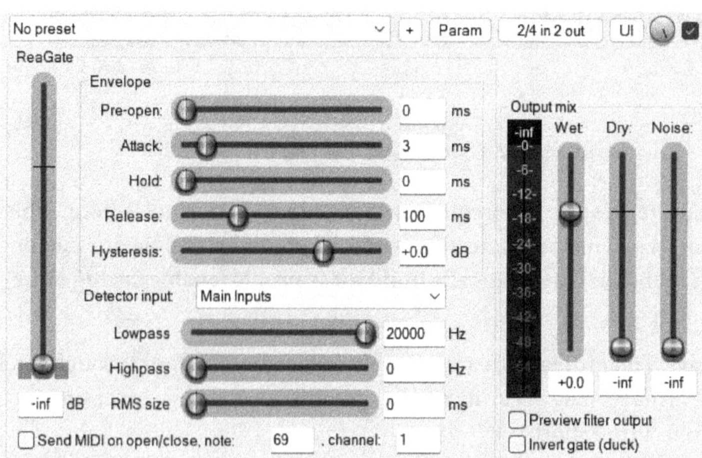

Figure 8.23 – ReaGate plugin

In the following list, we will explore each of the parameters offered by the **ReaGate** plugin:

- **Threshold**: This sets the dB level below which the gate will close.
- **Envelope**:
    - **Pre-open**: This analyzes the input signal ahead of time at the expense of latency. This allows for faster response time.
    - **Attack**: This sets how fast the gate will close when the signal falls below the threshold.
    - **Hold**: This determines how long the gate will remain at its closed state once triggered, regardless of input level.
    - **Release**: This sets how fast the gate will open.
    - **Hysteresis**: This allows the creation of a dB range within which the gate stays open even if the signal falls below the threshold. The threshold range is defined by our threshold +/- **Hysteresis** value.
- **Detector Input**:
    - **Lowpass/Highpass**: This allows filtering of the input signal for detection purposes. This won't affect the sound of our track but allows us to filter out high or low-frequency content to avoid unwanted gate opening. The resulting signal can be previewed by checking **Preview filter output**.
    - **RMS size**: This determines the window of time within which an average dB value is calculated that is then used as the input level value. This can help avoid gate misfires due to short transients or other peaks.
- **Output mix**:
    - **Wet**: Level of signal affected by the gate
    - **Dry**: Level of unaffected input signal
    - **Noise**: This allows for mixing white noise back into the signal to avoid absolute silence when the gate is closed
- **Invert gate (duck)**: It can be used to reference audio otherwise canceled out by the gate.

To find our ideal settings, we'll listen to our dialog and gently increase the **Threshold** setting to find our sweet spot where the gate closes during stretches of silence but not after each and every word.

After this, we will tweak our **Attack** and **Release** times. Very fast settings often result in an unnatural sound and lead to misfires caused by breathing or throat sounds. It is thus best to start with the default attack value and gently increase release first to avoid our dialog sounding *cut off*.

Adding some amount of **Hysteresis** (between -3 to -5 dB) is a best practice to avoid the gate closing unwantedly during slightly quieter segments. Additionally, widening our **RMS size** window to between 1 and 300 ms can help smooth out the gate's response.

Manual cleanup

The part of dialog cleanup we should arguably be most focused on is manual cleanup. Since automated tools lack our understanding of context and storytelling, they will only be able to get us so far before we have to resort to our own ears and sensibilities in order to get the most out of our recordings.

This involves trimming out longer stretches of silence, removing unwanted sounds, such as coughing or microphone handling noise, and *riding* the volume to achieve an even level throughout before applying further processing.

Volume envelopes

It is incredibly rare to receive a piece of recorded dialog that has been performed at a completely steady level, at a steady distance from the microphone, and without the performer moving around; however, that's probably for the best, since we want a performance that feels alive and dynamic rather than one that's clinical and *perfect*.

As such, most dialog recordings will require manual volume adjustments to ensure we get a good level throughout without having to immediately resort to compression and other processing.

These volume adjustments are best applied at the **item level** rather than on the channel fader. The latter can then be used to adjust the dialog volume in the grand context of our project.

REAPER has a very handy feature to automate volume changes for every item called **volume envelope**. These envelopes are similar to automation in the way they are drawn but act directly upon the volume of the item – prior to any signal making its way to our plugin chain and routings. This means they allow us to determine how *hot* our signal is hitting our processing plugins and create an ideal volume curve before adjusting things such as compression.

To show an item's volume envelope, right-click the item and select **Take** | **Take volume envelope** in the context menu, as shown in *Figure 8.24*:

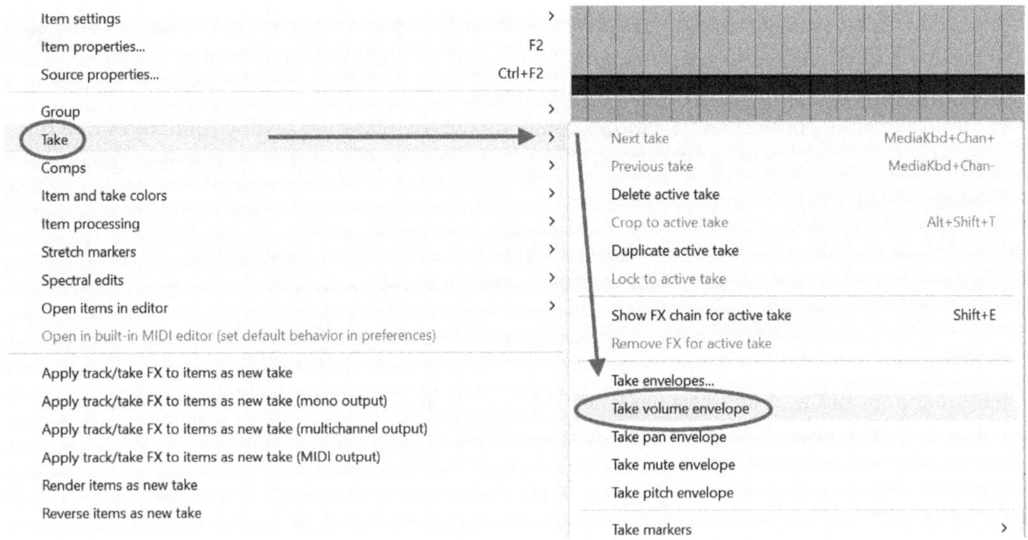

Figure 8.24 – Take envelopes in the item context menu

From here, we can adjust the volume of our dialog throughout by using the same techniques we've previously learned for working with automation. We will have to raise the volume in quieter parts as well as lower it as the level increases when our speaker (me) moves closer to the mic:

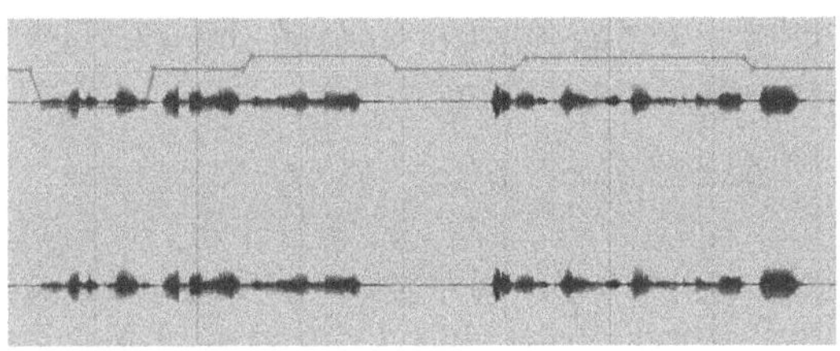

Figure 8.25 – Volume envelope used to even out dialog level

This envelope can also be used to completely mute longer stretches of silence rather than doing so by cutting out sections of audio. While it is slightly more work, this makes it easier to maintain the timing of our dialog if it is to be synced to video.

After editing, we can make sure our video and dialog stay locked together by **grouping** them. To do so, we select both and press *G* on the keyboard.

Voice processing

Now that we have sufficiently cleaned up any undesirable artifacts in our dialog, it is time to make it sound professional through thoughtful processing. Many of the tools used here will be familiar to you from previous chapters and the main difference is the context we're using them in.

Unlike in music, we strive for a less stylized sound with dialog and focus on maintaining constant intelligibility and clarity while supporting our means of storytelling. Occasionally, however, our processing approach will have to be more heavy-handed. Imagine, for example, the character in a short film is wearing a helmet and the other characters in the scene are having difficulties making out what they're saying. Context like this will require more significant processing than characters chatting over a cup of coffee.

In this section, we will explore the fundamentals of dialog processing, general guidelines, as well as some more drastic approaches for situations, such as the one just mentioned.

> **Remember**
>
> Note that none of the absolute values listed are prescriptive and we should always be trusting our ears when adjusting our processing for each speaker's individual voice.

Compression

When compressing dialog, we want to aim for **compression** without *pumping* artifacts. This is done by aiming for between -2 and -4 dB of gain reduction per compressor, using a ratio of 4:1 or below, an **Attack** time between 3 and 20 ms, and setting our **Release** time to a very fast setting under 100 ms.

Should more drastic compression be needed (for example in an action scene), a common technique in audio post-production for film, video games, and other spoken word-focused media is to stack multiple compressors with different settings to *share the load*. This will allow us to create a consistent level without producing overbearing compression artifacts.

De-essing

De-essers are to be used *sparingly* with dialog as harsh settings can lead to a highly processed-sounding tonality and negatively affect intelligibility. In many cases, dialog recorded with a lavalier microphone, as in our example, will not even require any de-essing. Should our voiceover or dialog contain a few *esses* that sound too harsh, they should be treated using the **Take volume envelope** option as described earlier.

For very harsh-sounding recordings, several de-essers with milder settings can again be stacked in a load-sharing matter to tame sibilance without producing an artificial lisp.

EQ

Equalization for dialog follows similar principles as compression: Intelligibility and natural tonality are key. Our brains are especially good at picking up on weird resonances and aggressive EQ moves on speaking voices since we listen to them every day of our lives. As such, it's important to regularly reference other, professional media (film, podcasts, videos, TV shows) to avoid *EQ fatigue* and retain objectivity.

The bulk of our EQ moves should be subtractive, with boosting only used if our voice recordings are distinctly lacking in a certain frequency band.

The ideal high-pass filter frequencies discussed in *Chapter 4* apply here as well. Where our approach will likely differ is in how we treat our low-pass filter. As, unlike in pop music, dialog often does not benefit from ultra-crisp high-end, it is commonplace to filter it quite aggressively – some post-production veterans even set their filters as low as 10 kHz. This may sound radical on its own but is commonplace in most Hollywood movies.

This practice helps reduce noise and raspiness while making it easier to ensure a constant tonality across different microphones. *Figure 8.26* shows an example of what the EQ curve looks like when aiming for a balanced, natural dialog sound:

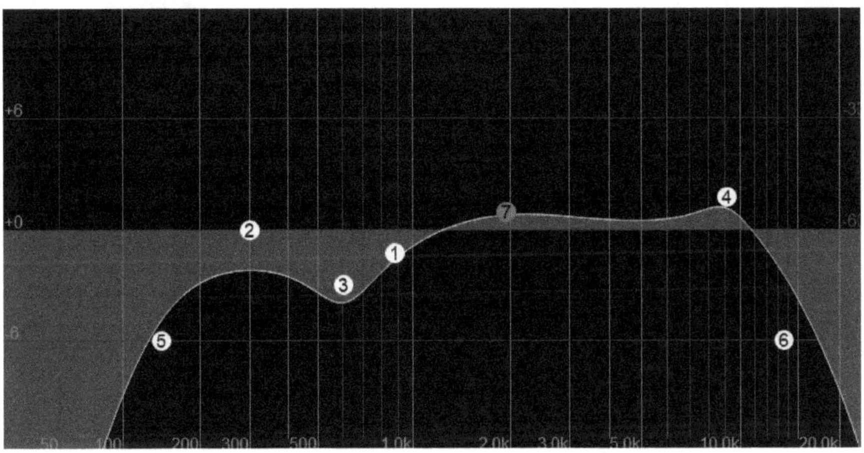

Figure 8.26 – Example EQ curve for the included audio recording

Reverb

The use of **reverb** for dialog is largely contextual as the location we are trying to portray is the key factor in choosing our reverb type. For isolated voices in podcasts, for example, a very subtle room reverb can help make our speakers sound like they're in the same space and aid intelligibility. If our character finds themselves in a chapel, we can utilize a reverb with a **long decay time** to *sell* that location more effectively.

Like with music, reverbs are best kept on **buses** (as sends) so they can be used across multiple tracks.

Handling music post-production for video

When working with music tracks in projects that feature video, sound effects, and possible dialog, we usually receive either finished recordings that are mixed and mastered, or **stems**, which are individual stereo files containing different instrument groups that create the original mix when played together.

Grouping stems

When working with stems, it's important to import them at once and select **Same time position on separate tracks** in the import dialog that opens when dragging them onto our timeline. Next, we want to make sure to group the individual stems by selecting them and pressing *G*. This will link them together and apply edits and movements across all of the items.

We then place them in a folder by selecting their tracks, right-clicking them, and selecting **Move tracks to folder | New folder track**, as shown in *Figure 8.27*:

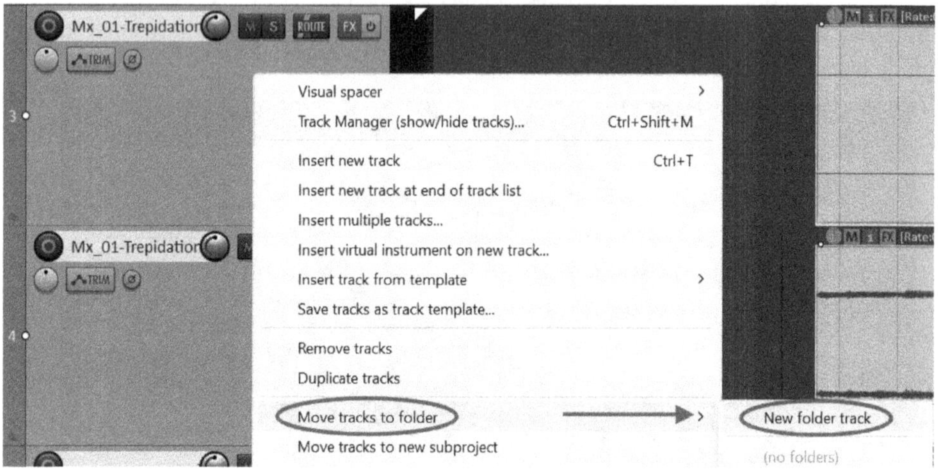

Figure 8.27 – Adding tracks to a folder

The resulting folder track will let you automate volume and other parameters for the sum of the music. The mix of all parts can then be tweaked by adjusting the individual channels.

Manual ducking

When a piece of media features both dialog and music, a best practice is to *lower* the music volume when dialog occurs and *raise* it slightly during sections without voice. This way, we can avoid awkward low-volume sections and maintain a natural flow to the narrative.

There is no definitive answer to how many dB to reduce music during dialog as it is highly dependent on the *tonality* and *intelligibility* of the dialog in question. Generally, when both dialog and music are playing, your overall project loudness should fall somewhere between -23 LUFS (a widely accepted standard for movies and video games and -14 LUFS (YouTube's current loudness target).

As discussed in *Chapter 5*, this can be measured with the **JS: Loudness Meter Peak/RMS/LUFS** plugin.

Side chaining

For content that is less story-driven, such as a podcast or online video that features background music during select parts, **side-chaining** can be a sufficient means of balancing voice and music levels.

By placing an instance of **ReaComp** on our *music (folder) track* and creating a routing connection by dragging the **Routing** button of our *dialog track* onto it, we can then switch **Detector input** to **Auxiliary inputs**. This will use our dialog as the signal triggering **ReaComp**'s detection algorithm.

By lowering the **Threshold** setting until our dialog begins attenuating our music and setting a fairly long **Release** time (500 – 2,000 ms or beyond), we can achieve ducking of the music whenever dialog occurs while making sure the music level recovers slowly – avoiding the *pumping* effect more appropriate in music.

Spotting sound effects and processing them

This brief section will explore bringing pre-made sound effects into our project and synchronizing them with events in our video. *Chapter 11* will dive deeper into sound effects creation and workflow considerations for film and games.

Sourcing sound effects

Free sound effects are commonplace all over the internet and can be sourced from many different websites. The important thing to note here is to be looking for sound effects that are *royalty-free* and can be used for *commercial projects* or fall under the CC-0 tier of the Creative Commons license. Any type of content created either as paid work or released with monetization enabled falls under commercial use.

Free sound effects for commercial and personal usage can be found at the following websites:

- **Freesound**: `https://freesound.org/search/` (be sure to select **Creative Commons 0** under licenses)
- **Sonniss**: `https://sonniss.com/gameaudiogdc`

Additionally, platforms such as **Soundly**, **Pro Sound Effects**, **Sound Particles Explorer**, and **Splice** offer cloud subscriptions that include large catalogs of professional-quality downloadable sound effects that can be used in commercial projects.

Sound effect "food groups"

To make mixing our sound effects easier, it is recommended to group them by category, or *food group*. These can range from general categories, such as ambiance, footsteps, explosions, and vehicles, to being grouped by individual characters onscreen. By grouping these tracks in folder tracks, we can control the volume of individual categories of sounds depending on their importance at any given moment.

Nudging

While we can easily drag our sound effects around on the timeline and reference our video to loosely synchronize them, most of the time, we will require greater precision.

To nudge an item is to move it left or right by a **predefined increment** in order to more precisely synchronize it to other events on our timeline – most commonly important **sound effects moments** in video content. Naturally, the ideal increment to choose when working with video is *frames*.

To do so, we'll press *N* or click **Edit** | **Nudge/Set Items**, which will open the nudging dialog. When clicking the right drop-down menu, we can select **frames** as our unit of measurement, as shown in *Figure 8.28*:

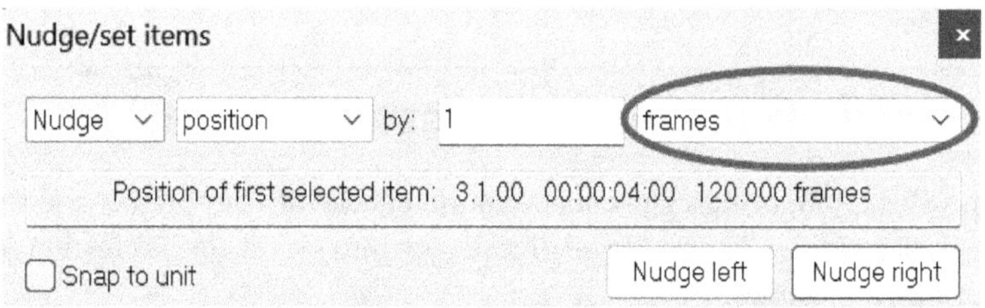

Figure 8.28 – The nudging dialog

From here, by clicking **Nudge left** or **Nudge right**, we can move our selected items on a per-frame basis while referencing our video to achieve perfect sync. These commands can also be assigned to keyboard shortcuts using the methods described in *Chapter 6*.

The actions to look for are **Item edit: Nudge left/right by last nudge dialog settings**.

Panning and spatialization

To reflect where a sound is coming from onscreen, panning is essential but should never be too drastic. A common rule of thumb in cinema is to never pan any sound effects *more than 60%* to each side of the stereo spectrum to avoid making the audience look away from the screen.

Similarly, most dialog in a cinematic context tends to be located entirely within the **center channel** of the surround mix unless its movement offscreen is directly relevant to the story.

To simulate distance, we can decrease a sound's volume, increase the amount of the signal sent to reverb (making it sound roomier), and gently roll off some high frequencies – simulating the natural air absorption of high-frequency energy over distance. A gentle low-pass filter will often do the trick, as shown in *Figure 8.29*:

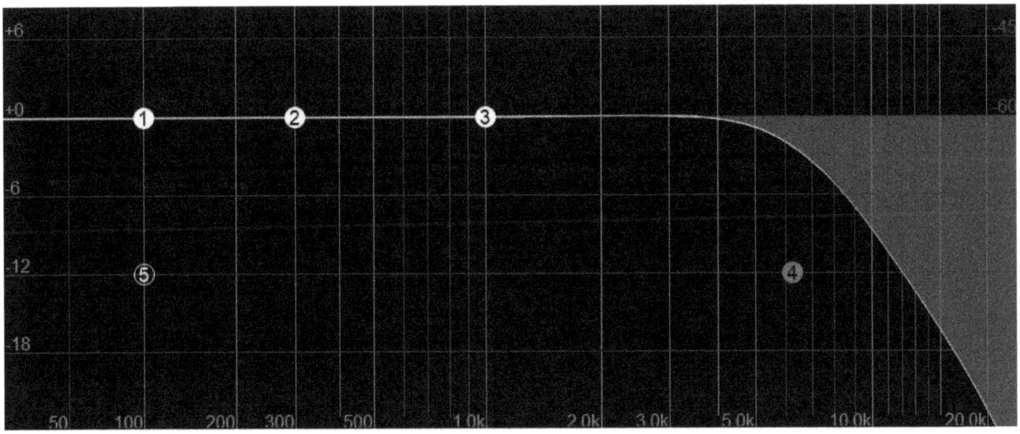

Figure 8.29 – Low-pass filter simulating high-frequency falloff over distance

With these essential techniques, we can process music and dialog alongside video effectively and tackle a wide range of projects that might come our way. Our final step in working on any video-based project will be rendering a new video file that contains all the new audio we've created.

Rendering video files

To finally render a video file of our work, we once again head into the **Render** window (*Ctrl*/*cmd* + *Alt* + *R*) and pick one of the following formats in the **Primary output format** tab:

- **Video (ffmpeg/libav encoder)**: This encoder offers the greatest flexibility but requires some experience with digital video formats to configure appropriately. We should avoid this one when just starting out.
- **MPEG-4/Windows Media** (Windows only): This encoder is greatly simplified and allows for easy creation of industry-standard videos encoded using the **h.264** compression algorithm.
- **AVFoundation** (Mac only): It provides a simple means to render `.m4v` or `.mov` video files.

When selecting one of the latter two encoders, it is crucial to match the original video file's format specifications (i.e., its *resolution* and *framerate*).

Similarly, we will want to set an appropriately high video bitrate in the **Video** line to avoid aggressive compression artifacts that would otherwise make our video look grainy and blurry. For `720` p video at 30 fps, we want our bitrate to be at least 2,000 kbps, twice that amount for a `1080` p video at the same framerate.

If our video is intended to be the final product of our project, it's best to err on the side of caution and export at a rather high bitrate, as shown in *Figure 8.30*:

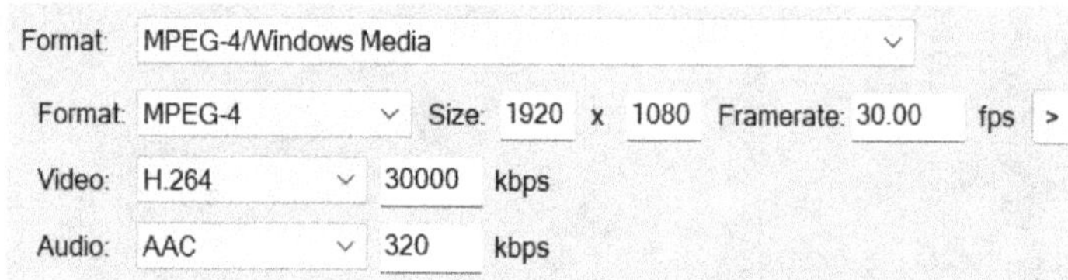

Figure 8.30 – Example settings for a high-quality export at 30 fps

This allows the proprietary encoders of platforms, such as YouTube or Vimeo, to work their best after we've uploaded our video.

To allow for the export of videos at near-lossless quality, allowing for color grading and heavier video processing later on, the FFmpeg codec allows for higher-quality compression methods, as shown in *Figure 8.31*:

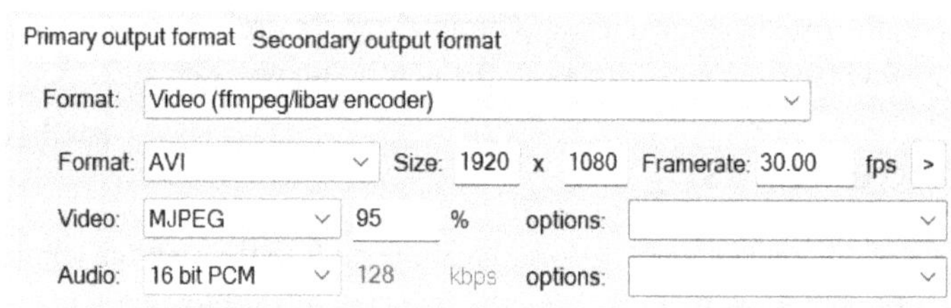

Figure 8.31 – Utilizing MJPEG compression

When selecting `Video (ffmpeg/libav encoder)` as our **Format** and `AVI` as our format wrapper, we will have the option of choosing `MJPEG` as our video codec.

MJPEG, short for **Motion-JPEG**, is a high-quality video codec derived from the JPEG image compression algorithm and is a popular archival format for video as it can maintain near-lossless video quality while being resource-efficient for playback devices and achieving smaller file sizes than fully uncompressed formats. Furthermore, we can also include uncompressed *PCM audio*, allowing ourselves and our collaborators to work with a truly lossless version of the audio we created alongside the video.

> **Important note**
>
> Note that if we export in this or one of the available lossless formats, our video cannot be played back properly in all common media players any longer and will require further encoding to a consumer codec (such as `h.264` or `h.265`) via a video editing app before being able to be distributed to video platforms or consumers.

Summary

In this chapter, we have explored the ins and outs of working with video in REAPER and touched on the fundamental principles of dialog, music, and sound effects processing, which will carry through to subsequent chapters on podcast production and sound design. Additionally, we learned how to perform essential video editing tasks right inside the DAW, using REAPER's uniquely comprehensive video toolset to our advantage.

These skills are essential for any audio professional as video content is now more widespread than ever. By being able to craft professional-quality audio to accompany just about any type of video, these skills will help you diversify your opportunities in the audio industry.

In the next chapter, we will be tackling music production techniques that will take us through the life cycle of a song from its initial idea all the way to a release-ready master.

Part 3: Specialized Applications

In this part, you will learn specialized techniques and procedures for certain types of audio projects, such as music production, podcast production, film and video game audio, as well as immersive sound. Additionally, you will learn best practices for working with audio and solving common problems in REAPER.

This part has the following chapters:

- *Chapter 9, Music Production Techniques*
- *Chapter 10, Podcast Production Workflows*
- *Chapter 11, Sound Design for Film and Games*
- *Chapter 12, Exploring Immersive Audio*
- *Chapter 13, Optimizing the Workflow and Troubleshooting in REAPER*

9

Music Production Techniques

In this chapter, we will see examples of REAPER being used for music production. Music production is one of the areas where REAPER can take full advantage of all its features.

With the information in this chapter, you will learn how to use REAPER to perform advanced mixing techniques used in music production. Additionally, you will learn the principles for creating musical ideas using MIDI programming.

This chapter will cover the following main topics:

- **Pre-production of a song**: You will learn the steps involved in the music pre-production process
- **Recording and producing the right sound**: You will learn how to use REAPER to record and find the right sound in a music production
- **Editing vocals and instruments**: You will learn techniques and tools to edit vocals and instruments that have been recorded
- **Classic music mixing techniques**: You will learn important and widely used techniques during the mixing of a music production
- **Mastering music for distribution**: You will learn the key points to consider when mastering and preparing a music production for distribution in modern media

By the end of this chapter, you will have seen how you can use REAPER to carry out a complete music production, from start to finish, applying various techniques used in professional productions.

Technical requirements

This chapter addresses music production starting from scratch and using only REAPER's native tools, so no additional materials are needed.

In order to implement the project in the chapter, you can download the following items from the `Chapter 9` folder of the book's GitHub repository at `https://github.com/PacktPublishing/Elevate-your-audio-production-with-Reaper`:

- Sample audio loops
- Audio phrase for editing vocals

Pre-production of a song

The traditional music production process involves three main stages:

1. **Pre-production**: This is the initial stage where basic ideas about the type of music, composition, instruments, arrangement, and so on are established. It is equivalent to creating a blueprint for building something. In this stage, REAPER is a very useful tool for starting to bring musical ideas to life.
2. **Production**: This is the stage where the recording or generation of the production's content takes place. Here, takes are made, and the best sound is sought for the original idea created in pre-production.
3. **Post-production**: This is the final stage, where the editing, mixing, and mastering of the recorded material is done. The quality of the result of this stage depends on the quality of the previous stages.

Each of these stages involves paying attention to specific details, as we will see throughout this chapter. Each of these stages contributes characteristics that will help shape the result of the music. First, let's look at how the music production process has been carried out over the past decades to understand its evolution and how we can approach the process in REAPER.

Traditional production stages

We say *traditional production stages* because they have commonly been carried out when producing music for decades. However, it is important to clarify that today, music production has become very dynamic, largely due to technological advances. For example, years ago, it was necessary to rent or own a professional recording studio to carry out the recordings of a production, due to the specialized and expensive equipment it entailed. Now, a complete production process can be done entirely using just a computer in an ordinary room.

On the other hand, in traditional production, it was common to have specialized personnel in each area: a songwriter, arranger, recording engineer, mixing engineer, and so on. Nowadays, it is very common for many of these roles to be carried out by the same person. In fact, the democratization of music production has allowed artists to carry out the production of their musical ideas completely by themselves, taking full control of the production process.

In this sense, we will see the process step by step. However, we will leave it up to each music producer to decide to what degree they want to get involved in each of the production stages, or whether they'd prefer to delegate some of them to other more experienced people.

Similarly, the order of the production process presented in this chapter is not an unbreakable rule. Music production is a creative process that allows for *skipping steps* or carrying out different stages in an order different from the one presented here. For example, someone might use effects and automation (typical mixing processes) in the pre-production stage while composing the musical piece. In the real world, it is valid to experiment in different ways if it leads to a satisfactory result.

Starting with pre-production

To carry out the examples in this chapter, we will start with a new project. The first step in musical creation is usually to decide what type of time signature we will use, as well as the tempo.

The most common time signature is **4/4**, but we can also create music in **3/4**, **2/4**, **6/8**, or any other time signature. The type of time signature depends on the rhythm we want to use.

> **Further reading**
> An explanation of the characteristics of each time signature goes beyond the objectives of this book. However, you can learn more about it at `https://www.oxfordmusiconline.com/grovemusic`.

In this project, we will choose a `4/4` time signature and a tempo of `95` BPM, adjusting these parameters in the spaces marked in *Figure 9.1*:

Figure 9.1 – Selecting the time signature and tempo

It is a good idea to listen to the tempo we choose to make sure it suits our musical idea. To listen to the click of our project, we activate the **metronome**, which is marked in the toolbar of *Figure 9.2*:

Figure 9.2 – Activating the metronome

In this way, if we play the project, we will hear a repeated clicking noise that marks the tempo. If we want to, we can adjust the tempo to suit our musical idea.

If we right-click on the *metronome* icon, the options shown in *Figure 9.3* will appear, allowing us to adjust the click volume and indicate whether we want to hear the clicking when playing the project or only when recording, among other options.

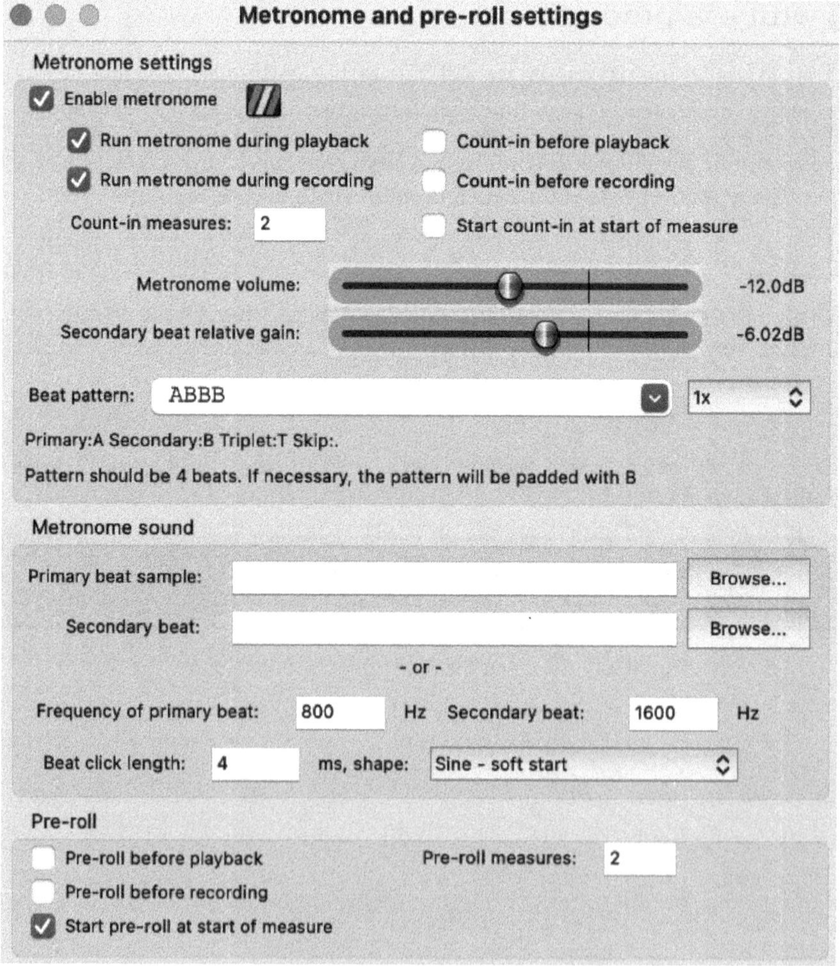

Figure 9.3 – Metronome settings

Once we have the tempo and time signature we want for our music, we can start the musical creation, either by recording audio or by programming MIDI notes.

Recording and producing the right sound

Let's begin the process of recording and adjusting the sounds to ensure they fit the project. We'll start with a basic rhythm, then add harmony and melody.

Creating a basic rhythm

Rhythm is the first element in musical creation, from which melody and harmony derive. The rhythmic base usually involves percussion instruments such as drums, shakers, tambourines, and so on, or electronic percussion using synthesized percussion or loops.

In this case, we'll use synthesized percussion and create a new track with a virtual instrument using the **Track | Insert virtual instrument on new track** command. This brings up the plugin selection window, where we'll choose the **ReaSynDr (Cockos) (4 out)** plugin from the **Cockos** category. REAPER will ask whether we want to add tracks for this effect, which we will confirm.

The **ReaSynDr** plugin is a simple percussion sound synthesizer that we'll use to create a basic rhythm. As shown in *Figure 9.4*, the **ReaSynDr** plugin is very straightforward and doesn't offer options to modify the percussion sounds. By opening the **Virtual MIDI keyboard** with the *Alt* + *B* command, or using a connected MIDI controller, we can hear the four percussion sounds of **ReaSynDr** by playing the C3, C#3, D3, and D#3 notes.

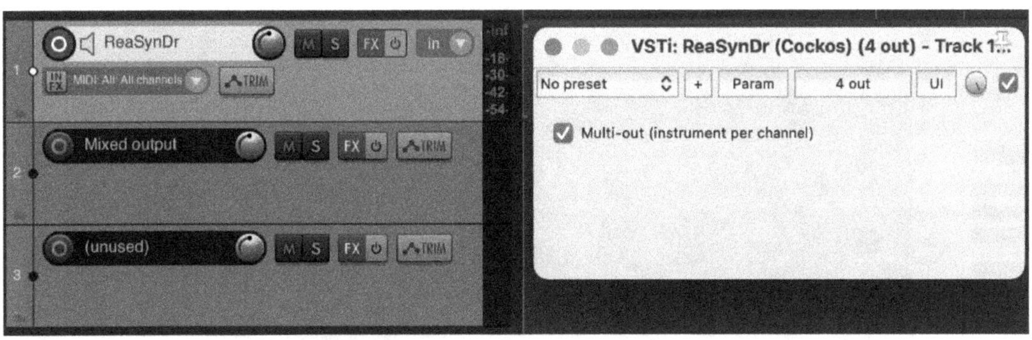

Figure 9.4 – ReaSynDr plugin

Now, we can input MIDI notes either by recording in real time while following the metronome clicks or by programming our rhythm, as shown next.

To program a rhythm using MIDI notes, we insert a MIDI item with the **Insert** | **New MIDI item** command. This creates an empty item in the **ReaSynDr** track. By double-clicking this item, we enter the **MIDI editor**, which displays the names of the four **ReaSynDr** sounds: **Kick**, **Snare**, **Blip**, and **Tick**, as shown in *Figure 9.5*:

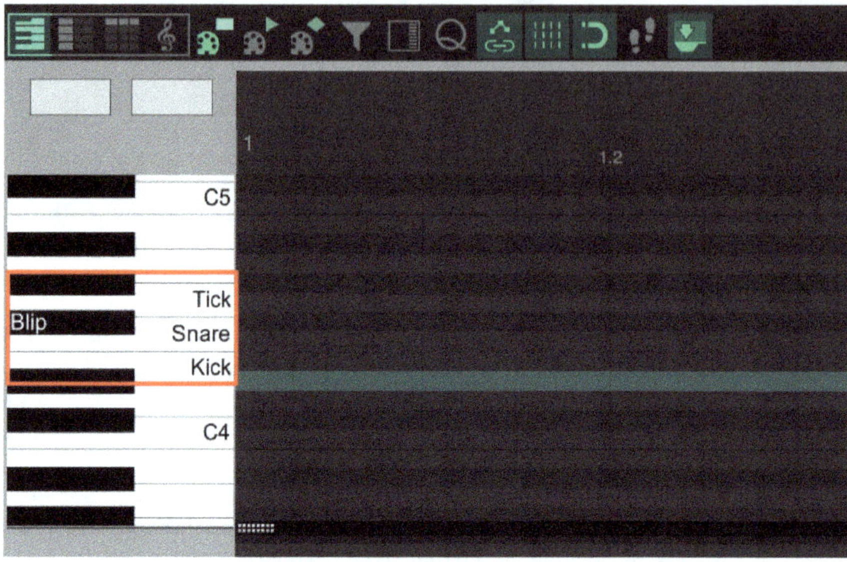

Figure 9.5 – ReaSynDr sounds

With these four sounds, we can create interesting rhythmic patterns. For instance, we can create a rhythm such as the one shown in *Figure 9.6*:

Figure 9.6 – Basic pop rhythm

Note that the **Grid** and **Notes** values are set to **1/16**, making note insertion easier. Also, the **Velocity** values at the bottom of the notes vary to give more groove to the rhythm, since uniform velocity makes the rhythm sound too flat. These decisions are subjective and can be adjusted according to taste or musical intention.

Although this rhythmic pattern lasts for only one measure, we will duplicate or copy it to cover two measures, as two-measure phrases work well as a base for many popular music genres.

If you listen to this rhythm, you'll notice that some sounds come from the left and others from the right. This is the default panning assignment of **ReaSynDr**. Let's see how to reassign these buses to change the panning.

Changing the panning

ReaSynDr has four percussion sounds, so the intention is to assign each sound to a different track to control the volume and panning of each sound individually.

To do this, we create two new tracks with the **Track | Insert new track** command. We then rename tracks **2** through **5** to **Kick**, **Snare**, **Blip**, and **Tick**, as shown in *Figure 9.7*:

Figure 9.7 – Renaming ReaSynDr tracks

Next, we left-click the area marked in *Figure 9.7* to show the routing menu of the track, as seen in *Figure 9.8*:

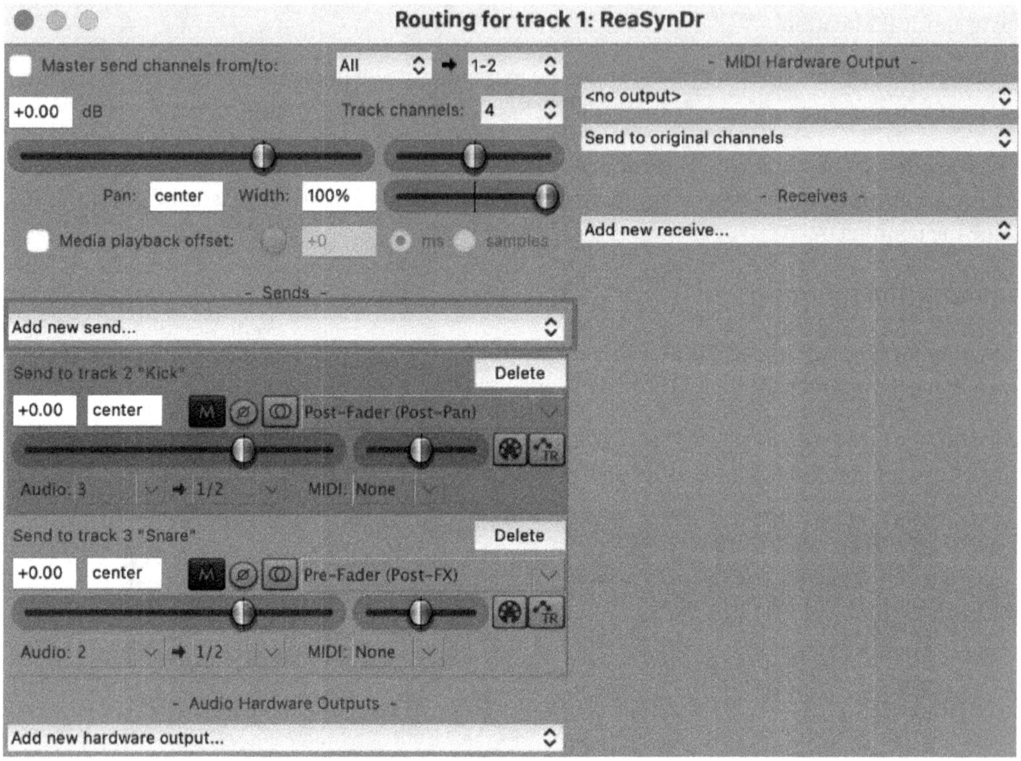

Figure 9.8 – Track routing window

In the **Routing for track 1: ReaSynDr** window, we add two new **Send** instances to the section marked in *Figure 9.8*. These will go to the **Blip** and **Tick** tracks. The purpose of these is to route the four **ReaSynDr** channels to four different tracks.

Once the sends are created, we assign them, as shown in *Figure 9.9*:

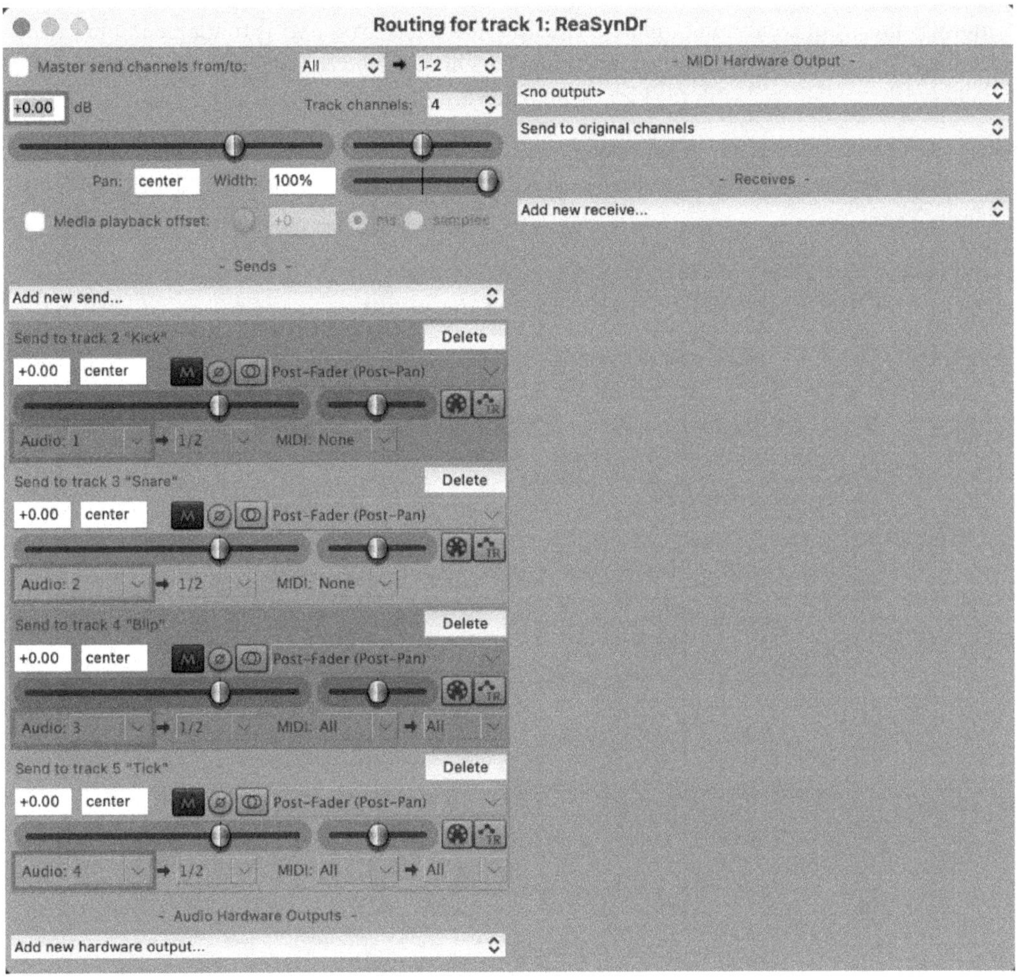

Figure 9.9 – Assigning track sends

In the **Audio** sections marked in *Figure 9.9*, we select **Mono source** and channels **1**, **2**, **3**, and **4**. This function sends each of the four **ReaSynDr** channels to each of our session tracks, allowing control over the volume and panning of each percussion sound. The next step is to adjust the volume and panning of the percussion sounds to achieve a proper balance, as explained in *Chapter 4*.

Once we have balanced the percussion sounds, the next step is to create a bass line.

Creating a bass line

Harmony is the art of combining different musical notes. The bass part is fundamental in music production as it provides the harmonic foundation. Bass lines should complement the rhythmic base, generally synchronizing well with the kick drum pattern.

The bass part can be played by various instruments, such as electric bass, double bass, synth bass, tuba, bassoon, and so on. In this case, we'll create a synth bass line using REAPER's included tools, specifically **ReaSynth**.

We create a new track with a virtual instrument, inserting **ReaSynth**. It's good practice to name each new track in a project appropriately, so we'll name this track `Bass`.

In ReaSynth, we select the **Square Bass** preset, as shown in *Figure 9.10*:

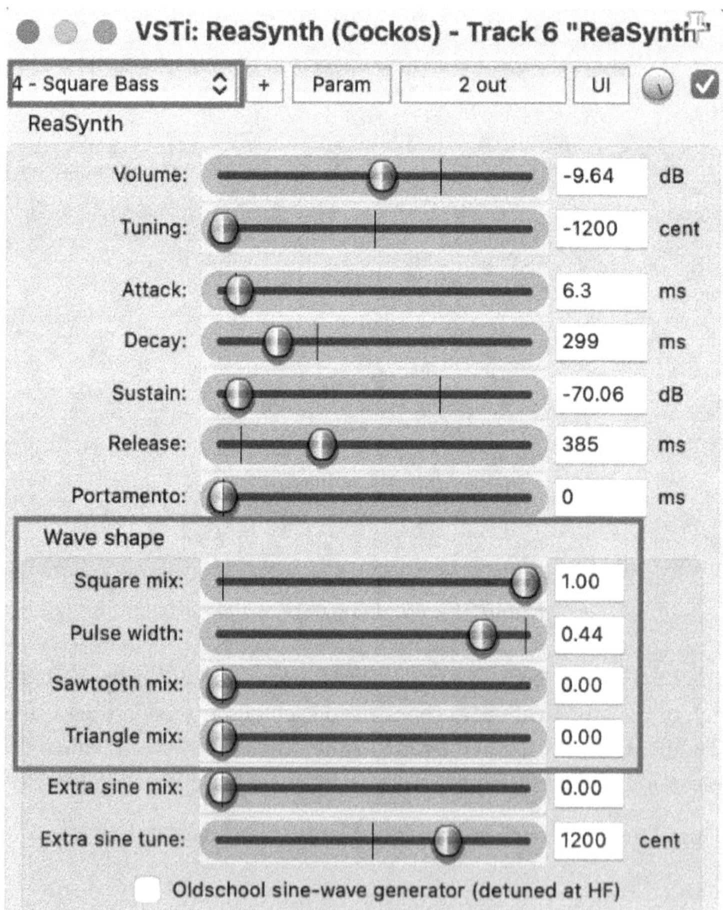

Figure 9.10 – ReaSynth bass preset

The **Square Bass** preset provides a synthesized bass sound using a square wave. Manipulating this sound in depth requires synthesis knowledge beyond this book's scope.

> **Further reading**
>
> You can read about synthesis and sound design at `https://www.soundonsound.com/series/synth-secrets-sound-sound`.

However, we can experiment by moving the **Wave shape** sliders marked in *Figure 9.10*, adjusting the sound balance. Each of these components contributes different characteristics to the final sound. Let's understand these in more detail:

- **Square mix**: It adjusts the square wave component in the sound
- **Pulse width**: It controls the width of the square wave pulse
- **Sawtooth mix**: It modifies the sawtooth wave component in the sound
- **Triangle mix**: It changes the triangle wave component in the sound

Once we have a pleasing sound, we can create a bass line by either playing and recording in real time or programming MIDI notes, as follows:

1. Create an empty MIDI item in the **Bass** track using the **Insert** | **New MIDI item** command.
2. Double-click the MIDI item to enter the **MIDI editor**.
3. Adjust the item's length to cover two measures (from the start of measure **1** to the start of measure **3**), as shown in *Figure 9.11*. Using two-measure phrases is an effective technique in music composition for structuring the composition.

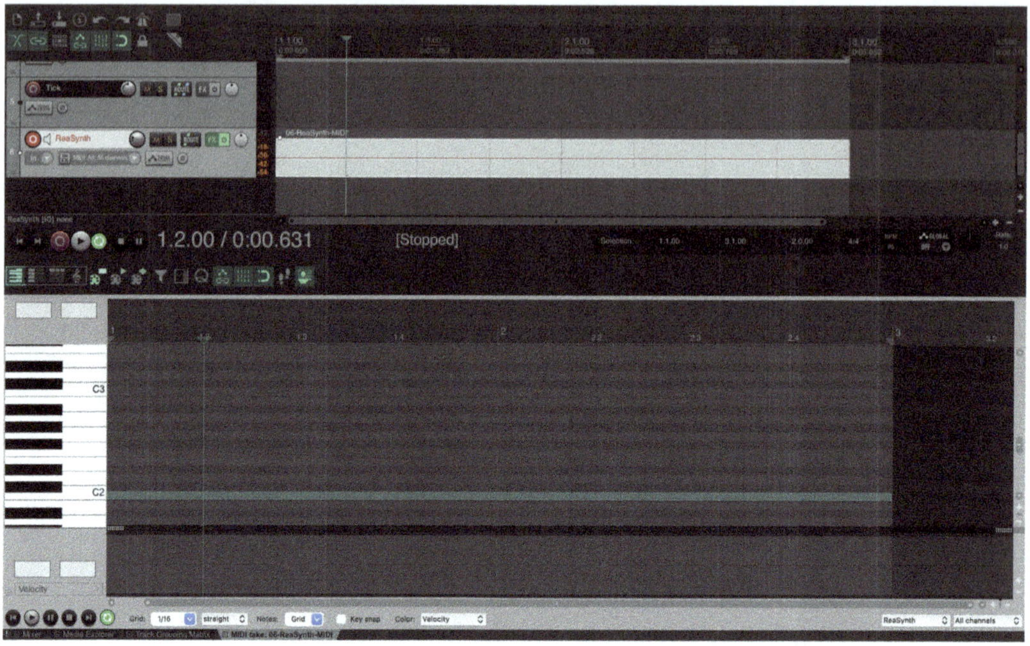

Figure 9.11 – Creating an empty MIDI item

Now it's time to input the notes. We can use a variety of **musical scales** as a basis for creating bass lines. However, to simplify things for those without knowledge of music theory, we'll focus on using only the white piano keys. This will result in music in the key of C major or A minor.

Bass lines typically are low-pitched, so it's recommended to restrict our notes to octave 2. Therefore, we'll base our bass pattern on the A2 note, referencing the kick rhythm, since the bass line should complement the kick pattern. This is shown in *Figure 9.12*:

Figure 9.12 – Bass line MIDI notes

> **Important note**
>
> The velocity of each note has been adjusted to vary the volume and enhance the groove. Experimenting with different velocity values and listening to the results is encouraged.

With a rhythmic base and a bass line, we can now add a harmonic element, creating chords.

Creating a harmonic pad

Technically, the bass provides a harmonic foundation in music. However, another element is needed to generate more notes to form chords. In this case, we'll use another synth sound to create a harmonic pad that provides the chords for our project.

First, add a new track with **ReaSynth**, naming it `Pad`. In **ReaSynth**, select the **Sustained** preset and make some adjustments to the sliders, as shown in *Figure 9.13*:

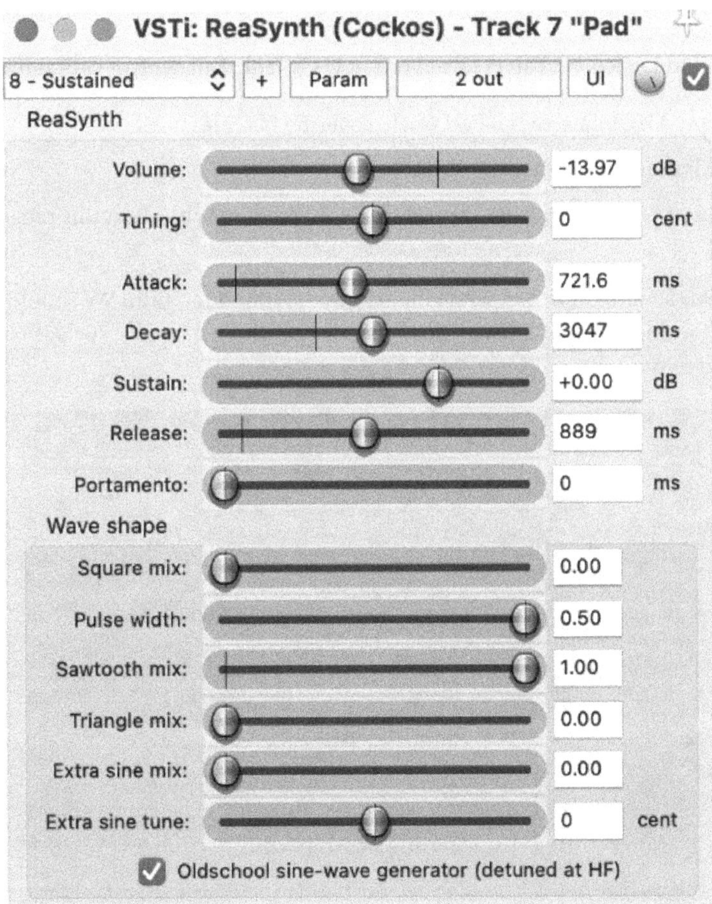

Figure 9.13 – Parameters of a pad sound

The adjustments needed in **ReaSynth** for a pad sound are discussed as follows. These settings are a starting point and can be tweaked according to personal preference:

- **Attack** (`700` *ms*): This time allows the sound to reach its maximum volume gradually. A longer attack time results in a slower sound response.
- **Decay** (`3000` *ms*): This is the time it takes for the sound to decay slightly.
- **Sustain** (`0` *dB*): This is the volume of the sound while the note continues to play.
- **Release** (`900` *ms*): This is the time it takes for the sound to fade out when the note is released.
- **Wave shape** (**Sawtooth**): For this pad sound, we'll use only the **Sawtooth** component for a fuller sound.

The **Attack**, **Decay**, **Sustain**, and **Release** parameters are also known as the **ADSR envelope**. These parameters are very common in most synthesizers and help control how a sound changes after it is triggered.

With this basic sound loaded, we can create chord notes by either playing or programming them:

1. Add an empty MIDI item to the **Pad** track, covering two measures.
2. Double-click the item to enter the **MIDI editor**.
3. Chord notes generally work best around C4, so create some chords in this range, as shown in *Figure 9.14*.

   Lower chords sound too dense, while higher chords sound too thin. We should stick to *white piano keys* for this example. Create chords by playing alternate notes, such as C, E, G; D, F, A; E, G, B, and so on.

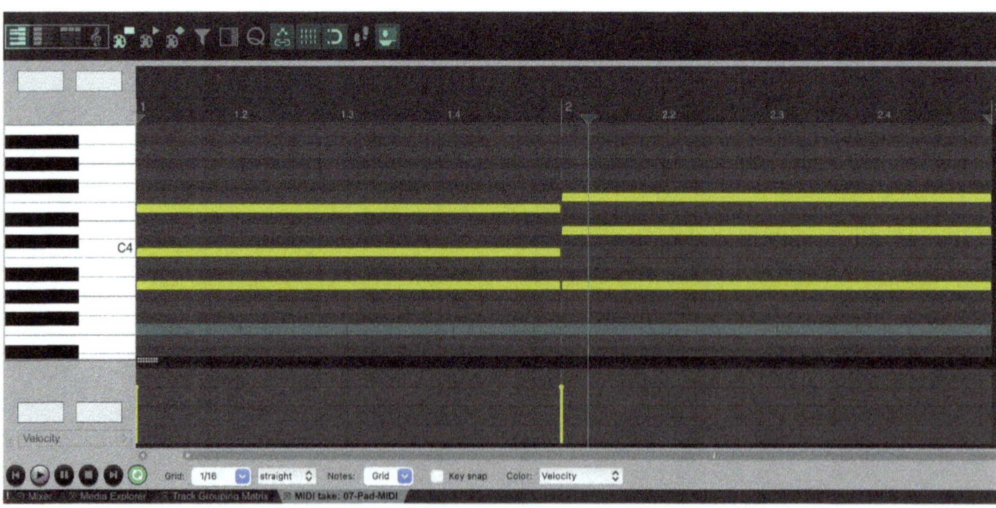

Figure 9.14 – Creating chord notes

In this case, since the bass line is based on note A, we will use chords that include that note. In the first measure, we have chosen the notes A, C, and E, which form the A minor chord. In the second measure, we have chosen the notes D, F, and A, which form the D minor chord.

A good practice when voicing **chord progressions** is to keep the common notes between chords and change the other notes with minimal movement (voice leading). In this case, note A is common to both chords and is therefore left in the same voice (the lowest voice), while note C moves to D, and note E moves to F.

There are many other possible chords that we could use that could also work, but we will leave that to your musical knowledge and judgment.

Now that we have several musical elements, we need to adjust their volume with the faders of each track to create a proper balance between the sounds. Once this is done, we can explore the options we have for creating a melody.

Creating a melody

The **melody** is the main musical element of a composition. Melodies consist of patterns of notes and rests that are related to each other, which gives cohesion to the musical idea. The melody can be the initial element in a musical production, and we can generate the other elements from there. However, the melody can also be created from a rhythmic and harmonic base, as we have worked on in this chapter.

To create a melody, we will use a new track with the **ReaSynth** synthesizer and choose the preset called **Belly**, which generates a bell-like sound. Then we will create an empty MIDI item to add notes to it.

The notes of the melody usually work best in the range between **G3** and **G5**, depending a lot on the type of sound being used. It is also common to base the melody on a musical scale; in this case, we are using the A minor scale (white piano keys), so we will only use these notes.

Using motifs

A common technique for creating melodic phrases is to use motifs. A **motif** is a small melodic structure, of two to four notes, that serves as the basis for creating a longer phrase.

Figure 9.15 shows an example of a motif; in this case, the motif includes the note A, which is the root of the scale we are using, and two other notes of the scale.

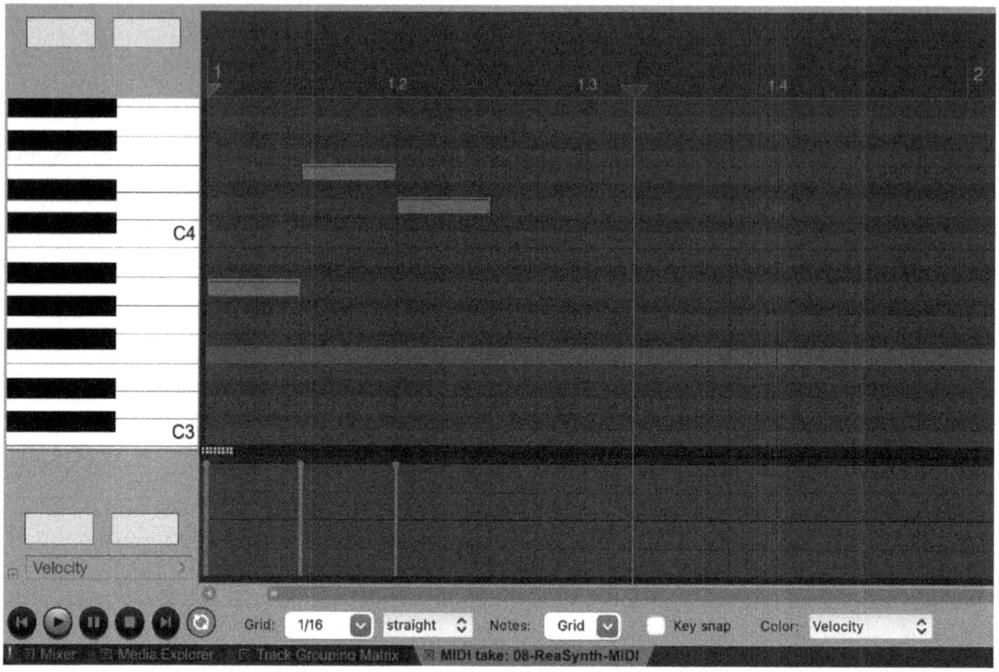

Figure 9.15 – Creating a motif

The choice of which notes to use, as well as their duration, can be different from what is shown. This is where musical creativity lies, as there are many different possibilities. The idea we must remember when deciding is that the motif will be the *basic cell* of our melody.

Once we have a motif that we like, we can do several things to form a longer phrase. *Figure 9.16* shows an example of some of these techniques for developing the same motif. Some of these techniques have been labeled in the screenshot:

- **Repetition**: It consists of repeating the motif more times, either leaving some space between each one or repeating it immediately (marked as **1**)
- **Augmentation**: It consists of increasing the values of the notes used (marked as **2**)
- **Diminution**: It involves reducing the values of the notes used
- **Sequence**: It consists of repeating the rhythm of the motif but using other notes and respecting the original trend (marked as **3**)
- **Inversion**: It consists of inverting the contour of the notes used (marked as **4**), that is, making the high notes low and vice versa

- **Reverse**: It consists of using the same notes but changing the order, from the last to the first (marked as **5**)

Figure 9.16 – Motif development

Generally, not all techniques are used at the same time; instead, the forms that are most pleasing to the composer are chosen. This way, we can create many melodic variants, all starting from the same unit. The **motivic technique** gives cohesion to the melodic idea and helps to avoid having your melody sound like random notes. In *Figure 9.16*, the velocity of the notes was adjusted to differentiate each technique used, but it would be appropriate to adjust the velocity to give dynamics to the sounds.

In *Figure 9.17*, we see an example of a better-developed musical phrase, four measures long. Here, only some of the techniques shown previously were used. The duration of a phrase typically can be two, three, or four measures. We can also see that the velocity of the notes in the phrase gives emphasis to the higher notes of each group. This technique helps create a natural dynamic in the musical phrase.

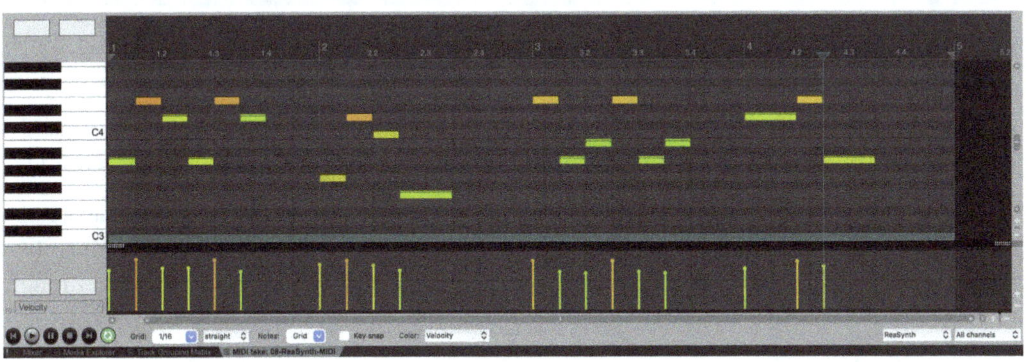

Figure 9.17 – Musical phrase using motif development

As we can see, the possibilities for composing melodies are broad using motif development techniques. Therefore, it is highly recommended to practice motivic techniques in different ways.

So far, our project includes percussion, bass, pad, and melody elements, the latter of which is a four-measure phrase. Now we need to copy and paste the percussion, bass, and pad items so that they also cover four measures, as shown in *Figure 9.18*. Additionally, we will use the track coloring techniques to color the tracks and make the session clearer.

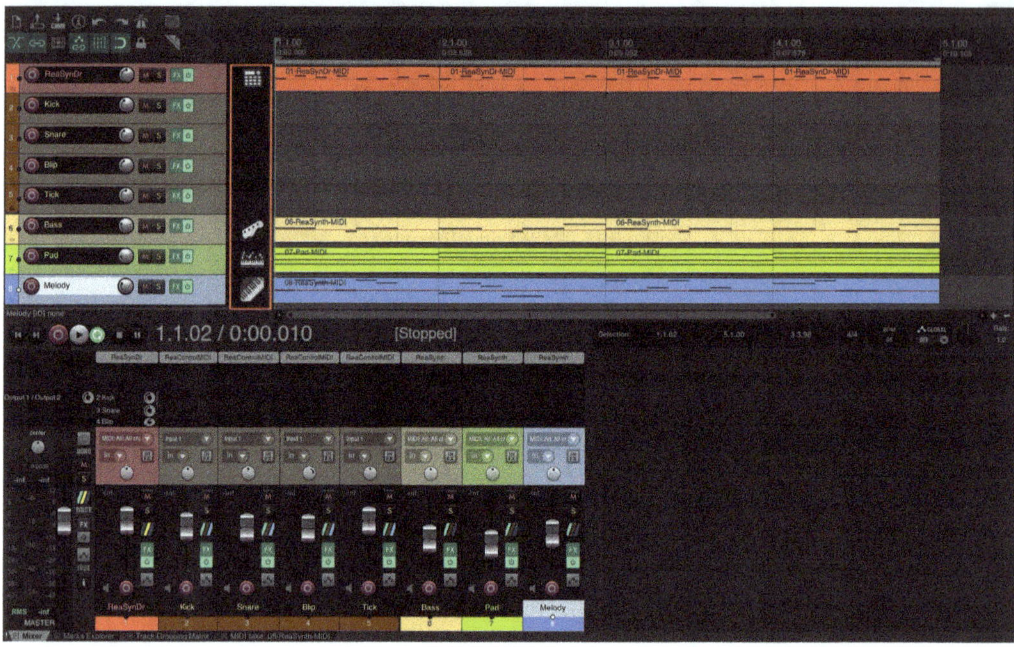

Figure 9.18 – Coloring the session and using track icons

If we right-click on a track, we can access the **Track icon | Set track icon** command. This command opens a window to select icons that we can use to identify the tracks more easily, as shown in *Figure 9.18*.

This four-measure section can serve as a starting point in our musical production. For example, it can function as half of a verse or chorus, as it is common for musical sections to last eight measures. To make an eight-measure section, we simply copy and duplicate all the items again so that everything covers eight measures.

Finally, we will add vocals, either by recording them or using a sample or audio loop (see the *Technical requirements* section) on a new track. With this, we will be ready to start editing and shaping the sounds we have used in our production.

Editing vocals and instruments

Now that we have a basic musical section, we can start editing and shaping its sounds. The goal is to achieve more interesting sounds that have their own distinctive character.

The adjustments we will see in this section are optional since modifying sounds is a subjective aspect of music production. However, the objective is to show techniques and resources that can broaden our perspective on what we can do with sounds.

Adjusting the pad sound

We will start by applying some equalization to the pad track, as it has a sound that is too bright.

We insert a **ReaEQ** equalizer and reduce the highs using a **Low Pass** filter of around 1,000 Hz, as shown in *Figure 9.19*:

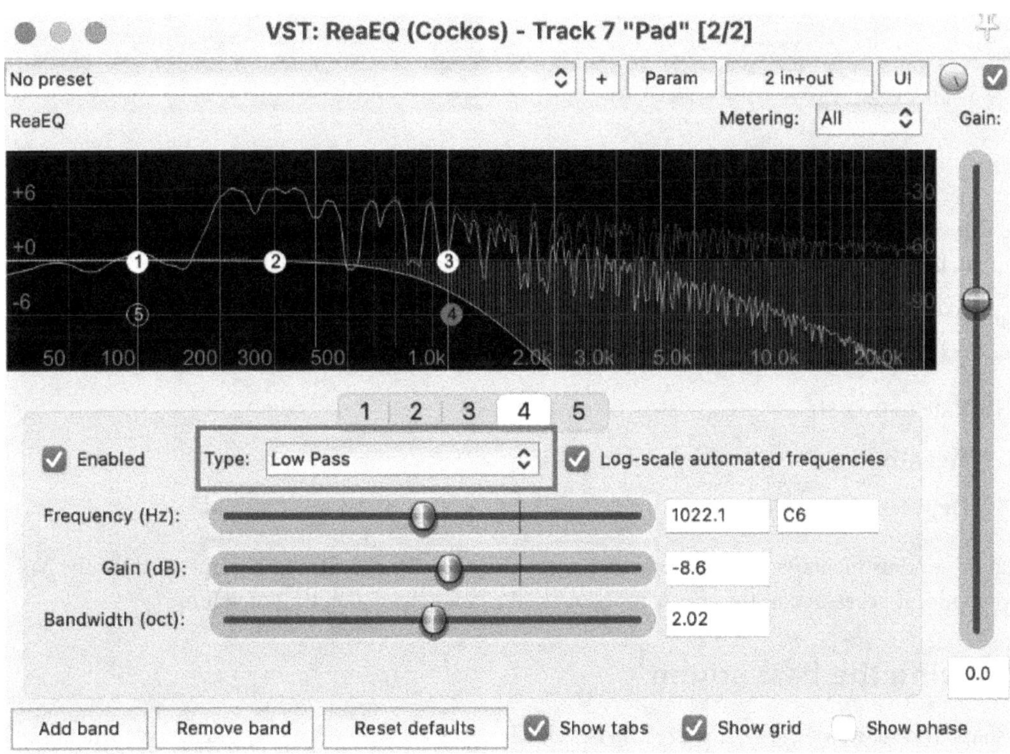

Figure 9.19 – Applying a Low Pass filter to the pad sound

The use of Low Pass filters is very common in synthesizer sounds as they help control the amount of harmonics in the sound.

After the **Low Pass** filter, we will insert a modulation effect called **chorus**. We can find this in the **JS effects** category as **JS: Chorus**. The chorus effect helps sounds appear wider, making it a good option for enhancing the pad sound.

As we saw in *Chapter 2*, **JS effects** are a type of plugin included in REAPER, and their source code can be edited by users with programming knowledge. In this case, we will just add the plugin and adjust its parameters, as shown in *Figure 9.20*:

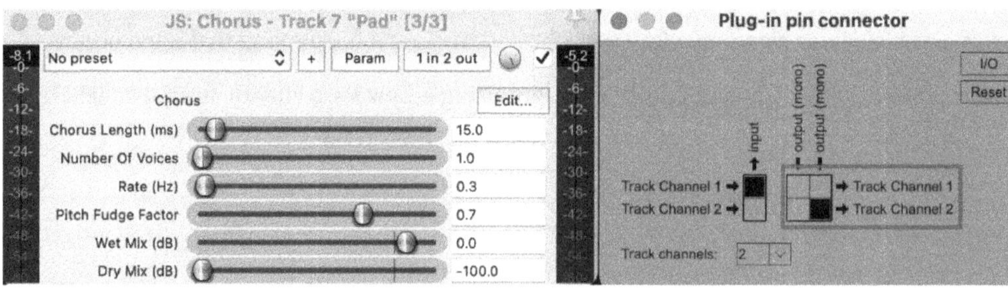

Figure 9.20 – JS Chorus plugin

The **Chorus** effect creates the impression that a sound is being played by several people at the same time, such as what happens with a choir of singers.

To properly appreciate this effect, we must deactivate **output 1** of the plugin, as marked in *Figure 9.20*. The other parameters to adjust are as follows:

- **Rate** to `0.3` Hz
- **Wet Mix** to `0` dB
- **Dry Mix** to `-100` dB

With these adjustments, we will have a wider stereo sound in the pad. It is important to adjust the pad track's fader if necessary, as the effects we have used change the perception of volume.

Adjusting the bass sound

To shape the sound of the synthesized bass, we will also start with a **ReaEQ** plugin. We will apply an HPF like we did with the pad, but this time, we will increase the filter's **resonance** with the **Bandwidth** parameter.

Increasing the filter's resonance creates a curve in it, as seen in *Figure 9.21*. The filter should have a cutoff frequency of around `800` Hz and a **Bandwidth** of around `0.7`.

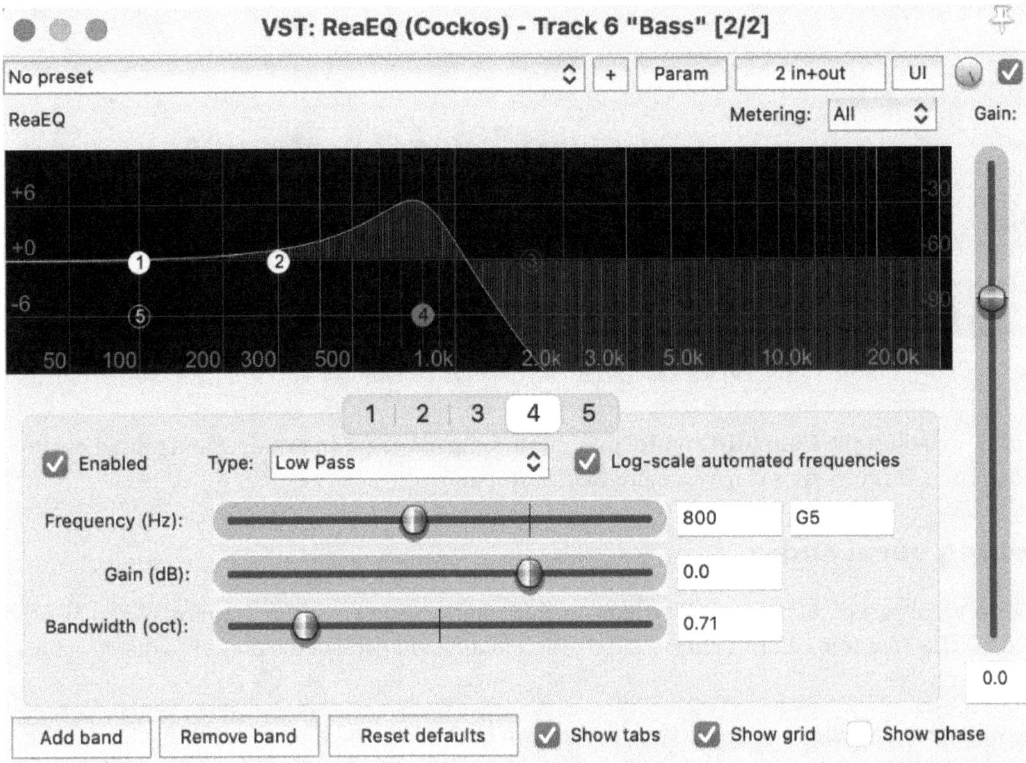

Figure 9.21 – Synth bass filtering

This resonant filter adjustment helps highlight the frequencies near `800` Hz and then abruptly cuts the higher harmonics. The result is a bass sound with greater definition in the mid frequencies, which helps the bass sound better when played on small speakers, such as those on a mobile phone, for example.

The next step in processing the bass will be to control its dynamics. For this, we will use a compressor: **JS: 1175 Compressor**. This plugin is a simple emulation of a famous hardware unit, the **Universal Audio 1176 compressor**. These compressors use FET transistors in their circuits and impart a characteristic sound that often works very well on many instruments, including bass.

We will insert the **JS: 1175 Compressor** plugin below the **ReaEQ** plugin and leave its parameters as their default values. We will only adjust the **Threshold** slider, which controls the amount of compression, aiming for the **Gain Reduction** meter at the bottom of the plugin to read around `-6` dB, as shown in *Figure 9.22*:

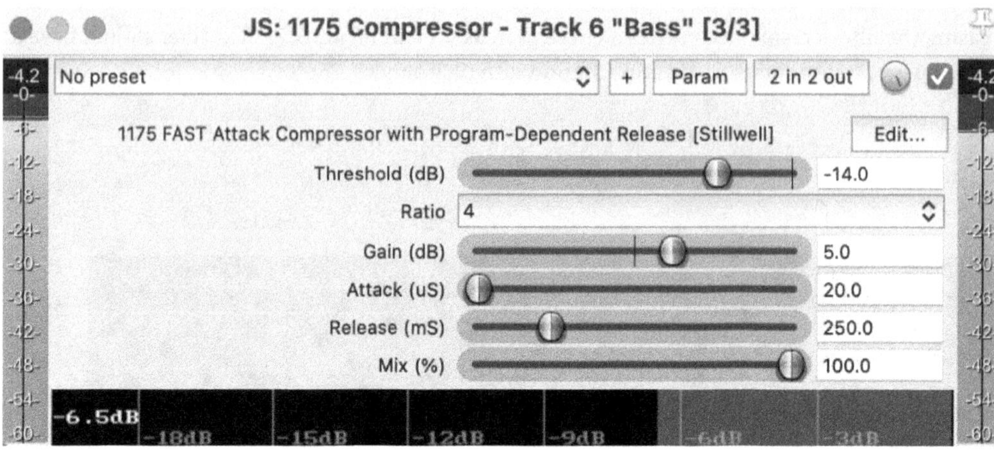

Figure 9.22 – Adjusting the 1175 compressor

Finally, we adjust the **Gain (dB)** control to 5 dB to compensate for the volume loss caused by the compressor. This way, we will have a more solid bass sound.

Editing vocal audio

For the vocal part of this project, we will use a short audio phrase (see the *Technical requirements* section). The idea is to edit this phrase and repeat it in different parts of the project so that it can be used creatively.

We will use audio editing to create the effect known as **stutter**, which takes small fractions of the audio that repeat quickly, creating this effect. *Figure 9.23* shows an example of how a vocal phrase or recording can be edited to generate the stutter effect.

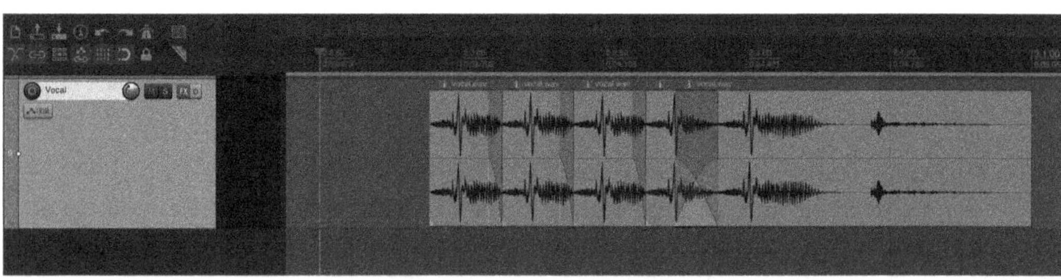

Figure 9.23 – Editing a vocal take

As we can see in *Figure 9.23*, there are several small audio items that repeat, and the original item is on the right side of the group. At the end of each item, a small fade-out is also used to smooth the transition between them.

We will then insert an instance of the **JS: 1175 Compressor** plugin on the vocal track too, using similar settings to those used on the bass track. This way, we will control the dynamics of the voice and give it more presence.

Another common task when using vocals in a music production is cleaning and editing the audio takes from a vocal recording. For example, we'll take the vocal take shown in *Figure 9.24* and edit it.

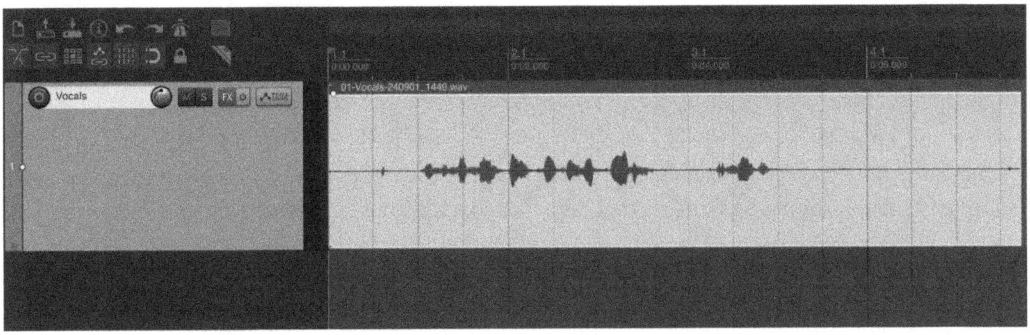

Figure 9.24 – A typical vocal take

First, we need to remove the parts of the audio that only contain background noise, whether at the beginning of the take, the end, or even in the spaces in the middle. We can use the **Split items at cursor** command (*S* key) to separate the vocal phrases and delete all the items without vocals, as shown in *Figure 9.25*:

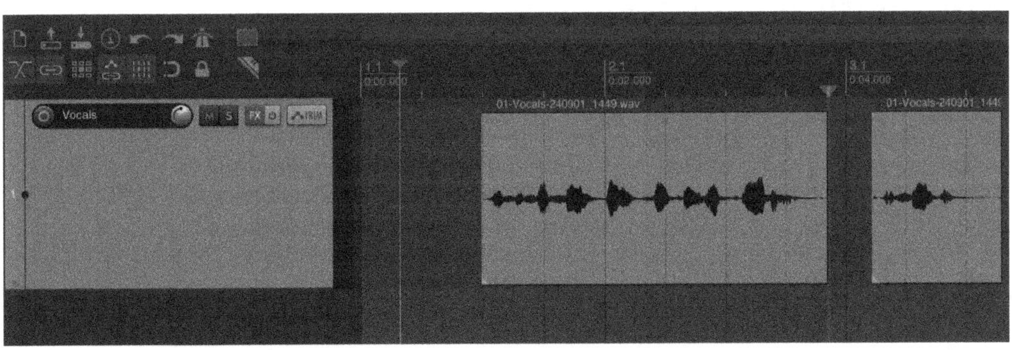

Figure 9.25 – Deleting empty spaces

Another common activity when editing vocals is adjusting the volume of different parts to balance their levels. To do this, we first need to identify the parts that sound louder and those that sound softer. We'll split the item into these parts and then adjust the volume of each one to even it out, as shown in *Figure 9.26*:

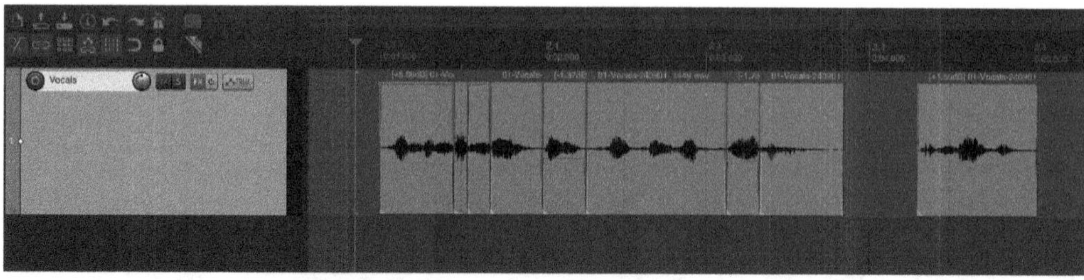

Figure 9.26 – Adjusting the volume of different items

As we can see, several items have been created in different parts of the phrase, and their volumes have been increased or decreased to balance everything out. The waveform can help us identify the louder or softer parts, but it should be our ears that help us make the final decision.

This technique, although a bit slow and tedious, is undoubtedly the best for fine-tuning a vocal take (or instrumental take), as we can separate words or even the sound of a consonant (for example, the *S* sound) that sounds too prominent, and reduce its volume, creating a *perfect* take.

Once the items have been edited, we can select them all and use the **Glue items** option from the right-click menu, which will create a new unified file that we can use for the rest of the project.

Now that we have edited and made some examples of sound production, we can focus on the mixing process.

Classic music mixing techniques

As we have seen, the sound production process involves adding effects to shape the original sound if necessary. This process can be as simple or as complex as creatively required. Once we have achieved a sound close to our liking, we can start making mixing adjustments.

In this section, we will look at a few widely used techniques in music mixing: adding effects using auxiliary sends and creating the ducking effect using compressors with sidechain input.

Using effect sends

One of the basic processes in mixing is adding reverb to create a sense of space. Although we can insert a reverb plugin on each channel, as we have seen before, a more convenient technique is to use a single reverb plugin and add effects using channel sends. Here are the steps for this process:

1. Create an empty track. This will be our master reverb control, so we will name it `Reverb`.
2. Insert an effect on this track. We will use **ReaVerbate**, but we could use any other effect we want to add to the mix.

3. Adjust the effect to have no **Dry** signal. This is an important step; we need the effect to be 100% wet, so it is necessary to completely reduce the **Dry** signal in the plugin.
4. Click on the sends section of the channel we want to add the effect to. For example, if we want the snare to have reverb, click on the sends section of the **Snare** track, as shown in *Figure 9.27*:

Figure 9.27 – Sends/Hardware output section

5. The **Track Routing** window will appear. Select the **Add new send** option and then the **Reverb** option, since that is the name of the track with the **Reverb** plugin. The controls shown in *Figure 9.28* will then appear:

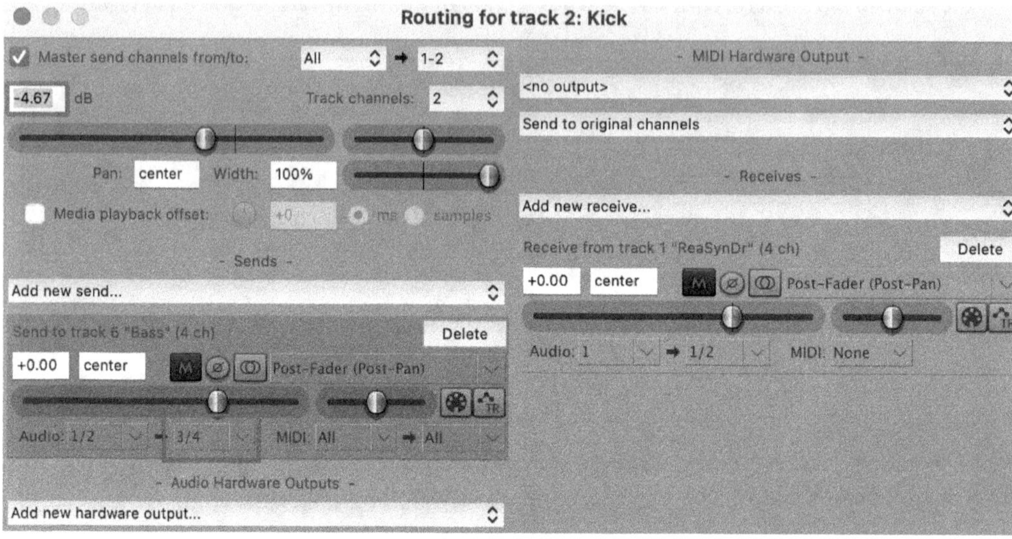

Figure 9.28 – Aux Send controls

We can use the newly created slider to control the amount of effect, or we can close this window and control the amount of effect with the send control marked in *Figure 9.29*:

Figure 9.29 – Track Send control

Now we can make adjustments to the **ReaVerbate** plugin to make the reverb sound the way we want it to.

The advantage of using this procedure is that if we want an effect on another track, we only need to add a new send to the desired track, as explained in *Step 4*. Then all the channels that use sends in this way will have the reverb effect created in *Step 2*. However, we can control the amount of effect independently for each track by adjusting each send.

We can also copy the send to another track by simply dragging and dropping it to the desired track. This way, we can quickly apply a certain effect to various tracks in the project. If we want to raise or lower the reverb level of all the channels at once, we can raise or lower the fader of the **Reverb** track created in *Step 1*.

Using effect sends helps achieve greater cohesion in the mix and optimizes CPU usage, as a single plugin can process all channels without needing to add multiple plugins.

Sidechain compression

As we have seen, the compressor is a very useful processor for controlling the dynamics of a sound and making it more even. Another popular use of the compressor is to create the *ducking effect*. This effect refers to reducing the volume of a track automatically when another track plays.

For example, when an announcer speaks on a radio station, the volume of the background music decreases each time the announcer speaks. In this case, the music has a compressor that reduces the volume, and the announcer's voice controls this compressor using a control called **sidechain**.

This ducking effect is also very common in music production. An example is when the bass reduces its volume each time the kick drum plays, giving the kick drum more clarity. Another example is when a pad reduces its volume each time the kick plays, creating more rhythm in the pad. Once you learn to use the sidechain technique, you can use it and experiment with various applications you can think of.

Let's see how to apply it in our project on the bass channel so that the bass attenuates a bit each time a kick drum plays, giving the kick more clarity:

1. Insert a **ReaComp** plugin on the bass channel, as this is the channel we want to automatically lower in volume.
2. Adjust the **ReaComp threshold** so that there is a gain reduction of approximately **6** dB. This time, we will not compensate for the **Output** mix, as we want it to remain attenuated.
3. Adjust the **Detector input** parameter of **ReaComp** and select **Auxiliary inputs**, as shown in *Figure 9.30*. This makes the compressor react to the signal that arrives through the auxiliary inputs of the compressor instead of the main inputs. These auxiliary inputs are what is known as sidechain in other compressors or DAWs.

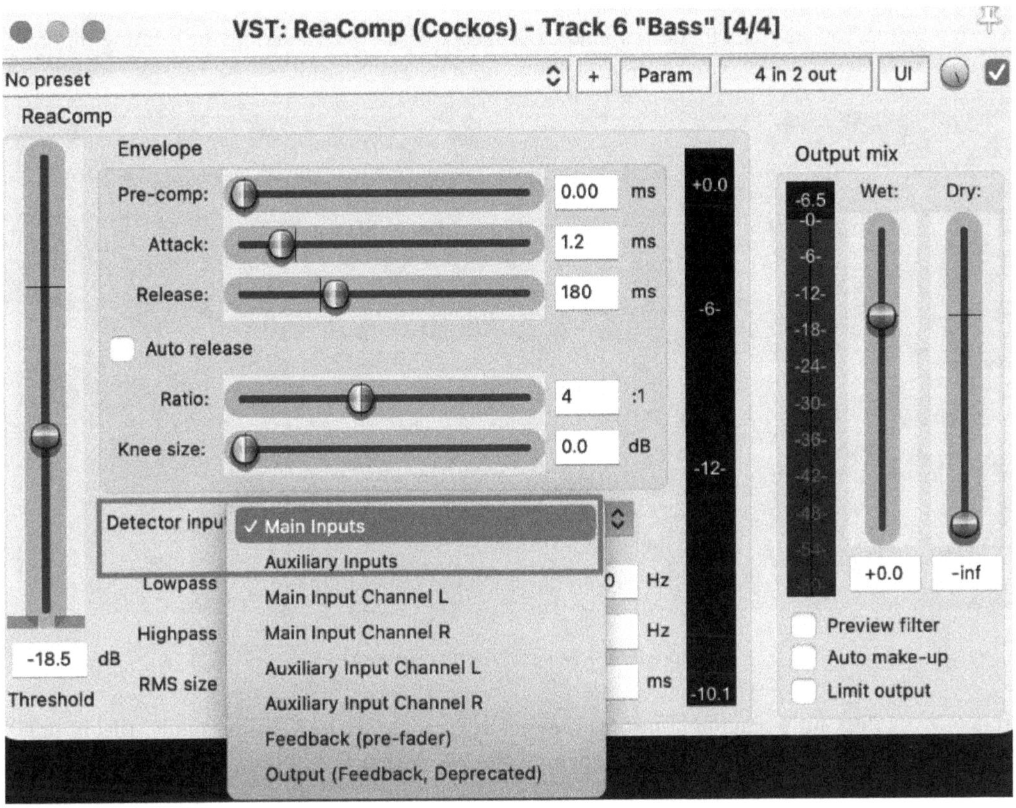

Figure 9.30 – Selecting detector inputs in the compressor

4. Click on the **Sends** section of the **Kick** drum channel, like how we did with the reverb in *Step 4* of the previous section.
5. In the **Routing** window, select **Add new send** and choose the **Bass** channel.

6. Ensure that you select **3/4** in the new send, as marked in *Figure 9.31*, and close the **Routing** window.

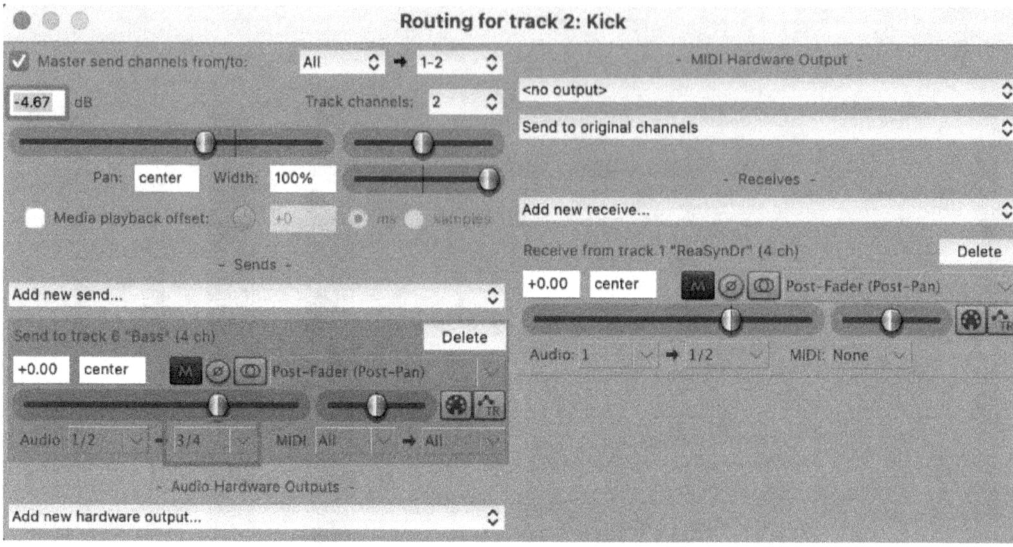

Figure 9.31 – Selecting send channels

In this way, the **ReaComp** plugin on the bass channel will react to the kick drum sounds. That is, only when a kick drum sounds will the compressor activate. We can verify this by opening the **ReaComp** plugin on the bass. We will see that the gain reduction meter only activates when the kick drum plays.

Similarly, we could assign compressors to different tracks and make them react to signals from other auxiliary sends, expanding our creative possibilities in both music and audio production.

Once we have adjusted levels, panning, effects, and automation in our mix, we can proceed to final mastering, as we will see in the next section.

Mastering music for distribution

As we have seen, **mastering** is the final stage of production and aims to achieve the best sound and volume for a project. We must remember that mastering should be done once the mix is fully finished, with the necessary effects and processors, as well as any required automation.

Compressor

For this project, we will use some audio processors on the **Master** track that we already know from *Chapter 5*, as well as some additional ones. Firstly, we will add a **ReaComp** plugin to the master and adjust it with the parameters explained in the chapter on mastering:

- **Attack**: `80` ms
- **Release**: `Auto release`
- **Ratio**: `2:1`
- **High pass**: `100` Hz
- **Auto make-up**: `On`

Remember that we must adjust the **Threshold** slider so that there is around **1** dB of gain reduction.

Exciter

The next step will be to add an **exciter**. The exciter is a processor that generates harmonics. These help to add more brightness and clarity to the sounds. Unlike an equalizer, which can only boost or cut the level of a signal's harmonics, the exciter creates new harmonics, so the result can enrich the final sound.

An exciter that works very well is **JS: Exciter**, found in the **JS effects** category. We will adjust its parameters as shown in *Figure 9.32*. This way, we can hear more brightness throughout the song. The general idea with exciters is not to overuse them, as although they may sound good initially, they can cause ear fatigue if overused.

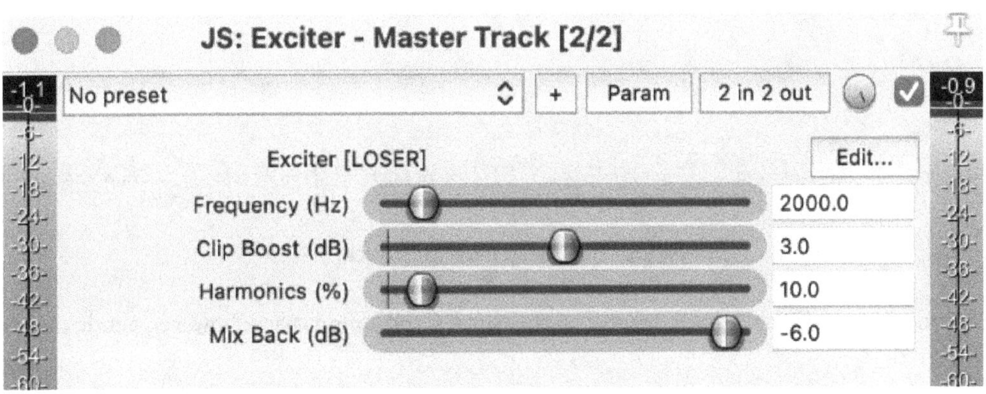

Figure 9.32 – Using an exciter effect

If desired, the effect of the exciter can be reduced by lowering the **Mix Back (dB)** slider so that the effect is very subtle.

Equalizer

After the exciter, we can use a **ReaEQ** plugin, as mentioned in *Chapter 5*, which focuses on mastering projects. For this song, it only seems necessary to apply an **HPF** at 30 Hz and a slight boost at 2 kHz, as shown in *Figure 9.33*:

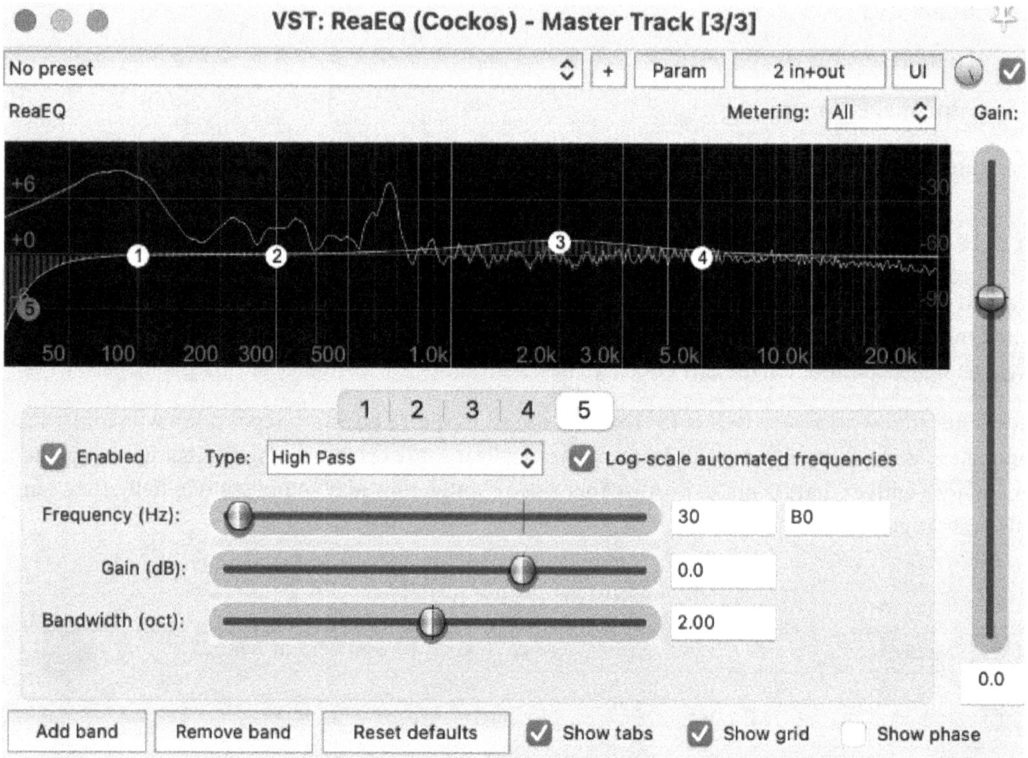

Figure 9.33 – EQ in the Master track

As we know, this equalization will depend on the balance and sounds used; however, gentle curves are preferred.

Limiter

The final step will be the **limiter**, which will allow us to increase the final volume and adjust it to a certain **LUFS-S** value. To date, most streaming platforms work with values of `-14` LUFS and `-1` dB maximum true-peak levels.

To properly adjust the limiter, we need to add a **Loudness** meter after the limiter and monitor that the mentioned levels are achieved, as shown in *Figure 9.34*:

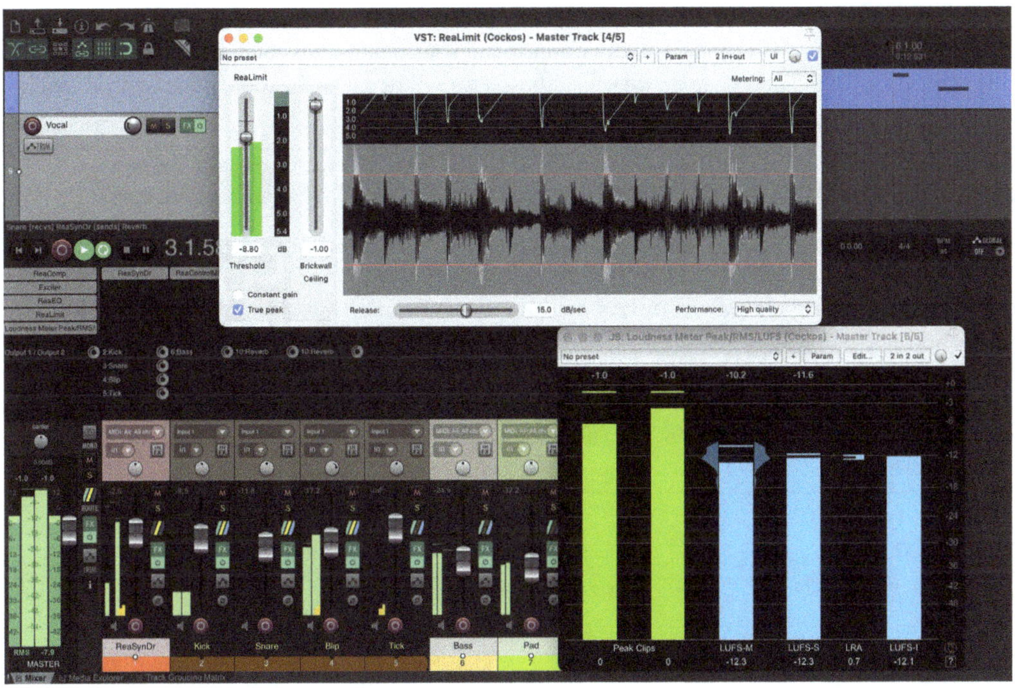

Figure 9.34 – Controlling the loudness level

As we can see, the **ReaLimit** limiter controls the signal peaks so that they do not exceed **-1** dB true-peak levels, while the **Loudness meter** allows us to verify this, as well as ensuring that the LUFS value is above `-14` LUFS-S.

Now the track is ready to be exported as an MP3 file for demonstration purposes or as a WAV file for final distribution.

Summary

In this chapter, we covered all stages of music production, starting with pre-production and MIDI recording. We learned the techniques used for musical composition and for creating rhythms, bass lines, and chords.

We also saw some special techniques used in music mixing, such as using sends and side-chain compression. Finally, we reviewed the parameters used in mastering a song so that it is suitable for use on current streaming platforms.

With the information in this chapter, you can now expand your creative possibilities when working on a music production. In the next chapter, we will address a very different application: podcast production.

10

Podcast Production Workflows

Today, podcasts have become more popular than ever. Once a niche product somewhere between talk radio and audiobooks, podcasts now occupy their own entertainment segment. Brands, solo creators, news anchors, authors – more people than ever have chosen to engage with their audience through this medium and there is no sign of stopping. From off-the-cuff interviews to highly polished investigative journalism series, the scope of what can be done in podcasts has never been broader.

In this chapter, we will explore how to take a podcast idea and turn it into a finished product ready for distribution.

Here are the topics that we will be covering in this chapter:

- **Introduction to podcast production**: You will learn the ins and outs of planning out your podcast episode and recording sessions so everything flows smoothly on the day of recording. This section will also explore some gear considerations.
- **Vocal recording techniques**: We will explore best practices for getting clean and intelligible audio and adopting workflow strategies that will ease editing and post-production.
- **Editing and mixing a podcast episode**: Finally, you will learn to take what you've recorded and turn it into a great-sounding product.

By the end of this chapter, you will be able to lay out a plan for your podcast idea; know best practices for achieving ideal recording quality; keep your recordings organized; and learn to mix and master your podcast to a competitive yet dynamic loudness.

Technical requirements

To create your first podcast, you will require a microphone and a means of connecting it to your computer. This means either an **XLR microphone** and an audio interface or a **USB microphone** that connects directly to your PC or Mac. When interviewing guests, it is best to have access to multiple microphones, each with its own respective input on your audio interface. This will allow for easier editing and cleanup during post-production. We will explore microphone choice and recording techniques later in this chapter.

> **Tip**
>
> A good way of practicing the methods outlined in this chapter is to record yourself or a friend reading a story or news article. An even better method is to record a dialog between multiple people, which gives you more of an accurate representation of the podcast format.

Introduction to podcast production

This section explores the inception phase of a podcast and how to turn a rough idea into a project outline that can be followed through upon. It will also explore some of the implications that different podcast formats have on the production timeline.

Creating a project outline document

In the beginning, there is always an idea. Turning this initial spark of inspiration into a finished project requires careful planning. It is important to make fundamental decisions about a show's format, rough episode length, release schedule, and overall scope as early as possible so that future planning for individual episodes can focus on their content and/or guests to be interviewed.

Here are some initial questions we should ask ourselves and write down in a document outlining our podcast:

- What is the theme and the podcast's main focus?
    - **Examples**: A movie series, a historical event, stories around certain subjects, politics, interviews with professionals in a certain segment, or just chat
- How long should each episode be?
    - **Examples**: Interview-based podcasts have a broad range from around 30 minutes to over an hour (or several) in length. Podcasts focusing on storytelling are often kept more concise, rarely lasting for more than 45 minutes.
- How frequently should episodes be released?
    - **Examples**: Monthly, weekly, bi-monthly, or on a loose schedule
- Will this project have seasons or an end?
    - **Example**: Limited series; a limited number of episodes per season recorded in quick succession and released on a regular schedule; intended to run as long as possible

- Will guests be featured and how will they join?
    - **Examples**: Zoom interviews, in-person chats, live panels
- Will there be a video component?
    - **Considerations**: Where will videos be distributed? What kind of snippets could be repurposed for social media content, such as reels?
- Where will the podcast be hosted?
    - **Considerations**: Conduct some research on **podcast hosting providers** and compare pricing, ad-supported tiers, and technical requirements. Some offer ad-free paid plans while others can host your podcast for free but will insert targeted ads.
- What will the intro be?
    - **Considerations**: Do you need someone to create a theme song? Will there be one intro re-used across episodes? Does the guest introduce themselves and the podcast in each episode?

This list of questions is by no means comprehensive and should be just a starting point for creating our initial **project outline document**. The more prepared we can be when starting a new project, the more likely we are to keep at it and follow through with working toward our goals. Clearly defining our goals will also help us find a shared language with our collaborators and guests and avoid miscommunication.

Having a clear outline will also make it easier for us to pitch our show to potential interviewees and other guests as we will be able to communicate its strengths much better.

Planning a timeline

While there are an infinite number of ways to create a podcast and just as many approaches to the production timeline, there tend to be two distinct styles that are most common: **interview-based**, and **storytelling-focused** podcasts (also including journalism-centric content).

A key difference between these two is that interview-based podcasts tend to center on the material captured in one long recording session while storytelling-focused podcasts, such as *This American Life* or *Lore*, and journalistic formats, such as *The Daily*, include many pieces of recordings captured at different times, often in different locations and featuring different people in a single episode.

As such, the production timelines for these two formats are very different. The following examples showcase the differences between two hypothetical podcast episodes: one centering around an *interview*, the other one on a central *story* told through various recordings.

Example timeline – interview-based podcast

Figure 10.1 shows an example of a typical timeline for an interview-based podcast:

Pre-Production	Production	Post-Production	Release
• Reaching out to potential interviewees • Securing guests • Researching guests and formalizing a list of interview questions • Reaching out to potential sponsors	• Recording interview • Q & A	• Dialog cleanup • First edit • Review of the first edit by stakeholders and (optionally) guests • Subsequent or final edit	• Distributing final master to hosting platforms • Writing ad copy and producing marketing material • Creating soundbites to use in social media content

Figure 10.1 – Timeline for an interview-based podcast

As an interview-focused podcast mainly focuses on the material gathered in a single recording session, the pre-production phase can be fairly brief and interviews could even be arranged spontaneously. Editing will mostly consist of cutting out *dead air*, unnecessary filler words, and "uhmms" and "erms," and maintaining a smooth flow to the conversation.

Example timeline – storytelling podcast

Figure 10.2 shows an overview of the timeline for a storytelling podcast:

Pre-Production	Production	Post-Production	Release
• Finalizing topic for episode • Researching topics and finding authority figures • Scriptwriting • Reaching out to interviewees • Sourcing archival material and negotiating rights • Planning recording sessions and/or creating plans for virtual interviews • Outlining episode structure	• Recording on-location interviews • Conducting virtual interviews via video conferencing • Assembling all archival material • Finalizing episode structure	• Cleanup of onsite recordings • Cleanup of video conferencing interviews • Cleanup of archival material • First edit • Review of first edit by stakeholders and (optionally) guests • Peer review, fact-checking, and final corrections • Subsequent or final edit	• Distributing final master to hosting platforms • Writing ad copy and producing marketing material • Creating soundbites to use in social media content

Figure 10.2 – Timeline for a storytelling podcast

With storytelling-focused podcasts, pre-production is a much more elaborate effort as it involves research, writing a script, securing interviewees and planning their interviews, and sometimes even sourcing and licensing archival materials, such as historic recordings, old interviews, and news reports. Establishing this sort of podcast requires a considerable amount of work, consideration, and, quite often, funding.

As you can see, timelines and the scope of podcasts can vary a great deal. As such, we will focus mainly on the recording and post-production portions within the scope of this book.

Vocal recording techniques

The human voice is at the center of every podcast, and thus capturing it as naturally and cleanly as possible is key. Of course, circumstances can often lead us to end up recording Zoom conversations, phone calls, or interviewing people at busy conferences.

The key is not to end up with a sterile, squeaky-clean recording, but rather to capture everyone's voices in ways that make the most of the situation we're given and allow them to remain intelligible for our audience.

This section will explore which gear and recording techniques are best suited to podcast-making, as well as how to set up your own space or on-location sessions for ideal audio.

Microphone choice and positioning

Recording voices for podcasts is less about capturing crisp high-end audio and every single minute detail than recording vocals in music often is. Instead, we want a natural, pleasing vocal sound, decent environmental noise rejection, and less cleanup work in post-production.

Whenever we are talking about gear, it is important to remind ourselves that we shouldn't let our creativity be held back by the fancy equipment we *don't* own. If you have a microphone – be it a handheld one or a large diaphragm condenser – you are already set to start working on your podcast.

The following sections provide recommendations that simply act as a guidepost if you're starting from scratch or planning to expand your setup.

Dynamic microphones

Dynamic microphones, previously already prevalent in radio, have become a staple in podcasting since their sound is not overly bright and doesn't emphasize the less desirable aspects of the voice, such as sibilance and raspiness. Additionally, many dynamic microphones are highly affordable and nearly indestructible.

The following microphones are some of the ones most commonly seen and heard in popular podcasts:

- **Shure SM58**: This mic has been sold for $99 for years and is an absolute classic with an overall balanced and pleasant sonic signature.
- **Shure SM7B**: This mic has become a staple with podcasters and is instantly recognizable due to its cylindrical shape designed to face the person speaking. It is much pricier and requires a higher-end interface or preamp to achieve a sufficient input level for speech. It is also great at rejecting environmental noise.
- **Shure MV7X**: A more affordable and smaller version of the SM7B specifically tuned for podcast production.

- **ElectroVoice RE-20**: Another classic, somewhat pricey, microphone that has been famously used in radio stations all across the USA for decades.
- **RØDE PodMic**: An affordable mic designed to somewhat mimic the look and tonality of the ElectroVoice RE-20 in a smaller design.

Lavalier microphones

Lavalier or **lapel microphones** (see *Figure 10.3*) are popular because their distance from the speaker's mouth gives them a very realistic tonality, which is closer to hearing someone speak from a natural distance. They are also easy to conceal, which is why they are used in pretty much every movie and TV production today. They are small microphones that can be clipped onto shirt collars, pockets, or attached to a headset.

Figure 10.3 – A lavalier microphone with foam wind protection

As these mics rarely sit in front of a speaker's mouth, they will not pick up plosives and often don't require de-essing in post-production. However, because they commonly feature an **omnidirectional pickup pattern** (meaning they pick up sound equally from all directions), they are somewhat more susceptible to picking up environmental noise.

Lavalier mics are commonly used with small wireless transmitters, so they usually feature **mini XLR** or **1/8" connectors** that won't connect to a regular audio interface without the necessary adapters.

In recent years, compact all-in-one wireless microphone kits have become incredibly popular since they are now more affordable than ever and can be connected directly to iOS and Android devices. This allows for high-quality audio to be recorded right alongside video captured in the phone's native camera app.

With these kits, the microphone is integrated into the transmitter and can be clipped to a collar, shirt pocket, tie, or scarf. While their size makes them harder to conceal, their all-in-one nature greatly simplifies setup. Additionally, many of these transmitters allow for connecting regular lavalier mics or headsets via a 1/8" TRS input.

Popular all-in-one microphone systems that support connecting external lavalier mics include the **RØDE Wireless** (see *Figure 10.4*) and **DJI Mic** series, which support up to two microphones per receiver and charge via USB-C.

Figure 10.4 – RØDE Wireless Go II, a popular integrated wireless mic solution

These microphones have become very popular for any on-location content accompanied by video and are easy to use for all involved regardless of their previous podcasting experience. Their somewhat higher price makes them a less ideal fit for any podcasts recorded in a studio, where practical needs outweigh the benefits of wireless connectivity.

USB microphones

USB microphones seem like a very attractive solution due to only requiring one cable to connect to any computer. However, this also means that they cannot be expanded into multi-mic setups quite as easily as any regular audio interface. Very few of them feature additional inputs, and microphone quality is often not on par with *regular* microphones costing the same or less. Additionally, some USB microphones might be susceptible to unpleasant high-frequency interference when connected to laptop USB ports.

So, while they are a decent choice for streamers narrating gameplay or for getting better conferencing audio, they are not the ideal solution for podcasting if guests are involved.

Microphone positioning

Whether microphones should be mounted on boom stands or be handheld largely depends on the type of microphone used and your budget for additional hardware. Desk-mounted arms have increased in popularity and allow participants to sit across from each other at a table, while microphone stands offer flexibility of placement if participants are seated on a couch or armchair.

If a very direct, radio-style sound is desired, we will have all podcast participants stay very close to their microphones and speak into them the same way a singer would on a pop production. This proximity to the microphones will require a **pop filter** to be placed in front of handheld or condenser microphones to avoid harsh plosives. Some microphones, such as the Shure SM7B, are somewhat immune to this phenomenon due to their integrated pop shield.

If the overall sound and feel of the podcast should be more natural, speaking into the microphones from a distance of 10" to 20" is preferable but will require higher input gain on our interface or mixer. This distance means that a non-pop filter will be required and de-essing will be less necessary in post-production.

Room acoustics

The way our room sounds will have a direct impact on the quality of our recordings. Acoustically untreated rooms with lots of hard surfaces and flat walls will lead to unwanted acoustic reflections and resonances that can lead to cancellation or exaggeration of certain frequency ranges and unwanted reverberation making its way onto the recording.

When planning to set up a space for podcasting, simple steps, such as adding a substantial rug, bookshelves, and some decor, will already serve to tame some acoustic reflections. To take it further, acoustic paneling can help to specifically target certain acoustic problems in our room, such as frequency buildup or cancellation.

While treating a room to combat room modes and standing waves can be costly, this will often not be required for voice recordings in a podcast format, and focusing on reducing early reflections will yield the most noticeable improvement.

Acoustic panels of 2" (5 cm) thickness and above made of fiberglass, rock wool, or other insulating materials will yield significant improvements to early reflections while pyramid foam and other thin foam panels often only lead to marginal improvements.

Panels can easily be built by layering rigid fiberglass panels (such as *Corning 703*), which can be sourced from certain home improvement stores and acoustics specialists and framed using metal studs or wooden planks, or even craft fabric to wrap them. This DIY method allows for building 4" thick 2' x 4' panels for a price of around $70 a piece, compared to buying premade ones at prices ranging from $100 to over $300 each.

These panels can then be placed at critical points that sound waves will bounce off of. This can be the walls the individual speakers are facing, the ceiling above the speakers, and larger, open wall spaces.

Signal flow

Ideally, we want to have every participant on their own track when recording a podcast. This can be achieved with an audio interface that offers us two or more XLR inputs, or a mixer with a USB connection that lets us record multiple channels at the same time.

This way, we can edit out noise from other mics that could be caused by non-speaking participants coughing, shuffling around, or whispering to each other. It also allows for more creative freedom during post-production as all voices can be treated in their own way. *Figure 10.5* compares the routing of a USB mic and running two microphones via an interface.

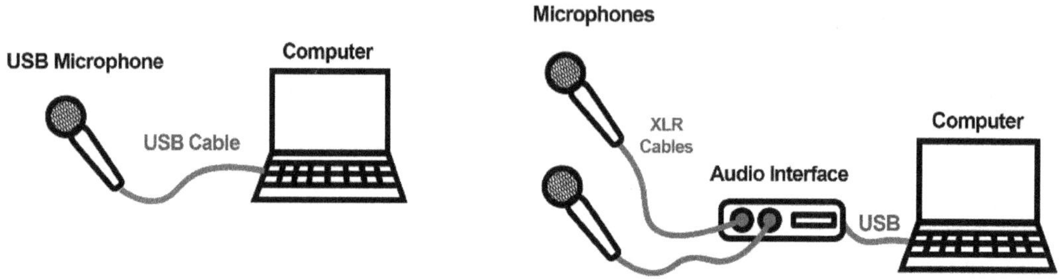

Figure 10.5 – USB microphone versus multiple microphones connected to an audio interface

Recording video conferencing via Loopback

No matter what topic our podcast is about, it's only a matter of time before we have to record an interview conducted via video conferencing platforms (such as Zoom, Skype, FaceTime, Webex, etc.). Luckily, this has become easier than ever before, thanks to the **Windows Audio Session API** (**WASAPI**) loopback feature, apps such as **VoiceMeeter**, and the fact most newly released audio interfaces are now shipping with **loopback** functionality.

Interfaces with integrated loopback

Many current audio interfaces ship with an integrated **loopback** feature that allows us to capture any audio output from our computer using any DAW or live streaming software. This feature has gained popularity with the rise of streaming and podcasting.

Since every manufacturer implements this feature in a different way, you will have to consult your audio interface manual to find out how to set it up.

Enabling WASAPI loopback in Windows

The WASAPI allows us to record any audio that is output by any app using *Windows System Audio*, including games, video conferencing, and web browsers.

To enable this feature in REAPER, we will have to follow these steps:

1. Enter **Preferences** and navigate to the **Audio Device** settings. Here, we will select **WASAPI** as our **Audio system** and **Shared loopback** as **Mode**.

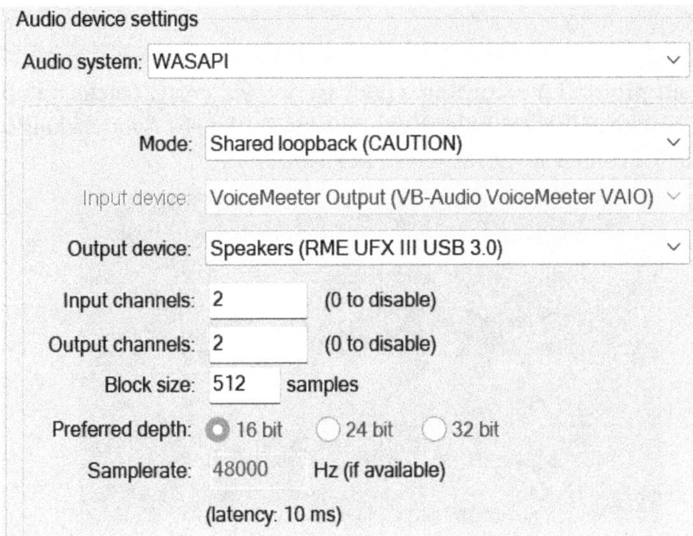

Figure 10.6 – Enabling WASAPI loopback

2. We will then select our desired audio interface as **Output device** and return to our project.
3. Before arming any track for recording, make sure it is muted as it will otherwise cause a feedback loop!

We will now be able to record any audio coming from our system right into REAPER. While WASAPI loopback is active, REAPER will not be able to record audio from our microphones. However, we can use another app, such as **Audacity**, or a second instance of REAPER to still record our own voice.

The recording process

Before we record any audio, we want to make sure to save our project under an appropriate name so that if there are any stability issues during a long recording, whatever we have captured up until that point will be located in a known folder. It is a best practice to always lead with our podcast name and episode number so that keeping track of our episodes will be easy in the future.

Here is an example: `PodcastName-10_Topic_GuestNameA_GuestNameB[...].rpp`.

An alternative would be to keep the full podcast name in the parent folder and to use an abbreviated version for project and file names.

In the subsequent sections, we will explore setting up our session to make our first podcast recordings, keep them organized, and finally mix and master them for distribution.

Session prep

When setting up our project for recording a podcast, we will create **tracks** for all participants, name them appropriately, and set our ruler measurements to time by right-clicking it and selecting **Minutes:Seconds** in the context menu, as shown in *Figure 10.7*:

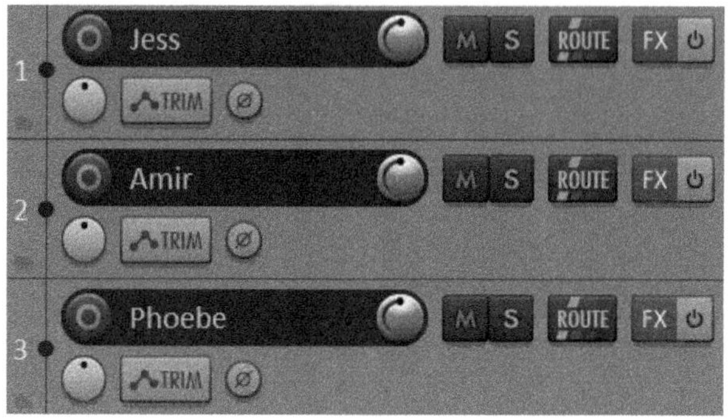

Figure 10.7 – Tracks named after podcast participants

Next, we will make sure all tracks have their appropriate inputs selected. We do so by opening our **Mixer** (*Ctrl/Cmd + M*) and choosing the correct input for each participant's microphone from the top dropdown found in each channel header, as shown in *Figure 10.8*:

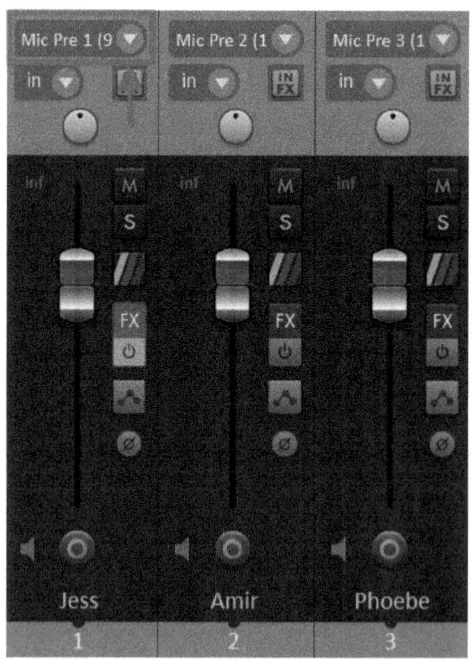

Figure 10.8 – Selecting inputs for participant tracks

Grouping tracks

To always ensure that all microphone tracks are armed for recording, we will select all our tracks and right-click them. In the resulting context menu, we will click **Track grouping | Track grouping parameters**.

In the following window, we will check both **Record Arm Lead** and **Record Arm Follow**, as shown in *Figure 10.9*. This will arm all of our selected tracks for recording if we click the circular *record arm* button on any of them, thus avoiding any microphone accidentally not being captured.

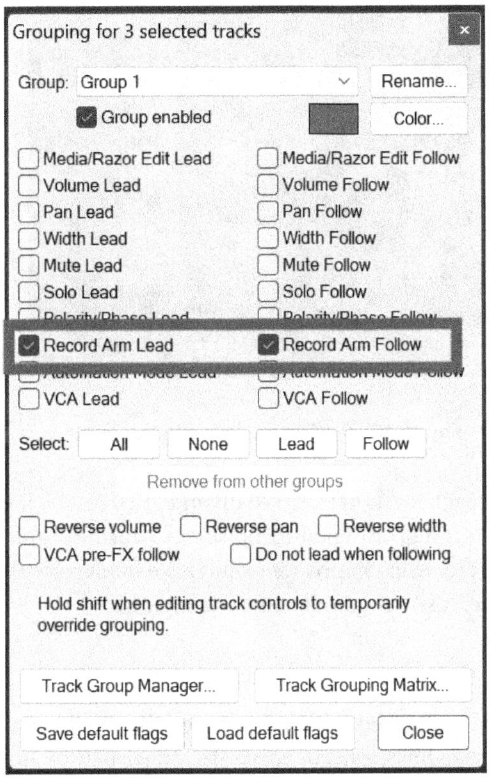

Figure 10.9 – Track grouping parameters window

Checking levels

With all tracks properly routed and their recording states linked, it is time for us to adjust the gain on our interface or mixer to get the best possible level on each microphone.

By clicking each track's *record arm* button, we will now see their levels and can ask our participants to speak into their mics at a normal conversational volume. Using the mixer (*Ctrl*/*cmd* + *M*), we can get the best view of our input levels:

Figure 10.10 – Getting levels in the mixer

Generally, we should aim to reach levels between -6 dB and -12 dB, which will avoid clipping during energized moments and provide a great signal-to-noise ratio during regular conversation. So, if our levels were as pictured in the preceding figure, we would have to increase the gain for **Jess**, check our connection for **Amir**, and decrease our gain for **Phoebe** slightly.

Ready to roll!

Once we are ready to roll, we can hit record! Once we are rolling, it is usually a best practice to just keep recording even if someone misspeaks or there are longer pauses as these issues can easily be remedied during editing. This ensures that no potentially interesting material is lost and prevents accidentally deleting a take for good that could have been useful in the final edit.

We need to regularly double-check our input levels and ensure that no one's microphone signal is clipping or unexpectedly absent and adjust the gain on the fly if needed.

As always, we should save whenever we can, especially right after any part of the recording is done.

Creating markers while recording

If you or someone else will be managing the REAPER session actively during recording, you or they can ease future editing by placing markers in real time during the recording by pressing the *M* key when there is a moment that we would want to be highlighted for later.

Pressing *Shift* + *M* will allow the person running the session to also quickly add a name to their marker, allowing them to highlight shifts in topic or parts to edit out later. *Figure 10.11* shows what these editorial markers can look like:

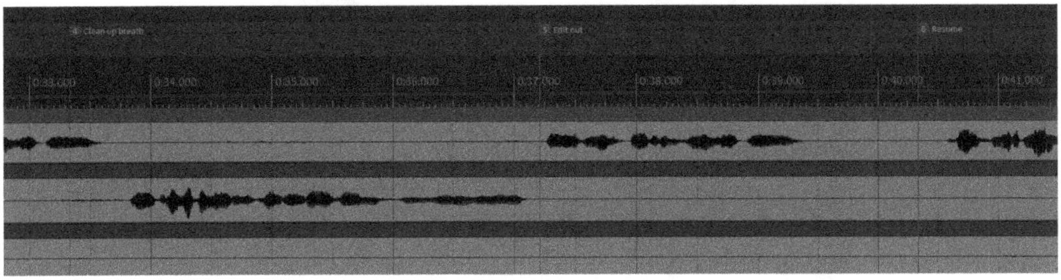

Figure 10.11 – Example of contextual markers aiding later editing

With these methods, we will be able to keep our sessions running smoothly and save ourselves time during the editing phase later. The more diligent we are before and during recording, the less guesswork is involved in post-production.

Next, we will tackle editing and mixing the material that we have recorded.

Editing and mixing a podcast episode

The bulk of time working on a podcast episode is usually spent in post-production as we will have to clean up our recordings, edit the material, and process our recordings to sound professional. Luckily, you will become much faster at this the more routine you have, and many settings can be brought over from previous episodes once your sound and workflow are established.

Stashing away original takes

Before jumping into editing, it is best to create a duplicate of all our tracks that should remain unedited in case of any misunderstandings and to avoid losing track of what has been recorded. The easiest way to do so is to select all our current tracks and add them to a folder. To do so, right-click them and select **Move tracks to folder | New folder track**.

We can then right-click the *folder track* and click **Duplicate tracks**. The old folder can then be named something like `Original Takes` or `UNEDITED` to remind us not to touch them unless needed. We can then collapse the contents of this folder by clicking the *arrow* on the right side of the track header and muting it, as shown in *Figure 10.12*:

Figure 10.12 – To collapse folders, click the left arrow button in the track header

This folder track can now be muted as we proceed to edit our podcast audio.

Cutting

When editing single or multi-mic podcasts, we should group our recorded items so that any edits we make will be applied across all recordings that were captured simultaneously. This maintains our sync and ensures no material gets moved out of context.

To do so, we select our recordings and press the *G* key to group them. Their linked status will be shown with a small *chain link* icon appearing in the item headers, as shown in *Figure 10.13*:

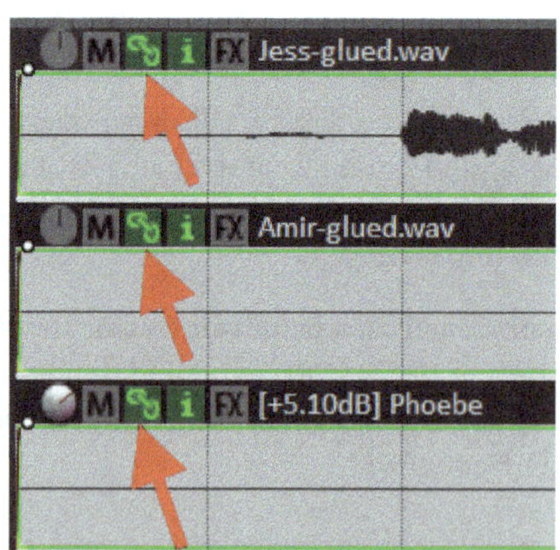

Figure 10.13 – The item link icons

Furthermore, we want to enable **Ripple editing all tracks** so that any material being cut won't create gaps. To review how this feature works, refer to *Chapter 8*.

Note that this mode of ripple editing will move all our previously placed makers along with our items, allowing us to keep an overview of our editing to-dos.

From here, we will listen to our episode and remove any unwanted sections, sidebars, extended pauses, or remarks that we or our guests don't want on the show. At the end of this process, we should be left with a conversation that flows smoothly, without unnecessary tangents.

Some cleanups may still be needed but this should be performed once the flow and timing of our episode has been established, allowing us to not spend time cleaning up segments that might not even make it onto the show.

> **Important note on grouping**
>
> When working with grouped items, always remember that any trimming applied to one item will be applied equally to all others within the group. This can lead to unintentional trimming, and it is thus a best practice to temporarily unlink items when we want to trim items mid-edit.

Cleanup

With our editing complete, we can disable **Ripple editing** as we might be removing smaller chunks of audio but no longer adjusting any timings or performing editorial tasks. Similarly, we will **disable item grouping** by pressing the *U* key or clicking the *green link* icons (see *Figure 10.13*) of the items. This prevents any edits made at this stage from affecting any timings previously established during editing.

Much like with dialog, the cleanup of podcast audio is best done in **passes**, where each run-through focuses on specific areas of *undesirables* to be removed attenuated.

This process could be structured as follows:

1. **First pass**: This involves finding appropriate gate settings for each track. Using volume envelopes to maintain a steady level on each voice throughout (see the *Working with dialog from editing to post-production* section in *Chapter 8*).
2. **Second pass**: It involves the removal of silence in the non-active speaker's tracks, the cleanup of breaths, coughs, and other mouth sounds, and the fine-tuning of volume envelopes.
3. **Final pass**: This focuses on manually reducing harsh essing and plosives, removing any remaining unwanted interjections and mouth sounds.

This is by no means a prescriptive list as some people might be better at focusing on many different tasks at once while others like to direct their focus on a smaller set of them to work more diligently.

Avoiding ear fatigue

Listening to a recording of the same, lengthy conversation for hours on end can lead to us focusing too much on tiny details and losing track of the bigger picture. When cleaning up dialog, it is especially important to frequently take breaks and listen to our edits in context. Remember, we want to achieve a natural listening experience, not an overproduced and overly sterile one.

Mixing

This section builds on the principles explored in the *Working with dialog from editing to post-production* section of *Chapter 8* and will thus focus primarily on principles and mixing philosophy in podcasting.

When mixing podcasts, we should apply the same dedication to a natural, conversational sound that we learned about in the *Working with dialog from editing to post-production* section of *Chapter 8*. Through the use of volume envelopes in combination with subtle, ideally load-sharing compression, we will maintain a steady level throughout without voices sounding overly compressed like they so often do on FM radio. An FX chain for a natural-sounding voice could look like what we see in *Figure 10.14*:

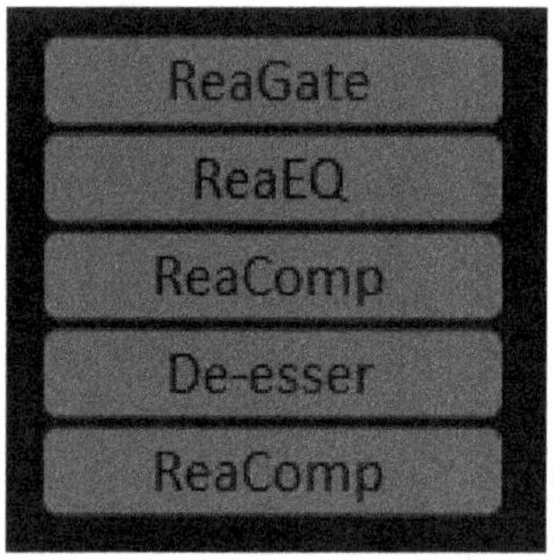

Figure 10.14 – An example FX chain for a podcast participant

Noise reduction with REAPER's integrated ReaFir plugin should be used very sparingly as voices often stand in complete isolation, making the plugin processing artifacts much more noticeable than with dialog in a dramatic context. In fact, if the podcast was recorded in a quiet space, this would not be necessary at all as we can utilize **gating** to handle the bulk of our background noise reduction.

Equalization can be used to tame harshness and boxiness, as well as to apply our go-to low-pass and high-pass filter frequencies. Just like with dialog, being somewhat aggressive in picking our low-pass frequency can lessen our need for de-essing and lead to an overall more pleasant tonality. Try setting it between 10 and 14 kHz. Reducing very high top-end, especially when recording with condenser microphones, will create some natural *distance* between the listener and our podcast participants. We will want to avoid excessive boosting and cutting and not try to impart a specific color to the signal as these can lead to listener fatigue.

Prior to applying any compression, we should have already started smoothing out our levels using *take volume envelopes* during the cleanup phase. As overly compressed dialog can easily lead to ear fatigue in our listeners, our goal should be to get most of our leveling done before applying further processing.

For precisely that reason, compression is to be handled lightly, with relaxed attack times and fast release times of 100 ms or below. Each compressor should ideally only reduce the overall level by -1 to -3 dB during regular conversation with load-sharing techniques (use of multiple compressors in series) used to catch more drastic peaks from energetic participants. It is very rare that more than two compressors will be required in civilized conversation.

De-essing should be applied on an as-needed basis and only when sibilance is a constant issue with one or more of our participant's voices. Occasional harsh esses can be removed more transparently by lowering their level in our *take volume envelopes*.

Panning can be used to communicate each participant's position if they are sitting across from each other. However, if individual participants frequently tend to speak for extended periods of time, their constantly sounding *off-center* can be disorienting for the listener or even make them think there is a problem with their headphones or speakers. As such, panning should be kept *narrow* (+/- 15% maximum) and is best reserved for conversations with frequent back and forth.

Mastering

Unlike music, podcasts don't require much in the way of mastering as most of our work in achieving good levels should have been accomplished in the *cleanup* and *mixing* phases.

Since podcasts are being listened to on a large variety of speakers, ranging from car audio systems to built-in phone speakers, an important element to keep under control is *harshness* and *boxiness*. While your ears should decide where cutting is needed, focus on the areas around 500 Hz, 2.5 kHz, and 6 kHz and notice any excess energy that could do with a slight cut via your master track's EQ. Especially early on, listening back to our podcast on many different speakers (car, phone, soundbar, laptop) is our best bet in developing our sonic signature we can then carry forward into future episodes.

Our overall loudness should fall somewhere between -23 LUFS (EBU R128) and -16 LUFS (official recommendation by Apple Podcasts). Where exactly we should fall within that range is dependent on how broad our spectrum of expression is. If we go from somber moments to emotionally charged arguments, aiming for -23 LUFS will be a more realistic goal to strive for. If our conversation stays at a somewhat consistent level, we might be able to bring our content all the way up to -16 LUFS using additional limiting and processing, as described in *Chapter 5*.

Utilizing render statistics

A great way to get readings of both our integrated loudness and momentary values over time, we can perform a so-called dry-run render to produce **render statistics** – a unique and powerful REAPER feature still unique to this DAW.

By entering the **Render** window (*Ctrl*/*cmd* + *Alt*/*option* + *R*) and clicking the **Dry run (no output)** button, we can perform a render without producing an actual audio file.

The file we get instead will be an HTML document, giving us an interactive **loudness graph** of our project that we can mouse over to analyze momentary and integrated loudness.

In the window that opens after our dry run has finished, we can click **Stats/Charts | Open render statistics charts in web browser** to view our stats document.

By hovering our mouse over the loudness curve, we will see our momentary peak level in dB, and our momentary (**M**) and short-term (**S**) loudness for every given moment of the project and can reflect on sections we might have to lower or increase in volume to achieve our desired loudness. *Figure 10.15* shows the statistics of a podcast recording that has been minimally processed:

File	Length	Peak	Clips	max LUFS-M	max LUFS-S	LUFS-I	LRA
0_Dialogue Sample Project	1:11.283	-1.0	0	-11.9	-15.6	-18.4	7.2

☐ Display project regions
☐ Display project markers

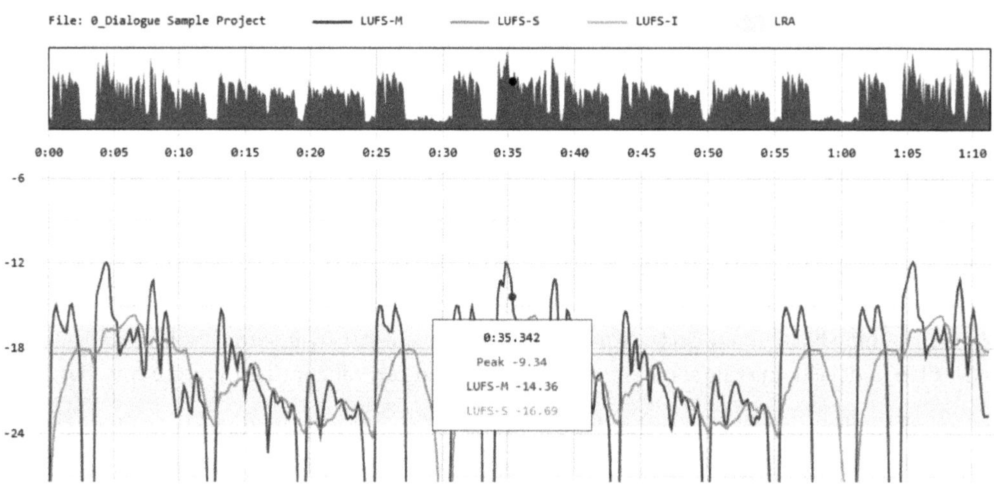

Figure 10.15 – Render stats of an unprocessed dialog recording

This document can also be saved by checking the **Save outfile render_stats.html** checkbox before initiating a render pass:

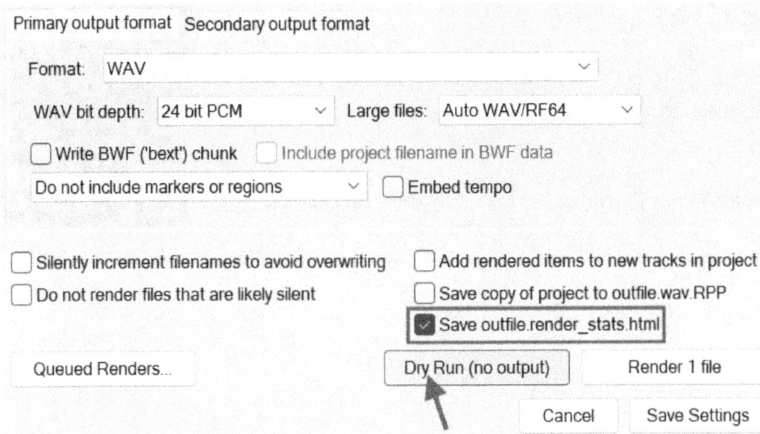

Figure 10.16 – Performing a render dry-run and saving our statistics

Using this handy feature to keep tabs on our overall loudness will help us establish our go-to processing methods over time and is an easy way to reference previous episodes' loudness measurements outside of the DAW.

Summary

In this chapter, we learned how to plan out our podcast idea and formalize our intentions for it. We learned which microphones can be used for recording podcasts and how to utilize them most effectively. We explored how to prepare for the recording sessions and keep our material organized while keeping the following editing process in mind.

We learned how to best approach the editing phase and avoid fatigue in the process while also building upon different editing techniques previously explored in *Chapter 8*.

Finally, we learned how to approach the mixing and mastering of podcasts from an intelligibility-first perspective, ensuring that they will sound engaging on any playback medium.

In the next chapter, we will explore the topic of sound design for film and video games. Many of these techniques can also be applied to the medium of podcasts and audio dramas and will be worth exploring for any aspiring audio professional.

11

Sound Design for Film and Games

Sound design is the practice of bringing stories to life through sound. Watch any movie or play any game with the sound off and you will immediately notice how big an effect the many creative choices made in sound design have on the emotional impact of the story being told.

While the practice of sound design has already filled several books on its own, this chapter will provide an essential primer to helping you get started in the matter and empower you to take your craft further. It will also showcase some incredibly powerful features unique to REAPER that have played a big part in its emergence to become the industry standard DAW for video game sound design around the globe.

In this chapter, we will cover the following main topics:

- **Sound design basics:** We explore the fundamentals and different philosophies of sound design, learn where and how to gather sonic source material, and we will be laying the groundwork for further editing and processing
- **Editing and effects:** Here, we explore editing and processing techniques ranging from layering and editing to utilizing FX plugins, transforming the source material we have gathered into entirely new soundscapes
- **Exporting and rendering considerations:** Finally, we explore best practices for exporting and managing our final audio assets, exporting stems, and developing naming schemes to fit the projects we're working on

By the end of the chapter, you will have a solid foundational understanding of how to approach the sound design process in REAPER from ideation to the rendering of final assets, harnessing REAPER's powerful wildcards and region render matrix features in the process. It will provide a solid basis to allow you to go further and experiment to find your own voice.

Technical requirements

To get started in sound design and tackle the topics explored in this chapter, you won't need much more than REAPER, some sound effects sourced from the internet or recordings you made yourself, and your imagination. Some examples of professionally recorded source material typically used to create sound effects are contained in the GitHub repository for this book: `https://github.com/PacktPublishing/Elevate-your-audio-production-with-Reaper`.

These recordings are royalty-free and can be used for any personal and commercial projects. Further free sound effects and raw recordings can be found at the following links:

- **GDC 2024 - Game Audio Bundle**: `https://gdc.sonniss.com/`
- **Freesound**: `https://freesound.org` (select **Creative Commons 0** in the *licensing* search filters)

Diving further into sound design, a microphone and audio interface, a handheld recorder, *or* a phone with high-quality mics will be important tools in allowing you to create sound effects out of your own unique recordings. While there are countless free and paid libraries out there for us to draw recordings from, the more we can bring our own distinct voice and aesthetic into what we do, the easier it will be for us to craft a style that's uniquely ours.

Sound design basics

With movies and video games, most of the time we can only stimulate two of our audience's senses: *sight* and *sound*. It is easy to see then why it is often stated that sound makes up at least 50% of movie and gameplay experiences. While the aspect of haptic feedback comes into play in games, these systems are increasingly handled by a game studio's audio department as well and are, one could argue, an extension of the game's soundscape.

Contrary to popular belief, all movies and games start off pretty much entirely silent. In the case of **film**, the focus of the location sound recording crew is entirely on capturing as much usable dialog as possible during the shooting process in order to avoid having to bring actors back into the studio for costly and time-consuming recording sessions. Even in busy scenes with lots of extras seemingly chatting and enjoying themselves in the background, it is commonplace for all background actors to simply mouth their conversations without actually saying anything. Combine this with a usually noisy set thanks to fans, generators, directors yelling instructions, and environmental factors, and you can see why the only audio making it to post-production is **on-set dialog** from the primary actors.

In animation as well as in games, the audio team starts with an entirely blank slate – often creating initial sound effects and temporary dialog to accompany a slideshow of storyboards or very rudimentary animations created in the game engine. It is also not uncommon to start sound design work based solely on concept artwork and loose ideas, envisioning what a character or location might sound like when brought to life onscreen.

The "food groups" of sound design

Taking any scene of gameplay from a completely silent state to living in a believable soundscape requires careful interplay of many elements that can be loosely categorized into three major *food groups*:

- **Ambience/backgrounds**: Ambiences fundamentally describes the sound and feel of an environment and can range from real-life nature recordings to highly designed futuristic soundscapes. They help create a sonic world that feels alive and omnipresent and can range from largely unprocessed, looping wind and birdsong to highly stylized drones and otherworldly synth textures.
- **Foley**: This category of sound design broadly describes any naturally occurring sound resulting from characters, creatures, and objects interacting with and moving through the world. Traditionally, Foley is performed in real time by highly specialized artists (often called *Foley walkers*) manipulating props or food items, walking on specially prepared surfaces, and many other techniques. In video games, Foley performances often serve as the basis for further sound design. Typical applications of Foley are the sounds of characters handling objects, footsteps, combat, and gore. The line between Foley and sound design is often a blurry one as they frequently play off of each other.
- **Sound effects/hard effects**: In movies, the term *sound effects* is often reserved for sounds that had to be *designed* to fulfill a specific purpose and could not be achieved through pure Foley performance. Examples of this are futuristic weapons and vehicles, giant creatures, or magic spells. In games, it is not uncommon to see the term used to refer to nearly all audio outside of music and ambiences.

> Note
>
> In the course of this chapter, when talking about games, the term **audio assets** will be used to refer to any and all audio files created during the sound design process.

Film versus games – key differences in sound design

While the same fundamental principles of sound design apply to both mediums, films and games pose entirely different requirements for how they are applied. **Films** are by and large a *linear medium*, meaning that the sequence of events and the storyline are clearly laid out. As such, sound design and audio post-production happen on a linear timeline, and many sound effects will only be heard one single time over the entire duration of the film. Every piece of sound can be precisely tuned to exactly hit the story beats and emotional moments we want to highlight, and they will play at exactly the same time regardless of where the movie is being shown.

Games, on the other hand, are highly interactive and *nonlinear*. Even with the most linear and predictable gaming experience, the player still has ultimate control over when and how they perform certain actions, how long they remain in a certain area, and where they will be going next. Players will also end up failing and replaying areas of the game over and over and generally play the game in ways that might be hard for the developers to predict.

With this in mind, it becomes clear that designing a single sound effect for something, such as a footstep or gunshot, would quickly lead to incredibly fatiguing repetition and a stilted, robotic feel that would break any immersion immediately. Thus, *variations* are key when creating sound effects for video games and it's not uncommon for games to utilize dozens of individual assets for something as simple as a character's footsteps on concrete.

While in movies, every single footstep and sound effect can be carefully considered and precisely placed to sound perfect in a very *specific moment*, in games, we have to create high-quality assets with numerous variations so that they can sound natural and non-repetitive regardless of how the game is being played. Similarly, we want to strive to create assets and systems that can be *reused* across different gameplay areas and create user interface and notification sounds that provide important feedback to the player on how well (or poorly) they are doing.

It is not rare for a game to feature thousands, if not tens of thousands, of individual sound effects upon release, and the need for organic variations is a key factor contributing to this. Furthermore, sound designers have to consider the available hardware resources of their target platform. Mobile games will have a much tighter memory budget and stricter CPU usage targets than AAA console titles, for example.

Implementation

Another way in which game sound design differs from working with movies is the process of **audio implementation**. While all sound for a film is traditionally laid out on a linear timeline, the way sound effects make their way into a game is through implementation via middleware or directly in the game engine. Let's have a look at these in more detail as follows:

- **Middleware** is essentially an engine purpose-built for audio that offers sound designers a graphical interface that allows for the creation of dynamic audio systems largely without any need for coding. The most commonly used middleware applications are **Audiokinetic Wwise** (see *Figure 11.1*) and **Firelight Technologies FMOD**.

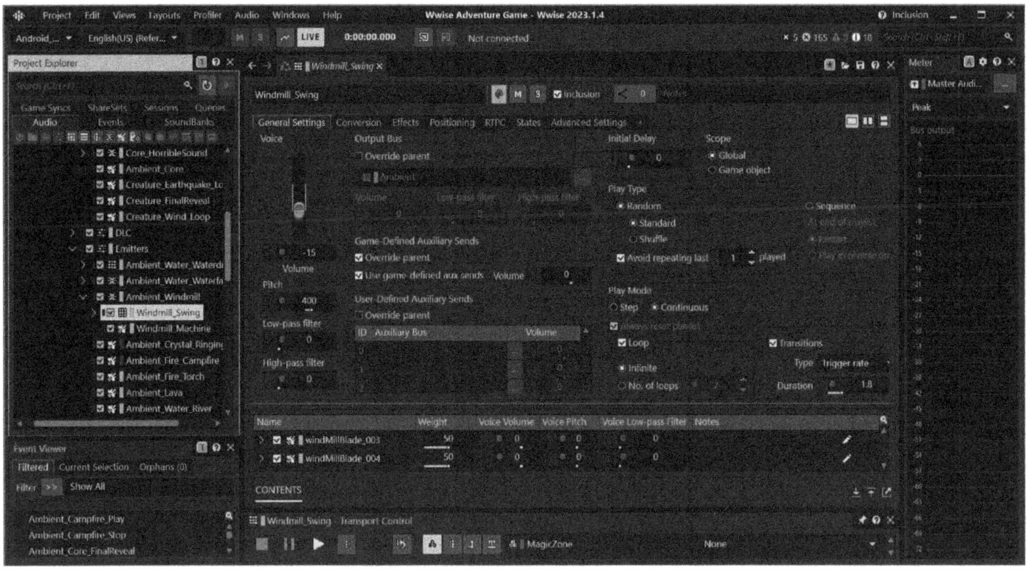

Figure 11.1 – An overview of Audiokinetic Wwise middleware

- **Game engines** also offer built-in audio functionality, but these features are often rudimentary, and implementation will require some degree of coding or scripting. The most commonly used game engines are **Unreal Engine** and **Unity**. Resources for all these apps can be found on vendor websites and in a myriad of places online, such as YouTube. Which tool will be used is ultimately up to the development team's preferences and budget as licensing middleware can incur substantial costs based on the production's budget and the number of platforms it will be released to.

  Some developers, particularly large studios, may be using only proprietary game engines and audio middleware. As those tools are usually shrouded in secrecy, the best we can do is learn our way around industry-standard tools as many of their features and workflows will more or less translate to proprietary ones. Note that these studios will usually train new hires on their tools and won't expect us to magically know all about their secret sauce.

Next, we will look at how game audio projects are planned through the process of spotting and how we keep track of the assets we're working on.

Spotting

The process of deciding which sounds should play when is usually referred to as **spotting**. During a spotting session for a film, the sound team or supervising sound editor will sit down with the director and potentially editors to discuss which moments of a film should be highlighted sonically and create a *cue sheet* containing all important sounds that need to be added to the picture with their precise *timecode*.

In games, the audio team's involvement in this decision-making process can happen at different points during the development cycle. In many cases, audio professionals are brought onto the team once the game's vision has been largely established, while in others, audio might play a key role from the very beginning of pre-production.

Regardless of what stage of development a game is in, at some point, a so-called **asset list** will have to be devised. This document should not only contain a list of all audio assets needed to complete the game's soundtrack but also provide a way to track the status and level of completion of every one of these sounds.

When joining a game's development as a contractor, it is not unusual to receive a previously created **audio asset list** we will have to follow and work through.

An example of an audio asset tracking sheet you can use as a template can be found in the GitHub repository accompanying this book at the following link:

`https://github.com/PacktPublishing/Elevate-your-audio-production-with-Reaper`

This document should be a continuously updated resource that can help communicate the progress and current challenges of the audio department across teams and collaborators and will also allow different team members to assign priorities to specific elements. Traditionally, these sheets are shared via Google Docs, Dropbox, or within the project's repository in order to allow for real-time collaboration and to track changes made by team members.

Now that the project has more clearly defined needs that its audio department (in this case us) has to fulfill, our next step will be to assemble the source material we will be using to create all of our sound effects, Foley, and ambiences.

Source material

Based on the demands of the project, we can now begin sourcing audio material that we can manipulate, edit, and process to shape into the sounds we're imagining. Typically, sound designers will resort to a combination of the following sources to build a catalog or library of source material for the project at hand:

- Sound effects libraries they have purchased
- Personal field recordings
- Material provided by Foley artists
- Sound effects they previously created through synthesis or processing

While your library might be somewhat small in the beginning, there are many ways to expand it through resources previously shared in the *Sourcing sound effects* section of *Chapter 8*. The more varied our library, the more creative freedom it allows us with our sound design.

All of the sounds in our library should live in one location on our computer or external storage so that we can easily access all of them using REAPER's **Media Explorer**. This will also make it easier to migrate this library in case its size eventually exceeds the remaining space on our drive of choice.

Working with the Media Explorer

As explored in *Chapter 2*, REAPER's **Media Explorer** is a tremendously helpful tool for managing our sound library. Furthermore, we can create our own databases and add notes and tags that will help us create pools of recordings and sound effects for specific projects that we can easily retrieve later in the sound design process.

The **Media Explorer** can be brought up using the *Ctrl* + *Alt* + *X* shortcut (replace *Ctrl* with *cmd* and *Alt* with *option* on Mac) and will appear at the bottom of the window by default. If you're using multiple displays or prefer a different layout, you can *right-click* the top bar of the Explorer panel and uncheck **Dock media explorer in Docker**, as shown in *Figure 11.2*:

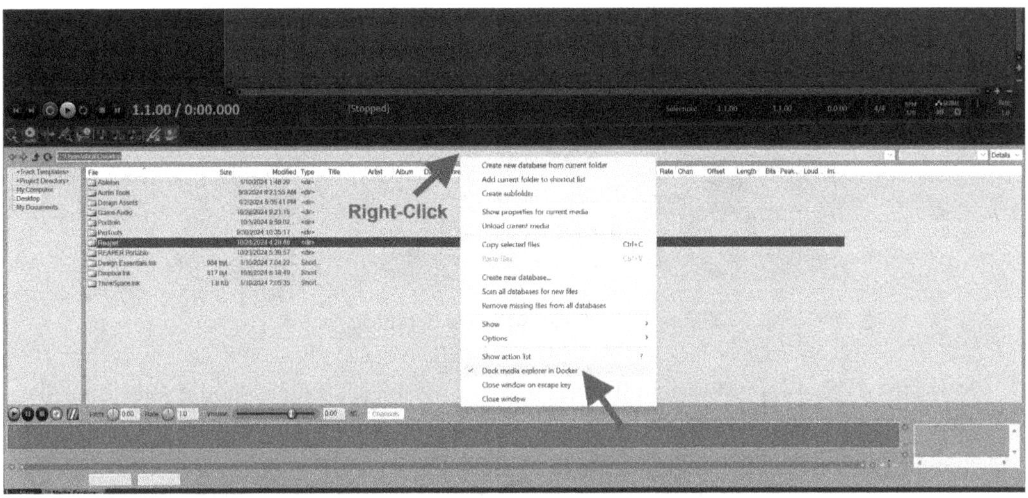

Figure 11.2 – Undocking the Media Explorer

This will move it into a floating window that can be placed anywhere. With the **Media Explorer** open, we can now begin scanning for the sounds in our library.

Scanning our library

To have access to our sound library through the **Media Explorer**, we first need to scan it. By creating a database in the **Media Explorer**, we establish a record of all sounds in our library and can have it update whenever we add new material. To do so, we need to do the following:

1. Right-click within the locations panel on the left side and click **Create new database...**.

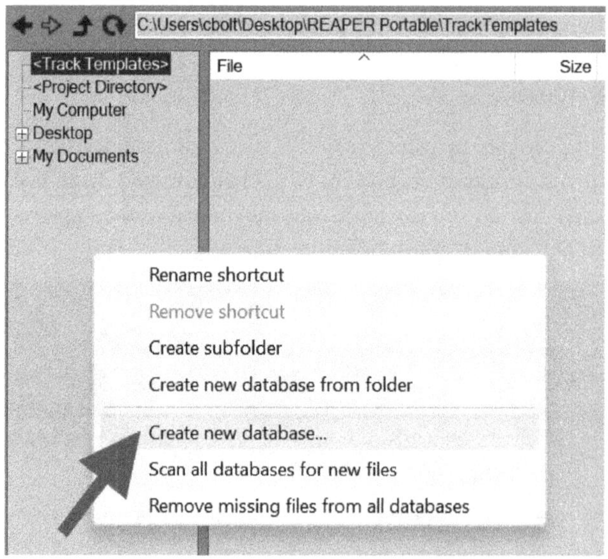

Figure 11.3 – Creating a new database

2. Name the database appropriately. If your library is in a single location, choose something like `SFX Library` or `Sound Library`, as shown in *Figure 11.4*. If you would like to index multiple libraries in different locations (for keeping musical samples and sound effects separate for example), you will need to repeat this process for each location and name them appropriately.

Figure 11.4 – Naming our new database

3. Now, we right-click the new database we just created in the left side panel and click **Add path to database...**, which is where we will be specifying the location of our sound library on our drive.

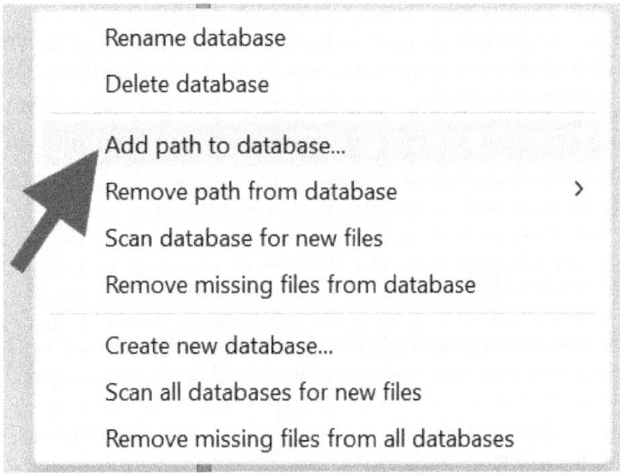

Figure 11.5 – Adding a file path to our database

Now, REAPER will scan the selected folder for all audio files and eventually produce a list of all of them in the **Media Explorer**, as shown in *Figure 11.6*:

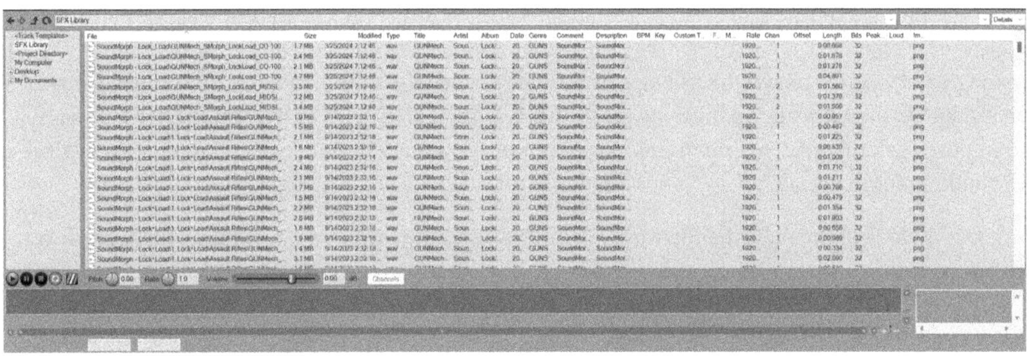

Figure 11.6 – Overview of the Media Explorer, now populated with files

Now that our library has been scanned, by clicking any audio file and skimming through files using our arrow keys, every sound selected will be previewed immediately, making it much easier to quickly find the material we need.

Using the columns, we can sort files by different pieces of metadata, such as description, comments, artist, and so forth. For work with sound effects, we will drag the **Description** and **Comment** columns closest to our file name and *expand* them in size. Most professionally created sound effects will have an informative description that tells us about the nature of the sound and how it was created. By double-clicking any column, we can also add our own comments and notes to any field to help us find sounds in the future.

Creating collections of sounds

When searching for sonic source material to use for our specific projects, it's best to keep all the sounds we like in a dedicated database to find them more easily later. This can be achieved in a few simple steps:

1. Create a new database as before and name it appropriately. If we are specifically looking for a certain category of sounds, we can name it `Project Name_Footsteps`, for example. Keeping the name of the project in the name of the database will make it easier to keep track of later on.
2. With the new database created, we can simply drag and drop any sound we think will be useful for our project right into it. This will not copy the file to another location and thus not consume any additional drive space until we actually insert the file into our REAPER project.

Creating databases for new projects helps us ultimately spend less time looking for sounds at a later stage when we should really be focusing on **sound design**. It also helps us overcome choice paralysis and imposes helpful creative limitations as we are not browsing our entire sound library every time we're looking for materials.

Next, we will look at the many handy ways in which we can move material from the **Media Explorer** into our project.

Getting sounds onto our timeline

To import sounds from the **Media Explorer** into our timeline, we have a handful of options:

- Dragging and dropping them from our explorer window or panel right onto the timeline is the quickest way to freely position our sound in the project.
- Spotting them via the **Insert** button allows us to position our chosen sound based on our timeline selection. When clicking the **Insert** button in the top toolbar of the **Media Explorer**, the sound will be inserted at the location of our edit cursor, as shown in *Figure 11.7*:

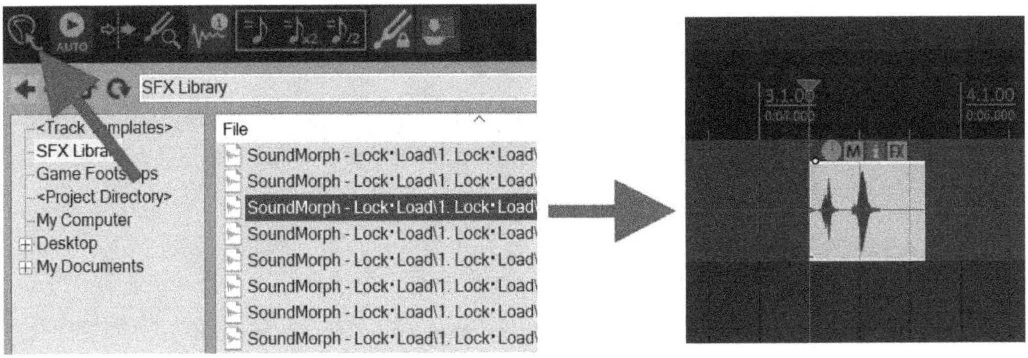

Figure 11.7 – Spotting sounds to the timeline via the Insert button

By right-clicking the sound in question, we will be presented with more specific inserting options:

- **Insert into project** functions the same way as the previously mentioned Insert button.
- **Insert at time selection (stretch/loop to fit)** will conform the sound to exactly match the duration of the *time selection* we made on our timeline. If the selection is *shorter* than our sound, it will be compressed in time and playback faster. If the selection is *longer*, the sound will loop to fill it.
- **Insert on a new track** will insert our sound on a new track at our edit cursor position.
- **Insert into sample player** will create an instance of the **ReaSampleOmatic5000** plugin on our current track or a new one, allowing us to perform the sound via our MIDI controller. This is handy if we will be playing a sample musically or quickly want to try performing it alongside our video.
- **Insert in selected media** items allows us to either replace an item with a new one of our choosing, add the new sound as another *take*, or replace the old item in a way that matches its length like in *item 2*.

If we wish to only bring a portion of our audio file into our timeline, we can *drag* across the waveform along the bottom of the **Media Explorer** to select the desired portion and either utilize dragging and dropping, or inserting via one of the ways described earlier. This is shown in *Figure 11.8* as follows:

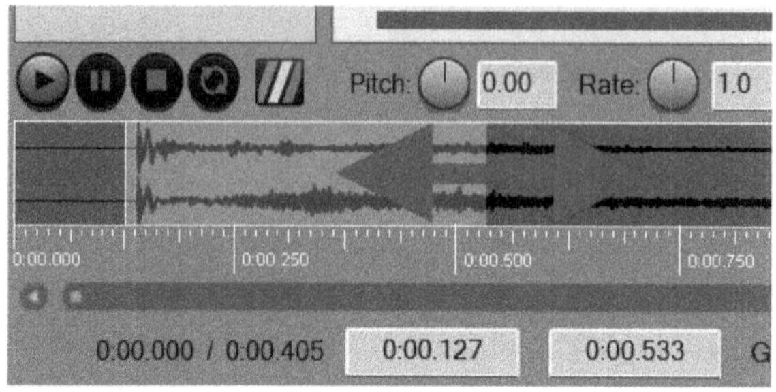

Figure 11.8 – Selecting pieces of audio by dragging across the waveform

The **Media Explorer** is a powerful tool that will be our constant companion when working on sound design projects. With our library indexed, and our favorite material collected in a dedicated database, we can move forward and process our sounds to create new sound effects, ambiences, and Foley.

Editing and effects

While the source material is one ingredient for sound design, the real magic happens in layering and processing, where we get to recontextualize our source material and create entirely new sounds through different combinations of sounds and processing techniques. We will explore some of the fundamentals of designing effective and impactful sound effects and create the foundation for you to go ahead and explore further.

Layering

The most essential sound design technique and one that has been practiced since the dawn of the craft is **layering** – combining different sounds to create entirely new ones. Whether it's layering lion roars with engines revving to create more menacing car sounds, to layering the recordings of popping bubble wrap with clothes rustling to recreate the sound of a campfire. Our imagination is the limit when it comes to finding combinations of seemingly disparate sounds that can reveal entirely new sonic worlds.

The best way to determine how many layers a sound needs is to separate it into its individual core components, as shown in *Figure 11.9*:

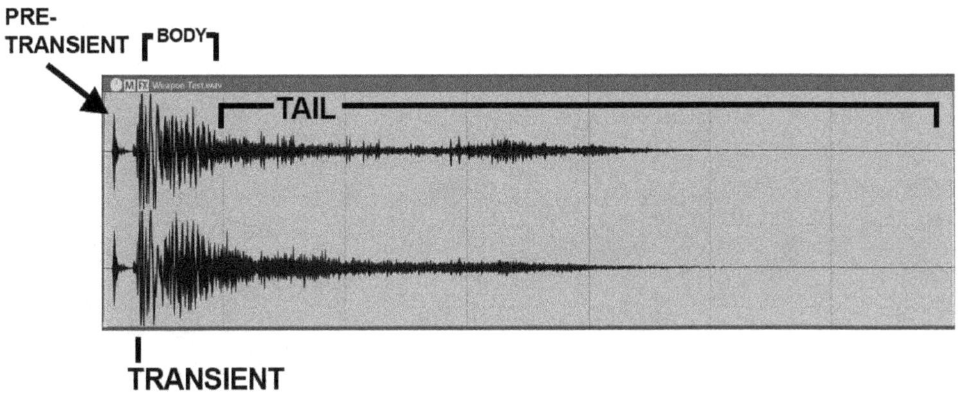

Figure 11.9 – A gunshot sound effect

While there are an innumerable number of different categories and styles of sound effects, many of them share the following components:

- **Pre-Transient**: The *wind-up* to a sound, say the *woosh* immediately before the impact of a large axe hitting a tree, can be called the **pre-transient** area. This includes any and all sound happening before the main transient.
- **Transient**: The **transient** is the initial *impact* and often the loudest peak of a sound effect. For weapons, it would be the sound of the initial muzzle blast, in a footstep, it would be the moment the person's heel touches the ground and produces an audible *thump*.
- **Body**: The **body** of a sound is what happens after the transient and its duration can vary greatly based on the source and intensity of the sound.
- **Tail**: What happens as a sound fades into silence is often called the **tail**. Its length can vary greatly based on the source of the sound and it can range from the echoes of a gunshot bouncing off of a cliffside to the winding down of a turbine.

Not all sound effects require all four components and it is common for these components to be treated as separate sound files in video games, which allows for a greater degree of randomization as each component can have independent variations. Regardless of whether they will all be rendered as one audio file or as individual layers, we should design them in context and audition all parts together before delivering them in the format our team requires.

Keeping these layers in mind, we can establish a clearer vision of what our sound effect needs. Let's look at the weapon sound effect from before on the timeline:

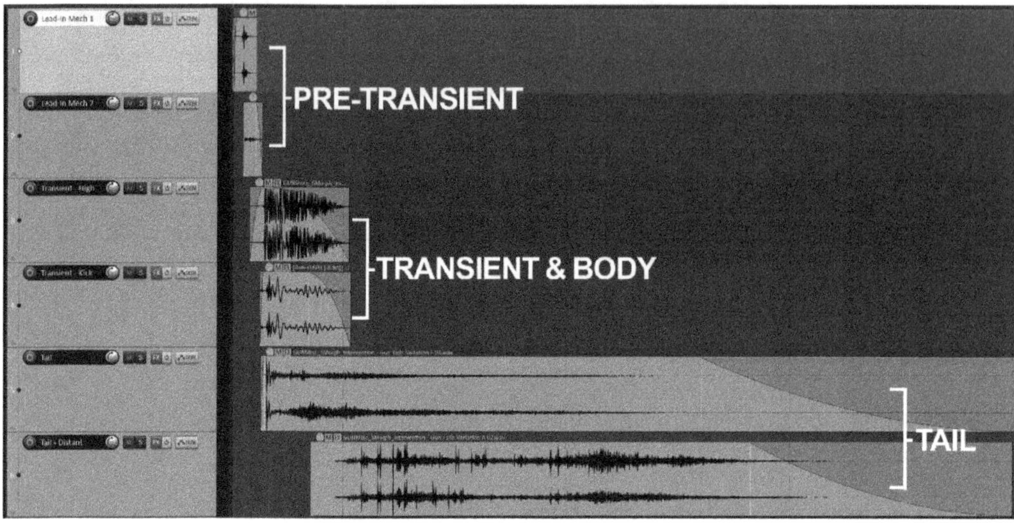

Figure 11.10 – A simple gunshot designed in six layers

This specific sound starts with a brief mechanical click that signifies the player character pulling the trigger during the pre-transient phase. Very shortly after follows a bombastic transient with a few further mechanical sounds representing the mechanical components of the weapon moving as the charge is fired. The two recordings making up the tail are each recording of the same, real-life gunshot from a medium and far microphone position respectively. In this case, the medium position recording is also used to further sweeten the main transient as it contains the initial *pop* of the gun, while the far recording primarily captures the complex echoing and reverberation caused by the gunshot.

Again, there is no definitive rule on how many layers any specific sound effect needs to sound convincing, but it is always advisable to not overcrowd each part of the sound and, more importantly, the **frequency spectrum**. Try **muting** each layer once you have landed on a combination of sounds you enjoy and see whether they still hold the same value in context or are unnecessarily crowding your sound effect and taking away from its impact.

Another important aspect to master in sound design is creating loops, which we will explore in the next section.

Looping

Creating seamless loops could be called the *bread and butter* of sound design for video games as looping assets are crucial in creating immersive soundscapes. Of course, we cannot create endless audio assets but still need to build a soundscape that doesn't show obvious signs of looping that our players would easily notice and get tired of.

Common uses for looped assets include nature ambiences, engines, bodies of water, and continuously firing weapons or magic spells that shoot for as long as the player holds down a button. This section will help demystify the creation of looping assets.

If we are looping an asset that we've already created or simply want to loop a nature recording, the easiest way to do so is by simply *cutting* off a small section at the end of the item, *pasting* it to the beginning on a new track, and *adjusting* the item fades to create a seamless transition.

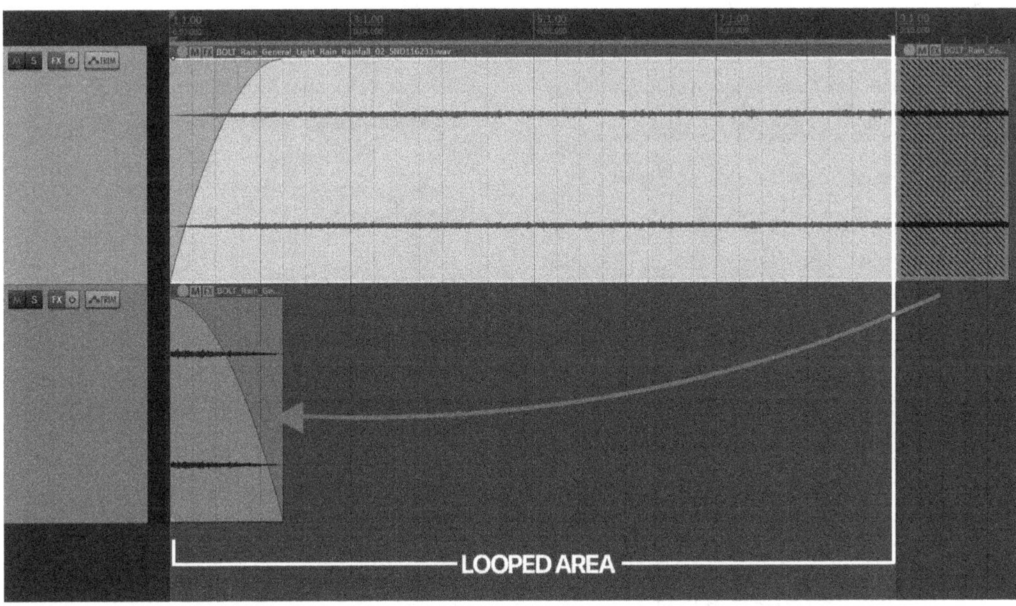

Figure 11.11 – Looping assets by cutting and pasting their end to make a new beginning

Adjusting the fades can sometimes take a lot of trial and error as recordings with any sort of constant noise, such as wind, rain, or engines, are prone to phasing issues during fades. Play your loop on repeat and try different fade-in and fade-out curve shapes via the **Media Item Properties** panel as well as fade lengths and listen to which sounds most natural.

To perform this action with material that we're actively designing, we will first have to render our current design as a mono or stereo file as follows:

1. Make an appropriate time selection to include the area we want to loop later.
2. Enter the **Render** dialog via *Ctrl + Alt + R* (substitute *cmd* for *Ctrl* and *option* for *Alt* on Mac).
3. Check **Add rendered items to new tracks in project**, as shown in *Figure 11.12*:

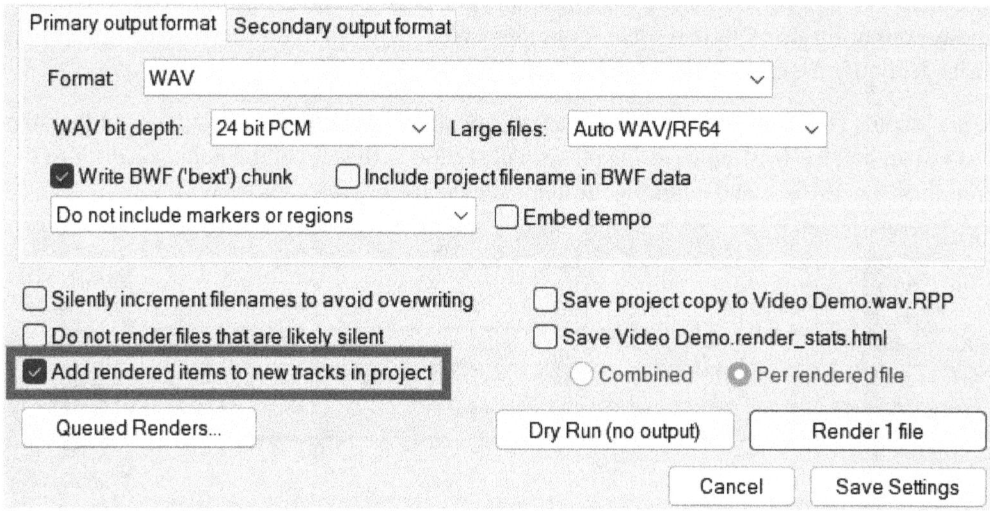

Figure 11.12 – Checking the Add rendered items to new tracks [...] button

4. Click the **Render [x] file(s)** button to render the audio file and have it automatically added to our session on a new track.

Now, we can proceed to create a loop of our sound design exactly as described before. Another benefit to rendering our creations to audio and bringing them back into the same project is that we can now apply further processing to the material, such as pitch shifting and effects processing. Next, we will explore one of the oldest tricks in the book: Slowing things down.

Slowing it down

Slowing recordings down and in turn lowering them in pitch is one of the most used techniques in sound design and has been used since the early days of film. Originally, this effect was achieved by simply playing back the audio tape at a slower speed – hence, this practice often being called **varispeed**.

This practice is not to be confused with the now popular method of **time stretching**, which aims to let us manipulate the timing and duration of recordings while maintaining their original pitch and sonic characteristics.

Slowing recordings down helps us discover new potential in recordings, makes things sound weightier and more intimidating, and, most commonly, lets us turn a normal human voice into what sounds much more like a large creature.

A great deal of all sounds used by professional sound designers will end up slowed down or sped up before they make it into a finalized sound effect and REAPER makes it easy for us to quickly alter the speed and pitch of a recording.

> **Higher sample rates and varispeed**
>
> The prevalence of the **varispeed process** in sound design is the major reason why most contemporary sound effects libraries are distributed at high sample rates of 96 kHz or above. At 48 kHz, the highest frequency that can be reproduced is 24 kHz – or half the sample rate. Slow a sound down by half and now the highest frequency in that same recording will be 12 kHz. We would notice a lack of high-end.
>
> Take a recording captured at 96 kHz and slow it down to half speed, and our highest possible frequency moves from 48 kHZ to 24 kHz, still well above what the human ear can perceive.
>
> Simply put, working with higher sample rate audio files will allow us to retain greater fidelity when we slow these recordings down, given that they have been created using microphones or other techniques that capture or yield usable information outside of the audible spectrum.

To quickly slow down any item within REAPER, we can use the following steps:

1. Double-click the item in question to open the **Media Item Properties** window.
2. Here, type in a value into the **Playback Rate** field and uncheck **Preserve pitch when changing rate**. This value should be below `1.000` [...] to slow the item down or higher when speeding up. A good starting point is slowing down or speeding up a sound in 10% increments (i.e., `0.9` or `1.1`).

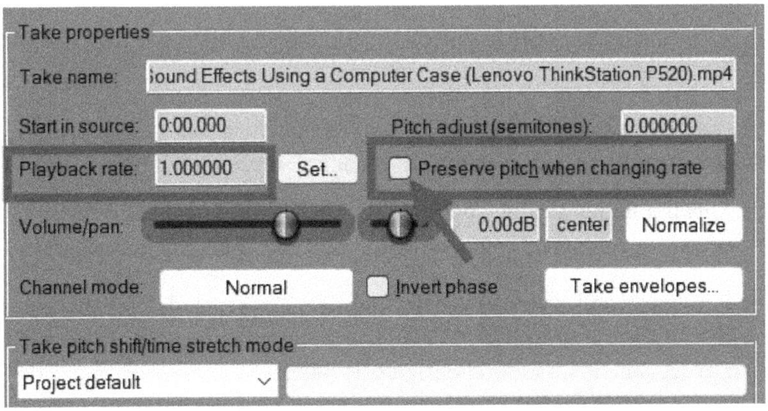

Figure 11.13 – Changing playback rate and disabling time stretching

3. Click **Apply** to commit our changes and play back the sound to hear how its tonality has changed. This change can be reversed at any time and playback rate changes are entirely non-destructive to our items.

From the sounds of handling metal chains to explosions and voices, changing an item's playback rate can unveil entirely new sonic perspectives and is something we will resort to constantly when trying to come up with new and interesting ways to approach our sound design projects.

Next, we will explore some of the many ways effects plugins can be utilized to further manipulate and shape our sound effects.

Utilizing effects

When it comes to effects, there is truly no limit to how wild we can get in sound design. Just about every kind of effects plugin has been used to create memorable sound effects heard in blockbuster movies and AAA video games and the key to harnessing our plugins to their fullest potential is to be willing to experiment and learn how they behave with different settings and source material.

This section will provide some ideas on what REAPER's included plugins can be used for in sound design:

- **ReaComp** or **ReaLimit** can be used with extreme settings to achieve larger-than-life sounding weapons, explosion, and impact sound effects.
- **Parallel compression** (see *Chapter 13*) can be utilized to give sounds great amounts of beefiness without destroying their transients
- **JS: Ring Modulator**: This can be used to make voices and other source materials sound metallic, robotic, or choppy by playing with its parameters.
- **JS: Saturation**: This offers simple saturation that will add additional harmonic content and subtly smooth our transients, allowing us to make recordings sound weightier and louder without applying compression and achieve varying degrees of audible yet desirable distortion. This is especially helpful on sounds with overbearing transients, such as gunshots, explosions, or crashes.
- **JS: Flanger and JS: Chorus**: These can help us widen sounds and make them sound futuristic or even mimic the way a large creature's mouth affects the sound of its voice and breathing.
- **ReaPitch**: This is a highly flexible, polyphonic **pitch shifter** that also allows us to perform **formant shifting** on voices and sound effects, drastically changing their character.

While most sound designers will eventually go beyond REAPER's included plugins and effects, they provide an incredible amount of sound design potential right out of the gate. The key to discovering how best to utilize processing in our sound design is to always be experimenting and not be afraid of making mistakes. Remember, the most interesting sounds are often the result of happy accidents!

Exporting and rendering considerations

Once we have created the sound effects for our game, film, or video, the next step will be to render them so that they can be sent to our collaborators and/or integrated into the final product.

This section will tackle exporting and rendering considerations for motion picture and game projects separately as there are key differences in how audio assets are delivered.

Rendering sound effects for film and video

When handling sound design for film and video, we will most commonly be asked to either deliver a complete sound effects mix or **stems** to whoever will be assembling and mixing the soundtrack for the project. If we oversee all audio, we would be delivering a final **master mix** or stems to the person editing the project so that they can sync it to their video timeline and deliver the final exported video for distribution or delivery to their client.

When we are exporting stems, it is once again important to have all sonic *food groups* of our project grouped in *folder tracks*. By utilizing the region render matrix, we can automatically render all these folder tracks as individual stems for delivery. To set up our matrix, we will follow these steps:

1. Create a region representing the entire duration of the project. If we're working with video, *Shift* + double-clicking the video file will automatically create a time selection for its duration. By pressing *Shift* + *R*, we will create a region matching our time selection.
2. By *Shift* + clicking this new region, we can change its name to something like `Project Duration` or `Export Range`, as shown in *Figure 11.14*:

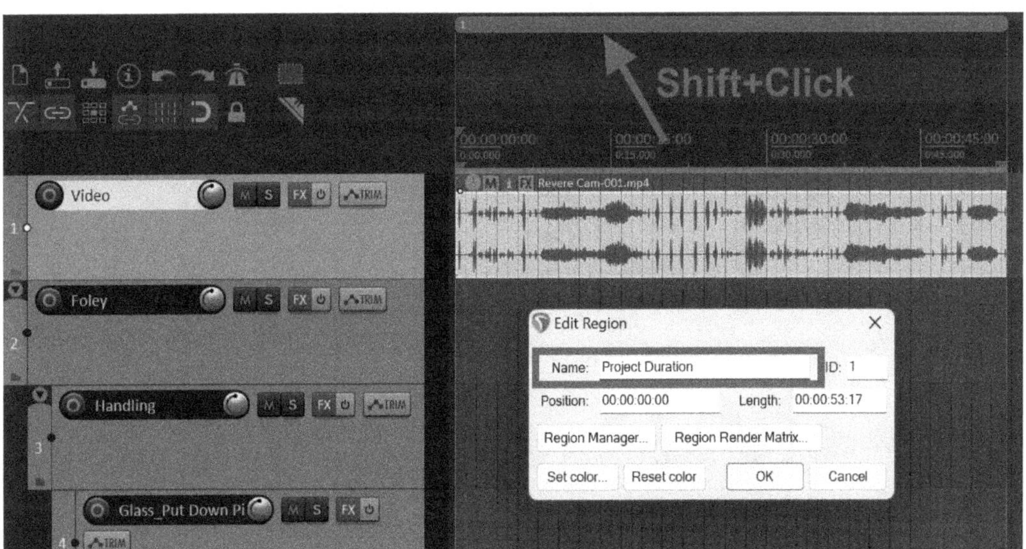

Figure 11.14 – Renaming our region

3. Now, we will bring up the **Render to File** window via *Ctrl* + *Alt* + *R* (*cmd* + *option* + *R* on Mac) and select **Region render matrix** as our **Source** option. Since the regions will define our **export range**, we don't need to choose any specific **Bounds** setting.

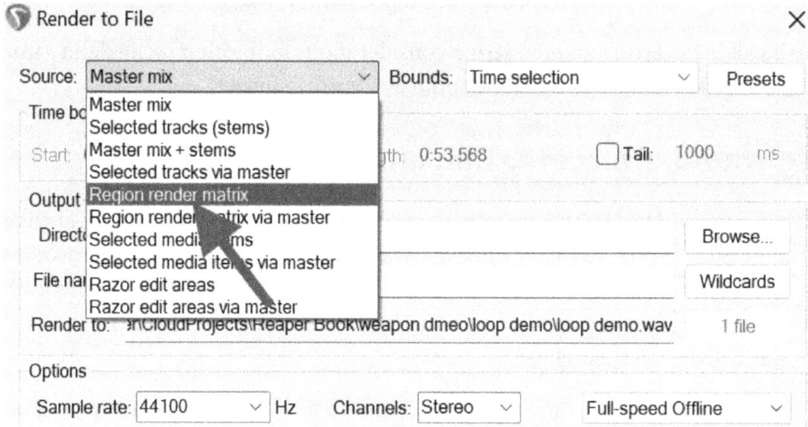

Figure 11.15 – Selecting Region render matrix as our Source

4. The **Render to File** window will now show buttons for **Region Manager** and **Region Render Matrix**, as shown in *Figure 11.16*. We will click on the latter to show the matrix. This will show a list of all tracks in our project as well as *columns* for each of our regions and render checkboxes for track and region combination.

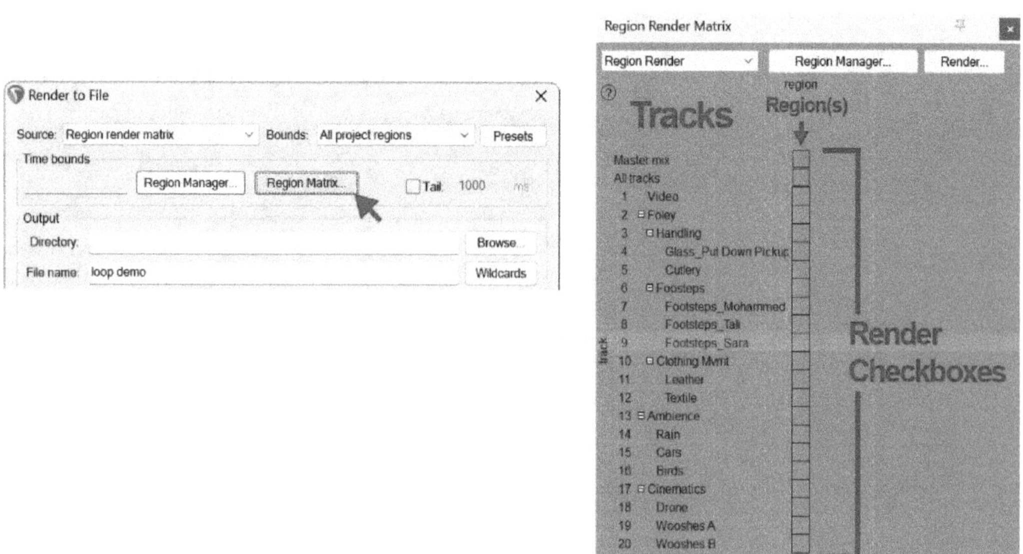

Figure 11.16 – Opening the region render matrix

5. Next, we will check the checkboxes next to the folder tracks we want to render as stems within the **Project Duration** region we just created. It is up to our discretion how granular we want to be with this, but it is generally common to group the major categories together, as shown in *Figure 11.17*:

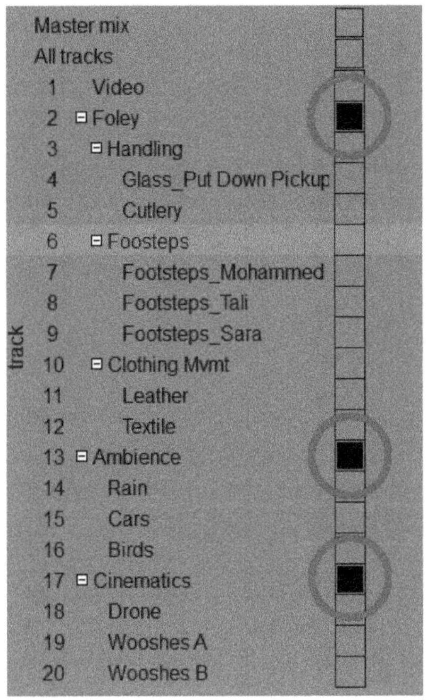

Figure 11.17 – Selecting which folders should be rendered as stems

We can now close **Region Render Matrix** and utilize REAPER's **wildcards** feature to automatically name our stems based on the folders they originate from:

1. In our **Directory** field, we will make sure to specify the folder in which we want to export our stems.
2. To dynamically add the name of a given track to our filename, we just have to type the `$track` wildcard into our desired part of the name and REAPER will automatically add it to the name of our file upon rendering. As seen in *Figure 11.18*, our example name will be `MyMovieProject_Stem_$track_MonthDD-YY`:

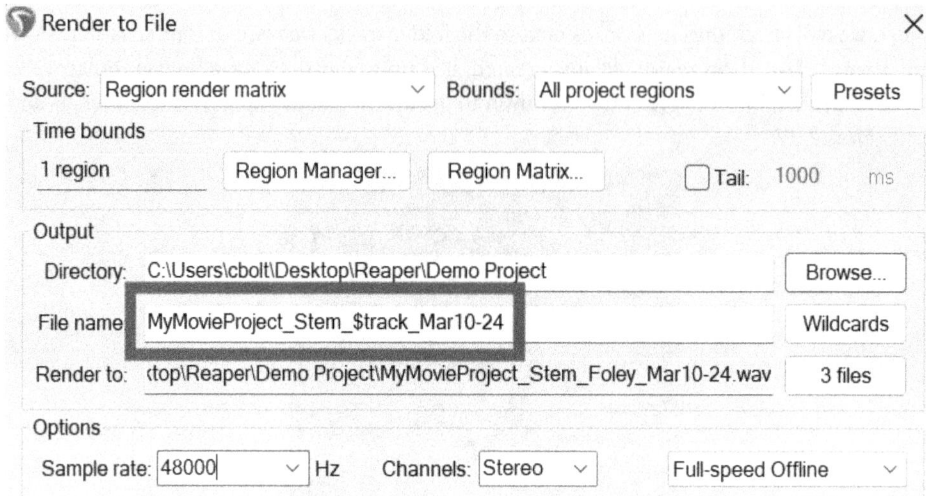

Figure 11.18 – The $track wildcard in action

3. By clicking the *x* **files** (where *x* = number of regions to render) button, we can verify the files REAPER will create and double-check whether they will be named correctly.

From here, we can proceed to set our desired audio rendering settings and proceed to create the final stems for our project. For video projects, it is customary for audio to be rendered at 48,000 Hz and for there to be no normalization or limiting applied during the render phase.

Rendering sound effects for video games

When working on a video game project, all of our sound effects will have to be rendered as individual files. The exception to this is cinematic cutscenes where audio is often handled in a linear manner similar to film.

It is not rare for a game's soundtrack to consist of tens or hundreds of thousands of individual sound effects. Even smaller, mobile titles frequently feature several hundred audio assets that all need to be delivered to our team at a consistent quality and with appropriate file names.

Luckily, REAPER's powerful naming features allow us to automate much of this process and ensure that even if we render all our work at once, all assets will be where we want them to be.

Splitting up the workload

Since video games require so many different kinds of assets and projects can easily become overly large and convoluted, it can be beneficial to create separate projects for each category of sound. For example, for an adventure game, we might create individual projects for `Weapons`, `Foley`, `Magic`, and `Ambiences`. Doing so will also make it easier to automate our file naming and rendering regimes.

Asset naming schemes

In games, there is no hard and fast rule for how audio assets should be named. Generally, the scope and scale of our project should be the main determining factor for how granular and detailed our file names and folder structures should be. Let's look at these two examples:

- **A**: `Sx_Mvmt_JumpLand_Dirt.wav`
- **B**: `Sx_Foley_Locom_Steve_JumpLand_Sand.wav`

In cases where different characters (be it the player or NPCs) share a lot of sound effects, we don't always need to specify which character a sound originates from. Naming scheme *A* would therefore be sufficient.

If we have to take many different player characters or unique NPCs into account, it will serve us well to include exactly whom a sound will be dedicated to right in our filename – in this case, `Steve`. Furthermore, the category of Foley could have many different subcategories, such as `Handle`, `Locomotion`, and `Interact`. Naming scheme *B* would allow us to get a clearer picture when managing thousands of assets for different characters.

Both of these two naming schemes would also allow us to simply render all files into the same folder and pick out the ones we need based on their name. Depending on how sounds will be integrated into the game, however, it may be beneficial for us to create a **folder structure** mirroring our categories so that folders can be imported into our middleware or game engine at once.

Luckily, REAPER can help us automate both of these methods and even create a folder structure for us. By organizing our tracks in folders and utilizing markers and regions, we have several project parameters we can utilize as wildcards in our file naming.

The following example showcases one of many ways to utilize folders, regions, and markers to implement our folder structure and file naming:

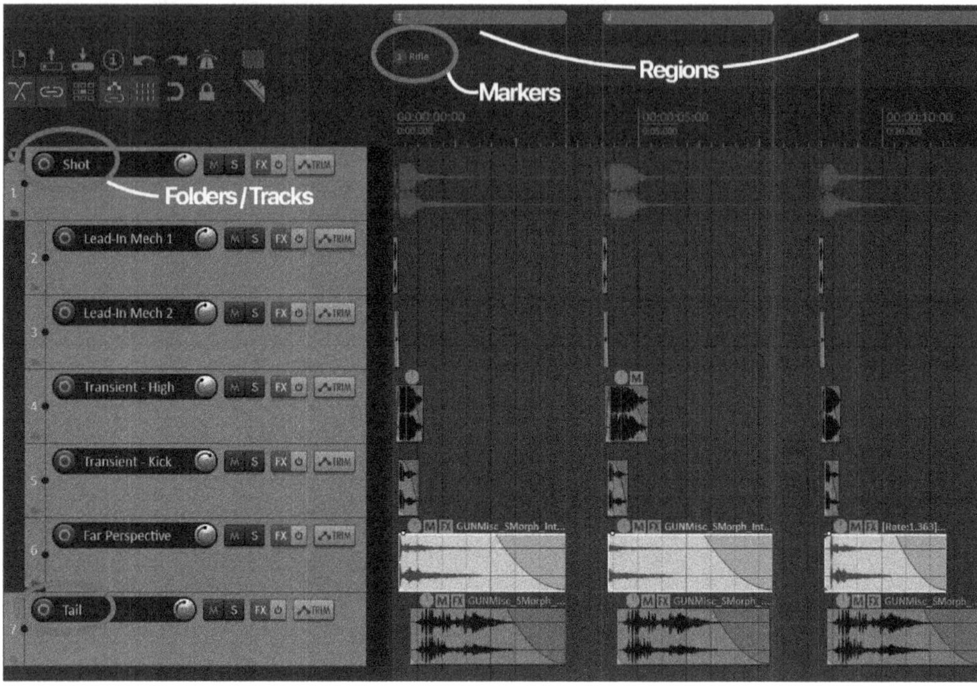

Figure 11.19 – An example of using markers, regions, and track names for file naming

In *Figure 11.19*, we see three variations of a *weapon sound effect*, each encased by a region. By using regions in this way, they allow us to utilize the region render matrix once again to render all variations in one go.

You'll also notice that, in the beginning, there is a marker with the name `Rifle`, denoting our weapon type. Furthermore, all layers involved in the gunshot sound are contained in the folder track named `Shot`, while tails reside on the track labeled `Tail`.

To now utilize these variables in our folder structure, we will follow these steps:

1. Open the **Render to File** window and select **Region Render Matrix** as the **Source** option, as described in the *Rendering sound effects for film and video* section.
2. In **Matrix**, we will make the following selection to create separate renders of the `Shot` and `Tail` sounds:

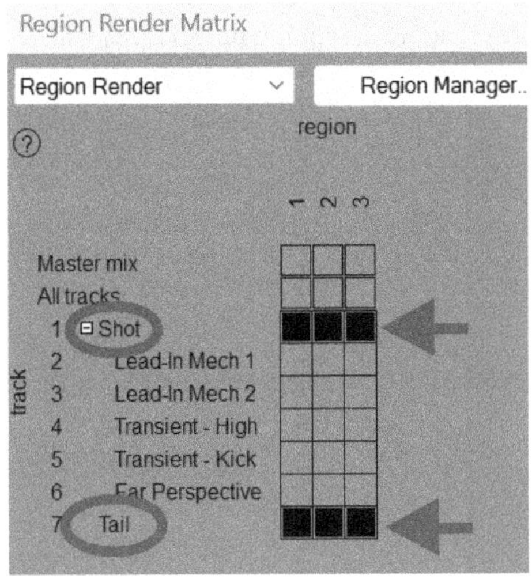

Figure 11.20 – Selecting the rendering checkboxes per desired tracks/folders

3. Next, in the render window, we will define the root folder that will house all of our game's sound effects under **Directory**. This will commonly be called `Audio Assets`.
4. For our file name, we will type in `Weapons\$marker\Sx_$marker_$track` (replace \ with / on Mac).

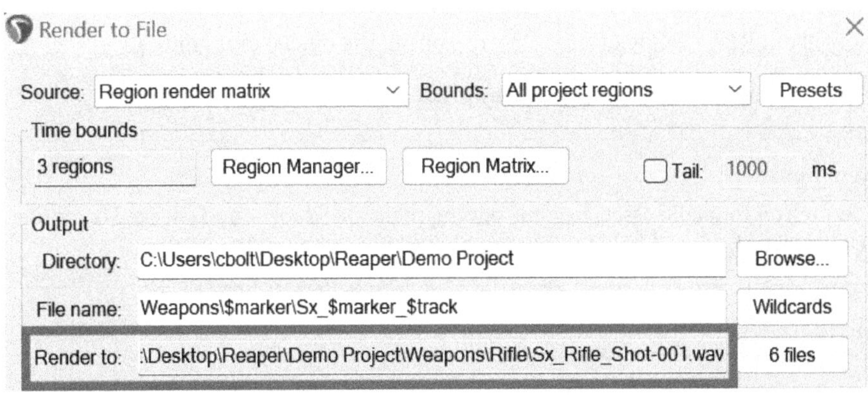

Figure 11.21 – Setting our folder structure and filename via Wildcards

The only manually specified aspects of our file name and folder structure will be that we would like our parent folder to be called `Weapons`, and for our files to have the `Sx_` prefix (for *sound effects*). By inserting slashes, we can define subdirectories to be created by REAPER. These can also be based on Wildcards, as shown here.

The `$marker` wildcard ensures that our weapon type, `Rifle`, will be made a new subfolder. By including `$marker` and `$track` in the file name, we ensure that both the weapon type as well as the element of the sound (`Shot` versus `Tail`) are reflected in the name of our final assets.

> **Important note**
>
> Note that REAPER will automatically add increment suffixes to files that would otherwise have the same name.

Upon rendering these files, the resulting folder structure and filenames will look as follows:

```
Audio Assets > Weapons > Rifle > Sx_Rifle_Shot-001.wav

Sx_Rifle_Shot-002.wav
Sx_Rifle_Shot-003.wav
Sx_Rifle_Tail-001.wav
Sx_Rifle_Tail-002.wav
Sx_Rifle_Tail-003.wav
```

As you can see, REAPER's rendering features allow for an incredible amount of functionality and automation and, given the limited page count, this section only scratches the surface of what's possible. Every sound designer has their own preferred methods of approaching the topic of rendering and asset naming, and it is up to you to experiment and find the one that works best for you.

To learn more about REAPER's wildcards feature, consult the official user guide at:

`https://www.reaper.fm/userguide.php`.

> **Common prefixes**
>
> Common prefixes for audio assets in game development are **Sx** for sound effects, **Dx** for dialog, and **Mx** for music; hence why dialog editing is often referred to as **Dx editing**.

File formats

In most cases, we should export all audio assets at 24-bit, 48 kHz WAV files to provide lossless quality assets for the audio implementation process. Further compression can then be handled by our game engine or middleware to make sure all audio assets stay within the allocated memory and performance budgets and these settings can even be customized per category of assets and even different target platforms (i.e., console, desktop, mobile, etc.).

In some cases (such as in browser-based games or with proprietary game engines), a developer might require us to deliver our assets already compressed. The most commonly used file format for this is **Ogg Vorbis**, a format which offers a simple quality parameter ranging from `0` to `10` (or `0.0` to `1.0` in the case of REAPER), is very efficient in terms of processing power required to decode it, and, unlike mp3, allows for seamless looping without additional effort. REAPER allows us to encode files in this format by selecting **OGG Vorbis** as the **Format** option in the **Render to File** window and specifying our desired quality level, as shown in *Figure 11.22*:

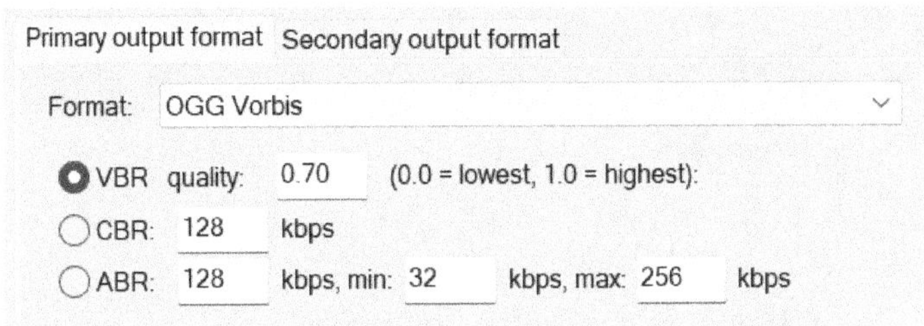

Figure 11.22 – The Ogg Vorbis settings

As a general rule of thumb, a quality level of `0.7` provides a decent balance of fidelity and compact file size for detailed sounds, such as Foley, ambiences, or weapons. Sounds of lesser importance, such as low, rumbling drones or humming appliances, will often sound just fine at lower-quality levels. This is yet another parameter that's best tweaked through trial and error, always trying to strike the ideal balance between quality and file size.

Even when delivering compressed assets, it's still best practice to always render WAV files as our **secondary output format** to have a lossless backup for every compressed file we create.

Loudness levels

When rendering out assets, setting ourselves loudness targets for each category of sound effects will make our lives a lot easier during the later stages of the project where we might be *revising* our previous creations and delivering alternative versions of assets.

Within the **Render to File** window, REAPER offers us the option to normalize and limit the files we will be rendering to different target values. The most important ones for sound design are **LUFS-I** (integrated loudness over the entire duration of the file) and **True Peak** (the highest peak level our file reaches).

By clicking the **Normalize/Limit/Fade** button, we can set these parameters to our liking.

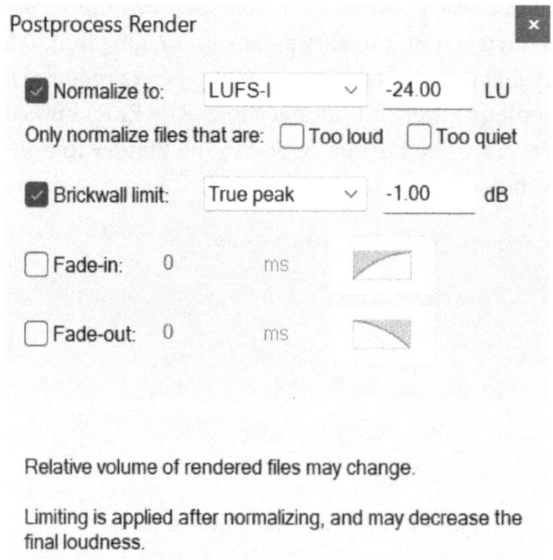

Figure 11.23 – The Postprocess Render dialog

Let's explore these options in more detail:

- **Normalize to**: This will adjust the overall volume of our file to meet our specified loudness target. Depending on the file in question, normalizing to a **LUFS** value might result in peaks above `0` dB, which would need to be limited to avoid clipping.
- **Brickwall limit**: This maintains the level previously achieved through normalization and hard-limits any peaks *above* the specified value. Note that if our sound is so loud that limiting is applied frequently, it will change the *tonality* and *dynamic range* of our sound noticeably, which can be undesirable. In this case, we need to adjust our processing to reach more consistent loudness before rendering our files.

Example loudness targets for different categories of sound effects can look as follows:

Sound Type	**Loudness Target**
Ambiences	`-32 LUFS-I`
Footsteps	`-16 dB True Peak`
Weapons	`-23 LUFS-I`
Magic Spells	`-23 LUFS-I`
User Interface Sounds	`-12 dB True Peak`

Figure 11.24 – Example loudness targets for sound effects

Sound categories that likely contain mostly very short files should generally be normalized to a dB True Peak target as LUFS measurements over time are not an accurate measure of perceived loudness for short durations. By keeping our general loudness targets at or below the European Broadcasting Union (EBU) recommendation of `-23 dB LUFS-I`, we ensure that our game project will not be unreasonably loud when initially importing our audio files. Additionally, we leave ourselves headroom to boost the levels of our sounds in middleware or the game engine without clipping.

Of course, these values are by no means prescriptive, and every project will pose unique requirements for how we deliver our files. They do, however, serve as a guideline to let us deliver our work in a consistent, predictable manner.

Summary

In this chapter, we explored the fundamentals of the sound design process for games and film from ideation to the delivery of our finished assets and saw how REAPER can help us establish highly efficient, automated workflows that let us deliver our work at a consistent quality and loudness.

We learned about key differences and commonalities between the two mediums and how they shape our workflow. Furthermore, we learned how to track our assets for game audio projects and utilize REAPER's powerful **Media Explorer** to manage our sound library.

Next, we learned about layering and processing techniques at the foundation of sound design, allowing us to shape our raw recordings into original soundscapes.

We explored how REAPER's region render matrix and wildcards features allow us to automate our rendering process and ensure that we can deliver our assets and stems consistently and into the correct drive locations.

Finally, we learned about rendering normalization and limiting features alongside helpful loudness targets for different categories of sound effects.

In the following chapter, we will be exploring immersive audio and how to create and work with projects that transcend the limits of conventional stereo playback.

Further reading

The subject of sound design is immense, and REAPER holds enormous potential beyond the scope of this chapter that can be explored in these reading recommendations:

- *The Ultimate REAPER Tools Guide for Game Audio* by Christopher Bolte. It's available at: `https://bolttracks.com/reaper-tools/`.
- *The REAPER Effects Guide*, Cockos, Inc. It's available at: `https://dlz.reaper.fm/userguide/REAPEREffectsGuide2021.pdf`.

- *The Game Audio Strategy Guide: A Practical Course* by Gina Zdanowicz, Spencer Bambrick, Routledge, ISBN 978-1138498341.
- *The Foley Grail: The Art of Performing Sound for Film, Games, and Animation* by Vanessa Theme Ament, Taylor Francis Publishing, ISBN 978-1003008439.
- *Sound Design: The Expressive Power of Music, Voice and Sound Effects in Cinema* by David Sonnenschein, Michael Wiese Productions, ISBN 978-0941188265.
- *Audiokinetic Wwise* Learning Portal. It's available at: `https://www.audiokinetic.com/en/learning`.
- *FMOD* documentation, `https://www.fmod.com/learn`.

12
Exploring Immersive Audio

In this chapter, we'll introduce immersive sound and the capabilities that REAPER offers for working with projects of this kind. Immersive sound may become the audio standard in the coming years as its ability to create realism surpasses the capabilities of a stereo system. This is why it's important to start exploring the production of immersive audio content, whether it's for music, series, podcasts, video games, or other sources.

As we'll see, REAPER comes with valuable tools that help us work on immersive audio projects. For this reason, REAPER is a DAW that's ready to face the challenges of sound production in both the present and the future.

In this chapter, we'll cover the following topics:

- **Basic concepts of immersive audio**: We'll start by providing a brief overview of the different technologies and systems for creating immersive audio so that you have a general understanding of the development of this technology
- **Creating immersive projects in REAPER**: In this section, you'll learn how to create projects in REAPER that allow you to produce immersive audio using the Ambisonics system
- **Mixing and mastering procedures**: Finally, you'll discover procedures that can help you mix and master your immersive audio projects in REAPER

By the end of this chapter, you'll know how to create immersive audio projects in REAPER, enabling you to experiment and let your creativity flow when you're working on projects that contain this type of sound.

Technical requirements

In this chapter, we'll develop immersive projects in REAPER using the **Ambisonics system**. Thus, it's necessary to install the free **IEM plugin suite** (`https://plugins.iem.at/`), which can be installed on Windows and Mac.

You can download the assets that are required to complete the example provided in this chapter from this book's GitHub repository: `https://github.com/PacktPublishing/Elevate-your-audio-production-with-Reaper`.

Basic concepts of immersive audio

Immersive sound is an auditory experience that aims to envelop the listener in a three-dimensional space, creating a sense of presence and realism that surpasses the limitations of traditional stereo sound.

This approach is based on the ability to position sound sources at any point in the space around the listener, both on the horizontal and vertical planes. Through the advanced techniques of recording, mixing, and playback, immersive sound allows for a richer and more enveloping experience, similar to how we perceive sound in the real world.

Here are some of the main characteristics of immersive sound:

- **360-degree spatiality**: Unlike stereo sound, which only offers a two-dimensional sound plane (left and right) with some depth perception, immersive sound can position sound sources anywhere along an imaginary sphere around the listener.
- **Height**: Immersive sound introduces an additional dimension by allowing sounds to be placed above and below the listener, adding a layer of realism that stereo and traditional surround sound can't provide.
- **Sound source mobility**: With immersive sound, it's possible to move sound sources throughout the three-dimensional space, creating dynamic and realistic effects that follow the natural movement of objects in the real world.

Now that we've covered the main features of immersive audio, let's look at some of its applications.

Applications of immersive sound

Immersive sound has numerous applications:

- **Film and television**: It enhances the visual experience by providing an auditory dimension that matches the on-screen action.
- **Virtual reality (VR) and augmented reality (AR)**: Sound immersion is crucial for creating credible and enveloping experiences in virtual environments.
- **Video games**: Immersive sound increases realism and immersion in gaming environments, allowing players to perceive the direction and distance of sounds more accurately.
- **Music**: Artists and producers can create richer and more enveloping soundscapes, providing a unique and memorable listening experience.

As we can see, the applications of immersive audio are very interesting. Now, let's look at the history of various sound systems that have led us to immersive sound.

History of immersive sound

The concept of immersive sound has evolved significantly since its inception. Here's a brief timeline of its development:

- **1950s – 1960s**: Stereophony, or stereo sound, marked the first step toward creating a more enveloping auditory experience. Techniques were developed to record and reproduce sound in two channels (left and right), providing a sense of directionality and depth.
- **1970s**: Quadraphonic sound was one of the first attempts to create a more immersive auditory experience. It used four channels (left, right, rear left, and rear right) to surround the listener. However, its adoption was limited due to a lack of standardization and the technical difficulties of the time.
- **1980s – 1990s**: The development of 5.1 surround sound, which uses five channels (left, right, center, left surround, and right surround), plus a subwoofer (the **.1** aspect), became the standard for cinema and later for home use. This format significantly improved the listening experience by allowing for better localization of sound sources around the listener.
- **2000s – present**: With the advent of high-definition and digital content, the demand for richer auditory experiences led to the development of immersive sound formats such as Dolby Atmos, DTS:X, and Ambisonics. These systems introduce the height dimension, allowing for more precise and realistic placement of sound sources.

Now that we've reviewed a bit of the history of immersive sound, let's take a look at the features of the most popular systems today.

Popular immersive audio systems

There are several immersive audio systems today, each with its characteristics and applications. We'll look at some of the most prominent ones in the subsequent sections.

Dolby Atmos

Dolby Atmos is one of the most well-known and widely used immersive sound systems in the film and entertainment industry. Introduced in 2012 by Dolby Laboratories, Dolby Atmos allows sounds to be placed anywhere within a three-dimensional space, using an object-based approach that positions sound based on *X*, *Y*, and *Z* coordinates, as well as **beds**, which use audio channels for each speaker. This allows Dolby Atmos to use the best of both approaches: **audio objects** and beds.

The following are some of the main features of Dolby Atmos:

- **Object-based audio**: Dolby Atmos uses objects to allow sounds to move freely within a three-dimensional space, creating an immersive audio experience without the need for a specific number of speakers.
- **Ceiling speakers**: While not mandatory, Dolby Atmos is known for its use of ceiling speakers or Atmos-enabled speakers that reflect sound from the ceiling, providing an additional vertical dimension to the audio.
- **Speaker configurations**: Dolby Atmos is compatible with a wide range of speaker configurations, from 2.0, 5.1, and 5.1.2 (five ear-level speakers, one subwoofer, and two height speakers) to more advanced configurations, such as 7.1.2, 7.1.4, and others.

Dolby Atmos supports up to 128 audio tracks and up to 64 independent speakers to create a fully immersive auditory experience. Its applications include cinema, television, video games, music, and mobile applications.

DTS:X

DTS:X is an immersive audio format developed by **Digital Theater Systems** (**DTS**). This format is designed to provide an immersive audio experience through object-based audio channels, allowing sounds to move freely through three-dimensional space, regardless of the number of speakers or their specific configuration.

Let's consider some of the main features of DTS:X:

- **Object-based audio**: Instead of assigning sounds to specific channels, sounds can be placed in three-dimensional space. This allows for greater flexibility in audio playback as sound objects can move around the sound scene accurately.
- **Adaptability**: DTS:X adapts to different speaker configurations. This means you can have a basic 5.1 setup or a more complex configuration, and the format will adjust the audio to provide the best possible experience. It doesn't require a specific speaker setup.

As we can see, Dolby Atmos and DTS:X are systems with some technological similarities that compete to be the market standard. In REAPER, we can create content with either of these systems, although it's necessary to purchase commercial plugins to do so, such as **Dolby Atmos Renderer** or **DTS:X Creator Suite**.

Let's look at another system that has a different approach from object-based audio: Ambisonics. This system can be easily integrated into REAPER, as we'll see in the next section.

Ambisonics

Ambisonics is an immersive sound approach that captures and reproduces a complete sound field rather than discrete channels. This system, developed in the 1970s, is based on a mathematical representation of the sound field, allowing for extreme flexibility in the reproduction and manipulation of sound.

The Ambisonics system allows for sound reproduction in any speaker configuration and is highly adaptable to different listening environments. It can have applications in VR, live concert recordings, and music, film, and television productions, as well as experimental sound applications.

The ability of Ambisonics to reproduce sound in any speaker configuration makes it extremely versatile and adaptable to different environments and applications. Additionally, the Ambisonics system is compatible with other immersive sound formats and can be converted to systems such as Dolby Atmos and DTS:X.

Ambisonics projects can be created from recordings made with special microphones, such as the **Røde NT-SF1** or the **Sennheiser AMBEO**, which generate recordings encoded in Ambisonics format, or with conventional mono or stereo sources, using encoders that transform these signals into Ambisonics format.

Ambisonics order

One of the main features of Ambisonics is that it operates with various degrees of precision, also known as the **order of the system**.

Ambisonics systems have various orders, up to the 7th order. The higher the order, the more channels are used to encode the position of each element. *Figure 12.1* shows the relationship between the order and the number of channels in an Ambisonics system:

Order	Number of Channels
1	4
2	9
3	16
4	25
5	36
6	49
7	64

Figure 12.1 – Ambisonics order and the number of channels

Thus, a *1st-order system* uses *four audio channels* to handle basic localization information in three dimensions, but it doesn't have very good precision in the positioning of sound elements. A *7th-order system* is the most precise, but it requires *64 audio channels*. The multichannel capabilities of REAPER make it an ideal DAW for working with Ambisonics systems up to the 7th order.

One advantage of Ambisonics is that higher-order encoded audio can be reduced to a lower order so that it's more compatible with systems with fewer channels, enhancing its compatibility.

Now that we've reviewed some of the main immersive sound systems, we'll learn how to set up REAPER so that we can carry out an immersive project using Ambisonics.

Creating immersive projects in REAPER

Let's learn how to create a new immersive project in REAPER using Ambisonics. This example shows the settings and plugins needed to create an Ambisonics project from conventional mono or stereo audio files:

1. To create an immersive sound project in REAPER, we'll start with a new empty project and add a track with a MIDI instrument or audio item (see the *Technical requirements* section to learn how to download the audio item). In this case, we'll use an instance of **ReaSynth** and program some MIDI notes.
2. Next, we'll click on the track's **Routing** button and change the number of channels on the track according to the Ambisonics order we want to use, as shown in *Figure 12.1*. For this example, we'll use a 3rd-order system, so we'll change **Track channels** to **16**, as shown in *Figure 12.2*:

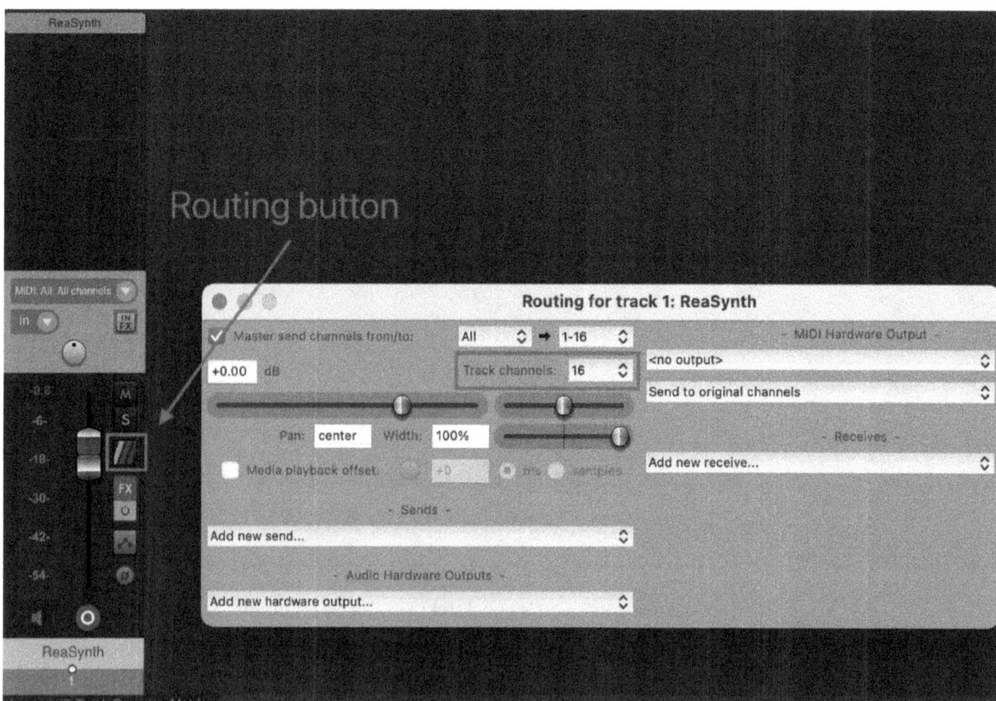

Figure 12.2 – Track channels

Here, we can see that REAPER allows us to have tracks with up to 128 channels, enabling us to work with 7th-order Ambisonics systems if desired.

3. Now, we'll insert one of the plugins from the **IEM** suite: **VST: StereoEncoder**. This plugin can be found in the **IEM** category, as shown in *Figure 12.3*:

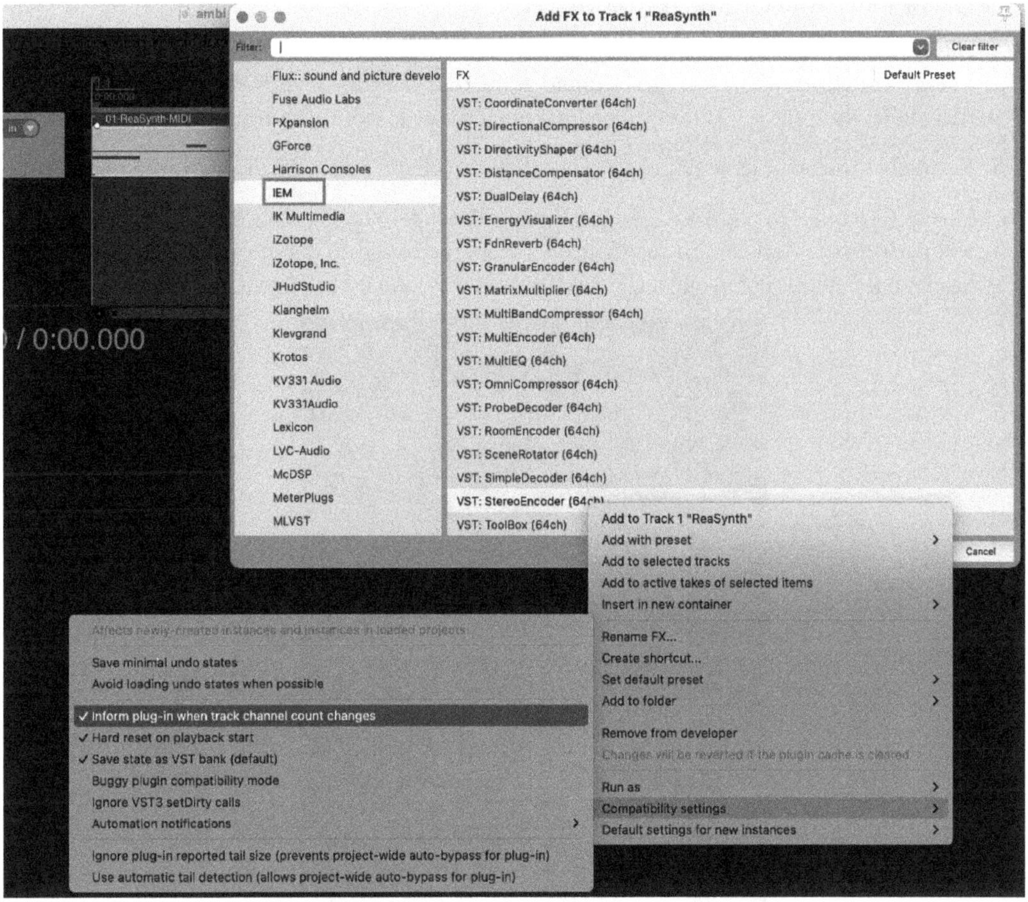

Figure 12.3 – Adding the IEM StereoEncoder plugin

This plugin encodes a conventional stereo sound and converts it into Ambisonics.

4. Before adding this plugin, we need to adjust its compatibility settings. Right-click on the plugin and select **Compatibility settings | Inform plug-in when track channel count changes**, as shown in *Figure 12.3*. This setting allows the IEM plugins to be aware when we change the number of channels on each track. This adjustment only needs to be done the first time an IEM plugin is inserted in REAPER.

The **StereoEncoder** plugin will serve as a 3D panning control, allowing us to position the audio of our track at any point within our 3D space, something we can visualize as a sphere surrounding us.

5. The next step will be to change the number of channels on the **MASTER** track to **16**, similar to how we did with the **ReaSynth** track.
6. Afterward, it's recommended to insert another **IEM** plugin on the **MASTER** track, **VST plugin: EnergyVisualizer**, which can also be found in the **IEM** category. **EnergyVisualizer** is a monitor that allows us to see a 3D energy map, making it easier to position a track during mixing.

   Remember to change its settings before inserting this plugin, just as we did with **StereoEncoder**.
7. Finally, we'll insert the IEM **VST plugin: BinauralDecoder** plugin on the **MASTER** track, which will perform the Ambisonics decoding and adapt the sound so that it can be listened to with headphones. At this point, our single-track project will contain the plugins shown in *Figure 12.4*:

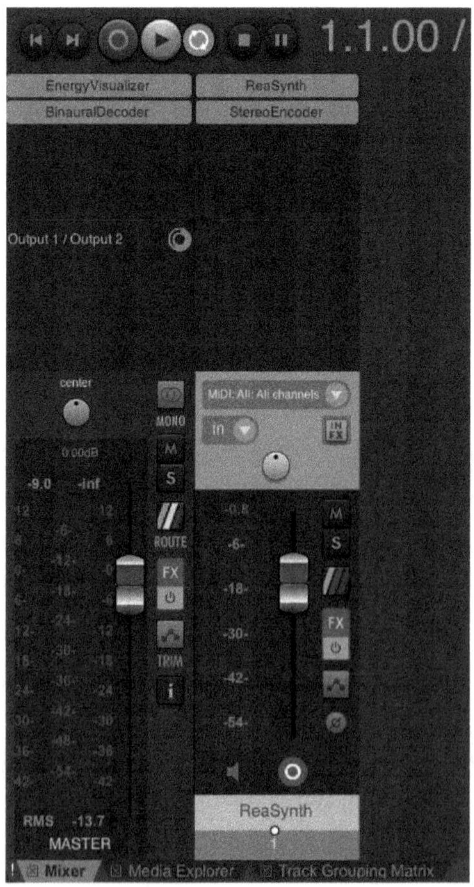

Figure 12.4 – Plugins for Ambisonics projects

With this setup, our project is ready to work with immersive sound using Ambisonics. Now, we can insert new tracks as needed for our project, adjusting the number of channels on each track and inserting the **VST: StereoEncoder** plugin on each track.

Now that we know how to prepare a REAPER project so that we can work with immersive sound, let's see how we can process and use 3D panning to add dimension to our sounds.

Mixing and mastering procedures

Once we've made the necessary adjustments to a new Ambisonics project in REAPER, we can proceed with the mixing and mastering processes.

Immersive mixing

In **immersive mixing**, the processes that are used are very similar to those used in stereo mixing. Let's take a look at them:

- **Level adjustment**: This involves adjusting the volume of each track to balance the levels of the various instruments. It's crucial to perform this adjustment while listening with headphones as this is the most common way immersive sound is consumed today. The type of headphones that are used will influence sound perception and mixing results, so it's recommended to work with the highest quality headphones available.
- **3D panning adjustment**: Panning is one of the vital components in an immersive system because it's precisely the characteristic that creates realism and impact in a three-dimensional sound.

  Let's use the IEM plugin suite (mentioned in the *Technical requirements* section) to enable immersive panning in REAPER:

  I. In our example project, we'll be using the IEM **VST: StereoEncoder** plugin, shown in *Figure 12.5*, to position the sound of each track at different 3D points:

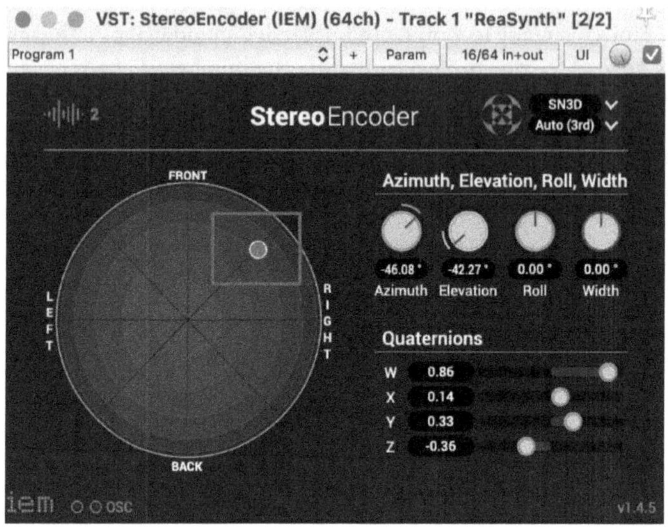

Figure 12.5 – The IEM StereoEncoder plugin

II. To move the audio of any track, simply move the circle marked in *Figure 12.5* and position it at different points on the sphere while monitoring with your headphones.

III. If the audio of our track comes from a stereo instrument or file, we can widen the stereo image by a certain number of degrees using the **Width** control, marked in *Figure 12.6*. This will show a pair of **L** and **R** position indicators, also shown in *Figure 12.6*:

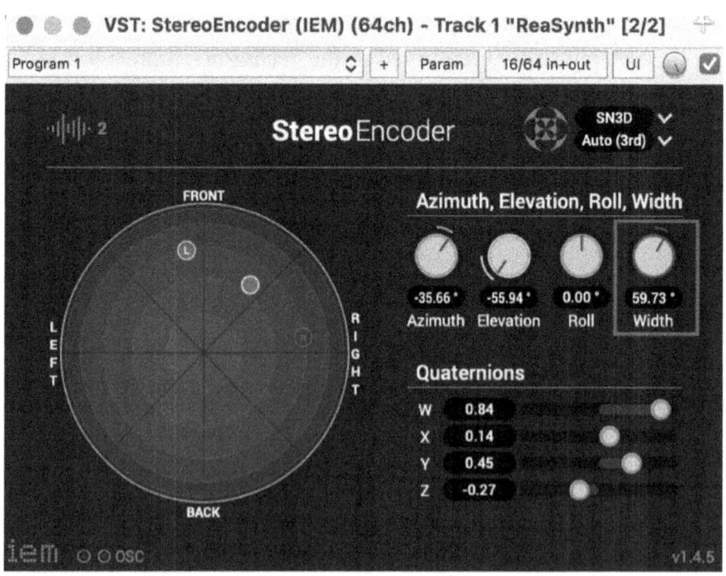

Figure 12.6 – Panning a stereo audio source

IV. If preferred, you can adjust the knobs for **Azimuth**, **Elevation**, and **Roll** to move the sound's position on the track more precisely.

V. A useful tool while adjusting the 3D panning is the IEM **VST: EnergyVisualizer** plugin, which we already inserted in the **MASTER** track. This plugin shows a heat map in the 3D virtual space, with the center of the graph representing our head, as shown in *Figure 12.7*:

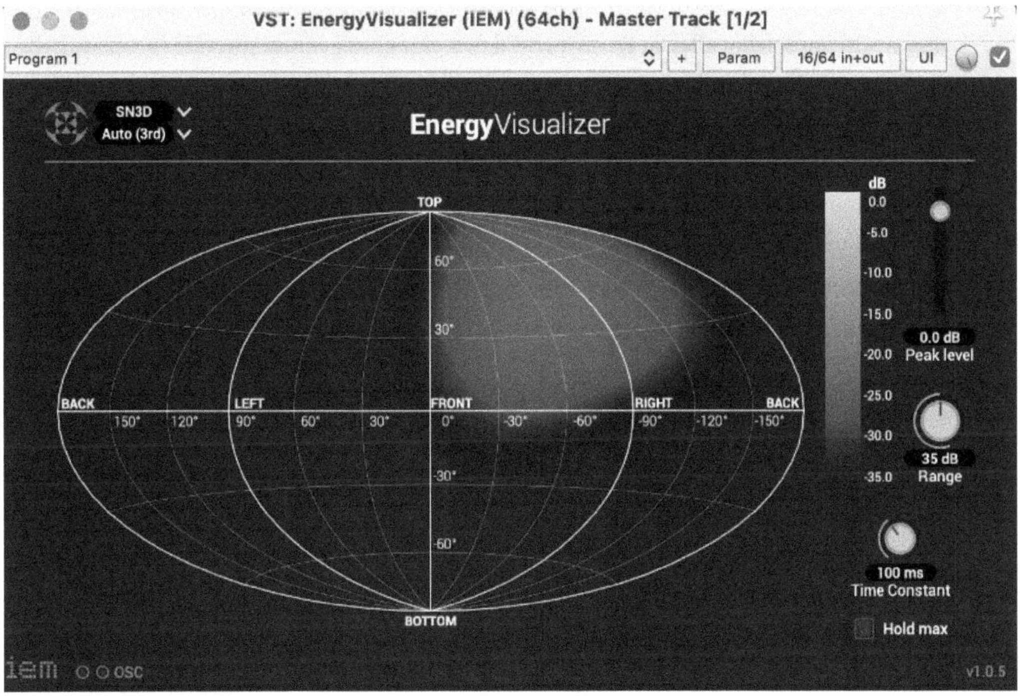

Figure 12.7 – The IEM EnergyVisualizer plugin

With this tool, we can visualize the energy distribution of the various tracks in an immersive project and ensure that the different sounds are panned in a balanced manner to achieve the desired effect.

- **Equalization and compression**: **Equalization** is a process that helps us adjust the frequency balance of the sounds in the project. For immersive projects, the equalization and compression techniques explained in *Chapters 4*, *7*, and *9* can be used.

  In the case of **compression**, this process helps control the dynamics or volume variations of the sounds. We can also use the techniques shown in the aforementioned chapters, remembering that if a sound has too many volume variations, to the point of losing detail in some parts, it's advisable to apply more compression to even out the perceived volume.

- **Automation**: In immersive projects, **automation** can be very important for creating the sensation of movement in 3D sounds. We can automate volume levels, panning, and any other effect or processing that's added to each track, always aiming for automation adjustments to help achieve a more impactful or realistic result, depending on what's being sought. The automation process in an immersive project in REAPER is the same as when automating any other plugin, whether it's mono or stereo.
- **Using reverb and delay effects**: **Reverb** and **delay** play a very important role in creating the sensation of depth and ambiance in a sound. To add reverb or delay to an Ambisonics project, follow these steps:

I. Create a new track and name it accordingly, depending on the effect you want to use – for example, `Reverb`.

II. Go to the **Routing** options for the track and change the number of channels according to the Ambisonics order you're using, as shown in *Figure 12.2*.

III. Insert the **VST plugin: ReaVerbate** plugin into the **Reverb** track and set the **Wet** level to **0** dB and the **Dry** level to the minimum. You can also adjust the **Room size** and **Initial Delay** values to create the sensation of a larger or smaller space, as shown in *Figure 12.8*:

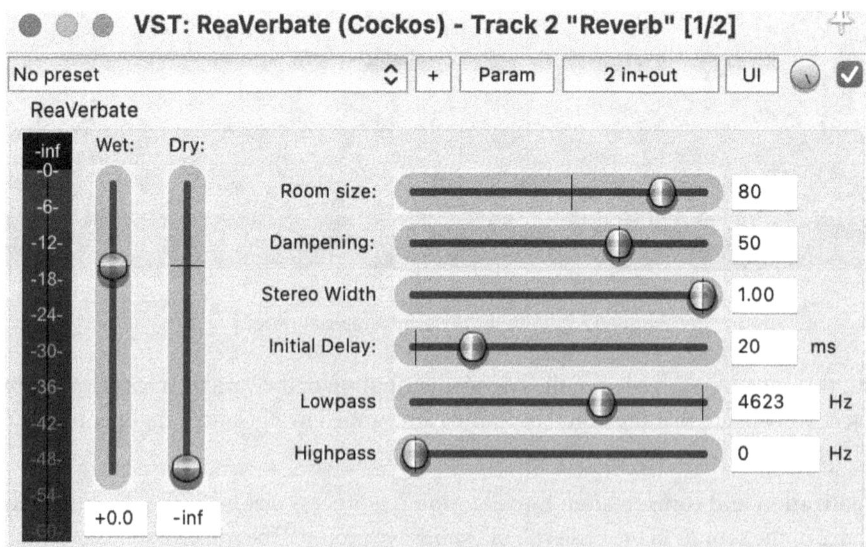

Figure 12.8 – ReaVerbate settings

IV. Insert the IEM **StereoEncoder** plugin below **ReaVerbate**. This will be your 3D panning control for the reverb.

V. Add a new send to the channel you want to have reverb and adjust the send channels to **16** (or the number of channels used by your project's Ambisonics order), as shown in *Figure 12.9*:

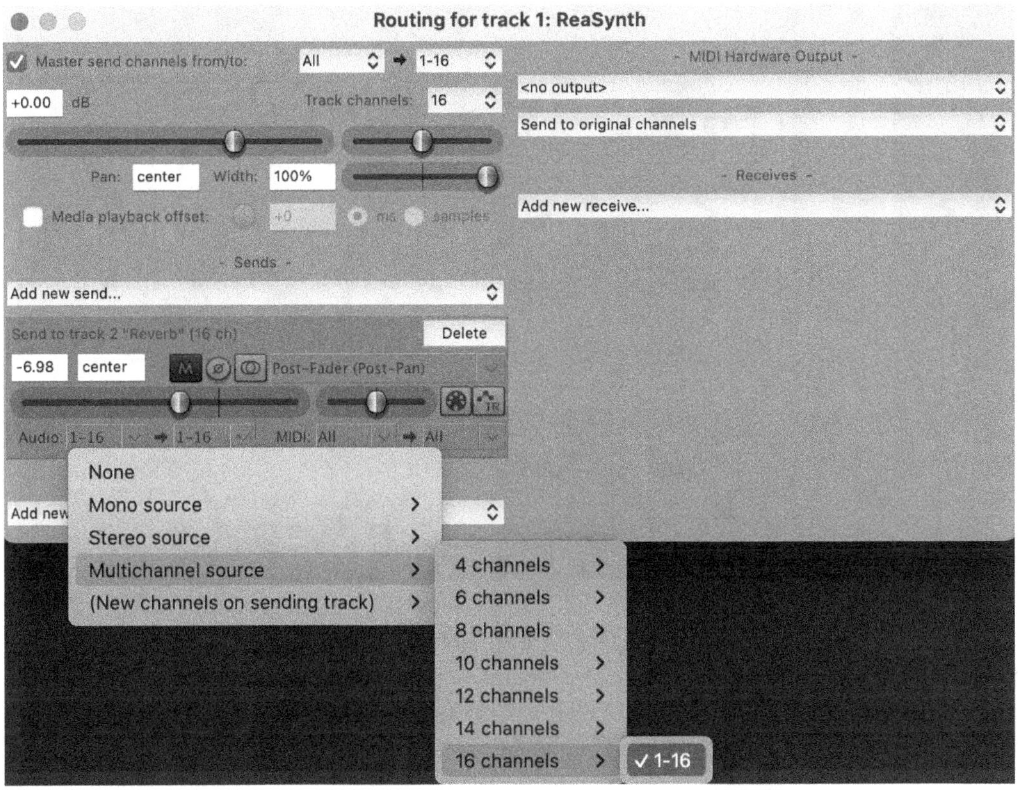

Figure 12.9 – Multichannel send

VI. By adjusting the level of this send, you can control the amount of reverb on your track. If you want to use the same effect on other tracks, simply repeat *Step 5* on the desired tracks.

Following these guidelines for immersive mixing, you can explore many possibilities for creating immersive projects with Ambisonics technology. Once the mixing process is complete, we can proceed with mastering considerations.

Immersive mastering

Mastering focuses on adjusting the final levels and other details of the file that will be exported, as we already saw in *Chapter 5*. In the case of an immersive project, REAPER provides options for rendering the final project, making it ready for distribution.

To ensure that the final file levels are appropriate, it's recommended to insert the **ReaLimit** plugin on the **MASTER** track, placing it just before the IEM **BinauralDecoder** plugin, as shown in *Figure 12.10*:

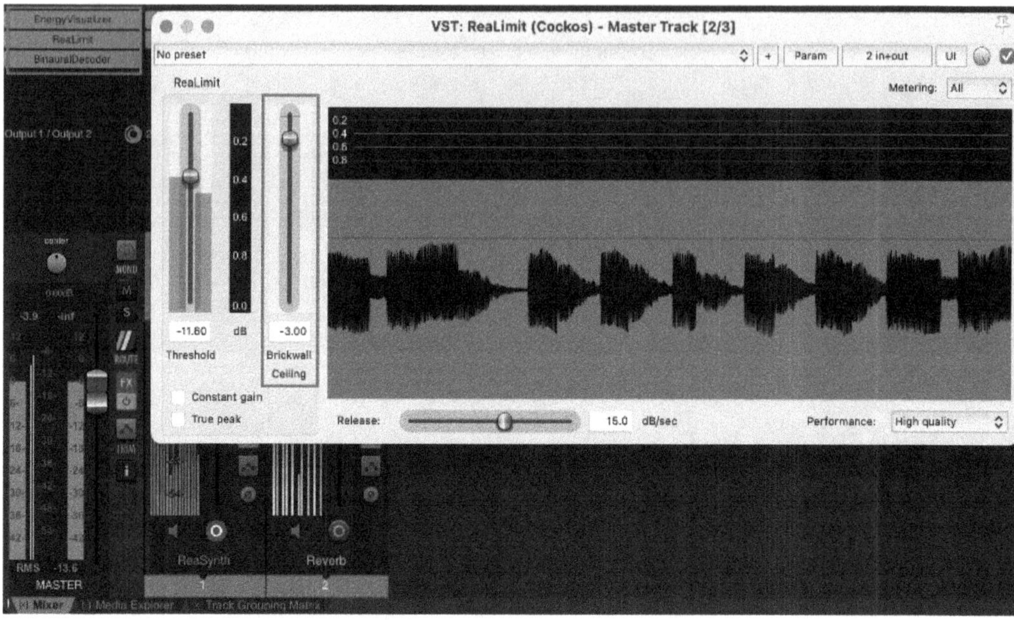

Figure 12.10 – ReaLimit on the MASTER track

You should also set the **Brickwall Ceiling** value of **ReaLimit** to **-3** dB, as shown in *Figure 12.10* since this is the maximum peak level recommended for the final file.

There are two ways you can render your final file:

- The first is to render it as a **binaural file**, which will create a stereo file that can be listened to with regular headphones by any user, though it may not have a strong sense of 3D realism.
- The second option is to create a **multichannel Ambisonics encoded file**, which can preserve much greater detail in 3D realism but will require the final user to decode it using Ambisonics decoding software.

Now, let's look at how we can create a binaural render and an Ambisonics render.

Creating a binaural render

If you want to create a binaural render, simply use the **File** | **Render** command and set the parameters to create a 24-bit WAV file at a 48,000 Hz sampling rate, as explained in *Chapter 5*.

Creating an Ambisonics render

If you want to create an Ambisonics encoded render, you must first disable **BinauralDecoder** on the **MASTER** track. Then, use the **File** | **Render** command and ensure you select the correct number of channels according to the Ambisonics order of your project, as shown in *Figure 12.11*:

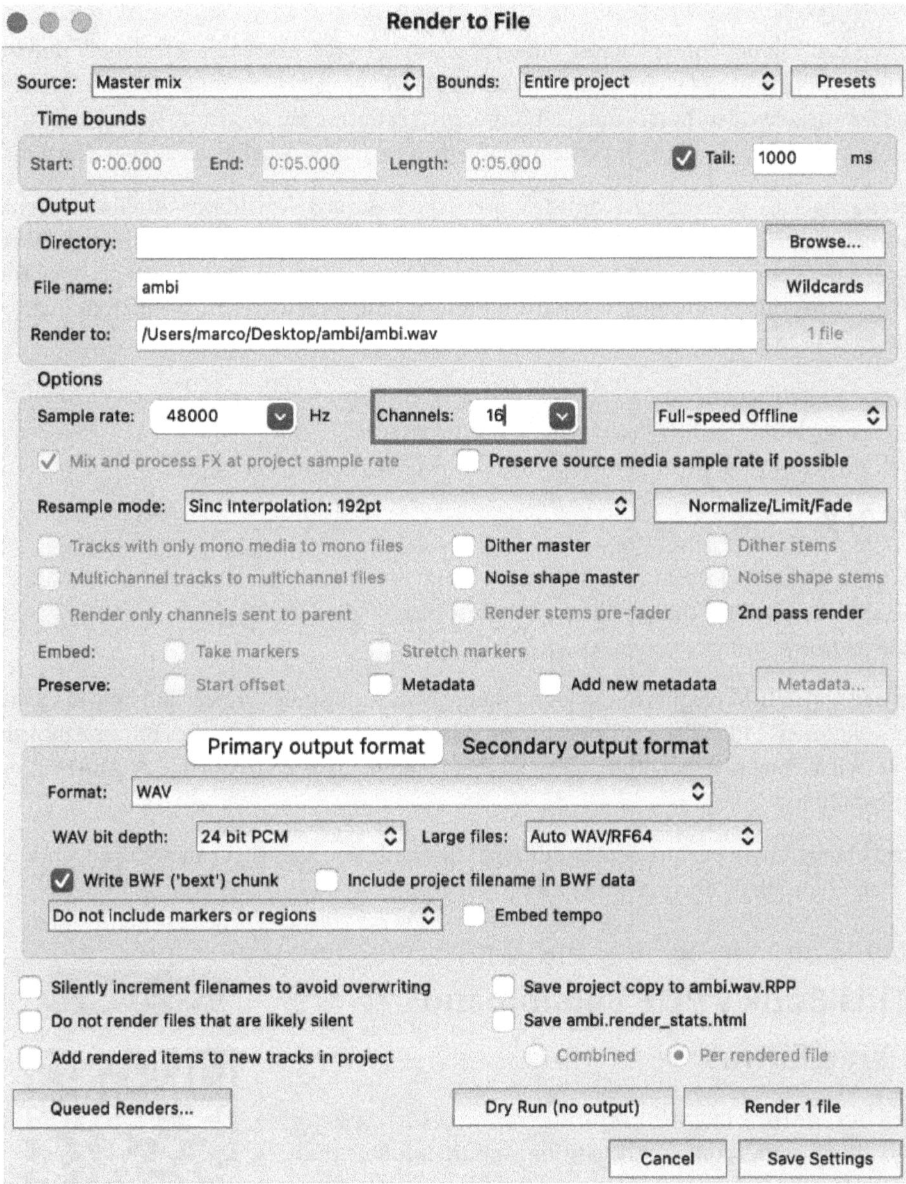

Figure 12.11 – Render settings

In our example, we used **16** channels since we're working with third-order Ambisonics, so the final file will be a 16-channel WAV file, ready for decoding.

This way, you can create files that have been leveled correctly and formatted for distribution.

Challenges distributing Ambisonics content

Distributing Ambisonics content across different platforms presents several challenges due to the system's unique spherical audio encoding. Ambisonics is widely used for immersive applications such as VR and 360-degree video, but its compatibility across platforms can be inconsistent. This is why it's important to know what kind of audio system will be used for playback before creating the final master.

Also, there's a challenge in ensuring a consistent user experience across platforms. Ambisonics is highly effective when experienced with headphones or dedicated VR systems, but playback on speakers or less advanced devices often leads to an inconsistent or diluted spatial effect. The system's open source nature also means there's no single standard for how it's implemented across different platforms, making it difficult to guarantee that content will sound the same for all users.

This lack of standardization, combined with varying levels of awareness and adoption of Ambisonics technology, complicates its distribution and may limit its reach.

Summary

In this chapter, we learned what immersive sound is and explored the most popular systems available today. We also examined the characteristics of these systems while focusing on the Ambisonics system, a powerful and easy-to-implement alternative in REAPER.

We discussed which IEM plugins to use for working on an Ambisonics project and how to configure REAPER's channels. Finally, we covered the mixing and mastering processes for an Ambisonics project, as well as how to export the project so that it can be listened to outside of REAPER or for public distribution.

In the next chapter, we'll explore some additional tips and processes that can help you work more efficiently and thoroughly on your REAPER projects.

13
Optimizing the Workflow and Troubleshooting in REAPER

We have reached the final chapter of this book. Throughout the previous chapters, we have explored various functions and applications of REAPER.

In this chapter, we will dive into tips and techniques that will help you improve your workflow while editing and mixing and making it more efficient to get better audio quality. Additionally, we will address some common problems when using REAPER, such as getting no sound when working or getting excessive noise in a recording.

We'll cover the following main topics in this chapter:

- **Enhancing workflow efficiency**: You will learn more advanced techniques to improve your workflow and polish the sound quality of your productions
- **Troubleshooting common issues**: You will discover procedures to solve common problems when working in REAPER

By the end of this chapter, you will be familiar with advanced techniques and functions in REAPER that will help you work more quickly and solve common issues.

Technical requirements

No special materials are needed to work with the contents of this chapter, as techniques and practices discussed here can be applied to any REAPER project.

Enhancing workflow efficiency

One of the most important points we need to develop when working on audio projects is improving our workflow, as this allows us to accomplish more in less time. In this section, we will explore various functions that help carry out specific tasks in REAPER efficiently. Let's start with dynamic split, which allows us to automatically split items.

Dynamic split

Dynamic splitting is a powerful feature that automatically detects **transients** (sharp changes in amplitude) or specific audio thresholds within an audio item and splits the item accordingly. This is particularly useful for tasks such as drum editing, removing silence, and creating accurate timing adjustments without manual slicing.

Dynamic splitting can save a lot of time by quickly breaking down a long recording into smaller, manageable pieces based on the audio's dynamics.

To apply dynamic splitting, follow these steps:

1. **Select the items to split**: Click on the audio item you want to split. You can select multiple items if you want to apply dynamic splitting across multiple tracks simultaneously.
2. Right-click on the selected items and choose **Item Processing | Dynamic Split Items...**.
3. **Configure split parameters**: Adjust the following parameters to ensure the desired parts of the audio remain selected:
    - **Gate Threshold**: Adjust the **Gate Threshold** sliders to set the minimum and maximum volume levels that will trigger a split. This is useful for isolating transients (such as drum hits) or ignoring noise and quiet parts.
    - **Hysteresis**: This parameter allows the gate to remain open, meaning the sound is maintained even if the signal drops below the threshold. It helps prevent the sound from being cut off.
    - **Min Slice Length**: This determines the minimum length in milliseconds of the slices generated.
    - **Min Silence Length**: This determines the minimum length in milliseconds of the silences generated.
4. **Apply the splits**: Once you're satisfied with the settings, click **Split** to apply the changes. REAPER will split the items based on the parameters you've set, as shown in *Figure 13.1*:

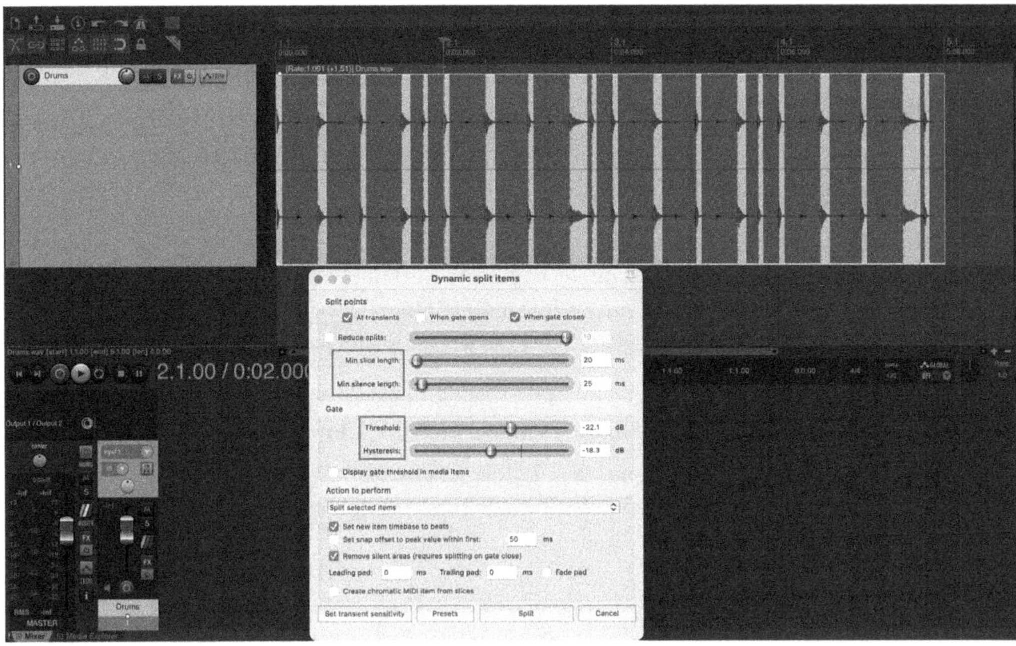

Figure 13.1 – Dynamic split

The use of dynamic splitting can be very helpful for tasks, such as the following:

- **Tightening drum performances**: Automatically slice a drum track into individual hits for precise timing corrections
- **Removing silence**: Clean up vocal tracks by splitting and removing silent sections
- **Sample extraction**: Extract individual sounds from a continuous recording, such as chopping up loops or breaks

Dynamic splitting is a versatile tool that can significantly speed up the editing process while maintaining accuracy and control.

Now, let's look at another type of process that falls under the category of dynamic processors, the de-esser.

De-esser

Some voices can have an overly accentuated *s* sound, known as **sibilance**. Sibilance can become more noticeable or bothersome due to the type of microphone used during recording, as well as the microphone's position.

While an equalizer can be used to reduce the sharp *s* sound, there is a specific processor for this purpose: the **de-esser**. The **de-esser** is an advanced audio process that applies compression to signals with very intense high frequencies.

In *Chapter 8*, we saw how to use the de-esser for dialogue post-production applications; now let's see how to use it in music applications.

In pop music, where clear, upfront vocals are crucial, de-essers are frequently applied to ensure intelligibility and listener comfort. For example, engineers working with artists such as Dua Lipa or Billie Eilish use de-essers to manage sibilance while maintaining the vocal's natural clarity. In Eilish's intimate vocal style, this technique helps balance delicate whispers with brighter consonants, delivering a polished, professional sound.

In REAPER, there is a de-esser included in the **JS** plugin category, shown in *Figure 13.2*:

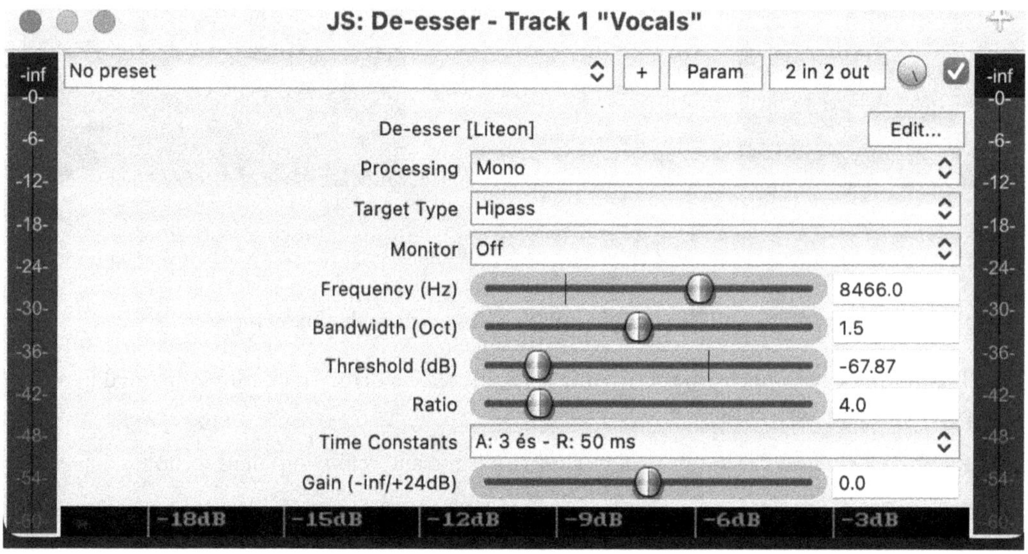

Figure 13.2 – JS: De-esser

To use this de-esser, follow these steps:

1. Insert the **JS: De-esser** plugin into the channel you want to process.
2. Activate the **Monitor** parameter by setting it to **On**. This will allow you to hear only the high frequencies.
3. Adjust the **Frequency (Hz)** parameter to find the high frequencies that stand out the most or are the most bothersome.
4. Set the **Monitor** parameter back to **Off**.

5. Lower the **Threshold** control to start compressing the high frequencies. The more you lower the threshold, the more compression will be applied.
6. You can adjust the **Bandwidth** and **Ratio** settings to make the de-esser effect more or less intense.

Using the de-esser allows you to control vocal sibilance quickly and effectively, making it a highly recommended tool for editing vocals in music, podcasts, videos, and so on.

Now, let's explore another essential and helpful process in mixing: parallel compression.

Parallel compression

There are certain audio processes considered *secret weapons* by many audio engineers to enhance sound or create more impact in a mix. One of these processes is **parallel compression**.

This technique retains the dynamic range and natural feel of the performance while adding power and density. For example, in pop and rock productions, engineers often use parallel compression on drums to enhance their punch without squashing their transients. Musical artists have benefited from this approach, where the vocals and drums maintain clarity and energy, giving the mix more impact without losing the musicality.

This type of compression, also known as *upward compression*, is a technique that involves combining a heavily compressed signal with the original uncompressed signal. The result is a fuller sound that works wonderfully on almost any type of audio source. The most common applications of parallel compression are vocals, bass, drums, subgroups, and the master track.

Using parallel compression on various tracks or groups within a project will help you achieve a more present, rich sound.

REAPER has an excellent feature that allows us to create parallel compression easily. Here are the steps to apply this type of compression to a track:

1. Add an instance of **ReaComp** to the track you want to compress.
2. Adjust the following compressor parameters to create aggressive compression:
    - **Attack**: `1` ms
    - **Release**: `200` ms
    - **Ratio**: `6:1`
    - **Threshold**: Lower the threshold to start compressing the signal until the compressor's gain reduction meter shows around `10` dB, as seen in *Figure 13.3*
    - **Output Wet**: Adjust the **Wet** output control to about `8` dB to compensate for the volume loss

3. The most important step is to adjust the *dry/wet* knob on the plugin, which is marked in *Figure 13.3*, to around `50%`. This knob allows you to control the degree of the plugin's effect.

   Note that if the knob is at `0%` (fully counterclockwise), the plugin will have no effect on the sound; if the knob is at `100%` (fully clockwise), the plugin will fully affect the sound.

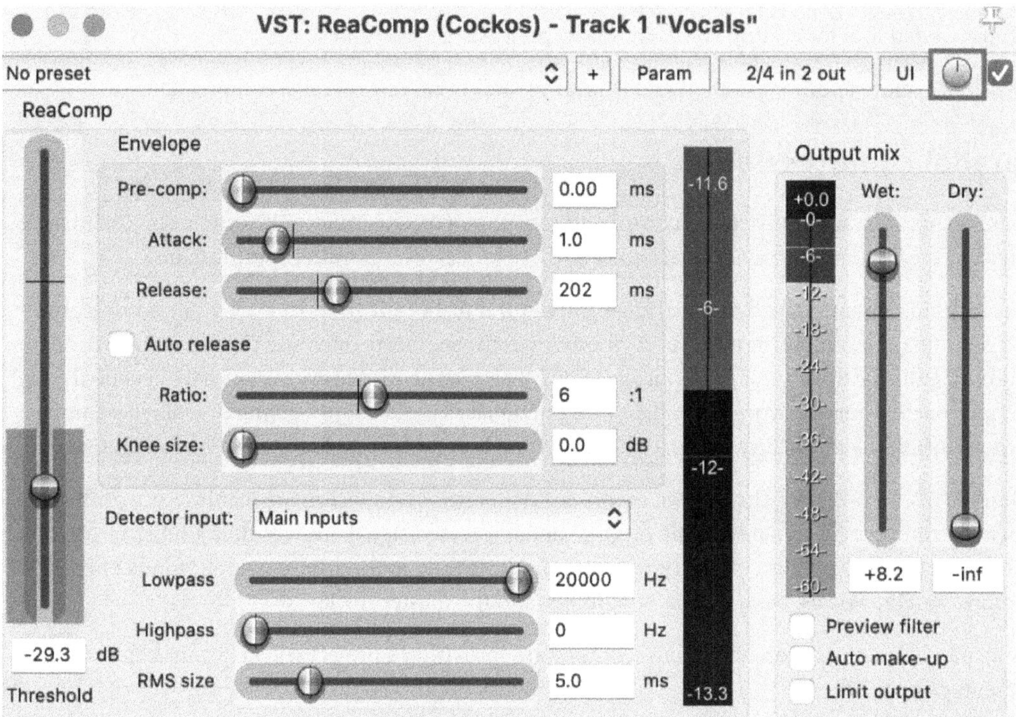

Figure 13.3 – Parallel compression

The key to parallel compression is setting the dry/wet control to around `50%`, as shown in *Figure 13.3*. This means that what we hear is 50% of the heavily compressed signal combined with 50% of the original signal, creating the parallel compression effect.

If we temporarily disable or bypass the compressor, we can hear the difference that parallel compression makes to the sound.

One of REAPER's great features is that this dry/wet knob is a native part of the plugin interface. This means we have access to this knob with any plugin we insert! This function allows us to apply any other processor or plugin in parallel, giving us more sonic possibilities.

For example, we can use parallel equalization by simply adding an equalizer, adjusting its parameters aggressively, and then setting the dry/wet knob to our liking. Similarly, we can manage any other processor or plugin.

Parallel processes have the advantage of preserving part of the original (dry) signal, so the result tends to sound more natural than when using the processor at 100% wet, but with more impact than the unprocessed signal.

Now, let's look at another tool that isn't about processing but rather a way to organize tracks visually.

Visual spacer

A visual tool that can be helpful is the **Visual spacer**. This is a visual element that creates a division between tracks, as shown in *Figure 13.4*:

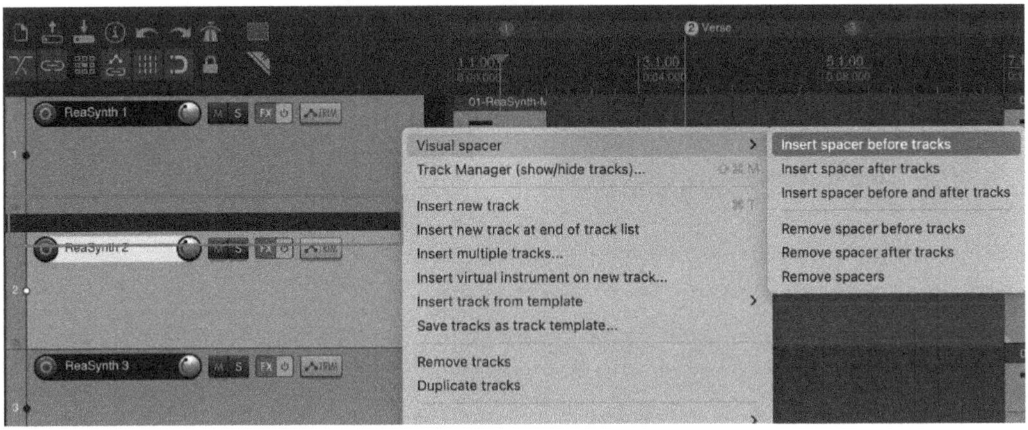

Figure 13.4 – Visual spacer

For example, we can use a visual spacer to separate drum tracks, choir tracks, sound effect groups, and so on. To add or remove a visual spacer, simply right-click on the track where you want to place it and access the **Visual spacer** menu, where you can choose to insert a spacer before or after the track, as well as remove spacers.

Now, let's look at another visual option that will help us understand the performance of our system when using REAPER.

Performance meter

When using REAPER and adding different plugins or performing audio processing, the computer's CPU will gradually take on more work. In this sense, it is important to monitor its performance to determine whether any plugin or track is causing more CPU load, or if we still have enough processing power to keep adding plugins, virtual instruments, and tracks.

If we use the **View | Performance Meter** command, a window will appear with useful information that lets you know not only the CPU load, but also the read and write performance of the hard drive or solid-state drive, and the RAM usage. We can also see the load that each track puts on the CPU, as well as the number of plugins used in each track, as shown in *Figure 13.5*.

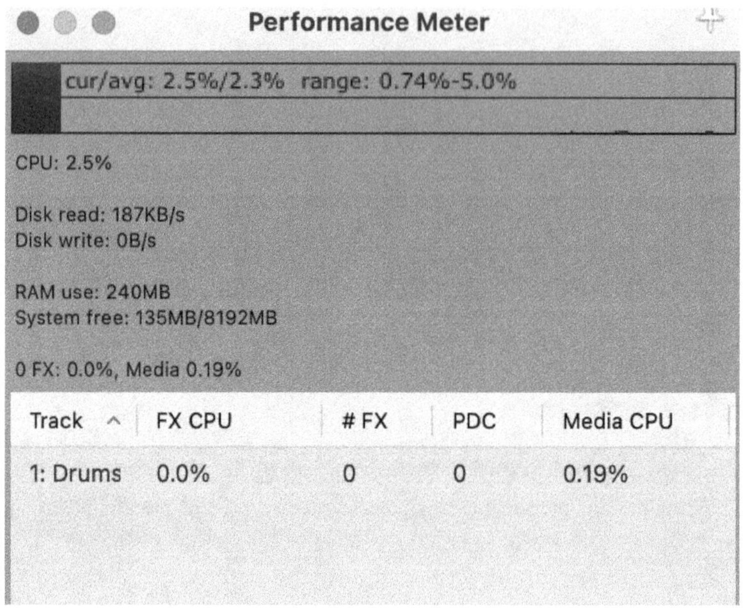

Figure 13.5 – Performance Meter

This monitoring tool is very useful for evaluating the performance of our system when running a REAPER project, especially if our computer is not the latest model. With the information from the **Performance Meter** window, we can optimize our system's resources by enabling or disabling unnecessary processes, as well as identifying the capabilities of our computer when working with REAPER projects.

Next, let's look at a function that will help us be more precise when automating a parameter in our mix: envelopes.

Automation envelopes

As we saw in *Chapter 8*, among REAPER's automation features, we have **automation envelopes**. An **envelope** is a curve that represents the change of a parameter over time. For example, a volume envelope can raise or lower the volume of a track at specific points in the project.

Using automation envelopes can help us make more precise adjustments to the automation of any parameter (volume, pan, effects, etc.).

Let's see how we can edit automation envelopes:

1. Click on the **TRIM** (or envelope) button on the track you want to automate, as shown in *Figure 13.6*. A menu will open where you can select which parameter you want to automate, such as **Volume**, **Pan**, or any parameter of the effects inserted on the track.

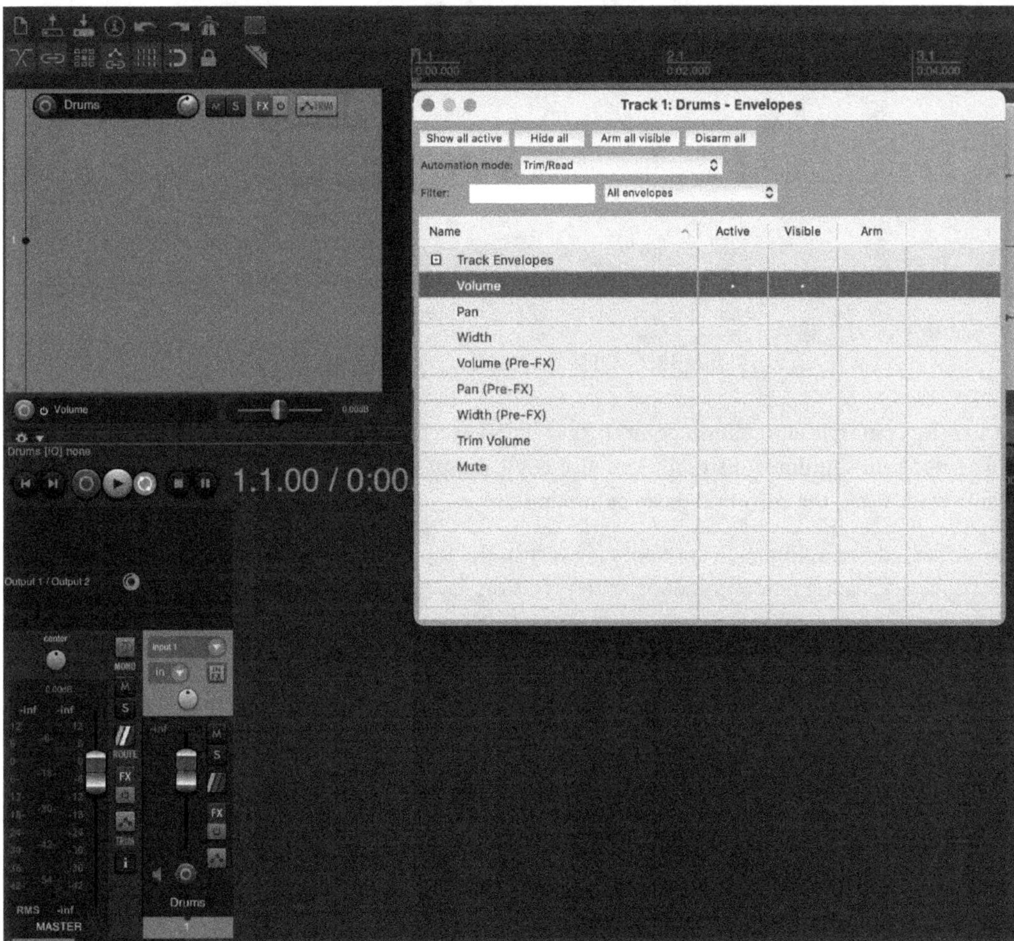

Figure 13.6 – The Envelopes window

2. Check the **Active** box next to the parameter you want to automate so that the automation line appears below the track.

3. To add an automation point, right-click on the envelope line and select **Insert point**, or simply *Shift + left-click*.
4. Move the points up or down to adjust the parameter's value at that point. Dragging a point along the timeline changes when the change occurs.

You can create smooth transitions (curves) between points for gradual changes using the *Alt/Option* key, as shown in *Figure 13.7*:

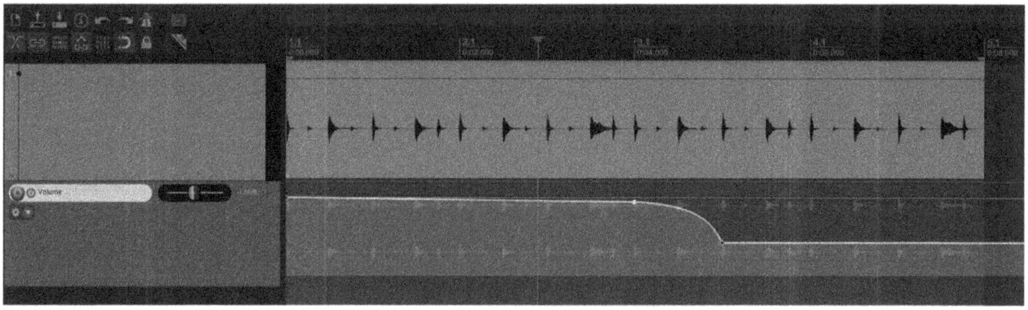

Figure 13.7 – Editing automation envelopes

You can select multiple automation points by holding down the *Shift* key and moving them together or changing them simultaneously. You can also copy and paste envelopes between tracks or within the same track using the **copy** and **paste** commands.

As we can see, editing automation envelopes is a very useful tool for refining a mix, editing pre-recorded automation, or creating new automation with precision.

Now that we've explored various tools to make our work in REAPER more efficient, let's look at how to solve some common issues that might arise when working on our projects.

Troubleshooting common issues

In this final part, we'll explain some of the most common problems that can arise when using REAPER, as well as their possible solutions.

No sound when playing the session

The *play* button is pressed, but no sound is heard, even though the tracks seem to be playing correctly.

Solution

This issue is usually due to an incorrect audio output configuration. To fix it, do the following:

1. Go to the **Options** | **Settings** | **Audio** | **Device** menu.
2. Ensure the output device is correctly set (e.g., the computer speakers or audio interface).
3. Verify that the tracks are not muted and that the main volume control (**MASTER**) is not at a minimum.

Plugins don't appear or don't work

VST plugins have been installed, but they don't appear in the effects list or don't work correctly when inserted into a track.

Solution

This issue usually occurs due to an incorrect location or improper configuration in REAPER. You have to check the following points:

- Go to the **Options** | **Settings** | **Plug-ins** | **VST** menu.
- Ensure that the folder where you installed the plugins is included in the **VST plug-in paths** list. If it's not, add it manually and click **Re-scan**.
- If the plugins still don't appear, make sure they are compatible with your operating system (32-bit versus 64-bit). If you have the wrong version, you'll need to reinstall the plugins using the correct version.

Missing tracks or audio files when opening a project

When opening a project, REAPER cannot find some tracks or audio files and displays error messages asking for the location of the missing files.

Solution

This usually happens when audio files have been moved, renamed, or deleted outside of REAPER. To solve this issue, do the following:

- If the files have been moved to a new location, use the **Browse for file** option in the error dialog to manually locate the files.
- To avoid this issue in the future, ensure that all project files are saved within the same project folder. When creating a new project, enable the **Copy all media into project directory** option in the **File** | **Save project as** menu.

- If you can't find the files, check your temporary files folder to see if REAPER saved backups there, or use your operating system's file search tool or REAPER's **Media Explorer** search, as shown in *Figure 13.8*:

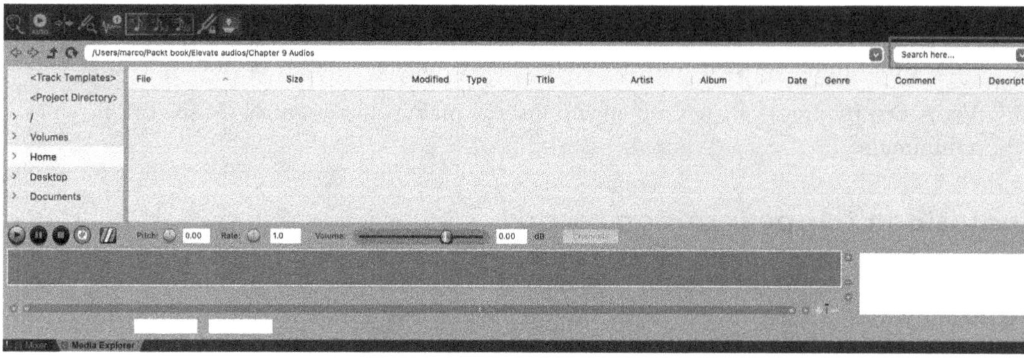

Figure 13.8 – Searching files in Media Explorer

Once you find the file in the system, move it to a dedicated folder and link it from there.

Clipping or distortion in the final mix

When playing the mix, distortion or clipping is heard, especially in the louder sections of the song or project.

Solution

This problem occurs when the signal level exceeds `0` dB on the **MASTER** or another track, causing distortion (clipping). The steps to address this issue are as follows:

1. Check the level meters on each track and the **MASTER** bus. If they are reaching or exceeding `0` dB, lower the levels with the faders.
2. Use the **ReaComp** or **ReaLimit** plugin on the track or master bus to control signal peaks, as explained in *Chapter 5*.
3. If several tracks are too loud, consider reducing the volume of all tracks together by selecting them all or using a group fader or VCA, as explained in *Chapter 7*.
4. Check if any plugin is adding unwanted gain and adjust its output levels.

These problems are common when starting with REAPER. With some practice and attention to the recommendations provided, it will be possible to solve or avoid these problems, allowing you to continue working in REAPER smoothly.

Summary

In this chapter, we covered some advanced tools that will help improve our audio processing in various projects. We saw how to quickly split audio items using dynamic split. We also learned how to reduce sibilance issues in vocals using a de-esser and how to enhance the impact of sounds through parallel compression.

Additionally, we explored how to use and adjust automation envelopes for more precision and control in parameter automation in our mix. Finally, we discussed some common issues that may arise when using REAPER and their typical solutions.

I hope the information you've found in this book is useful for starting to use REAPER in your audio projects. Learning to fully master a DAW as extensive as REAPER requires time, practice, and exploration of many other functions. However, you now have the basic resources to carry out your work following procedures used in the professional audio world. So, go ahead!

Index

Symbols

A

B

C

D

M

S

T

X

Z

Other Books You May Enjoy

If you enjoyed this book, you may be interested in these other books by Packt:

The Music Producer's Creative Guide to Ableton Live 11

Anna Lakatos

ISBN: 978-1-80181-763-9

- Understand the concept of Live, the workflow of recording and editing Audio and MIDI, and Warping
- Utilize Groove, MIDI effects, and Live 11 s new workflow enhancements to create innovative music
- Use Audio to MIDI conversion tools to translate and generate ideas quickly
- Dive into Live's automation and modulation capabilities and explore project organization techniques to speed up your workflow
- Utilize MIDI Polyphonic Expression to create evolving sounds and textures
- Adopt useful techniques for production and discover the capabilities of live performance

The Ultimate Studio One Pro Book

Doruk Somunkiran

ISBN: 978-1-80324-101-2

- Configure Studio One and run it smoothly in your production environment
- Record and edit MIDI using Studio One's excellent manipulation tools
- Record audio and edit confidently using Melodyne and Audio Bend
- Work with Studio One's stock virtual instruments to create an arrangement
- Mix a song with Studio One's stock effects plugins
- Master a song using the Project window
- Take your music on stage with the Show window

Packt is searching for authors like you

If you're interested in becoming an author for Packt, please visit `authors.packtpub.com` and apply today. We have worked with thousands of developers and tech professionals, just like you, to help them share their insight with the global tech community. You can make a general application, apply for a specific hot topic that we are recruiting an author for, or submit your own idea.

Share Your Thoughts

Now you've finished *Elevate Your Audio Production with REAPER*, we'd love to hear your thoughts! Scan the QR code below to go straight to the Amazon review page for this book and share your feedback or leave a review on the site that you purchased it from.

`https://packt.link/r/1835885438`

Your review is important to us and the tech community and will help us make sure we're delivering excellent quality content.

www.ingramcontent.com/pod-product-compliance
Lightning Source LLC
LaVergne TN
LVHW080806011026
849160LV00015B/1547